The European Union

To
Lois Nelsen and Göran Stubb
and to the memories of
Christel Stubb and Frank C. Nelsen

Contents

PART 2   EARLY CURRENTS IN INTEGRATION THEORY

PART 3   EUROPE RELAUNCHED

Introduction

Brent F. Nelsen and Alexander Stubb

More than a decade has passed since the third edition of this
book was published. Faithful users of the book will immediately realize that
this new edition has a new structure. We still have sections presenting
"visions" of Europe, early currents in theory, and contemporary theoretical
debates. But we have added a section called "Europe Relaunched" containing
pieces from the mid-1980s to the end of the twentieth century—a period of
increased integration in Europe and new efforts to explain it. We felt that to
jump directly from classic theoretical statements of the 1950s and 1960s to
the present without providing a few of the "greatest hits" of the relaunch era
would mystify rather than enlighten students and scholars. The new Part 3
thus opens the door to the intense—and intensely creative—debates of the
late twentieth century by bringing back seminal works from previous editions
of the book.

Crisis is the theme that unites the new selections reprinted in this edition.
In Part 1, Jürgen Habermas and Jacques Derrida (Chapter 11) explore a possible new identity for Europe after the mass protests against the Iraq War put
the United States and much of Europe on different foreign policy trajectories.
The following chapter takes up the constitutional crisis of the first decade of
the twenty-first century by presenting the controversial preamble to the failed
constitutional treaty and the very brief preamble to the successful Lisbon
treaty. Part 1 concludes with a chapter on the euro crisis, featuring the conflicting views of several prominent politicians as they outline their suggestions for heading off catastrophe.

Several of the selections featured in Part 4 are connected by their
attempts to make sense of the EU's current economic and political woes.
Nicolas Berggruen and Nathan Gardels (Chapter 27) chart a federalist course
through the turmoil, while economist Enrico Spolaore (Chapter 32) explains
the crisis in terms of the costs and benefits of integrating heterogeneous peoples and economies. Liesbet Hooghe and Gary Marks (Chapter 29) with their

1

"postfunctionalist" theory of integration and Gary Marks (Chapter 31) with his discussion of the European Union as an empire examine the political blowback against integration. They seem to agree that efficient governance has bumped into identity. Ideas may also play an independent role in the construction of Europe, as Craig Parsons argues (Chapter 28), making the way out of the European crisis more than a matter of cost-benefit analysis.

As with previous editions, the book records a conversation among political leaders and scholars about the possibility, purpose, and process of unifying Europe. From the close of World War II, European politicians have been articulating a vision of a united Europe and taking practical steps to achieve it. Scholars have also been known to prescribe courses of action for Europe, but more often than not have confined themselves to describing and explaining the process and progress of integration. The conversation has never been one-way: officials have very often taken their cues from theoretical work done by scholars, and scholars have often allowed political notions to inform their theoretical ruminations. Nor has the conversation proceeded without heated debates. Some of the heat has come from scholars who look to the politicians for greater progress toward integration; some has come from policymakers who lament the abstract nature of much of the scholarly work (a familiar refrain). Most of the conversational heat, however, comes from internal debates. European politicians have disagreed deeply over the nature and purpose of postwar integration, and scholars have divided over everything from the best method of integration, to who controls integration, to what the EU actually is. This book offers a window on this conversation over time and allows readers to enter the debate that continues to shape contemporary Europe.

* * *

Readers should be aware of several protocols that we employed when constructing the book. First, the introductions that begin each chapter set the context and summarize the argument of the selection. These prologues are designed to amplify the dialogue among the authors of the selections. They should not substitute for a broader discussion of the historical or theoretical contexts, nor should they replace a close reading of each piece. Second, we have abridged each selection. Centered bullets mark significant abridgments; less significant abridgments (i.e., less than a paragraph) are marked with ellipses; brackets mark our own additions; and notes are omitted to save space. We have taken great care to preserve the core—and much more—of each author's argument, but readers should consider the original sources before making definitive (i.e., published) statements about the selections reprinted here.

Part 1
Visions of a United Europe

1

Ventotene Manifesto

Altiero Spinelli and Ernesto Rossi

Visions of a united Europe have their roots in the political and cultural unity of ancient Rome and medieval Christendom. In the twentieth century these visions grew to maturity in the harsh climate of modern war. When the Allies began to turn back Hitler's armies, Europeans of many political persuasions commenced arguing for a united Europe as a means of eliminating the possibility of war and thus preserving European civilization. The resistance movements fighting fascist occupation were especially vocal in their criticism of the nation-state system and their support for a unified Europe. Leading the way was a small group of left-wing intellectuals from the Italian Resistance Movement who illegally launched their drive for a federated Europe from a political internment center on the island of Ventotene.

Altiero Spinelli (1907–1986), a former communist and future academic and politician (see Chapter 14), and Ernesto Rossi (1897–1967), an anti-fascist journalist, in consultation with several other prisoners, drafted what came to be known as the Ventotene Manifesto in June 1941. Ada Rossi smuggled the Manifesto to the Italian mainland, where the underground press published it in late 1941.[1] In August 1943 Spinelli founded the European Federalist Movement, which adopted the Manifesto as its political program.

The Manifesto is ultimately a call to action. It begins with a critique of totalitarianism and its causes, then proceeds to call for a movement of workers and intellectuals to seize the opportunity offered by the war to create a "European Federation" equipped to provide security and social justice for all Europeans. The section of the Manifesto reprinted here—which appeared under the heading "Post-war Duties: European Unity"—assesses the coming postwar crisis and asserts that a European Federation would easily solve "the multiple problems which poison international life on the continent." Finally, the authors sketch the outline of a federal state that controls the armed forces of Europe, its economy, and its internal security,

Translated by Emma Urgesi. Reprinted with permission from *Centro Italiano di Formazione Europea*, Rome, Italy, www.altierospinelli.org/manifesto/en/manifesto 1944en_en.html.

while leaving the states with sufficient autonomy to develop the political life of their people.

.   .   .

Germany's defeat would not automatically lead to the reformation of Europe according to our ideal of civilisation.

In the brief, intense period of general crises (during which the States will lie broken, during which the popular masses are anxiously awaiting for a new message and will, meanwhile, like molten matter, burn, being easily poured into new moulds, capable of welcoming the guidance of serious internationalists) the classes which were the most privileged under the old national systems will attempt, underhanded or violently, to moderate the feelings, the internationalist passions and they will ostentatiously begin the [sic] reconstruct the old, State institutions. And the English leaders, perhaps in agreement with the Americans, may try to push things in this direction, in order to restore the policy of the balance of power, in the apparent and immediate interests of their empires.

The conservative forces, that is: the directors of the basic institutions of the national States; the top-ranking officers in the armed forces up to, where possible, monarchies; the groups of monopolistic capitalism that have bound their profits to the fortunes of the States; the big landowners and the ecclesiastical hierarchy, who can expect their parasitical income only in a stable, conservative society; and following these, the interminable band of people who depend on them or who are simply misled by their traditional power. All these reactionary forces already feel the structure is creaking, and are trying to save their skins. A collapse would deprive them all of a sudden of all the guarantees they have enjoyed up to now, and would expose them to the attack of the progressive forces.

.   .   .

A real revolutionary movement must rise from among those who were able to criticise the old, political statements; it must know how to collaborate with democratic and with communist forces as well as with all those who work for the break-up of totalitarianism, without becoming ensnared by the political practices of any of these.

The reactionary forces have capable men and officers who have been trained to command and who will fight ruthlessly to preserve their supremacy. When circumstances are very hard, deceitfully they will show themselves as the lovers of liberty, of peace, of general well-being, of the poorer classes.

Already in the past we have seen how they made use of popular movements, and they paralysed, deflected and transformed them into exactly the opposite of what they were. No doubt they will be the most dangerous forced [sic] to be faced.

The point they will seek to exploit is the restoration of the national State. Thus they will be able to grasp the most widespread of popular feelings, most deeply offended by recent events, most easily handled to reactionary purposes: the patriotic sentiment. In this way they can also hope to confuse their adversaries' ideas more easily, since for the popular masses, the only political experience acquired up to this time has been within the national context, it is therefore fairly easy to direct them and their more shortsighted leaders towards the reconstruction of the States "felled" by the tempest.

If this purpose were to be reached, the reaction would have won. In appearance, these States might well be broadly democratic and socialist; it would only be a question of time before power returned into the hands of the reactionaries. National jealousies would again develop, and each State would again express its satisfaction only in its armed strength. In a more or less brief space of time their most important duty would be to convert populations into armies. Generals would again command, the monopoly holders would again draw profits from autarkies, the bureaucracy would continue to swell, the priests would keep the masses docile. All the initial conquests would shrivel into nothing, in comparison to the necessity of preparing for war once more.

The question which must be resolved first, failing which progress is but mere appearance, is definitive abolition of division of Europe into national, sovereign States. The collapse of the majority of the States on the continent under the German steam-roller has already placed the destinies of the European populations on common ground: either all together they will submit to Hitler's dominion, or after his fall, all together they will enter a revolutionary crisis, and they will not find themselves adamantly distinct in solid, state structures. The general spirit today is already far more disposed than it was in the past towards a federal reorganisation of Europe. The hard experience of the last decades has opened the eyes even of those who refused to see, and has matured many circumstances favourable to our ideal.

All reasonable men recognise that it is impossible to maintain a balance of power among European States with militarist Germany enjoying equal conditions, nor can Germany be broken up into pieces once it is conquered. We have seen a demonstration that no country within Europe can stay on the sidelines while the others battle: declarations of neutrality and non-aggression pacts come to naught. The uselessness, even harmfulness, of organisations like the League of Nations has been demonstrated: they pretended to guarantee an international law without a military force capable of imposing its decision, by respecting the absolute sovereignty of the member States. The principle of non-intervention turned out to be absurd. According to it each population should be left free to choose the despotic government it thought best, as if the constitution of each of the single States were not a question of vital interest for all the other European nations. The multiple problems which poison international life on the continent have proved to be insoluble: tracing boundaries through areas inhabited by mixed populations, defence of alien minorities, seaports for landlocked countries, the Balkan Question, the Irish problem, and so on. All these matters would find easy solutions in the European Federation, just as corresponding problems, suffered by the small States which became part of a vaster national unity, lost their harshness as they were transformed into problems regarding relationship between various provinces.

.   .   .

[O]nce the horizon of the Old Continent is passed beyond, and all the people who make up humanity join together for a common plane, it will have to be recognised that the European Federation is the only conceivable guarantee that relationships with American and Asiatic peoples can exist on the basis of peaceful co-operation, while awaiting a more distant future, when the political unity of the entire globe becomes a possibility.

The dividing line between progressive and reactionary parties no longer follows the formal line of greater or lesser democracy, or of more or less socialism to be instituted; rather the division falls along the line, very new and substantial, that separates the party members into two groups. The first is made up of those who conceive the essential purpose and goal of struggle as the ancient one, that is, the conquest of national political power—and who, although involuntarily, play into the hands of reactionary forces, letting the incandescent lava of popular passions set in the old moulds, and thus allowing old absurdities to arise once again. The second are those who see the creation of a solid international State as the main purpose; they will direct popular forces toward this goal, and, having won national power, will use it first and foremost as an instrument for achieving international unity.

Through propaganda and action, seeking to establish in every possible way agreements and links among the single movements which are certainly being formed in the various countries, the foundation must be built now for a movement that knows how to mobilise all forces for the birth of the new organism which will be the grandest creation, and the newest, that has occurred in Europe for centuries; and the constitution of a steady federal State, that will have an European armed service instead of national armies at its disposal; that will break decisively economic autarchies, the backbone of totalitarian regimes; that will have sufficient means to see that its deliberations for the maintenance of common order are executed in the [individual] federal States, while each State will retain the autonomy it needs for a plastic articulation and development of a political life according to the particular characteristics of the various people.

If a sufficient number of men in the most important European countries understand this, then the victory will shortly be at hand, as both the situation and the spirit will be favourable to their project. They will have before them parties and factions that have already been disqualified by the disastrous experience of the last twenty years. It will be the moment of new action and it will also be the moment for new men: the MOMENT FOR A FREE AND UNITED EUROPE!

Note

1. Walter Lipgens, *Documents on the History of European Integration, Vol. 1: Continental Plans for European Union 1939–1945*, ed. Walter Lipgens (Berlin: Walter de Gruyter, 1985), pp. 471–73.

2

The Tragedy of Europe

Winston S. Churchill

Calls for a united Europe—like that of the Ventotene Manifesto—drew the attention of a wide range of political leaders and activists. Many were young idealists or politicians with limited influence; no leaders of undeniable political stature raised a strong voice in favor of a federated Europe—that is, until Winston Churchill (1874–1965) spoke from a platform in Zurich.

Churchill, the great wartime prime minister of Britain, found himself leader of the Conservative opposition in Parliament after Labour's victory in the 1945 general election. Despite his removal from office, Churchill remained a key architect of the postwar world by identifying the dangers facing the West and articulating a clear strategy for defending Western interests and values.

Churchill's speech at Zurich University on 19 September 1946 profoundly influenced the shape of postwar Europe. He began this speech with the refrain common to all the postwar integrationists: Europe must unite before war destroys the continent, its glorious civilization, and perhaps much of the rest of the world. He called specifically for a "United States of Europe" led by Europe's former antagonists, France and Germany, but he did not outline a detailed program for achieving unity. Rather, he argued simply and powerfully for Europe to adopt an ideal to guide its future. Interestingly, Churchill seems to exclude Britain from his grand European project, thus reflecting an ambiguity toward Europe that remains strong in Britain today.

Churchill's stature forced European leaders to take his Zurich call seriously. His efforts eventually led to the Hague Congress of May 1948 and the creation of the Council of Europe in 1949, both milestones in European integration.

I wish to speak to you today about the tragedy of Europe. This noble continent, comprising on the whole the fairest and the most cultivated regions of the earth, enjoying a temperate and equable climate, is the home of all the great parent races of the western world. It is the fountain of Christian faith and Christian ethics. It is the origin of most of the culture, arts, philosophy, and science both of ancient and modern times. If Europe were once united in the sharing of its common inheritance, there would be no limit to the happiness, to the prosperity and glory which its three or four hundred million people would enjoy. Yet it is from Europe that have sprung that series of frightful nationalistic quarrels, originated by the Teutonic nations, which we have seen even in this twentieth century and in our lifetime, wreck the peace and mar the prospects of all mankind.

And what is the plight to which Europe has been reduced? Some of the smaller states have indeed made a good recovery, but over wide areas a vast quivering mass of tormented, hungry, care-worn and bewildered human beings gape at the ruins of their cities and homes, and scan the dark horizons for the approach of some new peril, tyranny or terror. Among the victors there is a babel of jarring voices; among the vanquished a sullen silence of despair. That is all that Europeans, grouped in so many ancient states and nations, that is all that the Germanic Powers have got by tearing each other to pieces and spreading havoc far and wide. Indeed, but for the fact that the great Republic across the Atlantic Ocean has at length realized that the ruin or enslavement of Europe would involve their own fate as well, and has stretched out hands of succor and guidance, the Dark Ages would have returned in all their cruelty and squalor. They may still return.

Yet all the while there is a remedy which, if it were generally and spontaneously adopted, would as if by a miracle transform the whole scene, and would in a few years make all Europe, or the greater part of it, as free and as happy as Switzerland is today. What is this sovereign remedy? It is to re-create the European Family or as much of it as we can, and provide it with a structure under which it can dwell in peace, in safety and in freedom. We must build a kind of United States of Europe. In this way only will hundreds of millions of toilers be able to regain the simple joys and hopes which make life worth living. The process is simple. All that is needed is the resolve of hundreds of millions of men and women to do right instead of wrong and gain as their reward blessing instead of cursing.

Much work has been done upon this task by the exertions of the Pan-European Union which owes so much to Count Coudenhove-Kalergi and which commanded the services of the famous French patriot and statesman, Aristide Briand. There is also that immense body of doctrine and procedure, which was brought into being amid high hopes after the first world war, as the League of Nations. The League of Nations did not fail because of its principles or conceptions. It failed because these principles were deserted by those states who had brought it into being. It failed because the governments of those days feared to face the facts, and act while time remained. This disaster must not be repeated. There is therefore much knowledge and material with which to build; and also bitter dear-bought experience.

I was very glad to read in the newspapers two days ago that my friend President Truman had expressed his interest and sympathy with this great design. There is no reason why a regional organization of Europe should in any way conflict with the world organization of the United Nations. On the contrary, I believe that the larger synthesis will only survive if it is founded upon coherent natural groupings. There is already a natural grouping in the Western Hemisphere. We British have our own Commonwealth of Nations. These do not weaken, on the contrary they strengthen, the world organization. They are in fact its main support. And why should there not be a European group which could give a sense of enlarged patriotism and common citizenship to the distracted peoples of this turbulent and mighty continent and why should it not take its rightful place with other great groupings in shaping the destinies of men? In order that this should be accomplished there must be an act of faith in which millions of families speaking many languages must consciously take part.

We all know that the two world wars through which we have passed arose out of the vain passion of a newly-united Germany to play the dominating part in the world. In this last struggle crimes and massacres have been committed for which there is no parallel since the invasions of the Mongols in the fourteenth century and no equal at any time in human history. The guilty must be punished. Germany must be deprived of the power to rearm and make another aggressive war. But when all this has been done, as it will be done, as it is being done, there must be an end to retribution. There must be what Mr. Gladstone many years ago called "a blessed act of oblivion." We must all turn our backs upon the horrors of the past. We must look to the future. We cannot afford to drag forward across the years that are to come the hatreds and revenges which have sprung from the injuries of the past. If Europe is to be saved from infinite misery, and indeed from final doom, there must be an act of faith in the European family and an act of oblivion against all the crimes and follies of the past.

Can the free peoples of Europe rise to the height of these resolves of the soul and instincts of the spirit of man? If they can, the wrongs and injuries which have been inflicted will have been washed away on all sides by the miseries which have been endured. Is there any need for further floods of agony? Is it the only lesson of history that mankind is unteachable? Let there be justice, mercy and freedom. The peoples have to will it, and all will achieve their hearts' desire.

I am now going to say something that will astonish you. The first step in the re-creation of the European family must be a partnership between

France and Germany. In this way only can France recover the moral leadership of Europe. There can be no revival of Europe without a spiritually great France and a spiritually great Germany. The structure of the United States of Europe, if well and truly built, will be such as to make the material strength of a single state less important. Small nations will count as much as large ones and gain their honor by their contribution to the common cause. The ancient states and principalities of Germany, freely joined together for mutual convenience in a federal system, might each take their individual place among the United States of Europe. I shall not try to make a detailed program for hundreds of millions of people who want to be happy and free, prosperous and safe, who wish to enjoy the four freedoms of which the great President Roosevelt spoke, and live in accordance with the principles embodied in the Atlantic Charter. If this is their wish, they have only to say so, and means can certainly be found, and machinery erected, to carry that wish into full fruition.

But I must give you a warning. Time may be short. At present there is a breathing space. The cannon have ceased firing. The fighting has stopped; but the dangers have not stopped. If we are to form the United States of Europe or whatever name or form it may take, we must begin now.

In these present days we dwell strangely and precariously under the shield and protection of the atomic bomb. The atomic bomb is still only in the hands of a state and nation which we know will never use it except in the cause of right and freedom. But it may well be that in a few years this awful agency of destruction will be widespread and the catastrophe following from its use by several warring nations will not only bring to an end all that we call civilization, but may possibly disintegrate the globe itself.

I must now sum up the propositions which are before you. Our constant aim must be to build and fortify the strength of [the United Nations]. Under and within that world concept we must re-create the European family in a regional structure called, it may be, the United States of Europe. The first step is to form a Council of Europe. If at first all the states of Europe are not willing or able to join the union, we must nevertheless proceed to assemble and combine those who will and those who can. The salvation of the common people of every race and of every land from war or servitude must be established on solid foundations and must be guarded by the readiness of all men and women to die rather than submit to tyranny. In all this urgent work, France and Germany must take the lead together. Great Britain, the British Commonwealth of Nations, mighty America, and I trust Soviet Russia—for then indeed all would be well—must be the friends and sponsors of the new Europe and must champion its right to live and shine.

The Schuman Declaration

Robert Schuman

Efforts in the 1940s to realize Churchill's vision of a united Europe led to increased economic and political cooperation but did not yield anything like a United States of Europe. European leaders needed a new strategy to achieve such a goal. On 9 May 1950, Robert Schuman (1886–1963), France's foreign minister, outlined a plan to unite under a single authority the coal and steel industries of Europe's bitterest enemies, France and Germany. The purpose of the plan, which was developed by Jean Monnet, was to begin building a peaceful, united Europe one step at a time. European governments would start with two industries essential to the making of war, coal and steel, then add other economic and political sectors until all major decisions were taken at a European level. This would create, in Schuman's words, a "de facto solidarity" that would ultimately make war between France and Germany "materially impossible." The practical approach of Schuman and Monnet won favor on the European continent; France, Germany, Italy, and the Benelux countries eventually responded by creating the European Coal and Steel Community in 1952.

World peace cannot be safeguarded without the making of creative efforts proportionate to the dangers which threaten it.

The contribution which an organized and living Europe can bring to civilization is indispensable to the maintenance of peaceful relations. In taking upon herself for more than 20 years the role of champion of a united Europe, France has always had as her essential aim the service of peace. A united Europe was not achieved and we had war.

Europe will not be made all at once, or according to a single plan. It will be built through concrete achievements which first create a *de facto* solidarity. The coming together of the nations of Europe requires the elim-

---

ination of the age-old opposition of France and Germany. Any action taken must in the first place concern these two countries.

With this aim in view, the French government proposes that action be taken immediately on one limited but decisive point. It proposes that Franco-German production of coal and steel as a whole be placed under a common High Authority, within the framework of an organization open to the participation of the other countries of Europe.

The pooling of coal and steel production should immediately provide for the setting up of common foundations for economic development as a first step in the federation of Europe, and will change the destinies of those regions which have long been devoted to the manufacture of munitions of war, of which they have been the most constant victims.

The solidarity in production thus established will make it plain that any war between France and Germany becomes not merely unthinkable, but materially impossible. The setting up of this powerful productive unit, open to all countries willing to take part and bound ultimately to provide all the member countries with the basic elements of industrial production on the same terms, will lay a true foundation for their economic unification.

This production will be offered to the world as a whole without distinction or exception, with the aim of contributing to raising living standards and to promoting peaceful achievements.

In this way, there will be realized simply and speedily that fusion of interests which is indispensable to the establishment of a common economic system; it may be the leaven from which may grow a wider and deeper community between countries long opposed to one another by sanguinary divisions.

By pooling basic production and by instituting a new High Authority, whose decisions will bind France, Germany and other member countries, this proposal will lead to the realization of the first concrete foundation of a European federation indispensable to the preservation of peace.

.   .   .

Preambles to the Treaties Establishing the European Communities (The Treaties of Paris and Rome)

In Rome on 25 March 1957, the six member countries of the European Coal and Steel Community (ECSC) signed treaties establishing the European Economic Community (EEC) and the European Atomic Energy Community (EURATOM). These two treaties are often called the "Treaties of Rome" (the ECSC treaty was signed in Paris). The EEC treaty is also sometimes referred to as the "Treaty of Rome."

The preambles to each of the three original treaties reflect the founders' vision for building, through economic integration, "an ever closer union among the peoples of Europe." The deep desire for peace on the Continent runs through each of the preambles and links them to the visions articulated by Spinelli and Rossi, Churchill, Schuman, Monnet, and many others. But the documents also represent a subtle shift in emphasis away from peace to economic prosperity as the driving motive for unity. We can detect the shift in the Schuman Declaration and its parallel, the preamble to the ECSC treaty, but it becomes more evident in the preamble to the EEC treaty, where "economic and social progress" seems to take precedence over preserving and strengthening "peace and liberty." European leaders, while mindful of the dangers of violent conflict in Western Europe, were becoming more concerned with the material improvement of life on a peaceful continent.

European Coal and Steel Community

. . .

CONSIDERING that world peace can be safeguarded only by creative efforts commensurate with the dangers that threaten it,

---

CONVINCED that the contribution which an organized and vital Europe can make to civilization is indispensable to the maintenance of peaceful relations,

RECOGNIZING that Europe can be built only through practical achievements which will first of all create real solidarity, and through the establishment of common bases for economic development,

ANXIOUS to help, by expanding their basic production, to raise the standard of living and further the works of peace,

RESOLVED to substitute for age-old rivalries the merging of their essential interests; to create, by establishing an economic community, the basis for a broader and deeper community among peoples long divided by bloody conflicts; and to lay the foundations for institutions which will give direction to a destiny henceforward shared,

HAVE DECIDED to create a European Coal and Steel Community.

.   .   .

European Economic Community

.   .   .

DETERMINED to lay the foundations of an ever closer union among the peoples of Europe,

RESOLVED to ensure the economic and social progress of their countries by common action to eliminate the barriers which divide Europe,

AFFIRMING as the essential objective of their efforts the constant improvement of the living and working conditions of their peoples,

RECOGNIZING that the removal of existing obstacles calls for concerted action in order to guarantee steady expansion, balanced trade and fair competition,

ANXIOUS to strengthen the unity of their economies and to ensure their harmonious development by reducing the differences existing between the various regions and the backwardness of the less favored regions,

DESIRING to contribute, by means of a common commercial policy, to the progressive abolition of restrictions on international trade,

INTENDING to confirm the solidarity which binds Europe and the overseas countries and desiring to ensure the development of their prosperity, in accordance with the principles of the Charter of the United Nations,

RESOLVED by thus pooling their resources to preserve and strengthen peace and liberty, and calling upon the other peoples of Europe who share their ideal to join in their efforts,

HAVE DECIDED to create a European Economic Community.

.   .   .

European Atomic Energy Community

.   .   .

RECOGNIZING that nuclear energy represents an essential resource for the development and invigoration of industry and will permit the advancement of the cause of peace,

CONVINCED that only a joint effort undertaken without delay can offer the prospect of achievements commensurate with the creative capacities of their countries,

RESOLVED to create the conditions necessary for the development of a powerful nuclear industry which will provide extensive energy resources, lead to the modernization of technical processes and contribute, through its many other applications, to the prosperity of their peoples,

ANXIOUS to create the conditions of safety necessary to eliminate hazards to the life and health of the public,

DESIRING to associate other countries with their work and to cooperate with international organizations concerned with the peaceful development of atomic energy,

HAVE DECIDED to create a European Atomic Energy Community (EURATOM).

.   .   .

5

A Ferment of Change

Jean Monnet

Jean Monnet (1888–1979) was the "father of Europe." No single individual influenced the shape of the European Union more than this French civil servant and diplomat. Monnet convinced Robert Schuman to propose the European Coal and Steel Community and became the first president of its High Authority. Monnet convinced Johan Willem Beyen and Paul-Henri Spaak to propose EURATOM and the EEC, and then he established the influential Action Committee for a United States of Europe to pressure governments to accept the proposals. Monnet worked hard, and eventually successfully, to enlarge the Community by adding Britain, Ireland, and Denmark. And shortly before his death, Monnet persuaded EC governments to turn their regular summits into the European Council.[1]

Monnet was a pragmatic government official who quite naturally developed a strategy for uniting Europe that looked much like the step-by-step functionalism of David Mitrany (see Chapter 15). Monnet argued that problems of insecurity and human need in the world—and in Europe in particular— required radical changes in the way people thought. Nations, he believed, should adopt common rules governing their behavior and create common institutions to apply these rules. Such a strategy, even if applied on a small scale, would create a "silent revolution in men's minds" that would change the way people thought and acted. For Monnet, the European Communities of the early 1960s demonstrated that small collective steps set off "a chain reaction, a ferment where one change induces another." This ferment, he asserted, would not lead to another nineteenth-century–style great power— nor would it be confined to Europe. Integration was a process that may have started in Europe but would soon have to include the broader West, followed by the rest of the world, if humanity was to "escape destruction." In short, Monnet was calling for nothing less than a new, more civilized way of organizing and conducting international politics.

Reprinted with permission from *Journal of Common Market Studies* 1, no. 1 (1962): 203–211. Copyright 1962 by John Wiley and Sons.

This century has probably changed the manner of life more for every one of us than all the thousands of years of man's progress put together. In the past, men were largely at the mercy of nature. Today in our industrial countries of the Western world and elsewhere, we are acquiring an unprecedented mastery over nature. Natural resources are no longer a limitation now that we control more and more forms of energy and can use raw materials in more and more ways. We are entering the age of abundance where work, as we know it, will only be one of many human activities. For the first time we in the West are witnessing the emergence of a truly mass society marked by mass consumption, mass education and even mass culture.

We are moving, in the West, from a society where privilege was part of nature to one where the enjoyment of human rights and human dignity are common to all. Unfortunately, two-thirds of mankind have not shared in this process.

And now, on the very eve of creating unprecedented conditions of abundance, we are suddenly faced with the consequences of our extraordinary mastery over the physical forces of nature. Modern medicine is steadily increasing our prospects of life, so that the population of the world is increasing fantastically fast. This revolution is creating new explosive pressures of all kinds in the world. At the same time, science is repeatedly creating new powers of destruction. This faces us with the greatest threat humanity has ever had to deal with. The issue today is no longer peace or war, but the triumph or destruction of civilized life.

We cannot assume that we shall avoid such destruction. We have only to look back on the last fifty years to see how constant the risk of upheaval has become. No region of the world has escaped violence. One-third of mankind has become Communist, another third has obtained independence from colonialism, and even among the remaining third nearly all countries have undergone revolutions or wars. True, atomic bombs have made nuclear war so catastrophic that I am convinced no country wishes to resort to it. But I am equally convinced that we are at the mercy of an error of judgment or a technical breakdown, the source of which no man may ever know.

We are then in a world of rapid change, in which men and nations must learn to control themselves in their relations with others. This, to my mind, can only be done through institutions; and it is this need for common institutions that we have learnt in Europe since the war.

We are used to thinking that major changes in the traditional relations between countries only take place violently, through conquest or revolution. We are so accustomed to this that we find it hard to appreciate those that are taking place peacefully in Europe even though they have begun to affect the world. We can see the communist revolution, because it has been violent and because we have been living with it for nearly fifty years. We can

see the revolution in the ex-colonial areas because power is plainly changing hands. But we tend to miss the magnitude of the change in Europe
because it is taking place by the constitutional and democratic methods
which govern our countries.

Yet we have only to look at the difference between 1945 and today to
see what an immense transformation has been taking place under our very
eyes, here in what used to be called the old world. After the war, the nations
of continental Europe were divided and crippled, their national resources
were depleted and, in most of them, the peoples had little faith in the future.
During the last fifteen years, these countries have lost their empires. It
might have been expected they would be further depressed by what many
considered the loss of past greatness and prestige.

And yet, after all these upheavals, the countries of continental Europe,
which have fought each other so often in the past and which, even in peace-
time, organized their economies as potential instruments of war, are now
uniting in a Common Market which is laying the foundations for political
union. Britain is negotiating to enter this European Community and by this
very fact changing the tradition of centuries. And now the President of the
United States is already asking Congress for powers to negotiate with the
enlarged European Common Market.

To understand this extraordinary change in all its basic simplicity, we
must go back to 1950, only five years after the war. For five years, the whole
French nation had been making efforts to re-create the bases of production,
but it became evident that to go beyond recovery towards steady expansion
and higher standards of life for all, the resources of a single nation were not
sufficient. It was necessary to transcend the national framework.

The need was political as well as economic. The Europeans had to
overcome the mistrust born of centuries of feuds and wars. The governments and peoples of Europe still thought in the old terms of victors and
vanquished. Yet, if a basis for peace in the world was to be established,
these notions had to be eliminated. Here again, one had to go beyond the
nation and the conception of national interest as an end in itself.

We thought that both these objectives could in time be reached if conditions were created enabling these countries to increase their resources by
merging them in a large and dynamic common market; and if these same
countries could be made to consider that their problems were no longer
solely of national concern, but were mutual European responsibilities.

Obviously this could not be done all at once. It was not possible to create a large dynamic market immediately or to produce trust between recent
enemies overnight. After several unsuccessful attempts, the French Government through its Foreign Minister, M. Robert Schuman, proposed in
1950 what many people today would regard as a modest beginning but
which seemed very bold at the time; and the parliaments of France, Ger-

many, Italy and Benelux voted that, for coal and steel, their countries would form a single common market, run by common institutions administering common rules, very much as within a single nation. The European Coal and Steel Community was set up. In itself this was a technical step, but its new procedures, under common institutions, created a silent revolution in men's minds. It proved decisive in persuading businessmen, civil servants, politicians and trade unionists that such an approach could work and that the economic and political advantages of unity over division were immense. Once they were convinced, they were ready to take further steps forward.

In 1957, only three years after the failure of the European Army, the six parliaments ratified the Treaty of Rome which extended the Common Market from coal and steel to an economic union embracing all goods. Today, the Common Market, with its 170 million people that will become 225 million when Britain joins, is creating in Europe a huge continental market on the American scale.

The large market does not prejudge the future economic systems of Europe. Most of the Six have a nationalized sector as large as the British and some also have planning procedures. These are just as compatible with private enterprise on the large market as they are within a single nation. The contribution of the Common Market is to create new opportunities of expansion for all the members, which make it easier to solve any problems that arise, and to provide the rest of the world with prospects of growing trade that would not exist without it. In Europe, an open society looking to the future is replacing a defensive one regretting the past.

The profound change is being made possible essentially by the new method of common action which is the core of the European Community. To establish this new method of common action, we adapted to our situation the methods which have allowed individuals to live together in society: common rules which each member is committed to respect, and common institutions to watch over the application of these rules. Nations have applied this method within their frontiers for centuries, but they have never yet been applied between them. After a period of trial and error, this method has become a permanent dialogue between a single European body, responsible for expressing the view of the general interest of the Community, and the national governments expressing the national views. The resulting procedure for collective decisions is something quite new and, as far as I know, has no analogy in any traditional system. It is not federal because there is no central government; the nations take their decisions together in the Council of Ministers. On the other hand, the independent European body proposes policies, and the common element is further underlined by the European Parliament and the European Court of Justice.

This system leads to a completely changed approach to common action. In the past, the nations felt no irrevocable commitment. Their responsibility was strictly to themselves, not to any common interest. They had to rely on themselves alone. Relations took the form either of domination if one country was much stronger than the others, or of the trading of advantages if there was a balance of powers between them. This balance was necessarily unstable and the concessions made in an agreement one year could always be retracted the next.

But in the European Communities, common rules applied by joint institutions give each a responsibility for the effective working of the Community as a whole. This leads the nations, within the discipline of the Community, to seek a solution to the problems themselves, instead of trading temporary advantages. It is this method which explains the dramatic change in the relations of Germany with France and the other Common Market countries. Looking forward to a common future has made them agree to live down the feuds of the past. Today people have almost forgotten that the Saar was ever a problem and yet from 1919 to 1950 it was a major bone of contention between France and Germany. European unity has made it seem an anachronism. And today, at French invitation, German troops are training on French soil.

· · ·

We have seen that Europe has overcome the attitude of domination which ruled state policies for so many centuries. But quite apart from what this means for us in the old continent, this is a fact of world importance. It is obvious that countries and peoples who are overcoming this state of mind between themselves will bring the same mentality to their relations with others, outside Europe. The new method of action developed in Europe replaces the efforts at domination of nation states by a constant process of collective adaptation to new conditions, a chain reaction, a ferment where one change induces another.

Look at the effect the Common Market has already had on world tariffs. When it was set up, it was widely assumed the member countries would want to protect themselves and become, as some put it, an inward-looking group. Yet everything that has happened since has shown this view to be wrong. The Six have reduced the tariffs between themselves and towards other countries faster than expected. Now President Kennedy proposes America and Europe should cut tariffs on manufactures by half, and the Common Market will certainly welcome it. This leads to a situation where tariffs throughout the major trading areas of the world will be lower than they have ever been.

These changes inside and outside Europe would not have taken place without the driving force of the Common Market. It opens new prospects for dealing with problems the solution of which was becoming increasingly urgent. I am thinking of world agriculture in a more and more industrial civilization; of links between the new and the long-established industrial regions, and in particular of the need for growing trade between Japan and the United States and Europe together.

Naturally, increasing trade will also benefit the Commonwealth. The prospect of Britain's future entry into the Common Market has already made the Continent more aware than ever before of the problems of the Commonwealth. Clearly, for countries whose major need is to obtain more capital for development, the fact that Britain is part of a rapidly developing Europe holds great promise of future progress.

Similarly, problems are arising that only Europe and the United States together have the resources to deal with. The need to develop policies of sustained growth, which in large part depend on maintaining international monetary stability, is an example. Increasing the aid of the West to the underdeveloped areas on a large scale is another. Separately, the European nations have inevitably taken divergent views of aid policies. But tomorrow, the nations of Europe by acting together can make a decisive contribution. The necessary precondition of such a partnership between America and Europe is that Europe should be united and thus be able to deploy resources on the same scale as America. This is what is in the course of happening today.

That we have begun to cooperate on these affairs at the Atlantic level is a great step forward. It is evident that we must soon go a good deal further towards an Atlantic Community. The creation of a united Europe brings this nearer by making it possible for America and Europe to act as partners on an equal footing. I am convinced that ultimately, the United States too will delegate powers of effective action to common institutions, even on political questions. Just as the United States in their own day found it necessary to unite, just as Europe is now in the process of uniting, so the West must move towards some kind of union. This is not an end in itself. It is the beginning on the road to the more orderly world we must have if we are to escape destruction.

The discussions on peace today are dominated by the question of disarmament. The world will be more and more threatened by destruction as long as bombs continue to pile up on both sides. Many therefore feel that the hopes for peace in the world depend on as early an agreement on armaments as possible, particularly an agreement on nuclear arms. Of course we must continue to negotiate on these questions. But it is too simple to hope the problems that arise out of philosophic conflicts could be settled without a change in the view which people take of the future. For what is the Soviet objective? It is to achieve a Communist world, as Mr. Khrushchev has told us many times. When this becomes so obviously impossible that nobody, even within a closed society, can any longer believe it—when the partnership of America and a United Europe makes it plain to all that the West may change from within but that others cannot change it by outside pressures, then Mr. Khrushchev or his successor will accept the facts, and the conditions will at last exist for turning so-called peaceful coexistence into genuine peace. Then at last real disarmament will become possible.

Personally, I do not think we shall have to wait long for this change. The history of European unification shows that when people become convinced a change is taking place that creates a new situation, they act on their revised estimate before that situation is established. After all, Britain has asked to join the Common Market before it was complete. The President of the United States is seeking powers to negotiate with the European Community on steps to an Atlantic partnership even before Britain has joined. Can we not expect a similar phenomenon in the future relations with the Soviet Union?

What conclusions can we draw from all these thoughts?

One impression predominates in my mind over all others. It is this: unity in Europe does not create a new kind of great power; it is a method for introducing change in Europe and consequently in the world. People, more often outside the European Community than within, are tempted to see the European Community as a potential nineteenth-century state with all the overtones of power this implies. But we are not in the nineteenth century, and the Europeans have built up the European Community precisely in order to find a way out of the conflicts to which the nineteenth-century power philosophy gave rise. The natural attitude of a European Community based on the exercise by nations of common responsibilities will be to make these nations also aware of their responsibilities, as a Community, to the world. In fact, we already see this sense of world responsibilities developing as unity in Europe begins to affect Britain, America and many other areas of the world. European unity is not a blueprint, it is not a theory, it is a process that has already begun, of bringing peoples and nations together to adapt themselves jointly to changing circumstances.

European unity is the most important event in the West since the war, not because it is a new great power, but because the new institutional method it introduces is permanently modifying relations between nations and men. Human nature does not change, but when nations and men accept the same rule and the same institutions to make sure that they are applied, their behavior towards each other changes. This is the process of civilization itself.

Note

1. Richard Mayne, "Gray Eminence," in *Jean Monnet: The Path to European Unity*, ed. Douglas Brinkley and Clifford Hackett (New York: St. Martin's Press, 1991), 114–116.

6

A Concert of European States

Charles de Gaulle

Charles de Gaulle (1890–1970), French Resistance leader and first president of France's fifth republic, was above all a French nationalist. His overriding objective after the humiliation of World War II was to reestablish France as a great power, free from domination by the superpowers and once again the source of Western civilization's cultural and spiritual strength. De Gaulle's vision of France profoundly shaped his vision of Europe, and differed markedly from the views held by the founders of the European Communities, most noticeably Jean Monnet.

De Gaulle believed in European unity, but he criticized the supranational vision of Europe as unrealistic and undesirable. He argued instead for a "concert of European states" where national governments coordinated their policies extensively but did not give up their rights as sovereign entities to a European "superstate." De Gaulle's unwillingness to concede France's right to control its vital affairs led to the 1965 crisis in the Communities and eventually the Luxembourg Compromise, which in practice gave every member state the right to veto Community decisions. In effect, the Six were forced to accept de Gaulle's vision of an intergovernmental Europe.

War gives birth and brings death to nations. In the meantime, it never ceases to loom over their existence. For us French, the development of our national life, our political regimes and our world position from 1815 to 1870 was determined by the hostile coalition which united the nations of Europe against the Revolution, the dazzling victories and then the down-

From "Europe," in *Memoirs of Hope: Renewal and Endeavor,* by Charles de Gaulle, English translation by Terence Kilmartin. Copyright 1971 by George Weidenfeld and Nicolson Ltd. Originally published in French as *Mémoires d'Espoire: Le Renouveau 1958–1962, L'Effort 1962.* Copyright 1970 by Librairie Plon. Reprinted by permission of Georges Borchardt, Inc., for Librairie Plon, and The Orion Publishing Group, London.

fall of Napoleon, and finally the disastrous treaties which sanctioned so many battles. Thereafter, during the forty-four years of the "armed truce," it was our defeat, our secret desire to avenge it, but also the fear that a united Germany might inflict another on us, that dominated our actions at home and abroad. Although the gigantic effort put forth by our people in the First World War opened the way to renewal, we closed it upon ourselves by failing to consolidate our military victory, by forgoing the reparations which would have provided us with the means of industrializing our country and thus compensating for our enormous human and material losses, and, finally, by withdrawing into a passive strategic and foreign policy which left Europe a prey to Hitler's ambitions. Now, in the aftermath of the last conflict in which she had all but perished, on what premises was France to base her progress and her actions?

The first of these premises was that, in spite of everything, she was alive, sovereign and victorious. That was undoubtedly a marvel. Who would have thought that, after suffering an unparalleled disaster, after witnessing the subjection of her rulers to the authority of the enemy, after undergoing the ravages of the two greatest battles of the war and, in the meantime, prolonged plundering by the invader, after enduring the systematic abasement inflicted on her by a regime founded on surrender and humiliation, she would ever heal the wounds inflicted on her body and her soul? Who would not have sworn that her liberation, if it was to come, would be due to foreigners alone and that they would decide what was to become of her at home and abroad? Who, in the almost total extinction of her resistance, had not condemned as absurd the hope that one day the enemy would surrender to her at the same time as to her allies? Nevertheless, in the end she had emerged from the struggle with her frontiers and her unity intact, in control of her own affairs, and in the ranks of the victors. There was nothing, therefore, to prevent her now from being what she intended to be and doing what she wished to do.

This was all the more true because, for the first time in her history, she was unhampered by any threat from her immediate neighbors. Germany, dismembered, had ceased to be a formidable and domineering power. Italy regretted having turned her ambitions against us. The alliance with England, preserved by Free France, and the process of decolonization which had removed old grievances, ensured that the wind of mistrust no longer blew across the English Channel. Bonds of affection and common interest were bringing a serene France and a pacified Spain closer together across the Pyrenees. And what enmities could possibly spring up from the friendly lands of Belgium, Luxembourg, Holland or neutral Switzerland? Thus we were relieved of the state of constant tension in which dangerous neighbors once held us and which gravely hampered our activities.

It is true that, while France had lost her special vocation of being constantly in danger, the whole world was now haunted by the permanent fear of global conflict. Two empires, the American and the Soviet, now became giants in comparison with the old powers, confronted each other with their forces, their hegemonies and their ideologies. Both were in possession of nuclear armaments which could at any moment shake the entire world, and which made each of them omnipotent protectors in their respective camps. This perilous balance was liable to tip over eventually into limitless war unless it evolved into a general *détente*. For France, reduced in wealth and power by the conflicts in which she had been engaged over the past two centuries, dangerously exposed by her geographical position at the edge of the Old World and facing the New, mortally vulnerable by reason of her size and population, peace was obviously of vital importance. And, as it happened, circumstances now ordained that she should appoint herself its champion. For she was in the singular position of having no claims on what others possessed while they had nothing to claim from her, and of harboring no grievances on her own behalf against either of the giants, for whose peoples she cherished a traditional friendship confirmed by recent events, while they felt an exceptional attachment to her. In short, if there was a voice that might be listened to and a policy that might be effective with a view to setting up a new order to replace the Cold War, that voice and that policy were pre-eminently those of France. But only on condition that they were really her own and that the hand she held out in friendship was free.

At the same time, France now enjoyed a vast fund of interest and trust among peoples whose future was in gestation but who refused to pay allegiance to either of the rival dominations. China, endowed with such reserves of manpower and resources that limitless possibilities were open to her for the future; Japan, re-creating an independent world role on the basis of economic strength; India, at grips with problems of subsistence as vast as her size, but ultimately destined to turn towards the outside world; a great number of old and new states in Africa, Asia and Latin America which accepted aid from either or both of the two camps for the immediate needs of their development, but refused to align themselves—all these now looked by choice towards France. True, until she had completed the process of decolonization, they bitterly criticized her, but the criticisms soon ceased when she had liberated her former possessions. It remained for her to exploit the potential of respect, admiration and prestige which existed in her favor over a large part of the globe provided that, as the world expected of her, she served the universal cause of human dignity and progress.

Thus the same destiny which had enabled France to survive the terrible crisis of the war, offered to her afterwards, in spite of all she had lost over the past two centuries in terms of relative power and wealth, a leading international role which suited her genius, responded to her interests and matched her means. I was naturally determined that she should play this role, the more so since I believed that the internal transformation, the political stability and the social progress without which she would unquestionably be doomed to disorder and decline demanded that she should once again feel herself invested with world responsibility. Such was my philosophy. What was my policy to be as regards the practical problems that faced our country abroad?

Apart from that of Algeria and our colonies, which was for us to settle on our own, these problems were of such scope and range that their solution would be a very lengthy undertaking, unless a new war should chance to come and cut the Gordian knots tied by the previous one. Hence a sustained and continuous policy was required to deal with them, and this was precisely what, in contrast to the unending shifts and changes of the past, our new institutions made possible.

But what exactly were these problems? First of all there was Germany, divided into three by the existence of a parliamentary republic in the West, a Communist dictatorship in the East, and a special status for Berlin, a prey to the internal strains imposed by this state of affairs and the principal pawn in the rivalry between the two camps. There was Europe, impelled by reason and sentiment towards unification after the terrible convulsions which had torn it apart but radically divided by the Iron Curtain, the Cold War and the enforced subjection of its eastern half to Soviet domination. There was the organization imposed on the Atlantic alliance, which amounted to the military and political subordination of Western Europe to the United States of America. There was the problem of aid for the development of the Third World, which was used by Washington and Moscow as a battleground for their rivalry. There were crises in the East, in Africa, in Asia and in Latin America, which the rival interventions of the two giants rendered chronic and incurable. And there were the international institutions in which the two opposing camps polarized judgments on all subjects and prohibited impartiality.

In each of these fields, I wanted France to play an active part. In this poor world which deserved to be handled gently and each of whose leaders was weighed down with grave difficulties, we had to advance step by step, acting as circumstances demanded and respecting the susceptibilities of all. I myself had struck many a blow in my time, but never at the pride of a people nor at the dignity of its leaders. Yet it was essential that what we did and said should be independent of others. From the moment of my return to power, that was our rule—such a complete change of attitude on the part of our country that the world political scene was suddenly and profoundly transformed.

It is true that the Eastern camp at first confined itself to watching to see what new attitude emerged in Paris. But our Western partners, among whom up till then official France had submissively taken its place under the hegemony known as Atlantic solidarity, could not help being put out. However, they would eventually resign themselves to the new situation. It must be said that the experience of dealing with de Gaulle which some of them had had during the war, and all of them after it, meant that they did not expect this Republic to be as easy to handle as the previous one. Still, there was a general feeling in their chancelleries, their parliaments and their newspapers that the ordeal would be a brief one, that de Gaulle would inevitably disappear after a while, and that everything would then be as it had been before. On the other hand, there was no lack of people in these countries, especially among the masses, who were not at all displeased by France's recovery and who felt a certain satisfaction, or envy perhaps, when they saw her shaking off a supremacy which weighed heavily on the whole of the Old World. Added to this were the feelings which foreign crowds were kind enough to entertain for me personally and which, each time I came in contact with them, they demonstrated with a fervor that impressed their governments. On the whole, in spite of the annoyance that was felt, the malicious remarks that were made, the unfavorable articles and aggressive caricatures that proliferated, the outside world would soon accommodate itself to a France who was once more behaving like a great power, and henceforth would follow her every action and her every word with an attention that had long been lacking.

I was to find rather less resignation in what was said and written in quarters which had hitherto been looked upon as the fountainhead of French political thought. For there it had long been more or less taken for granted that our country should take no action that was not dictated to it from outside. No doubt this attitude of mind dated from the time when the dangers which threatened France forced her continually to seek support from abroad, and when the instability of the political regime prevented the government from taking upon itself the risks of major decisions. Even before the First World War, in its alliance with Russia, the Third Republic had had to undertake to respect the Treaty of Frankfurt and let St. Petersburg lead the way rather than Paris. It is true that, during the long battle subsequently fought on our soil in alliance with the English, the Belgians and finally the Americans, the leading role and then the supreme command fell to the French, who in fact provided the principal effort. But was it not primarily the Anglo-Saxons' cry of "Halt!" that brought the sudden cessation of hostilities on 11 November 1918, at the very moment when we were about to pluck the fruits of victory? Were not the wishes and promises of the American President the dominant factor in the Treaty of Versailles, which admittedly restored Alsace and Lorraine to us but left the enemy's unity, territory and resources intact? And afterwards, was it not to gratify the wishes of Washington and London that the government in Paris surrendered the guarantees we had secured and renounced the reparations which Germany owed us in exchange for specious schemes offered to us by America? When the Hitlerian threat appeared and the Führer ventured to move his troops into the Rhineland, and preventive or repressive action on our part would have been enough to bring about his retreat and discomfiture at a time when he was still short of armaments, did not our ministers remain passive because England failed to take the initiative? At the time of the Austrian Anschluss, then the dismemberment and annexation of Czechoslovakia by the Reich, from whence did French acquiescence stem if not from the example of the English? In the surrender of Vichy to the invader's law and in the "collaboration" designed to make our country participate in a so-called European order which in fact was purely Germanic, was there not a trace of this long inurement to satellite status? At the same time, even as I strove to preserve France's sovereign rights in relation to our allies while fighting the common enemy, whence sprang the reprobation voiced by even those closest to me, if not from the idea that we should always give way?

After so many lessons, it might have been thought that once the war was over, those who claimed to lead public opinion would be less inclined towards subordination. Far from it: for the leading school of thought in each political party, national self-effacement had become an established and flaunted doctrine. While for the Communists it was an absolute rule that Moscow is always right, all the old party formations professed the doctrine of "supranationalism," in other words France's submission to a law that was not her own. Hence the support for "Europe" seen as an edifice in which technocrats forming an "executive" and parliamentarians assuming legislative powers—the great majority of both being foreigners—would have the authority to decide the fate of the French people. Hence, too, the passion for the Atlantic organization which would put the security and therefore the policy of our country at the disposal of another. Hence, again, the eagerness to submit the acts of our government to the approval of international organizations in which, under a semblance of collective deliberation, the authority of the protector reigned supreme in every field, whether political, military, economic, technical or monetary, and in which our representatives would never dare to say "we want" but simply confine themselves to "pleading France's cause." Hence, finally, the constant fury aroused among the party-political breed by my actions in the name of an independent nation.

Nevertheless, I was to find no lack of support. Emotionally, I would have the backing of the French people, who, without being in the least inclined to arrogance, were determined to preserve their own identity, all the more so because they had nearly lost it and because others everywhere were ardently affirming theirs, whether in terms of sovereignty, language, culture, production or even sport. Whenever I expressed myself in public on these matters I felt a quiver of response. Politically, the organization which had been formed to follow me above and beyond all the old parties, and which had had a numerous and compact group elected to parliament, was to accompany me through thick and thin. Practically, I would have a stable government at my side, whose Prime Minister was convinced of France's right and duty to act on a world scale, and whose Foreign Minister displayed in his field an ability which few have equalled in the course of our arduous history.

Maurice Couve de Murville had the required gifts. Amid a welter of interlocking problems and tangled arguments he was immediately able to distinguish the essential from the accessory, so that he was clear and precise in matters which others deliberately made as obscure and ambiguous as possible. He had the experience, having dealt with many of the issues of the day and known most of the men in command in the course of a distinguished career. He had the confidence, certain as he was that the post to which I had nominated him would be his for a long time. He had the manner, being skillful at making contact by listening, observing and taking note, and then excelling, at the critical moment, in the authoritative formulation of a position from which he would never be deflected. He had the necessary faith, convinced as he was that France could survive only in the first rank of nations, that de Gaulle could put her back there, and that nothing in life was more important than working towards this goal.

This was what we were aiming for in the vast arena of Europe. I myself had always felt, and now more than ever, how much the nations which peopled it had in common. Being all of the same white race, with the same Christian origins and the same way of life, linked to one another since time immemorial by countless ties of thought, art, science, politics and trade, it was natural that they should come to form a whole, with its own character and organization in relation to the rest of the world. It was in pursuance of this destiny that the Roman emperors reigned over it, that Charlemagne, Charles V and Napoleon attempted to unite it, that Hitler sought to impose upon it his crashing domination. But it is a fact of some significance that not one of these federators succeeded in inducing the subject countries to surrender their individuality. On the contrary, arbitrary centralization always provoked an upsurge of violent nationalism by way of reaction. It was my belief that a united Europe could not today, any more than in previous times, be a fusion of its peoples, but that it could and should result from a systematic *rapprochement*. Everything prompted them towards this in an age of proliferating trade, international enterprises, science and technology which know no frontiers, rapid communications and widespread travel. My policy therefore aimed at the setting up of a concert of European states which in developing all sorts of ties between them would increase their interdependence and solidarity. From this starting point, there was every reason to believe that the process of evolution might lead to their confederation, especially if they were one day to be threatened from the same source.

In practice this led us to put the European Economic Community into effect; to encourage the Six to concert together regularly in political matters; to prevent certain others, in particular Great Britain, from dragging the West into an Atlantic system which would be totally incompatible with a European Europe, and indeed to persuade these centrifugal elements to integrate themselves with the Continent by changing their outlook, their habits and their customers; and finally to set an example of *détente* followed by understanding and cooperation with the countries of the Eastern bloc, in the belief that beyond all the prejudices and preconceptions of ideology and propaganda, it was peace and progress that answered the needs and desires of the inhabitants of both halves of an accidentally divided Europe.

At the heart of the problem and at the center of the continent lay Germany. It was her destiny to be the keystone of any European edifice, and yet her misdeeds had contributed more than anything else to tearing the Old World apart. True, now that she was sliced into three segments, with the forces of her conquerors stationed in each, she was no longer a direct threat to anyone. But how could the memory of her ambition, her audacity, her power and her tyranny be effaced from people's memories—an ambition which only yesterday had unleashed a military machine capable of crushing with one blow the armies of France and her allies; an audacity which, thanks to Italy's complicity, had carried her armies as far as Africa and the Nile basin; a power which, driving across Poland and Russia with Italian, Hungarian, Bulgarian and Rumanian aid, had reached the gates of Moscow and the foothills of the Caucasus; a tyranny whose reign had brought oppression, plunder and crime wherever the fortune of war took the German flag? Henceforth, every precaution must be taken to prevent Germany's evil genius from breaking loose again. But how could a real and lasting peace be built on foundations that were unacceptable to this great people? How could a genuine union of the continent be established without Germany being a part of it? How could the age-old threat of ruin and death be finally dispelled on either side of the Rhine as long as the old enmity remained?

On the all-important question of Germany's future, my mind was made up. First of all, I believed that it would be unjust and dangerous to revise the *de facto* frontiers which the war had imposed on her. This meant that the Oder-Neisse line which separates her from Poland should remain her definitive boundary, that nothing should remain of her former claims in respect of Czechoslovakia, and that a new Anschluss in whatever form must be precluded. Furthermore, the right to possess or to manufacture atomic weapons—which in any case she had declared her intention to renounce— must in no circumstances be granted to her. This being so, I considered it essential that she should form an integral part of the organized system of cooperation between states which I envisaged for the whole of our continent. In this way the security of all nations between the Atlantic and the Urals would be guaranteed, and a change brought about in circumstances, attitudes and relationships which would doubtless ultimately permit the reunion of the three segments of the German people. In the meantime, the Federal Republic would have an essential role to play within the Economic Community and, should it ever materialize, in the political concert of the Six. Finally, I intended that France should weave a network of preferential ties with Germany, which would gradually lead the two peoples towards the mutual understanding and appreciation to which their natural instinct prompts them when they are no longer using up their energies in fighting each other.

. . .

Cooperation between the two former enemies [France and Germany] was a necessary but by no means a sufficient precondition for organized European cooperation. It is true that, judging merely by the spate of speeches and articles on the subject, the unification of our Continent might well appear to be a matter as simple as it was foreordained. But when the realities of needs, interests and preconceptions came into play, things took on an altogether different aspect. While fruitless bargaining with the British showed the fledgling Community that good intentions are not enough to reconcile the irreconcilable, the Six found that even in the economic sphere alone the adjustment of their respective positions bristled with difficulties which could not be resolved solely in terms of the treaties concluded to that end. It had to be acknowledged that the so-called executives installed at the head of common institutions by virtue of the delusions of integration which had prevailed before my return, were helpless when it came to making and enforcing decisions, that only governments were in a position to do this, and then only as a result of negotiations carried out in due form between ministers or ambassadors.

In the case of the European Coal and Steel Community, for example, once it had used up the birthday presents bestowed upon it by its member states, none of them, be it said, for our benefit—French relinquishment of coke from the Ruhr, deliveries of coal and iron to Italy, financial subventions to the Benelux mines—the High Authority, although vested with very extensive theoretical powers and considerable resources, was soon overwhelmed by the problems presented by competing national requirements. Whether it was a matter of fixing the price of steel, or regulating fuel purchases from outside, or converting the collieries of the Borinage, the areopagus enthroned in Luxembourg was powerless to legislate. The result was a chronic decline in that organization, whose prime mover, Jean Monnet, had moreover resigned the presidency.

At the same time, in the case of EURATOM, there seemed an irremediable disparity between the situation of France, equipped for some fifteen years past with an active Atomic Energy Commissariat, provided with numerous installations and already engaged in precise and far-reaching programs of research and development, and that of the other countries which, having done nothing on their own account, now wanted to use the funds of the common budget to obtain what they lacked by placing orders with American suppliers.

Lastly, in the case of the Economic Community, the adoption of the agricultural regulations in conjunction with the lowering of industrial tariffs raised obstacles which the Brussels Commission was unable to overcome on its own. It must be said that in this respect the spirit and terms of the Treaty of Rome did not meet our country's requirements. The industrial provisions were as precise and explicit as those concerning agriculture were vague. This was evidently due to the fact that our negotiators in 1957, caught up in the dream of a supranational Europe and anxious at any price to settle for something approaching it, had not felt it their duty to insist that a French interest, no matter how crucial, should receive satisfaction at the outset. It would, therefore, be necessary either to obtain it *en route*, or to liquidate the Common Market. Meanwhile, determined though it was to have its way in the end, the French government was able to allow the machinery of the Treaty of Rome to be set in motion thanks to the recovery of our balance of payments and the stabilization of the franc. In December 1958 it announced that it would implement the inaugural measures which were scheduled for New Year's Day, in particular a 10 percent tariff cut and a 20 percent quota increase.

Once initiated, the implementation of the Common Market was to give rise to a vast outgrowth of not only technical but also diplomatic activity. For, irrespective of its very wide economic scope, the operation proved to be hedged about with specifically political intentions calculated to prevent our country from being its own master. Hence, while the Community was taking shape, I was obliged on several occasions to intervene in order to repel the threats which overshadowed our cause.

The first arose from the original ambivalence of the institution. Was its objective—in itself momentous enough—the harmonization of the practical interests of the six states, their economic solidarity in face of the outside world and, if possible, their cooperation in foreign policy? Or did it aim to achieve the total fusion of their respective economies and policies in a single entity with its own government, parliament and laws, ruling in every respect its French, German, Italian, Dutch, Belgian and Luxembourg subjects, who would become fellow citizens of an artificial motherland, the brainchild of the technocrats? Needless to say, having no taste for make believe, I adopted the former conception. But the latter carried all the hopes and illusions of the supranational school.

For these champions of integration, the European executive was already alive and kicking: it was the Commission of the Economic Community, made up, admittedly, of representatives nominated by the six states but, thereafter, in no way dependent on them. Judging by the chorus of those who wanted Europe to be a federation, albeit without a federator, all the authority, initiative and control of the exchequer which are the prerogatives of government in the economic sphere must in future belong to this brigade of experts, not only within the Community but also—and this could be indefinitely extensible—from the point of view of relations with other countries. As for the national ministers, who could not as yet be dispensed with in their executive capacity, they had only to be summoned periodically to Brussels, where they would receive the Commission's instructions in their specialized fields. At the same time, the mythmongers wanted to exhibit the Assembly in Strasbourg, consisting of deputies and senators delegated by the legislatures of the member countries, as a "European parliament" which, while having no effective power, provided the Brussels "executive" with a semblance of democratic responsibility.

Walter Hallstein was the Chairman of the Commission. He was ardently wedded to the thesis of the superstate, and bent all his skillful efforts towards giving the Community the character and appearance of one. He had made Brussels, where he resided, into a sort of capital. There he sat, surrounded with all the trappings of sovereignty, directing his colleagues, allocating jobs among them, controlling several thousand officials who were appointed, promoted and remunerated at his discretion, receiving the credentials of foreign ambassadors, laying claim to high honors on the occasion of his official visits, concerned above all to further the amalgamation of the Six, believing that the pressure of events would bring about what he envisaged. But after meeting him more than once and observing his activities, I felt that although Walter Hallstein was in his way a sincere European, he was first and foremost a German who was ambitious for his own country. For in the Europe that he sought lay the framework in which his country could first of all regain, free of charge, the respectability and equality of rights which the frenzy and defeat of Hitler had cost it, then acquire the preponderant influence which its economic strength would no doubt earn it, and finally ensure that the cause of its frontiers and its unity was backed by a powerful coalition in accordance with the doctrine to which, as Foreign Minister of the Federal Republic, he had formerly given his name. These factors did not alter my esteem and regard for Walter Hallstein, but the goals I was pursuing on behalf of France were incompatible with such projects.

The fundamental divergence between the way the Brussels Commission conceived its role and my own government's insistence, while looking to the Commission for expert advice, that important measures should be subordinated to the decisions of the individual states, nurtured an atmosphere of latent discord. But since the Treaty specified that during the inaugural period no decision was valid unless unanimous, it was enough to enforce its application to ensure that there was no infringement of French sovereignty. So during this period the institution took wing in what was and must remain the economic sphere without being subjected to any mortal political crisis, in spite of frequent clashes. Moreover, in November 1959, at the initiative of Paris, it was decided that the six foreign ministers should meet at three-monthly intervals to examine the overall situation and its various implications and to report back to their own governments, which would have the last word if the need arose. It may be imagined that ours did not allow itself to be led.

But it was not only from the political angle that the newfledged Community had to undergo the truth test. Even in the economic sphere two formidable obstacles, secreting all kinds of contradictory interests and calculations, threatened to bar its way. These were, of course, the external tariff and agriculture, which were closely bound up with each other. True, on signing the Treaty, our partners had seemed to accept that common taxes should be imposed upon foreign goods as customs duties were reduced within the Community. But although they all recognized in principle that this procedure was essential to their solidarity, some of them were nonetheless irked by it because it deprived them of trade facilities which had hitherto been intrinsic to their existence. They therefore wanted the common external tariff to be as low as possible and in any case so elastic that their habits would not be disturbed. The same countries, for the same reasons, were in no hurry to see the Six take upon themselves the consumption and, therefore, the cost of continental farm products, nearly half of which happened to be French. For instance, Germany, nearly two-thirds of whose food was imported cheaply from outside the Community in exchange for manufactured goods, would have liked to see a Common Market for industrial goods only, in which case the Federal Republic would inevitably have had an overwhelming advantage. This was unacceptable to France. We therefore had to put up a fight in Brussels.

The battle was long and hard. Our partners, who bitterly regretted our having changed Republics, had been counting on us once again to sacrifice our own cause to "European integration," as had happened successively with the Coal and Steel Community, in which all the advantages went to others at our expense; with EURATOM, for which our country put up practically the entire stake without a *quid pro quo,* and, moreover, submitted her atomic assets to foreign supervision; and with the Treaty of Rome, which did not settle the agricultural question which was of paramount importance to ourselves. But now France was determined to get what she needed, and in any case her demands were consistent with the logic of the Community system. So her requirements were eventually met.

In May 1960, at our urgent insistence, the Six agreed to establish the external tariff and to adopt a timetable for the decisions to be taken on agricultural policy. In December of the same year, while urging an acceleration of the process of lowering customs barriers between them, they agreed that all imports of foodstuffs from elsewhere should be liable to an enormous financial levy at the expense of the purchasing state. And in January 1962 they adopted the decisive resolutions.

For at this date, now that the first phase of application was completed, it had to be decided whether or not, in pursuance of the terms of the Treaty, to proceed to the second phase, a kind of point of no return, involving a 50 percent reduction in customs duties. We French were determined to seize the opportunity to tear aside the veil and induce our partners to make formal commitments on what we regarded as essential. When they proved reluctant to give way, and indeed showed signs of some disquieting reservations, I judged that now or never was the moment to take the bull by the horns. Our ministers in Brussels, Couve de Murville, Baumgartner and Pisani, made it quite clear that we were prepared to withdraw from the Community if our requirements were not met. I myself wrote in similar terms to Chancellor Adenauer, whose government was our principal antagonist in this matter, and repeated it by formal telegram on the evening of the final debate. Feeling ran high in the capitals of the Six. In France, the parties and most of the newspapers, echoing foreign opinion, were disturbed and scandalized by the attitude of General de Gaulle, whose intransigence was threatening "the hopes of Europe." But France and common sense prevailed. During the night of 13–14 January 1962, after some dramatic exchanges, the Council of Ministers of the six states formally decided to admit agriculture into the Common Market, laid down then and there a broad basis for its implementation, and made the necessary arrangements to establish the agricultural regulations on the same footing and at the same time as the rest. Whereupon the implementation of the Treaty was able to enter its second phase.

But how far could it go, in view of the difficulties which the British were doing their utmost to raise, and the tendency of our five partners to submit to their influence? It was not surprising that Great Britain should be radically opposed to the whole venture, since by virtue of her geography, and therefore her policy, she has never been willing to see the Continent united or to merge with it herself. In a sense it might almost be said that therein lay the whole history of Europe for the past eight hundred years. As for the present, our neighbors across the Channel, adapted to free trade by the maritime nature of their economic life, could not sincerely agree to shut themselves up behind a continental tariff wall, still less to buy their food dear from us rather than import it cheap from everywhere else, for example the Commonwealth. But without the common tariff and agricultural preference, there could be no valid European Community. Hence at the time of the preliminary studies and discussions that led up to the Treaty of Rome, the London government, which was represented at the outset, had soon withdrawn. Then, with the intention of undermining the project of the Six, it had proposed that they should join a vast European free trade area with itself and various others. Things had reached this stage when I returned to power.

As early as 29 June 1958, Prime Minister Harold Macmillan had come to see me in Paris. In the midst of our friendly discussions which touched upon a great many topics, he suddenly declared with great feeling: "The Common Market is the Continental System all over again. Britain cannot accept it. I beg you to give it up. Otherwise, we shall be embarking on a war which will doubtless be economic at first but which runs the risk of gradually spreading into other fields." Ignoring the overstatement, I tried to pacify the English premier, at the same time asking him why the United Kingdom should object to seeing the Six establish a system of preference such as existed inside the Commonwealth. Meanwhile, his minister, Reginald Maudling, was actively engaged inside the so-called Organization for European Economic Cooperation, to which Britain belonged, in negotiations which were keeping the Six in suspense, and delaying the launching of the Community by proposing that the latter should be absorbed and, consequently, dissolved in a free trade area. Harold Macmillan wrote me a number of very pressing letters in an effort to obtain my compliance. But my government broke the spell, and made it clear that it would not agree to anything which did not include the common external tariff and an agricultural arrangement. London then appeared to abandon its policy of obstruction and, suddenly changing course, set up its own European Free Trade Association, with the Scandinavians, Portugal, Switzerland and Austria. At once, our Brussels partners dropped all their hesitations and set about launching the Common Market.

But the match had merely been postponed. In the middle of 1961 the British returned to the offensive. Having failed from without to prevent the birth of the Community, they now planned to paralyze it from within. Instead of calling for an end to it, they now declared that they themselves were eager to join, and proposed examining the conditions on which they might do so, "provided that their special relationships with the Commonwealth and their associates in the free trade area were taken into consideration, as well as their special interests in respect of agriculture." To submit to this would obviously have meant abandoning the Common Market as originally conceived. Our partners could not bring themselves to do so. But, on the other hand, it was beyond their power to say "No" to England. So, affecting to believe that the squaring of the circle was a practical proposition, they proceeded to discuss a series of projects and counter-projects in Brussels with the British minister, Edward Heath, which threw nothing but doubt on the future of the Community. I could see the day approaching when I should either have to remove the obstruction and put an end to the tergiversation, or else extricate France from an enterprise which had gone astray almost as soon as it had begun. At all events, as could have been foreseen, it was now clear to all that in order to achieve the unification of Europe, individual states are the only valid elements, that when their national interest is at stake nothing and nobody must be allowed to force their hands, and that cooperation between them is the only road that will lead anywhere.

In this respect what is true of economics is even truer of politics. And this is no more than natural. What depths of illusion or prejudice would have to be plumbed in order to believe that European nations forged through long centuries by endless exertion and suffering, each with its own geography, history, language, traditions and institutions, could cease to be themselves and form a single entity? What a perfunctory view is reflected in the parallel often naively drawn between what Europe ought to do and what the United States have done, when the latter was created from nothing in a completely new territory by successive waves of uprooted colonists? For the Six in particular, how was it conceivable that their external aims should suddenly become identical when their origins, situations and ambitions were so very different? In the matter of decolonization, which France was about to bring to a conclusion, what part could her neighbors play? If, from time immemorial, it had been in her nature to accomplish "God's work," to disseminate freedom of thought, to be a champion of humanity, why should it *ipso facto* become the concern of her partners? Germany, balked by defeat of her hopes of supremacy, divided at present and suspected by many of seeking her revenge, was now a wounded giant. By what token should her wounds automatically be shared by others? Given the fact that Italy, having ceased to be an annex of the Germanic or the French empires, and thwarted of her Balkan ambitions, remained a peninsular power confined to the Mediterranean and naturally located within the orbit of the maritime nations, why should she throw in her lot with the Continentals? By what miracle would the Netherlands, which had always owed its livelihood to shipping and its independence to overseas resources, allow itself to be swallowed up by the land powers? How could Belgium, hard put to it to maintain the juxtaposition of Flemings and Walloons in a single entity ever since a compromise between rival powers had turned her into a State, genuinely devote herself to anything else? With Luxembourg lying at the center of the territorial arrangements which had succeeded the rivalries of the two great countries bordering on the Moselle, what major concern could its people have other than the survival of Luxembourg?

On the other hand, while recognizing that each of these countries had its own national personality which it must preserve, there was no reason why they should not organize concerted action in every sphere, arrange for their ministers to meet regularly and their Heads of State or Government periodically, set up permanent organs to discuss politics, economics, culture and defense, have these subjects debated in the normal way by an assembly of delegates from their respective parliaments, acquire the taste and habit of examining together problems of common interest, and as far as possible adopt a united attitude towards them. Linked with what was already being practiced in the economic sphere in Brussels and Luxembourg, might not this general cooperation lead to a European policy as regards progress, security, influence, external relations, aid to the developing countries, and finally and above all as regards peace? Might not the grouping thus formed by the Six gradually attract the other states of the Continent into joining in on the same terms? And perhaps in this way, by opposing war, which is the history of men, that united Europe which is the dream of the wise might ultimately be achieved.

.   .   .

In the course of a press conference on 5 September [1960], after saying that "to build Europe, which means to unite Europe, is an essential aim of our policy," I declared that to this end it was necessary "to proceed, not on the basis of dreams, but in accordance with realities. Now, what are the realities of Europe? What are the pillars on which it can be built? The truth is that those pillars are the states of Europe . . . states each of which, indeed, has its own genius, history and language, its own sorrows, glories and ambitions; but states that are the only entities with the right to give orders and the power to be obeyed." Then, while recognizing "the technical value of certain more or less extranational or supranational organisms," I pointed out that they were not and could not be politically effective, as was proved by what was happening at that very moment in the European Coal and Steel Community, EURATOM and the Brussels Community. I insisted that, "although it is perfectly natural for the states of Europe to have specialist bodies available to prepare and whenever necessary to follow up their decisions, those decisions must be their own." Then I outlined my plan: "To arrange for the regular cooperation of the states of Western Europe in the political, economic and cultural spheres, as well as that of defense, is an aim that France deems desirable, possible and practical. . . . It will entail organized, regular consultations between the governments concerned and the work of specialist bodies in each of the common domains, subordinated to those governments. It will entail periodic deliberations by an assembly made up of delegates of the national parliaments. It must also, in my view, entail as soon as possible a solemn European referendum, in order to give this new departure for Europe the popular backing which is essential to it." I concluded: "If we set out on this road . . . links will be forged, habits will be developed, and, as time does its work, it is possible that we will come to take further steps towards European unity."

.   .   .

7

Preamble to the Single European Act

Representatives of the twelve members of the European Community signed the Single European Act (SEA) in February 1986 and saw it implemented in July 1987. The SEA, the first major revision of the Treaties of Rome, brought together in one "single" act a treaty on European cooperation in the area of foreign policy and institutional and procedural reforms (such as the increased use of qualified majority voting and the introduction of the cooperation procedure) designed to facilitate the completion of the Single Market. The SEA, while not universally recognized as significant at the time, marked a milestone in the attempt by Community leaders to bury the legacy of Charles de Gaulle and "relaunch" Europe. The success of the SEA in facilitating the Single Market opened the way for further institutional reforms in the early 1990s.

The preamble to the SEA differs significantly from its predecessors. Gone is the vision of a united Europe as an alternative to war. In its place is a vision of an evolving European Union ready to act in the world as a single entity to protect the common interests of its members, promote democracy and human rights, contribute to the "preservation of international peace," and "improve the economic and social situation in Europe." The preamble assumed the European Communities now resembled a sovereign entity more than a mere collection of individual states, an evolution the signatories believed corresponded to the "wishes of the democratic peoples of Europe."

· · ·

MOVED by the will to continue the work undertaken on the basis of the Treaties establishing the European Communities and to transform relations as a whole among their States into a European Union, in accordance with the Solemn Declaration of Stuttgart of 19 June 1983,

RESOLVED to implement this European Union on the basis, firstly, of the Communities operating in accordance with their own rules and, secondly, of European Cooperation among the Signatory States in the sphere of foreign policy and to invest this union with the necessary means of action,

DETERMINED to work together to promote democracy on the basis of the fundamental rights recognized in the constitutions and laws of the Member States, in the Convention for the Protection of Human Rights and Fundamental Freedoms and the European Social Charter, notably freedom, equality and social justice,

CONVINCED that the European idea, the results achieved in the fields of economic integration and political cooperation, and the need for new developments correspond to the wishes of the democratic peoples of Europe, for whom the European Parliament, elected by universal suffrage, is an indispensable means of expression,

AWARE of the responsibility incumbent upon Europe to aim at speaking ever increasingly with one voice and to act with consistency and solidarity in order more effectively to protect its common interests and independence, in particular to display the principles of democracy and compliance with the law and with human rights to which they are attached, so that together they may make their own contribution to the preservation of international peace and security in accordance with the undertaking entered into by them within the framework of the United Nations Charter,

DETERMINED to improve the economic and social situation by extending common policies and pursuing new objectives, and to ensure a smoother functioning of the Communities by enabling the institutions to exercise their powers under conditions most in keeping with Community interests,

WHEREAS at their Conference in Paris from 19 to 21 October 1972 the Heads of State or of Government approved the objective of the progressive realization of Economic and Monetary Union,

HAVING REGARD to the Annex to the conclusions of the Presidency of the European Council in Bremen on 6 and 7 July 1978 and the Resolution of the European Council in Brussels on 5 December 1978 on the introduction of the European Monetary System (EMS) and related questions, and noting that in accordance with that Resolution, the Community and the Central Banks of the Member States have taken a number of measures intended to implement monetary cooperation,

HAVE DECIDED to adopt this Act.

.   .   .

8

A Family of Nations

Margaret Thatcher

Margaret Thatcher (1925–2013) served as Britain's prime minister from 1979 to 1990. During her eleven years in office, she attempted to reduce the role of government in British society, particularly the economy. Her distrust of big government extended to the institutions of the European Community, which she considered a threat to prosperity in Europe and her policy successes in Britain. While prime minister, Thatcher raised the ire of most EC leaders by working tirelessly and unapologetically for Britain's particular interests and by resisting, often alone, most attempts to expand the powers of EC institutions. After her elevation to the House of Lords, she furthered her reputation as a virulent Euroskeptic by leading a small group of parliamentarians in a loud but unsuccessful fight to block Britain's ratification of the Maastricht treaty in 1993.

Prime Minister Thatcher outlined her views on European integration in a speech at the College of Europe in Bruges, Belgium, on 20 September 1988. There she placed Britain firmly in Europe but rejected the notion that "Europe" meant the absorption of Britain—and all the other member states—into a single, bureaucratized European "superstate." The European Community, she argued, would succeed only if each member state was allowed to maintain its own identity. Her vision—which mirrors de Gaulle's—of Europe as a "family of nations" represented well the traditional British approach to integration but challenged the federalist vision of the founders and continental builders of the Community. For this reason, Margaret Thatcher's Bruges speech proved highly controversial.

Mr. Chairman, you have invited me to speak on the subject of Britain and Europe. Perhaps I should congratulate you on your courage. If you believe some of the things said and written about my views on Europe, it must seem rather like inviting Genghis Khan to speak on the virtues of peaceful coexistence!

I want to start by disposing of some myths about my country, Britain, and its relationship with Europe. And to do that I must say something about the identity of Europe itself. Europe is not the creation of the Treaty of Rome. Nor is the European idea the property of any group or institution. We British are as much heirs to the legacy of European culture as any other nation. Our links to the rest of Europe, the continent of Europe, have been the dominant factor in our history. For three hundred years we were part of the Roman Empire and our maps still trace the straight lines of the roads the Romans built. Our ancestors—Celts, Saxons and Danes—came from the continent. Our nation was—in that favorite Community word—"restructured" under Norman and Angevin rule in the eleventh and twelfth centuries. This year we celebrate the three hundredth anniversary of the Glorious Revolution in which the British crown passed to Prince William of Orange and Queen Mary. Visit the great churches and cathedrals of Britain, read our literature and listen to our language: all bear witness to the cultural riches which we have drawn from Europe—and other Europeans from us.

We in Britain are rightly proud of the way in which, since Magna Carta in 1215, we have pioneered and developed representative institutions to stand as bastions of freedom. And proud too of the way in which for centuries Britain was a home for people from the rest of Europe who sought sanctuary from tyranny. But we know that without the European legacy of political ideas we could not have achieved as much as we did. From classical and medieval thought we have borrowed that concept of the rule of law which marks out a civilized society from barbarism. And on that idea of Christendom—for long synonymous with Europe—with its recognition of the unique and spiritual nature of the individual, we still base our belief in personal liberty and other human rights.

Too often the history of Europe is described as a series of interminable wars and quarrels. Yet from our perspective today surely what strikes us most is our common experience. For instance, the story of how Europeans explored and colonized and—yes, without apology—civilized much of the world is an extraordinary tale of talent, skill and courage.

We British have in a special way contributed to Europe. Over the centuries we have fought to prevent Europe from falling under the dominance of a single power. We have fought and we have died for her freedom. Only miles from here in Belgium lie the bodies of 120,000 British soldiers who died in the First World War. Had it not been for that willingness to fight and to die, Europe would have been united long before now—but not in liberty, not in justice. It was British support to resistance movements throughout the last War that helped to keep alive the flame of liberty in so many countries until the day of liberation. It was from our island fortress that the liberation of Europe itself was mounted. And still today we stand together. Nearly 70,000 British servicemen are stationed on the mainland of Europe. All these things alone are proof of our commitment to Europe's future.

The European Community is one manifestation of that European identity. But it is not the only one. We must never forget that east of the Iron Curtain peoples who once enjoyed a full share of European culture, freedom and identity have been cut off from their roots. We shall always look on Warsaw, Prague and Budapest as great European cities. Nor should we forget that European values have helped to make the United States of America into the valiant defender of freedom which she has become.

This is no arid chronicle of obscure facts from the dust-filled libraries of history. It is the record of nearly two thousand years of British involvement in Europe, cooperation with Europe and contribution to Europe, a contribution which today is as valid and as strong as ever. Yes, we have looked also to wider horizons—as have others—and thank goodness for that because Europe never would have prospered and never will prosper as a narrow-minded, inward-looking club.

The European Community belongs to all its members. It must reflect the traditions and aspirations of all its members. And let me be quite clear. Britain does not dream of some cozy isolated existence on the fringes of the European Community. Our destiny is in Europe, as part of the Community. That is not to say that our future lies only in Europe. But nor does that of France or Spain or indeed any other member.

The Community is not an end in itself. Nor is it an institutional device to be constantly modified according to the dictates of some abstract intellectual concept. Nor must it be ossified by endless regulation. The European Community is the practical means by which Europe can ensure the future prosperity and security of its people in a world in which there are many other powerful nations and groups of nations. We Europeans cannot afford to waste our energies on internal disputes or arcane institutional debates. They are no substitute for effective action. Europe has to be ready both to contribute in full measure to its own security and to compete commercially and industrially, in a world in which success goes to the countries which encourage individual initiative and enterprise, rather than to those which attempt to diminish them.

This evening I want to set out some guiding principles for the future which I believe will ensure that Europe does succeed, not just in economic and defence terms but also in the quality of life and the influence of its peoples.

My first guiding principle is this: willing and active cooperation between independent sovereign states is the best way to build a successful European Community. To try to suppress nationhood and concentrate power at the center of a European conglomerate would be highly damaging and would jeopardize the objectives we seek to achieve. Europe will be stronger precisely because it has France as France, Spain as Spain, Britain as Britain, each with its own customs, traditions and identity. It would be folly to try to fit them into some sort of identikit European personality.

Some of the founding fathers of the Community thought that the United States of America might be its model. But the whole history of America is quite different from Europe. People went there to get away from the intolerance and constraints of life in Europe. They sought liberty and opportunity; and their strong sense of purpose has, over two centuries, helped create a new unity and pride in being American—just as our pride lies in being British or Belgian or Dutch or German.

I am the first to say that on many great issues the countries of Europe should try to speak with a single voice. I want to see us work more closely on the things we can do better together than alone. Europe is stronger when we do so, whether it be in trade, in defense, or in relations with the rest of the world. But working more closely together does not require power to be centralized in Brussels or decisions to be taken by an appointed bureaucracy. Indeed, it is ironic that just when those countries such as the Soviet Union, which have tried to run everything from the center, are learning that success depends on dispersing power and decisions away from the center, some in the Community seem to want to move in the opposite direction. We have not successfully rolled back the frontiers of the state in Britain, only to see them reimposed at a European level, with a European superstate exercising a new dominance from Brussels.

Certainly we want to see Europe more united and with a greater sense of common purpose. But it must be in a way which preserves the different traditions, parliamentary powers and sense of national pride in one's own country; for these have been the source of Europe's vitality through the centuries.

My second guiding principle is this: Community policies must tackle present problems in a practical way, however difficult they may be. If we cannot reform those Community policies which are patently wrong or ineffective and which are rightly causing public disquiet, then we shall not get the public's support for the Community's future development.

.   .   .

My third guiding principle is the need for Community policies which encourage enterprise. If Europe is to flourish and create the jobs of the future, enterprise is the key. The basic framework is there: the treaty of Rome itself was intended as a Charter for Economic Liberty. But that is not how it has always been read, still less applied.

The lesson of the economic history of Europe in the 1970s and 1980s is that central planning and detailed control don't work, and that personal endeavor and initiative do. That a state-controlled economy is a recipe for low growth; and that free enterprise within a framework of law brings better results. The aim of a Europe open to enterprise is the moving force behind the creation of the Single European Market by 1992. By getting rid of barriers, by making it possible for companies to operate on a Europewide scale, we can best compete with the United States, Japan and the other new economic powers emerging in Asia and elsewhere. And that means action to free markets, action to widen choice, action to reduce government intervention. Our aim should not be more and more detailed regulation from the center: it should be to deregulate and to remove the constraints on trade.

. . .

My fourth guiding principle is that Europe should not be protectionist. The expansion of the world economy requires us to continue the process of removing barriers to trade, and to do so in the multilateral negotiations in the GATT [General Agreement on Tariffs and Trade]. It would be a betrayal if, while breaking down constraints on trade within Europe, the Community were to erect greater external protection. We must ensure that our approach to world trade is consistent with the liberalization we preach at home.

We have a responsibility to give a lead on this, a responsibility which is particularly directed towards the less developed countries. They need not only aid; more than anything they need improved trading opportunities if they are to gain the dignity of growing economic strength and independence.

. . .

I believe it is not enough just to talk in general terms about a European vision or ideal. If we believe in it, we must chart the way ahead and identify the next steps. That is what I tried to do this evening.

This approach does not require new documents: they are all there, the North Atlantic Treaty, the Revised Brussels Treaty, and the Treaty of Rome, texts written by far-sighted men. However far we may want to go, the truth is that we can only get there one step at a time.

What we need now is to take decisions on the next steps forward rather than let ourselves be distracted by Utopian goals. Utopia never comes, because we know we should not like it if it did. Let Europe be a family of nations, understanding each other better, appreciating each other more, doing more together but relishing our national identity no less than our common European endeavor.

Let us have a Europe which plays its full part in the wider world, which looks outward not inward, and which preserves that Atlantic Community—that Europe on both sides of the Atlantic—which is our noblest inheritance and our greatest strength.

9

A Necessary Union

Jacques Delors

Jacques Delors assumed the presidency of the Commission of the European Community in January 1985 and served for ten years. Prior to his appointment to the Commission, he was elected to the European Parliament (1979) and served as minister of finance (1981–1984) in France. Delors's energetic and visionary leadership contributed significantly to the revival of the Community in the 1980s and early 1990s. Under his watch the Community took several significant steps, including the creation of the Single Market and the European Economic Area; expansion to Portugal, Spain, Austria, Finland, and Sweden; and negotiation and implementation of the Single European Act and the Maastricht treaty.

On 17 October 1989, one year after Margaret Thatcher made her Bruges speech, Jacques Delors traveled to the same spot and offered an alternative vision. His purpose was to convince the Community to seize the moment afforded by history and take a dramatic leap toward federalism. World events, particularly those in the East, and global interdependence necessitated the strengthening of Community institutions and the expansion of the "joint exercise of sovereignty." But true federalism, he asserted, included the principle of subsidiarity: "Never entrust to a bigger unit anything that is best done by a smaller one." Subsidiarity, he argued in response to Margaret Thatcher, made federalism the savior of pluralism, diversity, patriotism, and national identity in Europe. Indeed, the rejection of federalism, he warned, would mean the return of ugly nationalism.

Two years later, in Maastricht, EC leaders heeded Delors's Bruges call.

I am speaking to you today at the invitation of your Rector, Professor Lukaszewski, as the College of Europe celebrates its fortieth

---

Reprinted with permission from *Address by Mr. Jacques Delors, President of the Commission of the European Communities, Bruges, 17 October 1989.* Copyright 1989 by Agence Europe.

birthday. European integration has had its ups and downs over those forty years, its high seasons of hope and progress and its long winters of despondency and stagnation. But here, in Bruges, faith in the European ideal has never wavered. . . .

It is a happy coincidence that this year your College has chosen to pay tribute to Denis de Rougemont, an all too little-known figure, whose life-work and writings are a precious legacy. I would like to speak in more personal terms of Denis de Rougemont, I never had the good fortune to work with him, but I would like to tell you why I think so much of him, why I draw on his intellectual and political contribution.

First of all, as a militant European, I, like many others, am carrying on the work he began in his time. He was an ardent federalist. For him federalism was a many-splendored thing; he saw it as a method, an approach to reality, a view of society. I often find myself invoking federalism as a method, with the addition of the principle of subsidiarity. I see it as a way of reconciling what for many appears to be irreconcilable: the emergence of a United Europe and loyalty to one's homeland; the need for a European power capable of tackling the problems of our age and the absolute necessity to preserve our roots in the shape of our nations and regions; and decentralization of responsibilities, so that we never entrust to a bigger unit anything that is best done by a smaller one. This is precisely what subsidiarity is about.

[I speak] as a personalist, a disciple of Emmanuel Mounier, whose influence will, I am convinced, revive as Europeans become aware of the quandaries of frenzied individualism, just as, for some years now, they have been rejecting collectivism and, in its attenuated form, the benevolent State.

. . .

Denis de Rougemont believed in what I would call working from the bottom up, rebuilding from below, from small entities rooted naturally in a solidarity of interests and a convergence of feeling. That is of course essential, but it is not enough. Others, and I am one of them, must at the same time work from the top down, viewing the paths of integration from above. Otherwise the small streams of solidarity will never converge to form a wide river.

And de Rougemont abhorred power. Let me quote him again: "My philosophy comes down to this: power is the authority one would wield over others; freedom is the authority one can wield over oneself." Although I would not deny the philosophical value of this statement, I would beg to disagree with it from a political standpoint.

Politically speaking, power is not necessarily the obverse of freedom. Neither the European Community—nor the peoples and nations that form it—will truly exist unless it is in a position to defend its values, to act on them for the benefit of all, to be generous. Let us be powerful enough to command respect and to uphold the values of freedom and solidarity. In a world like ours, there is no other way.

I would link power with the necessity I have so often invoked to promote the revitalization of European integration. Today I would like to get power working for the ideal. Where would necessity take us had we no vision of what we want to achieve? And, conversely, what impact can an ideal have without the resolve and the means to act? The time has come, I feel, to reconcile necessity and the ideal.

We can do so by drawing on our own experiences, on our national heritages, and on the strength of our institutions. Let me underline the importance of this at a time when people can appreciate the limits of any action implemented with national resources alone. Our present concerns—be it the social dimension or the new frontier represented by economic and monetary union—offer a golden opportunity for the joint exercise of sovereignty, while respecting diversity and hence the principles of pluralism and subsidiarity.

There is a need for urgency, for history does not wait. As upheavals shake the world, and the other "Europe" in particular, our reinvigorated Community must work for increased cohesion and set objectives commensurate with the challenges thrown down by history.

History is only interested in the far-sighted and those who think big, like Europe's founding fathers. They are still with us today in the inspiration they provided and the legacy they left.

By "thinking big," I mean taking account of worldwide geopolitical and economic trends, the movement of ideas and the development of the fundamental values which inspire our contemporaries. The founding fathers wanted to see an end to internecine strife in Europe. But they also sensed that Europe was losing its place as the economic and political center of the world. Their intuition was confirmed before our very eyes, to the point in the 1970s when we had to choose between survival and decline. I shocked many people at that time by constantly arguing this point. Gradually, though, the need for a quantum leap became apparent and created a climate in which a single European market by 1992 could be accepted as an objective. The same dynamism led to revision of the Treaty of Rome—the Single Act—and to what is known as the Delors package, in other words the financial reforms necessary to pay for our ambitious plans. Necessity woke Europe from its slumbers.

By "far-sighted," I mean being simultaneously capable of drawing on our historical heritage and looking to the future. Futurology has a part to play but so has a code of ethics for the individual, society and the human adventure. This, frankly, is what we most lack today. I can say, with both feet on the ground, that the theory of the bogeyman-nation has no place in the life of our Community if it wants to be a Community worthy of the name. The inevitable conflicts of interest between us must be transcended by a family feeling, a sense of shared values. These include the enhancement of personality through mutual knowledge and exchange. The younger generation is very conscious of this new horizon. It rejects isolation, it wants to experience other ideas, to explore new territory. The time has come, my friends, to revive the ideal.

To get there, however, we must take the path of necessity. At a time when the Community is being courted by some, threatened by others; at a time when there are those who, with scant regard for the mortar which already binds us, advocate a headlong dash in the name of a greater Europe, or offer us as an ultimate reference nothing more than the laws of the market; to these we must say that our Community is the fruit not only of history and necessity, but also of political will.

Let us consider necessity for a moment. Since the turn-around of 1984–85 our achievements are there for all to see. The threat of a decline is receding. Businessmen and manufacturers are more aware of this than politicians, many of whom still underestimate the way in which the gradual achievement of the single European market and common policies have supported national efforts to adapt to the new world economic order. Yet all we need to do to see how far we have come is look beyond our frontiers: Europe is once again a force to be reckoned with and is arousing interest everywhere: in America, in Asia, in Africa, in the North and in the South.

Then there is political will. I know that the term has sometimes been abused, as a sort of incantation, but it is precisely political will that led first six, then nine, ten, twelve countries to decide to unite their destiny, with their eyes wide open. The contract binding them is clear, involving both rights and obligations.

Last of all, history. The Twelve cannot control history but they are now in a position to influence it once again. They did not want Europe to be cut in two at Yalta and made a hostage in the Cold War. They did not, nor do they, close the door to other European countries willing to accept the terms of the contract in full.

The present upheavals in Eastern Europe are changing the nature of our problems. It is not merely a matter of when and how all the countries of Europe will benefit from the stimulus and the advantages of a single market. Our times are dominated by a new mercantilism and our young people expect something better of us. Are we going to turn away?

Make no mistake about it. Behind triumphant nationalism and excessive individualism, ethics are making a comeback in the wake of scientific progress. How far, for example, are we prepared to allow genetic manipulation to go? We need a code of ethics for man, we need to promote our concept of the individual and his integrity. Nature, whether pillaged or neglected, strikes back with disturbances and upheavals. So we also need a code of ethics governing the relationship between man and nature. With millions of young people knocking in vain on the door of adult society, not least to find their place in the world of work, with millions of pensioners— still in the prime of life—cut off from any real role in society, we must ask ourselves what kind of society are we building. A society in which the door is always closed?

Europe has always been the continent of doubt and questioning, seeking a humanism appropriate to its time, the cradle of ideas which ultimately encircle the globe. The time has come to return to ideals, to let them penetrate our lives. Let us continue to consider, in everything we do in the field of politics, economics and social and cultural life, what will enable every man, every woman, to achieve their full potential in an awareness not only of their rights, but also of their obligations to others and to society as a whole. We must sustain our efforts to create a humane society in which the individual can blossom through contact and cooperation with others.

Of course any reference to humanism is bound to unleash a debate among Europeans. People will hold conflicting views, but a synthesis will emerge to the benefit of democracy and Europe itself. For the Community is a concept charged with significance. "Where there is no big vision, the people perish," as Jean Monnet said, making this saying of President Roosevelt's [and Prov. 29:18] his own.

In this respect we are engaged in a unique adventure. We are creating a model, admittedly by reference to inherited principles, but in circumstances so extraordinary that the end result will be unique, without historical precedent. We owe much to the strength of our institutions because our Community is a Community based on the rule of law. And the condition for success is the joint, transparent exercise of sovereignty.

Let us consider the strength of our institutions for a moment, beginning with legitimacy. Without legitimacy—as earlier attempts to unite nations have shown—no progress, no permanence is possible.

In the Community the progress of history is there for all to see. We have the Treaty duly ratified by all national parliaments, an expression of national will. The Court of Justice plays a vital role in dealing with differences of interpretation. The European Council—now institutionalized—allows Heads of State and Government to monitor progress, to pinpoint delays and failures to honor the contract that unites and binds us, to provide impetus and to make good any deficiencies. A new development is that the Commission now presents a balance sheet at each meeting of what has been accomplished and what remains to be done. The Commission takes the European Council's pronouncements very seriously and does not hesitate to remind the Twelve of undertakings given. In this way the Community is demonstrating more and more clearly that it has little in common with organizations that produce worthy resolutions that are rarely if ever acted upon.

· · ·

Many envy us our Community based on the rule of law and this explains its growing influence. What a model our institutions, which allow every country irrespective of its size to have its say and make its contribution, offer the nations of Eastern Europe. They, and many other nations besides, admire the practical, forward-looking application of pluralist democracy within our borders. In the circumstances how can anyone expect us to accept absorption into a larger, looser structure along intergovernmental lines? We would be abandoning a bird in the hand for two in the bush. It would be a tragic mistake for Europe.

Despite the success of our Community based on the rule of law, disputes about sovereignty continue. We need to face the issues squarely.

A dogmatic approach will get us nowhere. It will merely complicate the difficult discussions that lie ahead and make it even harder to remove the remaining obstacles on the road to the single European market and 1992.

The facts speak for themselves. Each nation needs to consider how much room for manoeuvre it genuinely has in today's world. The growing interdependence of our economies, the internationalization of the financial world, the present or growing influence of the main protagonists on the world stage—all point to a dual conclusion. Firstly, nations should unite if they feel close to each other in terms of geography, history, values—and also necessity. Secondly—and ideally at the same time—cooperation should develop at world level to deal with such matters as international trade, the monetary system, underdevelopment, the environment and drugs. The two are complementary rather than concurrent. Because in order to exist on a global level and to influence events, not only the trappings of power are needed, but also a strong hand—that is, a capacity for generosity which is essential to any great undertaking. Europe has little clout as yet, although, as I have said, our economic performance is impressing our partners and reassuring our own people. It is quite clear that the fault lies in the deliberately fostered fiction of full national sovereignty and hence of the absolute effectiveness of national policies.

. . .

The Commission has no intention of getting embroiled in insidious tactical manoeuvering designed to lead the member states in a direction they do not wish to take. Let me repeat that our Community is a community based on the rule of law, where we work by the book with complete openness. Indeed, this is the first rule for success. Everyone must acknowledge this in good faith. If I turn to the principles of federalism in a bid to find workable solutions, it is precisely because they provide all the necessary guarantees on pluralism and the efficiency of the emergent institutional machinery. Here, there are two essential rules:

1. the rule of autonomy, which preserves the identity of each member state and removes any temptation to pursue unification regardless;

2. the rule of participation, which does not allow one entity to be subordinated to another, but on the contrary, promotes cooperation and synergy, on the basis of the clear and well-defined provisions contained in the Treaty.

This is the starting point for an original experiment which resists comparison with any other models, such as the United States of America, for instance. I have always shied away from such parallels, because I know that our task is to unite old nations with strong traditions and personalities. There is no conspiracy against the nation state. Nobody is being asked to renounce legitimate patriotism. I want not only to unite people, as Jean Monnet did, but also to bring nations together. As the Community develops, as our governments emphasize the need for a people's Europe, is it heresy to hope that all Europeans could feel that they belong to a Community which they see as a second homeland? If this view is rejected, European integration will founder and the specter of nationalism will return to haunt us, because the Community will have failed to win the hearts and minds of the people, the first requirement for the success of any human venture.

The success of the Community is such that it is attracting interest from all quarters. It cannot ignore this without abandoning its claim to a universal dimension. But here again the question of "what should be done" is inseparable from the question of "how do we go about it."

History will not wait for the Single Act to work through the system. It is knocking at our door even now.

.   .   .

Communist Europe is exploding before our eyes. Gorbachev has launched Perestroika and Glasnost. Poland and Hungary are carrying out political reforms, ushering in an era of greater freedom and democracy. East Germany totters as tens of thousands of its people flee to the West. The virus of freedom has reached Leipzig and East Berlin.

As early as 1984 François Mitterrand, in a speech to the European Parliament, voiced his presentiment of a radical new departure in Europe. "It is clear," he said, "that we are moving away from the time when Europe's sole destiny was to be shared out and divided up by others. The two words 'European independence' now sound different. This is a fact that our century, which is nearing its end, will, I am sure, remember."

As many European leaders have already stressed, it is our Community, a Community based on the rule of law, a democratic entity and a buoyant economy, that has served as the model and the catalyst for these developments. The West is not drifting eastward, it is the East that is being drawn towards the West. Will the Community prove equal to the challenges of the future? This is the question we should ask ourselves today, whether we mean helping the countries of Eastern Europe to modernize their economies—a precondition for the success of political reforms—or getting to grips with the German question when the time comes—in other words, extending the right of self-determination to everyone.

I have no doubt that if we refuse to face up to these new challenges, not only will we be shirking our responsibilities but the Community will disintegrate, stopped in its tracks by the weight of unresolved contradictions. When I look around me now, as these events unfold, I see too much despondency, too much defeatist thinking, too much willingness paralyzed by passive acquiescence. . . . How are we to find a solution except by strengthening the federalist features of the Community which, to paraphrase Hans-Dietrich Genscher, offer the best possible guarantee of survival to all concerned? There, I am quite sure, lies the only acceptable and satisfactory solution to the German question.

How are we to shoulder our international responsibilities and at the same time pave the way for the emergence of a greater Europe, except by pressing ahead with European integration? Only a strong, self-confident Community, a Community which is united and determined, can truly hope to control that process.

The pace of change is gathering momentum and we must try to keep up. If our institutions are to adapt to the new situation, we cannot afford to shilly-shally about economic and monetary union. There is no question of shortening the time we need to test wide-ranging cooperation and move on to successive stages. That would be unrealistic. But time is running out for the political decision which will generate the dynamism necessary for success and lead to the creation of institutions with the capacity to face up to the demands imposed by our international responsibilities.

. . .

I have always favored the step-by-step approach—as the experiment we are embarked upon shows. But today I am moving away from it precisely because time is short. We need a radical change in the way we think of the Community and in the way we act on the world stage. We need to overcome whatever resistance we encounter. If only to adapt the instruments we already have, so that we can, for example, inject more substance into the Lomé Convention or make a success of our aid program for Poland and Hungary. We need to give countries that depend on exports for survival more access to our markets to prevent them plunging deeper into debt. We need financial instruments which will help these countries to adapt and modernize their economies.

I am concerned that we will never achieve all this with our present decision-making procedures. Thanks to the Single Act the Council, Parliament and the Commission are a more efficient institutional troika than they were a few years ago. But this is not enough to enable us to keep pace with events.

For the honor of your generation and mine, I hope that in two years' time we will be able to repeat the very words which another great European, Paul-Henri Spaak, spoke at the signing of the Treaty of Rome: "This time the people of the West have not lacked daring and have not acted too late."

It is time, then, for a new political initiative. The Commission is ready for it and will play its full part in pointing the way. It will propose answers to the questions raised by another quantum leap: who takes the decisions; how do the various levels of decision making intermesh (subsidiarity again!); who puts decisions into practice; what resources will be available; what will it mean in terms of democracy?

There is no doubt that we are living in exciting times, but they are dangerous times too. The Community is faced with the challenge of making a telling contribution to the next phase of our history.

As I stand before a predominantly young audience, I find myself dreaming of a Europe which has thrown off the chains of Yalta, a Europe which tends its immense cultural heritage so that it bears fruit, a Europe which imprints the mark of solidarity on a world which is far too hard and too forgetful of its underdeveloped regions.

I say to these young people: If we can achieve this Europe you will be able to stretch yourselves to the utmost, you will have all the space you need to achieve your full potential. For you are being invited to play your part in a unique venture, one which brings peoples and nations together for the better, not for the worse. It will bring you back to your philosophical and cultural roots, to the perennial values of Europe. But you will need to give of yourselves and insist that those who govern you display boldness tempered with caution, a fertile imagination and a clear commitment to making the Community a necessity for survival and an ideal towards which to work.

10

Preamble to the Treaty on European Union (The Maastricht Treaty)

↑
introduction

Several factors, including the success of the Single Market program and the collapse of communism, increased momentum for integration as the European Community entered the 1990s. In December 1990, the member states opened negotiations to complete economic and monetary union, reform EC institutions, and expand Community competence in foreign and security policy. Final negotiations took place in December 1991 in Maastricht, The Netherlands, and the Maastricht treaty was signed there on 7 February 1992. Ratification seemed certain until Danish voters rejected the treaty on 2 June 1992 and opened a debate in Europe over the merits of integration. Public dissatisfaction with the complex treaty combined with a currency crisis and a severe economic recession to sap popular and elite enthusiasm for the European project. Nevertheless, all twelve countries finally ratified the treaty, which came into force in late 1993.

The preamble to the Maastricht treaty reflects the essence of Jacques Delors's thinking: the need to construct a new Europe out of a formerly divided continent requires a leap to a new stage of integration through the creation of a European Union. The institutions of the Union will have responsibility for issue areas previously reserved for national governments. But respect for Europe's core values, increased accountability, and faithful application of the principle of subsidiarity will, according to the treaty, preserve democracy and diversity within the new Europe.

. . .

RESOLVED to mark a new stage in the process of European integration undertaken with the establishment of the European Communities,

RECALLING the historic importance of the ending of the division of the European continent and the need to create firm bases for the construction of the future Europe,

CONFIRMING their attachment to the principles of liberty, democracy and respect for human rights and fundamental freedoms and the rule of law,

DESIRING to deepen the solidarity between their peoples while respecting their history, their culture and their traditions,

DESIRING to enhance further the democratic and efficient functioning of the institutions so as to enable them better to carry out, within a single institutional framework, the tasks entrusted to them,

RESOLVED to achieve the strengthening and the convergence of their economies and to establish an economic and monetary union including, in accordance with the provisions of this Treaty, a single and stable currency,

DETERMINED to promote economic and social progress for their peoples, within the context of the accomplishment of the internal market and of reinforced cohesion and environmental protection, and to implement policies ensuring that advances in economic integration are accompanied by parallel progress in other fields,

RESOLVED to establish a citizenship common to nationals of their countries,

RESOLVED to implement a common foreign and security policy including the eventual framing of a common defence policy, which might in time lead to a common defence, thereby reinforcing the European identity and its independence in order to promote peace, security and progress in Europe and in the world,

REAFFIRMING their objective to facilitate the free movement of persons, while ensuring the safety and the security of their peoples, by including provisions on justice and home affairs in this Treaty,

RESOLVED to continue the process of creating an ever closer union among the peoples of Europe, in which decisions are taken as closely as possible to the citizen in accordance with the principle of subsidiarity,

IN VIEW of further steps to be taken in order to advance European integration,

HAVE DECIDED to establish a European Union.

.   .   .

11

February 15, or What Binds
Europeans Together

Jürgen Habermas and Jacques Derrida

The European Union at the turn of the century struggled to maintain the momentum generated in the late 1980s and early 1990s. There were bright spots: the EU continued to attract new members—Austria, Finland, and Sweden in 1995, and ten more in 2004; it successfully introduced the euro; it implemented two new treaties, Amsterdam (1999) and Nice (2001); and in late 2001 opened a constitutional convention. But referendum defeats in Denmark, Ireland, and Norway (which again rejected EU membership) and the emergence of Euroskeptical political movements in some parts of the EU indicated increased popular resistance to the reforms many argued were needed to manage an enlarged Union with enhanced responsibilities. Some pro-integration observers lamented the absence among European citizens of a collective European identity that could legitimate a federal democracy. How, they asked, could Europe forge a continental identity?

Two of Europe's most prominent philosophers, the German critical theorist Jürgen Habermas (b.1929) and the late French deconstructionist Jacques Derrida (1930–2004), saw an answer in Europe's popular protests against the US-led invasion of Iraq in early 2003. In this opinion piece, Habermas and Derrida—who were philosophical rivals in the 1980s but forged a personal friendship in the 1990s, which lasted until Derrida's death—asserted that the protests were a likely "sign of the birth of a European public sphere." But they also realized that the war had divided Europe and uncovered the failure of the EU's common foreign policy. What was needed, they argued, was a new commitment by a core group of member states to forge an independent and irresistible (to other member states) foreign and security policy that would provide the world with an effective counterweight to the "hegemonic unilateralism of the United States."

From *Constellations* 10, no. 3 (2003): 291–297. Translated by Max Pensky. Reprinted with permission from John Wiley and Sons. This piece originally appeared in the *Frankfurter Allgemeine Zeitung*, 31 May 2003.

Habermas and Derrida recognized that a European Union with a common foreign policy would have to be backed by a shared identity, a "feeling of common political belonging." Europeans, they believed, possessed the raw materials for a unique identity and a shared global vocation to "promote a cosmopolitan order on the basis of international law." Thus, they called Europeans not just to unite, but also to use their newfound confidence to lead the world—including the United States—toward a postnational global polity.

We should not forget two dates: not the day the newspapers reported to their astonished readers the Spanish prime minister's invitation to the other European nations willing to support the Iraq war to swear an oath of loyalty to George W. Bush, an invitation issued behind the back of the other countries of the European Union. But we should also remember February 15, 2003, as mass demonstrations in London and Rome, Madrid and Barcelona, Berlin and Paris reacted to this sneak attack. The simultaneity of these overwhelming demonstrations—the largest since the end of the Second World War—may well, in hindsight, go down in history as a sign of the birth of a European public sphere.

During the leaden months prior to the outbreak of the war in Iraq, a morally obscene division of labor provoked strong emotions. The large-scale logistical operation of ceaseless military preparation and the frenetic activity of humanitarian aid organizations meshed together as precisely as the teeth of a gear. Moreover, the spectacle took place undisturbed before the eyes of the very population which—robbed of their own initiative—was to be its victim. The precautionary mustering of relief workers, relief services, and relief goods dressed itself in the rash rhetoric of alleviation of suffering yet to be inflicted; the planned reconstruction of cities and administrations yet to be ruined. Like searchlights, they picked out the civilized barbarism of coolly planned death (of how many victims?), of torments long since totted up (of how many injured and mutilated, how many thirsty and hungry?), of the long-planned destruction (of how many residential districts and hospitals, how many houses, museums, and markets?). As the war finally began, the Ernst Jünger aesthetic of the skyline of the nighttime Baghdad, illuminated by countless explosions, seemed almost harmless.

A Common European Foreign Policy: Who First?

There is no doubt that the power of emotions has brought European citizens jointly to their feet. Yet at the same time, the war made Europeans conscious of the failure of their common foreign policy, a failure that has been a long time in the making. As in the rest of the world, the impetuous break with international law has ignited a debate over the future of the international order in Europe as well. But here, the divisive arguments have cut deeper, and have caused familiar faultlines to emerge even more sharply. Controversies over the role of the American superpower, over a future world order, over the relevance of international law and the United Nations—all have caused latent contradictions to break into the open. The gap between continental and Anglo-American countries on the one side, and "the old Europe" and the Central and East European candidates for entry into the European Union on the other side, has grown deeper.

In Great Britain, while the special relationship with the United States is by no means uncontested, the priorities of Downing Street are still quite clear. And the central and eastern European countries, while certainly working hard for their admission into the EU, are nevertheless not yet ready to place limits on the sovereignty that they have so recently regained. The Iraq crisis was only a catalyst. In the Brussels constitutional convention, there is now a visible contrast between the nations that really want a stronger EU, and those with an *understandable* interest in freezing, or at best cosmetically changing, the existing mode of intergovernmental governance. This contradiction can no longer be finessed. The future constitution will grant us a European foreign minister. But what good is a new political office if governments don't unify in a common policy? A [Joshka] Fischer with a changed job description would remain as powerless as [Javier] Solana.

For the moment, only the core European nations are ready to endow the EU with certain qualities of a state. But what happens if these countries can only find agreement on the definition of "self-interest"? If Europe is not to fall apart, these countries will have to make use of the mechanisms for "strengthened cooperation" created in Nice as a way of taking a first step toward a common foreign policy, a common security policy, and a common defense policy. Only such a step will succeed in generating the momentum that other member states—initially in the Eurozone—will not be able to resist in the long run. In the framework of the future European constitution, there can and must be no separatism. Taking a leading role does not mean excluding. The avant-gardist core of Europe must not wall itself off into a new Small Europe. It must—as it has so often—be the locomotive. It is from their own self-interest, to be sure, that the more closely-cooperating member states of the EU will hold the door open. And the probability that the invited states will pass through that door will increase the more capable the core of Europe becomes of effective action externally, and the sooner it can prove that in a complex global society, it is not just divisions that count, but also the soft power of negotiating agendas, relations, and economic advantages.

In this world, the reduction of politics to the stupid and costly alternative of war or peace simply doesn't pay. At the international level and in the framework of the UN, Europe has to throw its weight on the scale to counterbalance the hegemonic unilateralism of the United States. At global economic summits and in the institutions of the WTO, the World Bank, and the IMF, it should exert its influence in shaping the design for a coming global domestic policy.

Political projects that aim at the further development of the EU are now colliding with the limits of the medium of administrative steering. Until now, the functional imperatives for the construction of a common market and the Eurozone have driven reforms. These driving forces are now exhausted. A *transformative* politics, which would demand that member states not just overcome obstacles for competitiveness but form a common will, must take recourse to the motives and the attitudes of *the citizens themselves*. Majority decisions on highly consequential foreign policies can only expect acceptance assuming the solidarity of outnumbered minorities. But this presupposes a feeling of common political belonging on both sides. The population must so to speak "build up" their national identities, and add to them a European dimension. What is already a fairly abstract form of civic solidarity, still largely confined to members of nation-states, must be extended to include the European citizens of other nations as well.

This raises the question of "European identity." Only the consciousness of a shared political fate, and the prospect of a common future, can halt outvoted minorities from the obstruction of a majority will. The citizens of one nation must regard the citizens of another nation as fundamentally "one of us." This desideratum leads to the question that so many skeptics have called attention to: are there historical experiences, traditions, and achievements offering European citizens the consciousness of a political fate that has been shared together, and *that can be shaped together*? An attractive, indeed an infectious "vision" for a future Europe will not emerge from thin air. At present it can arise only from the disquieting perception of perplexity. But it well can emerge from the difficulties of a situation into which we Europeans have been cast. And it must articulate itself from out of the wild cacophony of a multi-vocal public sphere. If this theme has so far not even gotten on to the agenda, it is we intellectuals who have failed.

The Treacheries of a European Identity

It is easy to find unity without commitment. The image of a peaceful, cooperative Europe, open toward other cultures and capable of dialogue, floats like a mirage before us all. We welcome the Europe that found exemplary solutions for two problems during the second half of the twentieth century. The EU already offers itself as a form of "governance beyond the nation-state," which could set a precedent in the postnational constellation. And for decades, European social welfare systems served as a model. Certainly, they have now been thrown on the defensive at the level of the national state. Yet future political efforts at the domestication of global capitalism must not fall below the standards of social justice that they established. If Europe has solved two problems of this magnitude, why shouldn't it issue a further challenge: to defend and promote a cosmopolitan order on the basis of international law against competing visions?

Such a Europe-wide discourse, of course, would have to match up with existing dispositions, which are waiting, so to speak, for the stimulation of a process of self-understanding. Two facts would seem to contradict this bold assumption. Haven't the most significant historical achievements of Europe forfeited their identity-forming power precisely through the fact of their worldwide success? And what could hold together a region characterized more than any other by the ongoing rivalries between self-conscious nations?

Insofar as Christianity and capitalism, natural science and technology, Roman law and the Code Napoleon, the bourgeois-urban form of life, democracy and human rights, the secularization of state and society have spread across other continents, these legacies no longer constitute a *proprium*. The Western form of spirit, rooted in the Judeo-Christian tradition, certainly has its characteristic features. But the nations of Europe also share this mental habitus, characterized by individualism, rationalism, and activism, with the United States, Canada, and Australia. The "West" encompasses more than just Europe. Moreover, Europe is composed of nation-states that delimit one another polemically. National consciousness, formed by national languages, national literatures, and national histories, has long operated as an explosive force.

However, in response to the destructive power of this nationalism, values and habits have also developed which have given contemporary Europe, in its incomparably rich cultural diversity, its own face. This is how Europe at large presents itself to non-Europeans. A culture which for centuries has been beset more than any other by conflicts between town and country, sacred and secular authorities, by the competition between faith and knowledge, the struggle between states and antagonistic classes, has had to painfully learn how differences can be communicated, contradictions institutionalized, and tensions stabilized. The acknowledgement of differences—the reciprocal acknowledgement of the Other in his otherness—can also become a feature of a common identity.

The pacification of class conflicts within the welfare state, and the self-limitation of state sovereignty within the framework of the EU, are only the most recent examples of this. In the third quarter of the twentieth century, Europe on this side of the Iron Curtain experienced its "golden age," as Eric Hobsbawm has called it. Since then, features of a common political mentality have taken shape, so that others often recognize us as Europeans rather than as Germans or French—and that happens not just in Hong Kong, but even in Tel Aviv. And isn't it true? In European societies, secularization is relatively far advanced. Citizens here regard transgressions of the border between politics and religion with suspicion. Europeans have a relatively large amount of trust in the organizational and steering capacities of the state, while remaining skeptical toward the achievements of markets. They possess a keen sense of the "dialectic of enlightenment"; they have no naïvely optimistic expectations about technological progress. They maintain a preference for the welfare state's guarantees of social security and for regulations on the basis of solidarity. The threshold of tolerance for the use of force against persons lies relatively low. The desire for a multilateral and legally regulated international order is connected with the hope for an effective global domestic policy, within the framework of a reformed United Nations.

The fortunate historical constellation in which West Europeans developed this kind of mentality in the shadow of the Cold War has changed since 1989–90. But February 15 shows that the mentality has survived the context from which it sprang. This also explains why "old Europe" sees itself challenged by the blunt hegemonic politics of its ally. And why so many in Europe who welcome the fall of Saddam as an act of liberation also reject the illegality of the unilateral, pre-emptive, and deceptively justified invasion. But how stable is this mentality? Does it have roots in deeper historical experiences and traditions?

Today we know that many political traditions that command their authority through the illusion of "naturalness" have in fact been "invented." By contrast, a European identity born in the daylight of the public sphere would have something constructed about it from the very beginning. But only what is constructed through an arbitrary choice carries the stigma of randomness. The political-ethical will that drives the hermeneutics of processes of self-understanding is not arbitrary. Distinguishing between the legacy we appropriate and the one we want to refuse demands just as much circumspection as the decision over the interpretation through which we appropriate it for ourselves. Historical experiences are only *candidates* for self-conscious appropriation; without such a self-conscious act they cannot attain the power to shape our identity. To conclude, a few notes on such "candidates," in light of which the European postwar consciousness can win a sharper profile.

Historical Roots of a Political Profile

In modern Europe, the relation between church and state developed differently on either side of the Pyrenees, differently north and south of the Alps, west and east of the Rhine. In different European countries, the idea of the state's neutrality in relation to different worldviews has assumed different legal forms. And yet within civil society, religion overall assumes a comparably unpolitical position. We may have cause to regret this social *priva-*

tization of faith in other respects, but it has desirable consequences for our political culture. For us, a president who opens his daily business with open prayer, and associates his significant political decisions with a divine mission, is hard to imagine.

Civil society's emancipation from the protection of an absolutist regime was not connected with the democratic appropriation and transformation of the modern administrative state everywhere in Europe. But the spread of the ideals of the French Revolution throughout Europe explains, among other things, why politics in both of its forms—as the organization of power and as a medium for the institutionalization of political liberty—has been welcomed in Europe. By contrast, the triumph of capitalism was bound up with sharp class conflicts, and this fact has prevented an equally unprejudiced appraisal of the market. That different evaluation of *politics and market* may back Europeans' trust in the civilizing power of the state, and their expectations for its capacity to correct "market failures."

The party system that emerged from the French Revolution has often been copied. But only in Europe does this system also serve an ideological competition that subjects the socio-pathological results of capitalist modernization to an ongoing political evaluation. This fosters the sensitivity of citizens to the paradoxes of progress. The contest between conservative, liberal, and socialist agendas comes down to the weighing of two aspects: Do the benefits of a chimerical progress outweigh the losses that come with the disintegration of protective, traditional forms of life? Or do the benefits that today's processes of "creative destruction" promise for tomorrow outweigh the pain of modernization losers?

In Europe, those who have been affected by class distinctions and their enduring consequences understood these burdens as a fate that could be averted only through collective action. In the context of workers' movements and the Christian socialist traditions, an ethics of solidarity, *the struggle for "more social justice,"* with the goal of equal provision for all, asserted itself against the individualistic ethos of market justice that accepts glaring social inequalities as part of the bargain.

Contemporary Europe has been shaped by the experience of the totalitarian regimes of the twentieth century and through the Holocaust—the persecution and the annihilation of European Jews in which the National Socialist regime made the societies of the conquered countries complicit as well. Self-critical controversies about this past remind us of the moral basis of politics. A heightened sensitivity to injuries to personal and bodily integrity is reflected, among other ways, in the fact that both [the] Europarat [Council of Europe] and EU made the ban on capital punishment a condition for entrance.

A bellicose past once entangled all European nations in bloody conflicts. They drew a conclusion from that military and spiritual mobilization against one another: the imperative of developing new, supranational forms of cooperation after the Second World War. The successful history of the European Union may have confirmed Europeans in their belief that the *domestication of state power* demands a *mutual* limitation of sovereignty, on the global as well as the national-state level.

Each of the great European nations has experienced the bloom of its imperial power. And, what in our context is more important still, each has had to work through the experience of the loss of its empire. In many cases this experience of decline was associated with the loss of colonial territories. With the growing distance of imperial domination and the history of colonialism, the European powers also got the chance to *assume a reflexive distance from themselves*. They could learn from the perspective of the defeated to perceive themselves in the dubious role of victors who are called to account for the violence of a forcible and uprooting process of modernization. This could support the rejection of Eurocentrism, and inspire the Kantian hope for a global domestic policy.

12

Preambles to the Treaty Establishing a Constitution for Europe and the Treaty of Lisbon

The European Convention, under the leadership of former French president Valéry Giscard d'Estaing, drafted a constitution that was signed in Rome by representatives of the member states on 29 October 2004. The text proved controversial from the beginning, not least because some Catholic politicians and member states, following the lead of Pope John Paul II, objected to the absence of an explicit reference to Christianity as a source of Europe's values in the preamble. Despite the disagreements, eighteen member states ratified the constitutional treaty, including two that offered the treaty to their electorates in a referendum. But on 29 May 2005 the French voted decisively against the treaty and two days later the Dutch did the same, thus sealing the constitution's fate. After a period of reflection, the leaders of the member states reassembled most of the pieces of the failed constitution and renamed it the Treaty of Lisbon, which they duly signed in 2007 and implemented in December 2009.

The preamble to the constitutional treaty may not contain many memorable phrases, but it does offer a succinct summary of Europe's values and vocation—at least as seen through the eyes of European Union leaders. Europe stands for "universal values": human rights, freedom, democracy, equality, and the rule of law. Its hard-won achievements have made it "a special area of human hope" and its continued efforts "to forge a common destiny" from its diverse peoples will further the process of "civilization, progress and prosperity" across the European continent, even as Europe strives for "peace, justice and solidarity throughout the world."

The constitutional treaty gave Europe a grand vision. But its defeat required a more humble approach. The Lisbon treaty aims for efficiency, coherence, and democratic legitimacy.

Preamble to the Treaty Establishing a Constitution for Europe

. . .

DRAWING INSPIRATION from the cultural, religious and humanist inheritance of Europe, from which have developed the universal values of the inviolable and inalienable rights of the human person, freedom, democracy, equality and the rule of law,

BELIEVING that Europe, reunited after bitter experiences, intends to continue along the path of civilization, progress and prosperity, for the good of all its inhabitants, including the weakest and most deprived; that it wishes to remain a continent open to culture, learning and social progress; and that it wishes to deepen the democratic and transparent nature of its public life, and to strive for peace, justice and solidarity throughout the world,

CONVINCED that, while remaining proud of their own national identities and history, the peoples of Europe are determined to transcend their former divisions and, united ever more closely, to forge a common destiny,

CONVINCED that, thus "United in diversity," Europe offers them the best chance of pursuing, with due regard for the rights of each individual and in awareness of their responsibilities towards future generations and the Earth, the great venture which makes of it a special area of human hope,

DETERMINED to continue the work accomplished within the framework of the Treaties establishing the European Communities and the Treaty on European Union, by ensuring the continuity of the Community acquis,

GRATEFUL to the members of the European Convention for having prepared the draft of this Constitution on behalf of the citizens and States of Europe . . . [the representatives of the member states] have agreed as follows . . .

Preamble to the Treaty of Lisbon

. . .

DESIRING to complete the process started by the Treaty of Amsterdam and by the Treaty of Nice with a view to enhancing the efficiency and democratic legitimacy of the Union and to improving the coherence of its action,

HAVE RESOLVED to amend the Treaty on European Union, the Treaty establishing the European Community and the Treaty establishing the European Atomic Energy Community . . .

13

Reflections on the
Crisis in Europe (excerpts)

In 2010 the Great Recession, which began in the United States with the bursting of the housing bubble, rolled into Europe. The economic crisis, which affected the entire EU but centered on Ireland, Greece, Portugal, Spain, Latvia, Cyprus, and Italy, evolved into a sovereign debt crisis that threatened to break up the Eurozone. By 2012 the Eurozone countries, led by Germany, had stabilized the troubled economies but serious threats remained to the long-term viability of the euro. As the euro crisis progressed, most European leaders recognized the need to reform the Eurozone to improve economic governance. Some advocated minimal changes, while others called for a banking union, Eurobonds, and European control of member-state budgets. European federalists renewed their calls for a leap to a full political union. But not every political leader enthusiastically embraced deeper integration as the solution to European economic woes. The British in particular questioned the wisdom of granting European institutions greater authority.

The political leaders featured below outlined various responses to the economic crisis. Alexander Stubb, Finland's minister of European affairs and trade, represents the Eurozone's "northern" perspective (shared by the Germans and Dutch). He characteristically emphasized open markets as a means to improved competitiveness, stricter rules designed to prevent irresponsible spending by Eurozone governments, protections against transfers of wealth from disciplined northern to imprudent southern economies, and minimal EU institutional changes. A broader and more "southern" view was taken by former Portuguese prime minister and European Commission president José Manuel Barroso, who argued for a new treaty to establish a political union—a "federation of nation states"—that would provide the institutional structure necessary to create a full economic union with the capacity to pay back existing member-state loans and issue new debt. Such a view is anathema to British prime minister David Cameron, who responded to political pressure from within his own party by calling for a renegotiated relationship between Britain and its European partners—and a British referendum on the result. His speech, however, was more than a call for a referendum: it was also a carefully crafted Thatcheresque vision of a looser, less regulated, less Brussels-centered European Union. Finally, Poland's foreign minister Radek Sikorski provided a rather light-hearted but forceful response to Britain's possible secession: "DON'T DO IT!"

The European Union—from Crisis to Regeneration (17 November 2011) ■ *Minister for European Affairs and Foreign Trade of Finland, Alexander Stubb*

It is an honour to be given this chance to speak at the College of Europe in Bruges, my old school. This place gave me more than I bargained for— including my wife! I even had a chance to teach here for seven years. I simply love this place.

I remember my early years working with European integration as a time of great optimism, a leap from an economic community to European Union. Now, the EU is in the midst of an unprecedented crisis with the grave problems the euro area is facing. Optimism is no longer the main game in town.

We are living through a global financial crisis and a western debt crisis, already in its fourth year. The problems of the euro area are far from over with added Greek and Italian drama and brinkmanship. Nothing could be further from the festive mood of ten years back when the euro was launched.

However, this is not the first time the Union faces a big challenge. The history of European integration is paved with crises and challenges that have resulted in the Union taking bold new steps, steps forward. Be it with the crisis of the coal and steel industry that resulted in the community approach in the first place. Or the economic stagnation of the 1970s that led to the single market and consequently to monetary union. Or the end of the Cold War that prompted European unification across the old dividing line.

We have to look beyond the crisis into new European horizons. Today, I want to talk to you about the future, not just about next week. I want to talk about European regeneration. Don't blame my government for the positions I am going to outline, these views are strictly personal.

In crisis situations, the clear response has always been more Europe, not less. And so it must be today—the European Union needs to emerge from this crisis stronger than ever. A stronger Europe, a smarter Europe. This is the mood I want to share with you here today.

The European project works on many fronts, and I could talk for hours about its trade or foreign policy agenda, the need for more unity in external action, the multi-annual financial framework or innovation policy, but

---

Speech given at the College of Europe, Bruges, Belgium. Reprinted with permission from the author.

today I want to focus on economic governance. Namely on three aspects: i) Growth, ii) Rules, iii) Cohesion.

I will make the case for three concrete proposals: i) improve growth by realising the digital single market, ii) make stronger rules for the euro, and iii) provide institutional arrangements that will preserve institutional cohesion.

So let me come to my first point, the European growth agenda.

We all know that financial stabilisation will only produce results if economic growth is strong in Europe at large, not just in the select few, northern export-led economies. If growth does not resume, buying time with rescue packages has no point. It amounts to kicking the can farther down the road, but it does nothing to change the end state.

For the time being, dealing with the immediate crisis takes precedence over long-term growth plans. Plugging holes takes priority over destination when ships are in trouble. But we should also start looking beyond the crisis.

A while back Gideon Rachman argued in a *Financial Times* column that the United States is the military super power, China the economic super power and Europe has opted for being the lifestyle super power. I agree with this choice, but as Gideon pointed out, our lifestyle is dependent on economic dynamism. We need to have world-leading cutting-edge companies in Europe also during the next decade—and the next century.

We talk a lot about growth and competitiveness, but little concrete action is taken. We need more ambition. One dimension is of course firm structural reforms removing obstacles to growth. Another dimension is opening markets to European companies—the EU is remarkably open, but we should make extra efforts to achieve improved market access with our external partners. More efforts are needed with, for example, the United States, Russia and the emerging markets. Yes to free trade and investments, no to all forms of mercantilism and protectionism.

But above all, we should take better care of the internal market, the heart of the European economy, the world's biggest single market in terms of GDP or trade.

Let me clarify. If you are pro-internal market you are also pro-European. If you are against the internal market, you are in essence anti-EU. This is why Britain—to my mind—is an instinctively pro-EU country, as paradoxical as this may sound to many of you.

The internal market is a major European achievement and it is the foundation for the economic competitiveness of European companies. It should be the hassle-free home arena from where our start-up companies can launch their global success stories. And it should include a fully functioning European financial market guaranteeing access to finance for promising companies.

One of the biggest gaps missing from the single market is the digital dimension. You cannot believe the amount of red tape our promising digital companies have to deal with when they want to sell in the European market. Usually twenty-seven rule books, instead of unified European rules. The situation is no better for the European consumer—try buying music or applications and you face a wall of national restrictions. And the digital market is where growth is happening, where our promising companies should be thriving.

No wonder American companies rule the web. We have surrendered without even starting. This must change and we have called for the establishment of a Digital Single Market by 2015. A new big bang for the Single Market, like the original 1992 deadline.

.   .   .

My second point is about rules and treaty change. The euro was a fair-weather currency—running smoothly as long as the sun was shining. There were only carrots, no sticks. This has to change. What I propose is firmer sticks with stronger rules, but I also want to remind you about the existing carrots.

First, let me talk about rules.

The Greek debt crisis has very clearly demonstrated the fact that soft coordination is not credible when it comes to economics and financing, things that really matter. I cannot say that Greek problems should have come as a surprise to anyone—even with Greek accounting the numbers were clear enough for everyone to see—but nothing forced us to take the situation seriously. Markets were happy to lend money to Greece at 4%. We had rules to prevent euro-area countries from over-borrowing, but these rules became redundant the day that Germany and France decided that they did not need to respect them.

We need strong rules, strong enforcement of rules and a culture of rules. The strengthening of institutions upholding the rules should be an inseparable part of European regeneration.

I cannot downplay the shock that the Greek debt-crisis has caused with my Finnish electorate that believes in fair play and following the rules. People feel cheated because European rules were not followed and national authorities even gave false information. The EU rarely provokes an emotional reaction among Finns—this time is different. For us this is not really about money, but principles.

The European Union is a deeply integrated system where we are all interdependent. Nothing moves without having an effect on others. We have participated in rescuing euro members in difficulties. We have felt an obligation to do this because it was in our interest and because we are all responsible for the euro. However, this responsibility needs to be complemented by firmer obligations on all euro-area members to run their economies in a sustainable manner.

If there are rights, there have to be obligations. Freedom cannot mean the freedom to harm others.

We need to restore credibility to the Union as a rules-based institution. This is after all the fundamental mission of the Union—bringing European countries and citizens together in a constitutional civilization built on common rules, not the arbitrary rule of the strong and mighty.

We need a system where irresponsible economic behaviour can be stopped in its tracks. The no bail-out rule is clear, but the markets have until now failed to take its meaning fully into account. The recent six-pack legislative package on economic governance goes a long way. This was an excellent move and I pay my deep respect to the European Parliament for making the six-pack a legislative reality.

However, we should go further. I see no reason why sanctions should not be tougher if a euro-area member state deliberately or out of negligence puts the common currency in danger. I understand the Dutch reasoning on a gradual loss of national control if things get out of hand.

The Union needs a budget tsar, the economic affairs commissioner with beefed-up powers to keep member states on the straight and narrow path. And please remember, I am a Finn—I do not speak about tsars lightly.

.   .   .

The big picture is clear—we need to balance rights and responsibilities. The majority has had to make major commitments to safeguard the euro area. Now the minority has to recognise its responsibilities towards the area as a whole and make that responsibility as firm as possible. Solidarity is a two-way street.

Carrots for following the rules exist today. And they are market-based, as they should be.

Eurobonds have been busily debated, but I think that we have taken a wrong approach to the whole issue. Joint eurobonds are not a solution to the present crisis. We should not seek means of economic governance that would remove market discipline from the euro area. We need more competition, mobility and capitalism in Europe—not less.

During the debt crisis, the market has started to fully appreciate the differences between euro area countries' competitiveness and sustainability. The euro has become an essentially Darwinist currency. The market rewards the triple-A countries and punishes those who have been slack about their public finances. Survival of the fittest prevails.

As a consequence the core of Europe's core is economic, not political. It includes all the AAA-rated euro countries which fulfill the Maastricht criteria. Unfortunately this core is quite small.

The crisis has led to closer economic cooperation among the core countries and provided an additional incentive for all euro members to stick to the rules. All euro members need to strive for a triple-A credit rating.

The re-emergence of market discipline in Europe is definitely painful for many. And I have no doubt that we have during the past two years seen the market overreact as if to make up for past mistakes. Countries with a solid economic base have seen their bond interest rates spike. But eventually the market will calm down and learn. In the long run, raw market pressure is the only really effective tool to ensure the governments pursue sound good economic policy. The market is both the stick and the carrot.

Last, but not least, let me come to my third point, maintaining institutional cohesion, EU unity, even as the euro area moves forward.

I wrote my thesis at Bruges on the famous Schäuble-Lamers paper of 1994, which suggested a euro core of founding states minus Italy. Just to prove I am an institutional nerd, I continued on the theme of differentiated integration with my Ph.D. at the London School of Economics and Political Science.

Many debates have been fought over cores: should we have them or not? Every time institutions, enlargement, Schengen, the euro or foreign and security policy are mentioned, cores come up in the debate. So far an institutional core Europe has not really emerged, but this time it may be in the making—by the markets.

I think there is a clear case for deepening integration in the euro area. But a deepening EURO17 may pose risks and question marks for the well-being of EU27.

But before I turn to this issue, let me make one additional point about the euro and the union. This may sound strange as the crisis is still brewing, but do remember that all EU members are supposed to join the euro when they meet its conditions. And these conditions must not be fudged.

Only Britain and Denmark have negotiated the right to remain outside. Estonia showed the way quite recently, unafraid of assuming euro obligations. Sweden—and I do say this with deep neighbourly love—is in fact living in sin as it has not joined the euro, in spite of the fact that it has the ability to do so. I have the conviction that the euro area will grow, once the crisis is over. So the division between the 27 and the 17 should only be temporary—at least for a true believer like me.

So the deepening of the euro should not happen in a way that endangers the Union. We cannot introduce elements that would for instance harm the internal market. We need to find ways to make the development of the euro area compatible with our daily life at 27. I think that the key for this harmony lies in the way we construct new institutions for the euro area.

The general rule in developing EU institutions should be streamlining: more simplicity, more continuity, and more stability. This was in fact a guiding light in the constitutional process leading to the Lisbon treaty. But now the evolution of the euro area seems to be taking a new turn with the possibility of electing a separate president for the euro-area summits. We need fewer presidents, but are in fact opening the door to more.

There is something of an iron law in European organization—every time you create a new functionary, you create a new dimension of bureaucratic competition. We all recognise this. You only have to read the daily papers to witness it. And bureaucratic games are not conducive to decisive leadership in times of crisis.

I am convinced that entrenching the euro area with its own president would deepen the divide between the 17 and the 27. And just imagine future decision making: President of the Commission, President of the European Council, President of the Euro Area, President of the European Parliament, President of the European Central Bank, President of the Eurogroup, President of the Council. I am sure that I have forgotten someone, but this is already decisionmaking at seven presidents. You need a new building to house just the presidents.

We need to make a different choice—fewer presidents, not more. I think we should streamline decisionmaking in the euro area and at the same time ensure that the institutional setup leads to more coherence, not entrenchment and infighting.

My solution would be to combine the functions of the Presidents of the Commission, the European Council and Euro-Area Summits into one high post. In effect, not double-hatting, but triple-hatting the holder of office. As we have seen, combining the presidency of the European Council and Euro-Area Summits works.

You can just select the same person to all three posts. It does not require treaty change. But making this permanent and doing so in a clear and unequivocal manner—paying careful attention to procedures and structures—would require treaty change. It is worth exploring. My conviction is that this solution would be of great benefit to the Commission and the community method—the Commission would naturally take centre stage. Let's be frank, the financial crisis has not been good to the community method.

Careful attention should be given to how this European President would be elected and how he or she would work. And I do not pretend that I have a ready and detailed blueprint in my back pocket.

The exercise is worthwhile only if it brings more order and more harmony. Command, control and communication all need to be crystal clear. The President would in effect be Commission based, but would need a strong administration bringing together the preparations of the European Council, the Eurogroup and the leadership of the Commission.

I am not proposing institutional innovations just for the fun of it, but we need to remember that form follows function. There is a need for more leadership in Europe and I would rather have this leadership in the hands of a joint—perhaps elected—trustee, than self-anointed member states. I would rather choose an open rostrum than a smoke-filled backroom.

As we are in College, we need to keep academic standards and mind pedagogical method. So let me recapitulate my message. The EU faces an unprecedented crisis, but the way is forward. And this way consists of three steps: one—pay attention to growth, two—make rules work, and three—upgrade institutions in ways that are conducive to improved leadership. Sometimes less is more.

State of the Union Address (12 September 2012)
■ *President of the European Commission,*
José Manuel Durão Barroso

It is an honour to stand before you today to deliver this third State of the Union address. At a time when the European Union continues to be in crisis. A financial and economic crisis. A social crisis. But also a political crisis, a crisis of confidence.

At its root, the crisis results from:

• Irresponsible practices in the financial sector;
• Unsustainable public debt; and also
• A lack of competitiveness in some Member States.

On top of that, the Euro faces structural problems of its own. Its architecture has not been up to the job. Imbalances have built up.

This is now being corrected. But it is a painful, difficult effort. Citizens are frustrated. They are anxious. They feel their way of life is at risk. The sense of fairness and equity between Member States is being eroded. And without equity between Member States, how can there be equity between European citizens?

Over the last four years, we have made many bold decisions to tackle this systemic crisis. But despite all these efforts, our responses have not yet convinced citizens, markets or our international partners.

Why? Because time and again, we have allowed doubts to spread. Doubts over whether some countries are really ready to reform and regain competitiveness. Doubts over whether other countries are really willing to stand by each other so that the Euro and the European project are irreversible.

On too many occasions, we have seen a vicious spiral. First, very important decisions for our future are taken at European summits. But then, the next day, we see some of those very same people who took those decisions undermining them. Saying that either they go too far, or that they don't go far enough. And then we get a problem of credibility. A problem of confidence.

Speech given at the plenary session of the European Parliament/Strasbourg, 12 September 2012. Reprinted with permission. Copyright European Union, 1995–2014.

It is not acceptable to present these European meetings as if they were boxing events, claiming a knockout victory over a rival. We cannot belong to the same Union and behave as if we don't. We cannot put at risk nine good decisions with one action or statement that raises doubts about all we have achieved.

This, Honourable Members, reveals the essence of Europe's political crisis of confidence. If Europe's political actors do not abide by the rules and the decisions they have set themselves, how can they possibly convince others that they are determined to solve this crisis together?

A crisis of confidence is a political crisis. And, the good thing is that, in a democracy, there is no political problem for which we cannot find a political solution. That is why, here today, I want to debate with you the fundamental political questions—where we are now and how we must move forward. I want to focus on the political direction and the vision that shall inspire our policy decisions. . . .

My message to you today is this: Europe needs a new direction. And, that direction cannot be based on old ideas. Europe needs a new thinking.

When we speak about the crisis, and we all speak about the crisis, have we really drawn all the consequences for our action? When we speak about globalisation, and we all speak a lot about globalisation, have we really considered its impact on the role of each of our Member States?

The starting point for a new thinking for Europe is to really draw all the consequences of the challenges that we are facing and that are fundamentally changing our world. The starting point is to stop trying to answer the questions of the future with the tools of the past. Since the start of the crisis, we have seen time and again that interconnected global markets are quicker and therefore more powerful than fragmented national political systems. This undermines the trust of citizens in political decisionmaking. And it is fuelling populism and extremism in Europe and elsewhere.

The reality is that in an interconnected world, Europe's Member States on their own are no longer able to effectively steer the course of events. But at the same time, they have not yet equipped their Union—our Union—with the instruments needed to cope with this new reality. We are now in a transition, in a defining moment. This moment requires decisions and leadership.

Yes, globalisation demands more European unity. More unity demands more integration. More integration demands more democracy, European democracy.

In Europe, this means first and foremost accepting that we are all in the same boat. It means recognising the commonality of our European interests. It means embracing the interdependence of our destinies. And it means demanding a true sense of common responsibility and solidarity. Because when you are on a boat in the middle of the storm, absolute loyalty is the minimum you demand from your fellow crewmembers. This is the only way we will keep up with the pace of change. It is the only way we will get the scale and efficiency we need to be a global player. It is the only way to safeguard our values, because it is also a matter of values, in a changing world.

In the 20th century, a country of just 10 or 15 million people could be a global power. In the 21st century, even the biggest European countries run the risk of irrelevance in between the global giants like the US or China.

History is accelerating. It took 155 years for Britain to double its GDP per capita, 50 years for the US, and just 15 years for China. But if you look at some of our new Member States, the economic transformation going on is no less impressive.

Europe has all the assets it takes. In fact much more so than previous generations faced with similar or even greater challenges.

But we need to act accordingly and mobilize all these resources together.

It is time to match ambitions, decisions, and actions.

It is time to put a stop to piecemeal responses and muddling through.

It is time to learn the lessons from history and write a better future for our Europe.

What I demand and what I present to you today is a Decisive Deal for Europe.

A decisive deal to project our values, our freedom and our prosperity into the future of a globalized world. A deal that combines the need to keep our social market economies on one hand and the need to reform them on the other. A deal that will stabilise the EMU, boost sustainable growth, and restore competitiveness. A deal that will establish a contract of confidence between our countries, between Member States and the European institutions, between social partners, and between the citizens and the European Union.

The Decisive Deal for Europe means that: We must leave no doubt about the integrity of the Union or the irreversibility of the euro. The more vulnerable countries must leave no doubts about their willingness to reform. About their sense of responsibility. But the stronger countries must leave no doubts about their willingness to stick together. About their sense of solidarity. We must all leave no doubts that we are determined to reform. To REFORM TOGETHER. The idea that we can grow without reform, or that we can prosper alone is simply false. We must recognise that we are in this together and must resolve it together. This decisive deal requires the completion of a deep and genuine economic union, based on a political union.

Let me start with Europe's economy. Firstly, we need growth. Sustainable growth. Growth is the lifeblood of our European social market model: it creates jobs and supports our standard of living. But we can only maintain growth if we are more competitive.

. . .

Our agenda of structural reform requires a major adjustment effort. It will only work if it is fair and equitable. Because inequality is not sustainable.

In some parts of Europe we are seeing a real social emergency. Rising poverty and massive levels of unemployment, especially among our young people. That is why we must strengthen social cohesion. It is a feature that distinguishes European society from alternative models. Some say that, because of the crisis, the European social model is dead. I do not agree.

. . .

To deliver lasting results, we need to develop a fully equipped Community economic governance together with a genuine, credible Community fiscal capacity. We do not need to separate institutions or to create new institutions for that. Quite the contrary: for this to be effective and quick, the best way is to work with and through the existing institutions: The European Commission as the independent European authority, and overseen by the European Parliament as the parliamentary representation at the European level. And it is in such a framework that over time, steps for genuine mutualisation of debt redemption and debt issuance can take their place. So economic reform coupled with a genuine economic and monetary union: these are the engines to get our boat moving forward.

. . .

Ultimately, the credibility and sustainability of the Economic and Monetary Union depends on the institutions and the political construct behind it. This is why the Economic and Monetary Union raises the question of a political union and the European democracy that must underpin it. If we want economic and monetary union to succeed, we need to combine ambition and proper sequencing. We need to take concrete steps now, with a political union as a horizon.

. . .

A deep and genuine economic and monetary union, a political union, with a coherent foreign and defence policy, means ultimately that the present European Union must evolve. Let's not be afraid of the words: we will need to move towards a federation of nation states. This is what we need. This is our political horizon. This is what must guide our work in the years to come.

Today, I call for a federation of nation states. Not a superstate. A democratic federation of nation states that can tackle our common problems, through the sharing of sovereignty in a way that each country and each citizen are better equipped to control their own destiny. This is about the

Union with the Member States, not against the Member States. In the age of globalisation pooled sovereignty means more power, not less.

And, I said it on purpose, a federation of nation states because in these turbulent times, these times of anxiety, we should not leave the defence of the nation just to the nationalists and populists. I believe in a Europe where people are proud of their nations but also proud to be European and proud of our European values.

Creating this federation of nation states will ultimately require a new treaty. I do not say this lightly. We are all aware how difficult treaty change has become. It has to be well prepared.

Discussions on treaty change must not distract or delay us from doing what can and must be done already today. A deep and genuine economic and monetary union can be started under the current treaties, but can only be completed with changes in the treaties. So let's start it now but let's have the horizon for the future present in our decisions of today.

We must not begin with treaty change. We must identify the policies we need and the instruments to implement them. Only then can we decide on the tools that we lack and the ways to remedy this. And then there must be a broad debate all over Europe. A debate that must take place before a convention and an IGC is called. A debate of a truly European dimension.

. . .

This is our project. A project which is step by step but with a big ambition for the future with a Federation as our horizon for Europe.

Many will say that this is too ambitious, that it is not realistic. But let me ask you—is it realistic to go on like we have been doing? Is it realistic to see what we are seeing today in many European countries? Is it realistic to see tax-payers paying banks and afterwards being forced to give banks back the houses they have paid for because they cannot pay their mortgages? Is it realistic to see more than 50% of our young people without jobs in some of our Member States? Is it realistic to go on trying to muddle through and just to accumulate mistakes with unconvincing responses? Is it realistic to think that we can win the confidence of the markets when we show so little confidence in each other?

To me, it is this reality that is not realistic. This reality cannot go on.

The realistic way forward is the way that makes us stronger and more united. Realism is to put our ambition at the level of our challenges. We can do it! Let's send our young people a message of hope. If there is a bias, let it be a bias for hope. We should be proud to be Europeans. Proud of our rich and diverse culture. In spite of our current problems, our societies are among the most human and free in the world.

We do not have to apologise for our democracy, our social market economy and for our values. With high levels of social cohesion. Respect for human rights and human dignity. Equality between men and women and respect for our environment. These European societies, with all [their] problems, are among the most decent societies in human history and I think we should be proud of that. In our countries two or three girls do not go to prison because they sing and criticise the ruler of their country. In our countries people are free and are proud of that freedom and people understand what it means to have that freedom. In many of our countries, namely the most recent Member States, there is a recent memory of what was dictatorship and totalitarianism.

So previous generations have overcome bigger challenges. Now it is for this generation to show they are up to the task. Now is the moment for all pro-Europeans to leave business as usual behind and to embrace the business of the future. The European Union was built to guarantee peace. Today, this means making our Union fit to meet the challenges of globalization.

That is why we need a new thinking for Europe, a decisive deal for Europe. That is why we need to guide ourselves by the values that are at the heart of the European Union. Europe, I believe, has a soul. This soul can give us the strength and the determination to do what we must do.

You can count on the European Commission. I count on you, the European Parliament. Together, as Community institutions we will build a better, stronger and a more united Europe, a citizens' Union for the future of Europe but also the future of the world.

A British Referendum? (23 January 2013)
■ *Prime Minister of the United Kingdom,*
David Cameron

. . .

I am not a British isolationist. I don't just want a better deal for Britain. I want a better deal for Europe too.

So I speak as British prime minister with a positive vision for the future of the European Union. A future in which Britain wants, and should want, to play a committed and active part. Some might then ask: why raise fundamental questions about the future of Europe when Europe is already in the midst of a deep crisis?

Why raise questions about Britain's role when support in Britain is already so thin? There are always voices saying: "Don't ask the difficult questions." But it's essential for Europe—and for Britain—that we do because there are three major challenges confronting us today.

First, the problems in the eurozone are driving fundamental change in Europe. Second, there is a crisis of European competitiveness, as other

---

Speech given in London, 23 January 2013.

nations across the world soar ahead. And third, there is a gap between the EU and its citizens which has grown dramatically in recent years. And which represents a lack of democratic accountability and consent that is—yes—felt particularly acutely in Britain.

If we don't address these challenges, the danger is that Europe will fail and the British people will drift towards the exit. I do not want that to happen. I want the European Union to be a success. And I want a relationship between Britain and the EU that keeps us in it.

That is why I am here today: to acknowledge the nature of the challenges we face. To set out how I believe the European Union should respond to them. And to explain what I want to achieve for Britain and its place within the European Union.

.   .   .

So let me set out my vision for a new European Union, fit for the 21st century. It is built on five principles.

The first: competitiveness. At the core of the European Union must be, as it is now, the single market. Britain is at the heart of that single market, and must remain so. But when the single market remains incomplete in services, energy and digital—the very sectors that are the engines of a modern economy—it is only half the success it could be. It is nonsense that people shopping online in some parts of Europe are unable to access the best deals because of where they live. I want completing the single market to be our driving mission. I want us to be at the forefront of transformative trade deals with the US, Japan and India as part of the drive towards global free trade. And I want us to be pushing to exempt Europe's smallest entrepreneurial companies from more EU directives.

These should be the tasks that get European officials up in the morning—and keep them working late into the night. And so we urgently need to address the sclerotic, ineffective decision-making that is holding us back. That means creating a leaner, less bureaucratic union, relentlessly focused on helping its member countries to compete. In a global race, can we really justify the huge number of expensive peripheral European institutions? Can we justify a commission that gets ever larger? Can we carry on with an organisation that has a multibillion-pound budget but not enough focus on controlling spending and shutting down programmes that haven't worked? And I would ask: when the competitiveness of the single market is so important, why is there an environment council, a transport council, an education council but not a single market council?

The second principle should be flexibility.

We need a structure that can accommodate the diversity of its members—north, south, east, west, large, small, old and new. Some of whom are contemplating much closer economic and political integration. And many others, including Britain, who would never embrace that goal. I accept, of course, that for the single market to function we need a common set of rules and a way of enforcing them. But we also need to be able to respond quickly to the latest developments and trends.

Competitiveness demands flexibility, choice and openness—or Europe will fetch up in a no-man's land between the rising economies of Asia and market-driven North America. The EU must be able to act with the speed and flexibility of a network, not the cumbersome rigidity of a bloc. We must not be weighed down by an insistence on a one-size-fits-all approach which implies that all countries want the same level of integration. The fact is that they don't and we shouldn't assert that they do. Some will claim that this offends a central tenet of the EU's founding philosophy. I say it merely reflects the reality of the European Union today; 17 members are part of the eurozone, 10 are not. Twenty-six European countries are members of Schengen—including four outside the European Union—Switzerland, Norway, Liechtenstein and Iceland. Two EU countries—Britain and Ireland—have retained their border controls. Some members, like Britain and France, are ready, willing and able to take action in Libya or Mali. Others are uncomfortable with the use of military force.

Let's welcome that diversity, instead of trying to snuff it out. Let's stop all this talk of two-speed Europe, of fast lanes and slow lanes, of countries missing trains and buses, and consign the whole weary caravan of metaphors to a permanent siding. Instead, let's start from this proposition: we are a family of democratic nations, all members of one European Union, whose essential foundation is the single market rather than the single currency. Those of us outside the euro recognise that those in it are likely to need to make some big institutional changes. By the same token, the members of the eurozone should accept that we, and indeed all member states, will have changes that we need to safeguard our interests and strengthen democratic legitimacy. And we should be able to make these changes too.

Some say this will unravel the principle of the EU—and that you can't pick and choose on the basis of what your nation needs. But far from unravelling the EU, this will in fact bind its members more closely because such flexible, willing co-operation is a much stronger glue than compulsion from the centre.

Let me make a further heretical proposition. The European treaty commits the member states to "lay the foundations of an ever closer union among the peoples of Europe." This has been consistently interpreted as applying not to the peoples but rather to the states and institutions compounded by a European court of justice that has consistently supported greater centralisation. We understand and respect the right of others to maintain their commitment to this goal. But for Britain—and perhaps for others—it is not the objective. And we would be much more comfortable if the treaty specifically said so, freeing those who want to go further, faster, to do so, without being held back by the others. So to those who say we have no vision for Europe, I say we have.

We believe in a flexible union of free member states who share treaties and institutions and pursue together the ideal of co-operation. To represent and promote the values of European civilisation in the world. To advance our shared interests by using our collective power to open markets. And to build a strong economic base across the whole of Europe. And we believe in our nations working together to protect the security and diversity of our energy supplies. To tackle climate change and global poverty. To work together against terrorism and organised crime. And to continue to welcome new countries into the EU.

This vision of flexibility and co-operation is not the same as those who want to build an ever closer political union—but it is just as valid.

My third principle is that power must be able to flow back to member states, not just away from them. This was promised by European leaders at Laeken a decade ago. It was put in the treaty. But the promise has never really been fulfilled. We need to implement this principle properly. So let us use this moment, as the Dutch prime minister has recently suggested, to examine thoroughly what the EU as a whole should do and should stop doing.

In Britain we have already launched our balance-of-competences review—to give us an informed and objective analysis of where the EU helps and where it hampers. Let us not be misled by the fallacy that a deep and workable single market requires everything to be harmonised, to hanker after some unattainable and infinitely level playing field. Countries are different. They make different choices. We cannot harmonise everything. For example, it is neither right nor necessary to claim that the integrity of the single market, or full membership of the European Union requires the working hours of British hospital doctors to be set in Brussels irrespective of the views of British parliamentarians and practitioners.

In the same way, we need to examine whether the balance is right in so many areas where the European Union has legislated, including on the environment, social affairs and crime. Nothing should be off the table.

My fourth principle is democratic accountability: we need to have a bigger and more significant role for national parliaments.

There is not, in my view, a single European demos.

It is national parliaments, which are, and will remain, the true source of real democratic legitimacy and accountability in the EU. It is to the Bundestag that Angela Merkel has to answer. It is through the Greek parliament that Antonis Samaras has to pass his government's austerity measures. It is to the British parliament that I must account on the EU budget negotiations, or on the safeguarding of our place in the single market. Those are the parliaments which instill proper respect—even fear—into national leaders.

We need to recognise that in the way the EU does business.

My fifth principle is fairness: whatever new arrangements are enacted for the eurozone, they must work fairly for those inside it and out. That will be of particular importance to Britain. As I have said, we will not join the single currency. But there is no overwhelming economic reason why the single currency and the single market should share the same boundary, any more than the single market and Schengen.

Our participation in the single market, and our ability to help set its rules, is the principal reason for our membership of the EU. So it is a vital interest for us to protect the integrity and fairness of the single market for all its members. And that is why Britain has been so concerned to promote and defend the single market as the eurozone crisis rewrites the rules on fiscal co-ordination and banking union.

These five principles provide what, I believe, is the right approach for the European Union.

So now let me turn to what this means for Britain.

Today, public disillusionment with the EU is at an all-time high. There are several reasons for this. People feel that the EU is heading in a direction that they never signed up to. They resent the interference in our national life by what they see as unnecessary rules and regulation. And they wonder what the point of it all is. Put simply, many ask "why can't we just have what we voted to join—a common market?"

They are angered by some legal judgements made in Europe that impact on life in Britain. Some of this antipathy about Europe in general really relates of course to the European court of human rights, rather than the EU. And Britain is leading European efforts to address this. There is, indeed, much more that needs to be done on this front. But people also feel that the EU is now heading for a level of political integration that is far outside Britain's comfort zone.

They see treaty after treaty changing the balance between member states and the EU. And note they were never given a say. They've had referendums promised—but not delivered. They see what has happened to the euro. And they note that many of our political and business leaders urged Britain to join at the time. And they haven't noticed many expressions of contrition. And they look at the steps the eurozone is taking and wonder what deeper integration for the eurozone will mean for a country which is not going to join the euro. The result is that democratic consent for the EU in Britain is now wafer-thin.

Some people say that to point this out is irresponsible, creates uncertainty for business and puts a question mark over Britain's place in the European Union. But the question mark is already there and ignoring it won't make it go away. In fact, quite the reverse. Those who refuse to contemplate consulting the British people, would in my view make more likely our eventual exit. Simply asking the British people to carry on accepting a European settlement over which they have had little choice is a path to ensuring that when the question is finally put—and at some stage it will have to be—it is much more likely that the British people will reject the EU.

That is why I am in favour of a referendum. I believe in confronting this issue—shaping it, leading the debate. Not simply hoping a difficult situation will go away.

. . .

Let me finish today by saying this.

I have no illusions about the scale of the task ahead. I know there will be those who say the vision I have outlined will be impossible to achieve. That there is no way our partners will co-operate. That the British people have set themselves on a path to inevitable exit. And that if we aren't comfortable being in the EU after 40 years, we never will be.

But I refuse to take such a defeatist attitude—either for Britain or for Europe. Because with courage and conviction I believe we can deliver a more flexible, adaptable and open European Union in which the interests and ambitions of all its members can be met. With courage and conviction I believe we can achieve a new settlement in which Britain can be comfortable and all our countries can thrive.

And when the referendum comes let me say now that if we can negotiate such an arrangement, I will campaign for it with all my heart and soul. Because I believe something very deeply: That Britain's national interest is best served in a flexible, adaptable and open European Union and that such a European Union is best with Britain in it.

Over the coming weeks, months and years, I will not rest until this debate is won. For the future of my country. For the success of the European Union. And for the prosperity of our peoples for generations to come.

The Blenheim Palace Speech (on the UK and Europe) (21 September 2012)
■ *Foreign Minister of Poland, Radek Sikorski*

It's always wonderful to come back to Oxford. I remember my first day when I arrived here in 1982, for an interview at Pembroke College. I applied to read PPE. The examiners asked me about Marxism. I told them, *"I'm a refugee from Communist Poland. I haven't met a Marxist yet."* I'm sure they laughed into their sleeves at the thought of what was coming. Indeed, I was ill-prepared for the tutorials at the Soviet republic of Balliol. . . .

Since then, life has continued to bring new learning experiences. It's interesting what happens on your first day as Foreign Minister. Helpful officials flutter around you like so many butterflies. One of them produces a special secret red file marked *"How to be a Foreign Minister."* Inside the file are papers on the Dos and Don'ts of the office. But decades of bureau-

---

Speech given at Blenheim Palace, United Kingdom, 21 September 2012.

cratic experience are best summed up in the immortal lines from my favourite instalment of *Yes, Prime Minister: "Once you start interfering in the internal squabbles of other countries, you're on a very slippery slope. Even the Foreign Secretary has grasped that!"*

It is in that fine spirit that tonight I mean to interfere recklessly in the internal affairs of the United Kingdom. I want to offer some thoughts on a subject of considerable British domestic sensitivity: the UK's membership of the European Union. And I want to try to change some minds.

The unofficial results of last YouGov Survey 2012 confirm that 67% British people support the idea of holding a referendum on EU membership, with only 19% opposed; 42% say they would vote to stay in, while 34% would vote to leave.

Well, I would like to say to you: DON'T DO IT.

Let me be 100% clear right at the start where I am coming from on this subject. I am Polish, from the Solidarity generation that helped bring down the Soviet empire. From Oxford I went to Afghanistan, to report on the anti-Communist resistance there. I have lived in the USA, working for the right-wing American Enterprise Institute. I am a fervent believer in free markets. Lady Thatcher—may she live forever—acknowledges me in her book on "Statecraft." I represent a government which has won plaudits for its financial rectitude—our finance minister, Jacek Rostowski, is a former member of the British Conservative party.

In other words, I tick every box required to be a life-long member of London's most powerful Eurosceptics' club. The Travellers' used to be my London club, but Euroscepticism is not. On the contrary, I believe in the logic and justice of the modern European project. And my country, Poland, will do its utmost to help it succeed.

. . .

Here we are this evening, enjoying the splendour and hospitality of Blenheim Palace. It commemorates the superb leadership of the Duke of Marlborough back in August 1704, and his decisive victory in the War of the Spanish Succession.

This war dragged on for 13 years. It involved the countries of Western Europe and even spread as far as North and South America. Tens of thousands of Europeans and others died as the rival armies tramped to and fro. The point of the war? To stop France and Spain uniting under one monarch and so preserve the wider "balance of power" across Europe.

In the famous battle of Blenheim, England used its military skill to intervene on the continent of Europe. Now, Britain's leaders need to decide once again how best to use their influence in Europe. The EU is an English-speaking power. The Single Market was a British idea. A British commissioner runs our diplomatic service. You could, if only you wished, lead Europe's defence policy.

But if you refuse, please don't expect us to help you wreck or paralyze the EU. Do not underestimate our *determination* not to return to the politics of the 20th century. You were not occupied. Most of us on the continent were. We will do almost anything to prevent that from happening again.

It's not difficult to see why. Poland wants to be with Germany and France as partners, leading a strong, democratic European political-economic space. We do not want to be a buffer between Western Europe and a less democratic Eurasian political-economic space dominated by Russia.

More importantly, we believe the Eurozone will survive, because it is in its members' interest for it to survive. The leaders of Europe will step up operational integration at the European level. The new institutional arrangements within the EU will be different. But eventually they'll be strong. They'll work because Europe's leaders want them to work. And be careful what you read in your tabloids: No country has benefitted more from the single currency than Germany.

Since I first came to these shores over 30 years ago, Britain has become much more European. You've built the Channel-Tunnel, you got used to mixer taps, duvets and double glazing. Even your cooking has improved. Yet, your public opinion and politics is more Eurosceptic than ever. And I think I can guess why: Marxists at those Balliol tutorials taught me the term "false consciousness" which is when the ideological superstructure is out of sync with the economic base. Britain today is living with false consciousness. Your interests are in Europe. It's high time for your sentiments to follow.

Your leaders need to make a more vocal case for your European interests. Britain is famous through the ages for its practical good sense and policies based on reality, not myths. We hope you can return to this tradition soon.

Part 2

Early Currents in Integration Theory

14

Altiero Spinelli and the Strategy for the United States of Europe

Sergio Pistone

Integration theory describes and explains the process of unifying separate nation-states. Some "theories" of integration, however, are grounded in the social scientific method, while others are more philosophical, normative, and prescriptive. Early theories of integration tended in the latter direction with a strong emphasis on prescribing a course of action for Europe. These theorists were not explaining integration so much as offering a recipe for European union.

Altiero Spinelli, as we saw in Chapter 1, was an ardent federalist. As a founder of the European Federalist Movement, as an Italian deputy, and as a member of the European Parliament, Spinelli dedicated his life to the actual uniting of Europe. He criticized the slow and, in his view, undemocratic process that characterized postwar integration in Europe. He longed for a revolutionary leap to a federal state.

Spinelli elaborated his federalist vision of European integration in the years after the Ventotene Manifesto. His goal, like most federalists, was a new Europe composed of individual states that had ceded their sovereignty to common democratic institutions. What made his brand of federalism more than just a description of a European federation, however, was his strategy for achieving a united Europe, here summarized by his associate, Sergio Pistone (University of Turin). In Spinelli's view, overcoming resistance from national governments required a popular pan-European movement that demanded a US-style constitutional convention. This constituent assembly would command such democratic legitimacy that national governments would have to accede to its wishes and ratify the new European constitution. Spinelli believed that only a dramatic leap to federalism would succeed in

Reprinted from *Altiero Spinelli and Federalism in Europe and the World*, ed. Lucio Levi (Franco Angeli, 1990). Copyright 1990 by Franco Angeli. Notes omitted.

unifying Europe; functionalism's step-by-step approach would never create institutions strong enough to solve major problems and democratic enough to respond to the people.

Spinelli eventually saw the directly elected European Parliament (EP) as a possible constituent assembly and, as a member of parliament, set about writing a new constitution for Europe. Shortly before his death, he saw this document passed by the EP as the Draft Treaty on European Union (1984). Although the Draft Treaty was not ratified by the member states, many of the ideas contained in it found their way into subsequent treaty revisions. More important, Spinelli's dream of a constitutional process began in earnest in 2002 but failed in 2005, when the very citizens Spinelli counted on to press forward the federalist project failed to ratify the proposed constitution.

What distinguishes Spinelli's approach to European federalism from that of its former supporters is his commitment to turn it into an active movement with a political program. That is why his ideas about a campaign strategy for the United States of Europe, which he had always considered as a first stage in the process of unifying the whole world, are amongst the most important, if not the most important contributions to federalism. To illustrate the essential elements of these ideas is, in my view, a contribution to a clearer understanding of the problems of the struggle for European unification (still in progress), but also to help in the fight for world unity (now in its initial stages).

For the purposes of synthesis, my case will follow a logical rather than chronological course. In other words I will not trace the origins of Spinelli's strategic concepts, but the basic theses that emerged from his ideas and actions. In my view these boil down to three:

1. The autonomous nature of the movement for the European federation;
2. The European Constituent Assembly;
3. The exploitation of the contradictions of the functional approach to European unification.

The arguments in favor of the autonomy of the movement for the European federation stem from the belief that the national democratic governments are, simultaneously, the means and the obstacles to European unification.

They are the means because unification can only be achieved as a result of freely arrived at decisions by democratic governments. This implies the rejection of two other ways forward. Spinelli rejects any attempts to unite Europe by force, as Hitler tried, and against which European federalists fought in the Resistance during the Second World War. As a matter of principle he also rejects unification by illegal and violent means from below, because the federalist struggle takes place in Western Europe within democratic political systems which provide legal means for even the most radical change. Moreover such unification stems from the historical development of European democracy.

Whilst European unification can only be achieved by the free decisions of democratic national governments, by their very nature they represent obstacles to its attainment. As a direct consequence of the Second World War, which led to the collapse of the European nation states, they are obliged to face the alternative of "either unite or perish." Yet, at the same time, they are inclined to reject a genuine European federation involving the irreversible transfer of substantial parts of their sovereignty to a supranational authority.

With regard to this obstacle one must clarify Spinelli's important distinction between the permanent agents of executive power, such as diplomats, civil servants and the military, and those who wield political power temporarily, such as heads of governments and their ministers. The strongest opposition to the transfer of sovereignty usually comes from the former because they would suffer immediate and substantial loss of power and status. After all, the permanent agents of executive power were originally created to put into effect the unfettered sovereignty of the state, and they thus became the natural defenders of nationalist traditions. For the latter, wielders of temporary power, the situation is rather more complex for three reasons: (1) without permanent positions of power they have much greater opportunities of playing a role within a wider European political framework; (2) they represent democratic parties with international programs which usually include support for a European federation; (3) they are in direct touch with public opinion which, in countries suffering from the decline and crisis of the nation state, is generally favorable to European unification. This distinction is of great importance, as we shall see later, in considering procedures for the creation of institutions for European unity. Nevertheless, there remains the fact that democratic national governments, by the very nature of their structures, are unfavorably inclined towards federal unification. In the absence of ulterior reasons they are only likely to favor the type of unification which does not involve the irrevocable transfer of power.

A direct consequence springs from these structural problems: namely, that an essential condition for exercising pressure on governments and political parties in favor of genuine federal unification is the existence of an independent movement for a European federation, which is able to persuade them in favor of action they would not, otherwise, take readily on their own.

According to Spinelli, the basic features of such a movement must be:

1. it should not be a political party, but an organization aimed at uniting all supporters of a European federation, irrespective of their political beliefs or social background. This is because a political party seeking national power to achieve European unification would be fatally weakened by intending to transfer to supranational institutions substantial parts of the national power for which it would be competing;
2. it has to be a supranational organization uniting all federalists beyond their national allegiance, so as to imbue them with a supranational loyalty and enable them to organize political action at European level;
3. it must seek to establish direct influence on public opinion, outside national electoral campaigns, which would help it to exert effective pressure on the European policies of governments. One should remember that these have been the guiding principles of the Italian European Federalist Movement from its inception in 1943, even when Spinelli ceased to be its leader and continued to cooperate with the MFE [European Federalist Movement] as an ordinary member, while working in the European Commission or Parliament.

The existence of a European federal movement with these characteristics represents for Spinelli merely a subjective condition for effective federalist action. There is, however, also need for objective conditions for a successful struggle, such as those provided by crises within national political systems.

During periods of relative stability of national political systems, when governments appear able to deal with the principal political, economic or social problems, the movement for a European federation is unable to influence national governments effectively, because public opinion tends to support the latter and their policies. Only at times of acute crisis, when governments are unable to cope and this fact is generally evident, will public opinion be able to share the federalist point of view. At such times the federalist movement ought to be able to mobilize support for federal solutions and persuade governments in favor of them. Spinelli was always convinced that such crises were bound to arise because we are living during a historically critical stage for nation states which, after periods of relative and apparent stability, will be subject to intense crises of their political systems. And this is also true for policies of European unification based on the maintenance of absolute national sovereignty, because intergovernmental cooperation does not provide adequate means for facing such crises, which stem from an irreversible decline of national power of European states.

I will now deal with the second main theme of Spinelli's strategy—the concept of a European constituent assembly.

The fact that national governments are simultaneously the means and the obstacles to the federal unification of Europe carries important implications for the procedure needed to establish European institutions: if one wants federal institutions then one must proceed by way of a constituent assembly and not by the use of intergovernmental or diplomatic conferences.

In other words, Spinelli was always convinced that the creation of European institutions, being entrusted to representatives of national governments, and diplomats in particular, or if they have the last word over the constituent procedure, cannot bring about federal solutions, because the tendency of all such diplomatic negotiations will be the maintenance of absolute national sovereignty at the expense of effective unification. In contrast, in a constituent assembly, composed of people representing public opinion, a favorable attitude towards federal institutions is likely to be incomparably stronger than nationalist tendencies. This is for a number of reasons: (1) the great majority of public opinion (especially in countries first committed to European unification) is in favor of genuine unification and its representatives have to take account of this; (2) the parties and the principal democratic political trends have an international orientation which, by its very nature, would be favorable to a European federation, and would, therefore, back the creation of transnational groups within a European assembly working to strengthen pro-European attitudes; (3) those representing public opinion, unlike the diplomats, do not hold positions of power which are directly dependent on the maintenance of absolute national sovereignty.

Thus, in the event of a critical situation, the pre-eminent task of the movement for a European federation will be to persuade governments (which, at such moments, are susceptible to persuasion by the federalists) to initiate a constituent democratic procedure under which the ultimate responsibility for proposing the nature of the European institutions will be entrusted to the representatives of public opinion, and whose draft of the European constitution will then be directly submitted for ratification to the appropriate constitution organs of the member states, without being subjected to prior diplomatic negotiations.

The concept of a constituent European assembly was patterned by Spinelli on the way the first federal constitution in history was drawn up, namely that of the American constitution, worked out by the Philadelphia Convention in 1787. The example of Philadelphia which, according to him, should provide the model for a European constituent procedure contains three essential elements:

1. governments of individual states have the basic responsibility for initiating the process by conferring the constituent mandate upon the convention, but refrain from interfering in its deliberations;
2. the convention acts by majority votes in drawing up the constitution;

3. the ratification of the constitution is entrusted to the appropriate constitutional organs of individual states, and it comes into force once ratified by a majority of them (in the American case it required ratification by 9 out of the 13 states).

Throughout his federalist campaign Spinelli never ceased to press for the adoption of a constituent procedure on these lines. One needs to stress that for him the essence lay not in the form but the substance of the procedure, namely to give the last word on the constitutional project to a parliamentary assembly. During the various stages of his campaign he proposed various forms of political action, each adapted to prevailing circumstances, to advance the constituent procedure:

1. a constituent assembly elected by universal suffrage with the sole mandate of drawing up a European constitution;
2. the transformation of the consultative parliamentary assembly into a constituent one, either by its own action or by mandate conferred upon it by national governments;
3. by the direct election of a European parliament with a specific constituent mandate;
4. by a popular referendum which would confer the constituent mandate upon the European parliament.

But the substance remained unchanged.

Spinelli's constituent concept stemmed from his belief that the functional approach to European unification will not achieve profound and irreversible unity. He never shared the conviction of the supporters of the functional approach that one can integrate selected sectors of national activity without a federalist constitutional framework from the very start. And this for two fundamental reasons:

1. by refusing to start with a supranational authority of a democratic character, the principle of the national veto is retained (even with a formal acceptance of majority voting). This would deprive European institutions of the capacity to overcome special interests that arise from the exercise of unfettered national sovereignty, and to ensure the supremacy of the common European interest;
2. the chaos and inefficiency which result from the lack of common management of the interdependent economies of modern states and of their foreign and defense policies.

One needs to recognize, however, that Spinelli accepted that unification could start with effective supranational powers being first confined to economic issues, while postponing their immediate adoption in matters of foreign and security policies (as provided in the draft treaty for European Union). And this from the consideration that convergence in the latter sectors was already being influenced by American leadership. But he always stressed the need for genuine federal institutions which would ensure the ultimate extension of supranational powers from economic to defense and foreign policies. That is why he never ceased to insist on the constitutional approach, in place of the functional one, by calling for a federal constitution from the start, obtained by a democratic constituent procedure.

Spinelli's criticism of the functional method was not confined to a dialectical and doctrinaire preference for the constitutional approach. First he was clearly aware that the functional approach stemmed largely from the contradictory nature of the attitudes of national governments to European unification. As objective historical circumstances force them to face the need for supranational unification, whilst they resist giving up their sovereignty, it is natural that they prefer an approach that postpones indefinitely the establishment of an authentic supranational authority. At the same time he recognized that the functional approach could assist the constitutional process by exposing, due to its inadequacy, the contradictions of the former, that could be exploited in the course of the federalist struggle.

These contradictions boil down to two. The first stems from the precariousness and inefficiency of functional unification. Functional institutions established by the unanimous decisions of national governments have shown themselves to be weak and incapable of acting decisively at critical moments when particularly grave problems face them. As a consequence, positive results obtained in more favorable circumstances tend to be compromised or abandoned in time of crisis. This leads to the disappointment of expectations in the development of European integration and can lead to support for federal solutions. The second contradiction stems from the democratic deficit which arises when important responsibilities and powers are transferred to the supranational level without subjecting them to effective democratic control. This causes uneasiness among political parties and to democratically sensitive public opinion which can be thus influenced to favor the concept of supranational democracy. Spinelli's federalist campaign had always aimed at exploiting these contradictions in order to initiate the democratic constituent procedure.

. . .

15

A Working Peace System

David Mitrany

David Mitrany (1888–1975) was a Romanian-born academic who spent most of his adult life in Britain and the United States. During World War II, Mitrany—who had been profoundly influenced by the radical intellectual currents of interwar London—thought seriously about the shape of the postwar world and how to prevent future wars. The result of his reflection was a pamphlet entitled A Working Peace System, which he published in the summer of 1943, two years before the end of the war. In this pamphlet, Mitrany argued for a transformation of the way people think about international relations, particularly the prevention of war. His "functional alternative" aimed at world, not European, unity. Nevertheless, it had a profound effect on European activists and early integration theorists, especially the neofunctionalists (see Chapter 17).

Mitrany saw the division of the world into "competing political units" as the root of international conflict. A world federal government, he argued, would eliminate these divisions but would be impossible to establish given the modern "disregard for constitutions and pacts" and continuing nationalism. Mitrany called, instead, for a functional approach that would "overlay political divisions with a spreading web of international activities and agencies, in which and through which the interests and life of all the nations would be gradually integrated." Functional integration would be rational, pragmatic, technocratic, and flexible; it would deliberately blur national and international, public and private, and political and nonpolitical distinctions. As functional agencies were formed and joined, national divisions would become less and less important. Ultimately, a central authority might coordinate the various agencies, but such a government would not be necessary to successful international relations, and might not be desirable. Here Mitrany parted with many other functionalists (such as Monnet) and the neofunctionalists who believed federal institutions were essential to the success

Reprinted from *A Working Peace System* (Quadrangle Books, 1966). Copyright 1966 by The Society for a World Service Federation. Notes omitted.

of functional integration. Mitrany was far less sanguine about the value of the state and its institutions, reflecting an anarchic streak that led him to distrust political authority.

The General Problem

The need for some new kind of international system was being widely canvassed before the Second World War, in the measure in which the League of Nations found itself frustrated in its attempts to prevent aggression and to organize peace. Some blamed this failure on the irresponsibility of small states; others rather the egoism of the Great Powers. Still others imputed the League's failure more directly to weaknesses in its own constitution and machinery: the proper ingredients were there, but the political dosage was inadequate. It was especially among those who held this view that the idea of a wide international federation began to be embraced as a new hope.

Federation seemed indeed the only alternative to a League tried so far for linking together a number of political units by democratic methods. It would mean an association much closer than was the League, and its advocacy therefore takes it for granted that the League failed because it did not go far enough. In what way would federation go further? Federation would be a more intensive union of a less extensive group; the constitutional ties would be closer. Second, certain activities would be more definitely and actively tied together. More definite common action is clearly the end; the formal arrangements which the federalists put in the forefront would be merely a necessary adjunct, to ensure the reliable working of the federal undertakings. And that is as it should be for, leaving formal arguments aside, it is plain that the League failed not from overstrain but from inanition. It might have done more about sanctions, but that would not have been enough. Even if the League's action for "security" had been more fearless, that would not by itself have sufficed to give vitality to an international system that was to last and grow. To achieve that end, such a system must in some important respects take over and coordinate activities hitherto controlled by the national state, just as the state increasingly has to take over activities which until now have been carried on by local bodies; and like the state, any new international authority could under present conditions not be merely a police authority.

We realize now that the League failed because, whatever the reasons, it could not further that process of continuous adjustment and settlement which students of international affairs call "peaceful change." But they themselves, taking the form for the substance, all too often thought of it mainly as a matter of changing frontiers. We shall have to speak of this again, but what peaceful change should mean, what the modern world, so closely interrelated, must have for its peaceful development, is some system that would make possible automatic and continuous social action, continually adapted to changing needs and conditions, in the same sense and of the same general nature as any other system of government. Its character would be the same for certain purposes; only the range would be new. It is in that sense that the League's work has in truth been inadequate and ineffective, as one may readily see if one reflects whether a change of frontiers now and then would really have led to a peaceful and cooperative international society.

A close federation is supposed to do just what the League proved unable to do, and in a set and solid way. But to begin with, can we take a system which has worked well in one field and simply transplant it to another, so much wider and more complex? Federations have still been national federations; the jump from national states to international organization is infinitely more hazardous than was the jump from provincial units to national federations. None of the elements of neighborhood, of kinship, of history are there to serve as steps. The British Empire is bound closely by old ties of kinship and history, but no one would suggest that there is among its parts much will for federation. Yet apart from this matter of whether the federal idea has any great prospects, there is the more important question whether it would have any great virtues in the international sphere. If the evil of conflict and war springs from the division of the world into detached and competing political units, will it be exorcised simply by changing or reducing the lines of division? Any political reorganization into separate units must sooner or later produce the same effects; any international system that is to usher in a new world must produce the opposite effect of subduing political division. As far as one can see, there are only two ways of achieving that end. One would be through a world state which would wipe out political divisions forcibly; the other is the way discussed in these pages, which would rather overlay political divisions with a spreading web of international activities and agencies, in which and through which the interests and life of all the nations would be gradually integrated. That is the fundamental change to which any effective international system must aspire and contribute: to make international government coextensive with international activities. A League would be too loose to be able to do it; a number of sectional federations would, on the contrary, be too tight to be welded into something like it. Therefore when the need is so great and pressing, we must have the vision to break away from traditional political ideas, which in modern times have always linked authority to a given territory, and try some new way that might take us without violence toward that goal. The beginnings cannot be anything but experimental; a new international system will need, even more than national systems, a wide freedom of continuous adaptation in the light of experience. It must care as much as possible for common needs that are evident, while presuming as little as possible upon a global unity which is still only latent and unrecognized. As the late John Winant well said in a lecture at Leeds in

October 1942: "We must be absolute about our principal ends (justice and equality of opportunity and freedom), relative and pragmatic about the mechanical means used to serve those ends."

The need for a pragmatic approach is all the greater because we are so clearly in a period of historical transition. When the state itself, whatever its form and constitution, is everywhere undergoing a deep social and political sea-change, it is good statesmanship not to force the new international experiments into some set familiar form, which may be less relevant the more respectable it seems, but to see above all that these experiments go with and fit into the general trend of the time.

When one examines the general shape of the tasks that are facing us, one is, to begin with, led to question whether order could be brought into them by the device of formal written pacts. Why did written constitutions, declarations of rights, and other basic charters play such a great role during the nineteenth century? The task of that time, following the autocratic period, was to work out a new division of the sphere of authority, to determine new relationships between the individual and the state, to protect the new democracy. These relationships were meant to be fixed and final, and they had to rest on general principles, largely of a negative character. It was natural and proper that all that should be laid down in formal rules, meant to remain untouched and permanent. In much the same way the new nation state was in world society what the new citizen was in municipal society; and with the increase in their number, the liberal growth in international trade and cultural and social intercourse, the resulting international rules and a host of written treaties and pacts sought, like the national constitutions, to fix the formal relationship between the sovereign individual states and their collectivity; which in this case also was expected to be fixed and final, with international law as a gradually emerging constitution for that political cosmos.

Viewed in this light, the Covenant of the League is seen to have continued that nineteenth-century tradition. It was concerned above all with fixing in a definite way the formal relationship of the member states and in a measure also of non-members, and only in a very secondary way with initiating positive common activities and action. The great expectation, security, was a vital action, but a negative one; its end was not to promote the active regular life of the peoples but only to protect it against being disturbed. Broadly one might say that the Covenant was an attempt to universalize and codify the rules of international conduct, gradually evolved through political treaties and pacts, and to give them general and permanent validity. It was neither unnatural nor unreasonable to follow up that nineteenth-century trend and try to steady international relations by bringing them within the framework of a written pact, one provided with set rules for its working. But when it came to going beyond that, the League could not be more or do more than what its leading members were ready to be and do, and they were ready to do but little in a positive way. It was indeed characteristic of the post-Armistice period 1918–19 that even the victors hastened to undo their common economic and other machinery, such as the Allied Shipping Control, which had grown and served them well during the war. And that was at a time when within each country government action and control were spreading fast, causing many a private international activity also to be cut down or cut off. In other words, the incipient common functions, as well as many old connections, were disbanded in the international sphere at the very time when a common constitution was being laid down for it. It was that divorce between life and form that doomed the League from the outset, and not any inadequacy in its written rules.

Hence it is pertinent to ask: Would another written pact, if only more elaborate and stringent, come to grips more closely with the problems of our time? Let us by way of a preliminary answer note two things: First, the lusty disregard for constitutions and pacts, for settled rules and traditional rights, is a striking mark of the times. In the pressure for social change no such formal ties are allowed to stand in the way, either within the several countries or between them. It is a typical revolutionary mood and practice. If it does not always take the outward form of revolution, that is because the governments themselves act as spearheads of the trend, and not only in countries ruled by dictatorships. Those who lead in this rush for social change pride themselves indeed on their disregard for forms and formalities. The appeal which communism, fascism, and nazism had for youth in particular and for the masses in general lies in no small degree in that political iconoclasm. At the turn of the nineteenth century the radical masses were demanding settled rules and rights, and Napoleon could play the trump card of constitutional nationalism against the autocratic rulers. Now the masses demand social action without regard to established "rights," and the totalitarian leaders have been playing the strong card of pragmatic socialism against constitutional democracy.

That universal pressure for social reform, in the second place, has utterly changed the relation of nationalism to internationalism, in a way that could be promising if rightly used. In constitution-making there was a parallel between the two spheres, but nothing more, for they belonged politically to different categories. The nineteenth-century nationalism rested mainly on cultural and other differential factors, and the creation of the nation state meant inevitably a breaking up of world unity. A cosmopolitan outlook spread rapidly, but the nations at the same time balked at international political organization and control, and they could justify that refusal by seemingly good principle. At present the new nationalism rests essentially on social factors; these are not only alike in the various countries, thus paradoxically creating a bond even between totalitarian groups, but often cannot make progress in isolation. At many points the life of the nation state is overflowing back into that common world which existed before the rise of modern nationalism. At present the lines of national and international evolution are not parallel but converging, and the two spheres now belong to the same category and differ only in dimensions.

In brief, the function of the nineteenth century was to restrain the powers of authority; that led to the creation of the "political man" and likewise of the "political nation," and to the definition through constitutional pacts of their relation to the wider political group. The Covenant (and the Locarno and Kellogg pacts) was still of that species essentially, with the characteristic predominance of rules of the "thou shall not" kind. The function of our time is rather to develop and coordinate the social scope of authority, and that cannot be so defined or divided. Internationally it is no longer a question of defining relations between states but of merging them—the workday sense of the vague talk about the need to surrender some part of sovereignty. A constitutional pact could do little more than lay down certain elementary rights and duties for the members of the new community. The community itself will acquire a living body not through a written act of faith but through active organic development. Yet there is in this no fundamental dispute as to general principles and ultimate aims. The only question is, which is the more immediately practicable and promising way: whether a general political framework should be provided formally in advance, on some theoretical pattern, or left to grow branch by branch from action and experience and so find its natural bent.

The Functional Alternative

Can these vital objections be met, and the needs of peace and social advance be satisfied, through some other way of associating the nations for common action? The whole trend of modern government indicates such a way. That trend is to organize government along the lines of specific ends and needs, and according to the conditions of their time and place, in lieu of the traditional organization on the basis of a set constitutional division of jurisdiction and of rights and powers. In national government the definition of authority and the scope of public action are now in a continuous flux, and are determined less by constitutional norms than by practical requirements. The instances are too many and well known to need mentioning; one might note only that while generally the trend has been toward greater centralization of services, and therefore of authority, under certain conditions the reverse has also occurred, powers and duties being handed over to regional and other authorities for the better performance of certain communal needs. The same trend is powerfully at work in the several federations, in Canada and Australia, and especially in the United States, and in these cases it is all the more striking because the division of authority rests on written constitutions which are still in being and nominally valid in full. Internationally, too, while a body of law had grown slowly and insecurely through rules and conventions, some common activities were organized through ad hoc functional arrangements and have worked well. The rise of such specific administrative agencies and laws is the peculiar trait, and indeed the foundation, of modern government.

A question which might properly be asked at the outset in considering the fitness of that method for international purposes is this: Could such functions be organized internationally without a comprehensive political framework? Let it be said, first, that the functional method as such is neither incompatible with a general constitutional framework nor precludes its coming into being. It only follows Burke's warning to the sheriffs of Bristol that "government is a practical thing" and that one should beware of elaborating constitutional forms "for the gratification of visionaries." In national states and federations the functional development is going ahead without much regard to, and sometimes in spite of, the old constitutional divisions. If in these cases the constitution is most conveniently left aside, may not the method prove workable internationally without any immediate and comprehensive constitutional framework? If, to cite Burke again, it is "always dangerous to meddle with foundations," it is doubly dangerous now. Our political problems are obscure, while the political passions of the time are blinding. One of the misfortunes of the League experiment was that a new institution was devised on what have proved to be outworn premises. We might also recollect that of the constitutional changes introduced in Europe after the First World War, fine and wise though they may have been, none has survived even a generation. How much greater will that risk of futility be in Europe after the Second World War, when the split within and between nations will be much worse than in 1919? We know now even less about the dark historical forces which have been stirred up by the war, while in the meantime the problems of our common society have been distorted by fierce ideologies which we could not try to bring to an issue without provoking an irreconcilable dogmatic conflict. Even if an action were to be to some extent handicapped without a formal political framework, the fact is that no obvious sentiment exists, and none is likely to crystallize for some years, for a common constitutional bond.

In such conditions any pre-arranged constitutional framework would be taken wholly out of the air. We do not know what, if anything, will be in common—except a desperate craving for peace and for the conditions of a tolerable normal life. The peoples may applaud declarations of rights, but they will call for the satisfaction of needs. That demand for action could be turned into a historic opportunity. Again we might take to heart what happened to the U.S. in 1932–33 and think of what chances the Roosevelt administration would have to have had to achieve unity, or indeed to survive, if instead of taking immediate remedial action it had begun by offering constitutional reforms—though a common system was already in being. A timid statesman might still have tried to walk in the old constitutional grooves; Mr. Roosevelt stepped over them. He grasped both the need and opportunity for centralized practical action. Unemployment, the banking collapse, flood control, and a hundred other problems had to be dealt with by national means if they were to be dealt with effectively and with lasting results.

The significant point in that emergency action was that each and every problem was tackled as a practical issue in itself. No attempt was made to relate it to a general theory or system of government. Every function was left to generate others gradually, like the functional subdivision of organic cells; and in every case the appropriate authority was left to grow and develop out of actual performance. Yet the new functions and the new organs, taken together, have revolutionized the American political system. The federal government has become a national government, and Washington for the first time is really the capital of America. In the process, many improvements in the personnel and machinery of government have come about, and many restrictive state regulations have melted away. More recently there has been heard the significant complaint that the ties between cities and their states are becoming looser, while those with the national government become ever stronger. No one has worked to bring this about, and no written act has either prescribed it or confirmed it. A great constitutional transformation has thus taken place without any changes in the Constitution. There have been complaints, but the matter-of-course acceptance has been overwhelming. People have gladly accepted the service when they might have questioned the theory. The one attempt at direct constitutional revision, to increase and liberalize the membership of the Supreme Court, was bitterly disputed and defeated. Yet that proposal involved in effect much less of a constitutional revolution than has the experiment of the Tennessee Valley Authority. The first would not have ensured any lasting change in the working of the American government, whereas the second has really introduced into the political structure of the United States a new regional dimension unknown to the Constitution.

In many of its essential aspects—the urgency of the material needs, the inadequacy of the old arrangements, the bewilderment in outlook—the situation at the end of the Second World War will resemble that in America in 1933, though on a wider and deeper scale. And for the same reasons the path pursued by Mr. Roosevelt in 1933 offers the best, perhaps the only, chance for getting a new international life going. It will be said inevitably that in the United States it was relatively easy to follow that line of action because it was in fact one country, with an established Constitution. Functional arrangements could be accepted, that is, because in many fields the federal states had grown in the habit of working together. That is no doubt true, but not the most significant point of the American experiment; for that line was followed not because the functional way was so easy but because the constitutional way would have been so difficult. Hence the lesson for unfederated parts of the world would seem to be this: If the constitutional path had to be avoided for the sake of effective action even in a federation which already was a working political system, how much less promising must it be as a starting mode when it is a matter of bringing together for the first time a number of varied, and sometimes antagonistic, countries? But if the constitutional approach, by its very circumspectness, would hold up the start of a working international system, bold initiative during the period of emergency at the end of the war might set going lasting instruments and habits of a common international life. And though it may appear rather brittle, that functional approach would in fact be more solid and definite than a formal one. It need not meddle with foundations; old institutions and ways may to some extent hamper reconstruction, but reconstruction could begin by a common effort without a fight over established ways. Reconstruction may in this field also prove a surer and less costly way than revolution. As to the new ideologies, since we could not prevent them we must try to circumvent them, leaving it to the growth of new habits and interests to dilute them in time. Our aim must be to call forth to the highest possible degree the active forces and opportunities for cooperation, while touching as little as possible the latent or active points of difference and opposition.

There is one other aspect of the post-war period which has been much discussed and has a bearing on this point, and which helps to bring out the difference in outlook between the two methods contrasted here. Much has been heard of a suggestion that when the war ends we must have first a period of convalescence and that the task of permanent reorganization will only come after that. It is a useful suggestion, insofar as it may help to clear up certain practical problems. But it could also be misleading and even dangerous if the distinction were taken to justify either putting off the work of international government or differentiating between the agencies by which the new international activities are to be organized, into nurses for convalescence and mentors for the new life. A clean division in time between two such periods in any case is not possible, for the period of convalescence will be different for different activities and ends; but, above all, except for such direct and exceptional consequences of the war as demobilization and the rebuilding of damaged areas, the needs of society will be the same at once after the war as later on. The only difference will be the practical one of a priority of needs, the kind of difference which might be brought about by any social disturbance—an epidemic or an earthquake or an economic crisis—and the urgency of taking action. For the rest, one action and period will merge into the other, according to circumstances. Seed and implements will be as urgent for ensuring the food supply of Europe and Asia as the actual distribution of relief, and indeed more urgent if the war should end after a harvest. Again, both relief and reconstruction will depend greatly on the speedy reorganization and proper use of transport, and so on.

Both circumstances point again to the advantage of a functional practice and to the disadvantage, if not the impossibility, of a comprehensive attempt at political organization. To obtain sufficient agreement for some formal general scheme would, at best, not be possible without delay; at the same time, action for relief and reconstruction will have to start within the hour after the ceasefire. The alternatives would be, if a comprehensive constitutional arrangement is desired and waited for, either to put the immediate work in the hands of temporary international agencies or to leave it to the individual states. The one, in fact, would prepare for the other. Except in matters of relief—the distribution of food, fuel, and clothing and also medical help—*ad hoc* temporary agencies could have no adequate authority or influence; all of what one might call the society-building activities, involving probably considerable planning and reorganization within and between the several countries, would fall upon the individual states again, as in 1919, when they competed and interfered rather than cooperated with each other, to the loss of them all. Yet it is vital that international activity should be from the outset in the same hands and move in the same direction after the war as later; otherwise the chances of building up an international system would be gravely prejudiced. It is certain that one of the chief reasons for the failure of the League was that it was given a formal authority and promissory tasks for the future, while the immediate, urgent, and most welcome tasks of social reconstruction and reform were left to be attended to by national agencies. Later efforts to retrieve that mistake only led to a series of barren economic conferences, as by that time the policy of each country was set hard in its own mold. It is inevitable with any scheme of formal organization that the national states should have to re-start on their own, and natural therefore that refuge should be sought in the idea of a period of convalescence while the full-fledged scheme is worked out and adopted. But functional authorities would not need such political hospitalization, with its arbitrary and dangerous division of stages; they would merely vary, like any other agency anywhere and at any time, the emphasis of their work in accordance with the changing condition of their task, continuing to control and organize transport, for instance, after they had rebuilt it, and in the same way taking each task in hand with a plan and authority for continuing it. The simple fact is that all the re-starting of agriculture and industry and transport will either be done on some pre-arranged common program or it will have to be done, for it could not wait, on disjointed local plans; it will be done either by pre-established international agencies or it will have to be done by local national agencies—and the agencies which will act in the supposed convalescence period will also be those to gather authority and acceptance unto themselves.

.   .   .

The Broad Lines of Functional Organization

The problem of our generation, put very broadly, is how to weld together the common interests of all without interfering unduly with the particular ways of each. It is a parallel problem to that which faces us in national society, and which in both spheres challenges us to find an alternative to the totalitarian pattern. A measure of centralized planning and control, for both production and distribution, is no longer to be avoided, no matter what the form of the state or the doctrine of its constitution. Through all that variety of political forms there is a growing approximation in the working of government, with differences merely of degree and of detail. Liberal democracy needs a re-definition of the public and private spheres of action. But as the line of separation is always shifting under the pressure of fresh social needs and demands, it must be left free to move with those needs and demands and cannot be fixed through a constitutional re-instatement. The only possible principle of democratic confirmation is that public action should be undertaken only where and when and insofar as the need for common action becomes evident and is accepted for the sake of the common good. In that way controlled democracy could yet be made the golden mean whereby social needs might be satisfied as largely and justly as possible, while still leaving as wide a residue as possible for the free choice of the individual.

That is fully as true for the international sphere. It is indeed the only way to combine, as well as may be, international organization with national freedom. We have already suggested that not all interests are common to all, and that the common interests do not concern all countries in the same degree. A territorial union would bind together some interests which are not of common concern to the group, while it would inevitably cut asunder some interests of common concern to the group and those outside it. The only way to avoid that twice-arbitrary surgery is to proceed by means of a natural selection, binding together those interests which are common, where they are common, and to the extent to which they are common. That functional selection and organization of international needs would extend, and in a way resume, an international development which has been gathering strength since the latter part of the nineteenth century. The work of organizing international public services and activities was taken a step further by the League, in its health and drug-control work, in its work for refugees, in the experiments with the transfer of minorities and the important innovations of the League loan system, and still more through the whole activity of the ILO [International Labour Organisation]. But many other activities and interests in the past had been organized internationally by private agencies—in finance and trade and production, etc., not to speak of scientific and cultural activities. In recent years some of these activities have been brought under public national control in various countries; in totalitarian countries indeed all of them. In a measure, therefore, the present situation represents a retrogression from the recent past: the new turn toward self-sufficiency has spread from economics to the things of the mind; and while flying and wireless were opening up the world, many old links forged by private effort have been forcibly severed. It is unlikely that most of them could be resumed now except through public action, and if they are to operate as freely as they did in private hands they cannot be organized otherwise than on a nondiscriminating functional basis.

What would be the broad lines of such a functional organization of international activities? The essential principle is that activities would be selected specifically and organized separately—each according to its nature, to the conditions under which it has to operate, and to the needs of the moment. It would allow, therefore, all freedom for practical variation in the organization of the several functions, as well as in the working of a particular function as needs and conditions alter. Let us take as an example the group of functions which fall under communications, on which the success of post-war reconstruction will depend greatly. What is the proper basis for the international organization of *railway* systems? Clearly it must be European, or rather *continental*, North American, and so on, as that gives the logical administrative limit of coordination. A division of the Continent into separate democratic and totalitarian unions would not achieve the practical end, as political division would obstruct that necessary coordination; while British and American participation would make the organization more cumbersome without any added profit to the function. As regards shipping, the line of effective organization which at once suggests itself is *international*, or intercontinental, but not universal. A European union could not solve the problem of maritime coordination without the cooperation of America and of certain other overseas states. *Aviation* and *broadcasting*, a third example in the same group, could be organized effectively only on a *universal* scale, with perhaps subsidiary regional arrangements for more local services. Such subsidiary regional arrangements could in fact be inserted at any time and at any stage where that might prove useful for any part of a function. Devolution according to need would be as easy and natural as centralization, whereas if the basis of organization were political every such change in dimension would involve an elaborate constitutional re-arrangement. Similarly, it could be left safely to be determined by practical considerations whether at the points where functions cross each other—such as rail and river transport in Europe and America—the two activities should be merely coordinated or put under one control.

These are relatively simple examples. The functional coordination of production, trade, and distribution evidently would be more complex, especially as they have been built up on a competitive basis. But the experience with international cartels, with the re-organization of the shipping, cotton, and steel industries in England, not to speak of the even wider and more relevant experience with economic coordination in the two world wars—all shows that the thing can be done and that it has always been done on such functional lines. No fixed rule is needed, and no rigid pattern is desirable for the organization of these working functional strata.

A certain degree of fixity would not be out of place, however, in regard to more *negative* functions, especially those related to law and order, but also to any others of a more formal nature which are likely to remain fairly static. Security, for instance, could be organized on an interlocking regional basis, and the judicial function likewise, with a hierarchy of courts, as the need may arise—the wider acting as courts of appeal from the more local courts. Yet, even in regard to security, and in addition to regional arrangements, the elasticity inherent in functional organization may prove practicable and desirable, if only in the period of transition. Anglo-American naval cooperation for the policing of the seas may prove acceptable for a time, and it would cut across physical regions. Agreement on a mineral sanction would of necessity mean common action by those countries which control the main sources; and other such combinations might be found useful for any particular task in hand. That is security only for defense; security arrangements were conceived usually on a geographical basis because they were meant to prevent violence, and that would still be the task of sanctions, etc., based on some regional devolution. But in addition there is a growing functional devolution in the field of social security in connection with health, with the drug and white slave traffic, with crime, etc. In all that important field of social policing it has been found that coordination and cooperation with the police of other countries on functional lines, varying with each task, was both indispensable and practicable. There is no talk and no attempt in all this to encroach upon sovereignty, but only a detached functional association which works smoothly and is already accepted without question.

However that may be, in the field of more *positive* active functions—economic, social, cultural—which are varied and ever changing in structure and purpose, any devolution must, like the main organization, follow functional lines. Land transport on the Continent would need a different organization and agencies should the railways after a time be displaced by roads; and a Channel tunnel would draw England into an arrangement in which she does not at present belong, with a corresponding change in the governing organ.

Here we discover a cardinal virtue of the functional method—what one might call the virtue of technical self-determination. The functional *dimensions*, as we have seen, determine its appropriate *organs*. It also reveals through practice the nature of the action required under given conditions, and in that way the *powers* needed by the respective authority. The function, one might say, determines the executive instrument suitable for its proper activity, and by the same process provides a need for the reform of the instrument at every stage. This would allow the widest latitude for variation between functions, and also in the dimension or organization of the same function as needs and conditions change. Not only is there in all this no need for any fixed constitutional division of authority and power, prescribed in advance, but anything beyond the original formal definition of scope and purpose might embarrass the working of the practical arrangements.

The Question of Wider Coordination

The question will be asked, however, in what manner and to what degree the various functional agencies that may thus grow up would have to be linked to each other and articulated as parts of a more comprehensive organization. It should be clear that each agency could work by itself, but that does not exclude the possibility of some of them or all being bound in some way together, if it should be found needful or useful to do so. That indeed is the test. As the whole sense of this particular method is to let activities be organized as the need for joint action arises and is accepted, it would be out of place to lay down in advance some formal plan for the coordination of various functions. Coordination, too, would in that sense have to come about functionally. Yet certain needs and possibilities can be foreseen already now, though some are probable and others only likely, and it may help to round off the picture if we look into this aspect briefly.

1. *Within the same group* of functions probably there would have to be coordination either simply for technical purposes or for wider functional ends, and this would be the first stage toward a wider integration. To take again the group concerned with communications—rail, road, and air transport in Europe would need *technical* coordination in regard to timetables, connections, etc. They may need also a wider *functional* coordination if there is to be some distribution of passenger and freight traffic for the most economic performance—whether that is done by a superior executive agency or by some arbitral body, perhaps on the lines of the Federal Commerce Commission in America. Sea and air traffic across the Atlantic or elsewhere, though separately organized, probably would also benefit from a similar type of coordination. Again, various mineral controls, if they should be organized separately, would need some coordination, though this arbitrary grouping of "minerals" would be less to the point that the coordination of specific minerals and other products with possible substitutes—of crude oil with synthetic oil, of crude rubber with synthetic rubber, and so on.

2. The next degree or stage might be, if found desirable, the coordination of *several groups* of functional agencies. For instance, the communi-

cations agencies may not only work out some means of acting together in the distribution of orders for rolling stock, ships, etc., but they could or should work in this through any agencies that may have come into being for controlling materials and production, or through some intermediary agency as a clearinghouse. There is no need to prescribe any pattern in advance, or that the pattern adopted in one case should be followed in all the others.

3. The coordination of such working functional agencies with any *international planning* agencies would present a third stage, and one that brings out some interesting possibilities, should the ideas for an international investment board or an international development commission, as an advisory organ, come to fruition. One can see how such a development commission might help to guide the growth of functional agencies into the most desirable channels, and could watch their inter-relations and their repercussions. And an investment board could guide, for instance, the distribution of orders for ships, materials, etc., not only according to the best economic use but also for the purpose of ironing out cyclical trends. It could use, according to its nature, its authority or its influence to make of such orders a means additional to international public works, etc., for dealing with periods or pockets of unemployment. Coordination of such a general kind may in some cases amount almost to arbitration of differences between functional agencies; regional boards or councils like those of the Pan-American Union might be used to adjust or arbitrate regional differences.

4. Beyond this there remains the habitual assumption, as we have already said, that international action must have some overall *political authority* above it. Besides the fact that such a comprehensive authority is not now a practical possibility, it is the central view of the functional approach that such an authority is not essential for our greatest and real immediate needs. The several functions could be organized through the agreement, given specifically in each case, of the national governments chiefly interested, with the grant of the requisite powers and resources; whereas it is clear, to emphasize the previous point, that they could not allow such organizations simply to be prescribed by some universal authority, even if it existed. For an authority which had the title to do so would in effect be hardly less than a world government; and such a strong central organism would inevitably tend to take unto itself rather more authority than that originally allotted to it, this calling in turn for the checks and balances which are used in federal systems, but which would be difficult to provide in any loose way. If issues should arise in any functional system which would call either for some new departure or for the re-consideration of existing arrangements, that could be done only in council by all the governments concerned. Insofar as it may be desired to keep alive some general view of our problems, and perhaps a general watch over the policies of the several joint agencies, some body of a representative kind, like the League Assembly or the governing body of the ILO, could meet periodi-

cally, perhaps elected by proportional representation from the assemblies of the member states. Such an assembly, in which all the states would have a voice, could discuss and ventilate general policies, as an expression of the mind and will of public opinion; but it could not actually prescribe policy, as this might turn out to be at odds with the policy of governments. Any line of action recommended by such an assembly would have to be pressed and secured through the policy-making machinery of the various countries themselves.

These, then, are the several types and grades of coordination which might develop with the growth of functional activities. But there is, finally, in the political field also the problem of security, admittedly a crucial problem, for on its being solved effectively the successful working of the other activities will depend. At the same time, the general discussion of functional organization will have served to bring out the true place and proportion of security, as something indispensable but also as something incapable by itself of achieving the peaceful growth of an international society. It is in fact a separate function like the others, not something that stands in stern isolation, overriding all the others. Looking at it in this way, as a practical function, should also make it clear that we would not achieve much if we handled it as a one-sided, limited problem—at present too often summed up in "German aggression." German aggression was a particularly vicious outgrowth of a bad general system, and only a radical and general change of the system itself will provide continuous security for all. In this case also it would be useful to lay down some formal pledges and principles as a guiding line, but the practical organization would have to follow functional, perhaps combined with regional, lines. That is all the more necessary as we know better now how many elements besides the purely military enter into the making of security. The various functional agencies might, in fact, play an important role in that wide aspect of security; they could both watch over and check such things as the building of strategic railways or the accumulation of strategic stocks in metals or grains. Possibly they could even be used, very properly and effectively, as a first line of action against threatening aggression, by their withholding services from those who are causing the trouble. They could apply such preventive sanctions more effectively than if this were to wait upon the agreement and action of a number of separate governments; and they could do so as part of their practical duties, and therefore with less of the political reactions caused by political action.

Representation in Controls

One aspect likely to be closely examined is that of the structure of the functional controls, and here again the initial difficulty will be that we shall have to break away from attractive traditional ideas if we are to work out the issue on its merits. It is not in the nature of the method that representation on the controlling bodies should be democratic in a political sense, full and equal for all. Ideally it may seem that all functions should be organized on a worldwide scale and that all states should have a voice in control. Yet the weight of reality is on the side of making the jurisdiction of the various agencies no wider than the most effective working limits of the function; and while it is understandable that all countries might wish to have a voice in control, that would be really to hark back to the outlook of political sovereignty. In no functional organization so far have the parties interested had a share in control as "by right" of their separate existence—neither the various local authorities in the London Transport Board, nor the seven states concerned in the TVA [Tennessee Valley Authority]. And in any case, in the transition from power politics to a functional order we could be well satisfied if the control of the new international organs answered to some of the merits of each case, leaving it to experience and to the maturing of a new outlook to provide in time the necessary correctives.

.   .   .

Through Functional Action to International Society

The Way of Natural Selection

One cannot insist too much that such gradual functional developments would not create a new system, however strange they might appear in the light of our habitual search for a unified formal order. They would merely rationalize and develop what is already there. In all countries social activities, in the widest sense of the term, are organized and reorganized continually in that way. But because of the legalistic structure of the state and of our political outlook, which treat national and international society as two different worlds, social nature, so to speak, has not had a chance so far to take its course. Our social activities are cut off arbitrarily at the limit of the state and, if at all, are allowed to be linked to the same activities across the border only by means of uncertain and cramping political ligatures. What is here proposed is simply that these political amputations should cease. Whenever useful or necessary the several activities would be released to function as one unit throughout the length of their natural course. National problems would then appear, and would be treated, as what they are—the local segments of general problems.

.   .   .

Epilogue

Peace will not be secured if we organize the world by what divides it. But in the measure in which such peace-building activities develop and succeed, one might hope that the mere prevention of conflict, crucial as that may be, would in time fall to a subordinate place in the scheme of international things, while we would turn to what are the real tasks of our common society—the conquest of poverty and of disease and of ignorance. The stays of political federation were needed when life was more local and international activities still loose. But now our social interdependence is all-pervasive and all-embracing, and if it be so organized the political side will also grow as part of it. The elements of a functional system could begin to work without a general political authority, but a political authority without active social functions would remain an empty temple. Society will develop by our living it, not by policing it. Nor would any political agreement survive long under economic competition, but economic unification would build up the foundation for political agreement, even if it did not make it superfluous. In any case, as things are, the political way is too ambitious. We cannot start from an ideal plane but must be prepared to make many attempts from many points, and build things and mend things as we go along. The essential thing is that we should be going together, in the same direction, and that we get into step now.

.   .   .

Cooperation for the common good is the task, both for the sake of peace and of a better life, and for that it is essential that certain interests and activities should be taken out of the mood of competition and worked together. But it is not essential to make that cooperation fast to a territorial authority, and indeed it would be senseless to do so when the number of those activities is limited, while their range is the world. "Economic areas do not always run with political areas," wrote the *New York Times* (February 26, 1943) in commenting on the Alaska Highway scheme, and such cross-country cooperation would simply make frontiers less important. "Apply this principle to certain European areas and the possibilities are dazzling." If it be said that all that may be possible in war but hardly in peace, that can only mean that practically the thing is possible but that we doubt whether in normal times there would be the political will to do it. Now, apart from everything else, the functional method stands out as a solid touchstone in that respect. Promissory covenants and charters may remain a headstone to unfulfilled good intentions, but the functional way is action itself and therefore an inescapable test of where we stand and how far we are willing to go in building up a new international society. It is not a promise to act in a crisis, but itself the action that will avoid the crisis. Every activity organized in that way would be a layer of peaceful life; and a sufficient addition of them would create increasingly deep and wide strata of peace—not the forbidding peace of an alliance, but one that would suffuse the world with a fertile mingling of common endeavor and achievement.

This is not an argument against any ideal of formal union, if that should prove a possible ultimate goal. It is, above all, a plea for the creation now of the elements of an active international society. Amidst the tragedy of war one can glimpse also the promise of a broader outlook, of a much deeper understanding of the issues than in 1918. It is because the peoples are ready for action that they cannot wait. We have no means and no standing to work out some fine constitution and try to impose it in time upon the world. But we do have the standing and the means to prepare for immediate practical action. We do not know what will be the sentiments of the peoples of Europe and of other continents at the end of the war, but we do know what their needs will be. *Any* political scheme would start a disputation; *any* working arrangement would raise a hope and make for confidence and patience.

The functional way may seem a spiritless solution—and so it is, in the sense that it detaches from the spirit the things which are of the body. No advantage has accrued to anyone when economic and other social activities are wedded to fascist or communist or other political ideologies; their progeny has always been confusion and conflict. Let these things appear quite starkly for what they are, practical household tasks, and it will be more difficult to make them into the household idols of "national interest" and "national honor." The ideological movements of our time, because of their indiscriminate zeal, have sometimes been compared to religious movements. They may be, but at their core was not a promise of life hereafter. The things which are truly of the spirit—and therefore personal to the individual and to the nation—will not be less winged for being freed in their turn from that worldly ballast. Hence the argument that opposes democracy to totalitarianism does not call the real issue. It is much too simple. Society is everywhere in travail because it is everywhere in transition. Its problem after a century of laissez faire philosophy is to sift anew, in the light of new economic possibilities and of new social aspirations, what is private from what has to be public; and in the latter sphere what is local and national from what is wider. And for that task of broad social refinement a more discriminating instrument is needed than the old political sieve. In the words of a statement by the American National Policy Committee, "Part of the daring required is the daring to find new forms and to adopt them. We are lost if we dogmatically assume that the procedures of the past constitute the only true expression of democracy."

16

Political Community and the North Atlantic Area

Karl W. Deutsch et al.

In the 1950s, with memories of World War II still fresh and the Cold War threatening to burn hot, the issue of war and peace in Europe remained vital. European politicians were busy abolishing war between France and Germany by laying the foundation for a united Europe. In the meantime, US social scientists, many of them immigrants from the Continent, began systematically studying the European integration process to discover what propelled it and whether it would actually ensure peace.

One of these academics, a 1938 German-Czech refugee named Karl W. Deutsch (1912–1992), helped revolutionize the study of international relations by introducing scientific and quantitative methods. While at the Massachusetts Institute of Technology (he later taught at Yale and Harvard), he and seven of his colleagues applied their new social scientific skills to "the study of possible ways in which men someday might abolish war." The result of this study was Political Community and the North Atlantic Area (1957). The work did not focus on the new supranational institutions of Europe, but rather examined ten historical cases of integration to see if lessons could be applied to an area that included Western Europe, Canada, and the United States. After comparing these cases, they concluded that successful integration required a sense of community—a "we-feeling"— among the populations of the integrating territories, a core political area around which this community could coalesce, and a rise in administrative capabilities to meet the challenge of an enlarged domain. To meet these requirements for an "amalgamated security-community," Deutsch and his colleagues argued that the integrating territories must share a common set of values and that the communication and transactions between them must expand in numerous ways. This was their key insight: integration was a learning process that took place over a long period of extensive and sustained contact between people from the politically relevant strata of society. They were skeptical of the functionalists' claim (see Chapter 15) that integrating government tasks one step at a time would lead to more successful amalgamation, but they did confirm that functionalism had succeeded in the past.

Deutsch's transactionalist approach to integration was largely overshadowed by the rise of neofunctionalism (see Chapter 17) in the late 1950s and early 1960s, but more recently Deutsch has attracted attention from a new generation of scholars impressed by his prescient insights. His relevance seems to grow as the European Union continues to enlarge and the question of who is a "European" increases in importance.

The Problem

We undertook this inquiry as a contribution to the study of possible ways in which men someday might abolish war. From the outset, we realized the complexity of the problem. It is difficult to relate "peace" clearly to other prime values such as "justice" and "freedom." There is little common agreement on acceptable alternatives to war, and there is much ambiguity in the use of the terms "war" and "peace." Yet we can start with the assumption that war is now so dangerous that mankind must eliminate it, must put it beyond serious possibility. The attempt to do this may fail. But in a civilization that wishes to survive, the central problem in the study of international organization is this: How can men learn to act together to eliminate war as a social institution?

This is in one sense a smaller, and in another sense a larger, question than the one which occupies so many of the best minds today: how can we either prevent or avoid losing "the next war"? It is smaller because there will, of course, be no chance to solve the long-run problem if we do not survive the short-run crisis. It is larger because it concerns not only the confrontation of the nations of East and West in the twentieth century, but the whole underlying question of relations between political units at any time. We are not, therefore, trying to add to the many words that have been written directly concerning the East-West struggle of the 1940–1950's. Rather, we are seeking new light with which to look at the conditions and processes of long-range or permanent peace, applying our findings to one contemporary problem which, though not so difficult as the East-West problem, is by no means simple: peace within the North Atlantic area.

Whenever a difficult political problem arises, men turn to history for clues to its solution. They do this knowing they will not find the whole answer there. Every political problem is unique, of course, for history does not "repeat itself." But often the reflective mind will discover situations in the past that are essentially similar to the one being considered. Usually, with these rough parallels or suggestive analogies, the problem is not so much to find the facts as it is to decide what is essentially the same and what is essentially different between the historical facts and those of the present.

. . .

We are dealing here with political communities. These we regard as social groups with a process of political communication, some machinery for enforcement, and some popular habits of compliance. A political community is not necessarily able to prevent war within the area it covers: the United States was unable to do so at the time of the Civil War. Some political communities do, however, eliminate war and the expectation of war within their boundaries. It is these that call for intensive study. We have concentrated, therefore, upon the formation of "security-communities" in certain historical cases. The use of this term starts a chain of definitions, and we must break in here to introduce the other main links needed for a fuller understanding of our findings.

A SECURITY-COMMUNITY is a group of people which has become "integrated."

By INTEGRATION we mean the attainment, within a territory, of a "sense of community" and of institutions and practices strong enough and widespread enough to assure, for a "long" time, dependable expectations of "peaceful change" among its population.

By SENSE OF COMMUNITY we mean a belief on the part of individuals in a group that they have come to agreement on at least this one point: that common social problems must and can be resolved by processes of "peaceful change."

By PEACEFUL CHANGE we mean the resolution of social problems, normally by institutionalized procedures, without resort to large-scale physical force.

A security-community, therefore, is one in which there is real assurance that the members of that community will not fight each other physically, but will settle their disputes in some other way. If the entire world were integrated as a security-community, wars would be automatically eliminated. But there is apt to be confusion about the term "integration."

In our usage, the term "integration" does not necessarily mean only the merging of peoples or governmental units into a single unit. Rather, we divide security-communities into two types: "amalgamated" and "pluralistic."

By AMALGAMATION we mean the formal merger of two or more previously independent units into a single larger unit, with some type of common government after amalgamation. This common government may be unitary or federal. The United States today is an example of the amalgamated type. It became a single governmental unit by the formal merger of several formerly independent units. It has one supreme decision-making center.

The PLURALISTIC security-community, on the other hand, retains the legal independence of separate governments. The combined territory of the United States and Canada is an example of the pluralistic type. Its two separate governmental units form a security-community without being merged.

It has two supreme decision-making centers. Where amalgamation occurs without integration, of course a security-community does not exist.

Since our study deals with the problem of ensuring peace, we shall say that any political community, be it amalgamated or pluralistic, was eventually SUCCESSFUL if it became a security-community—that is, if it achieved integration—and that it was UNSUCCESSFUL if it ended eventually in secession or civil war.

Perhaps we should point out here that both types of integration require, at the international level, some kind of organization, even though it may be very loose. We put no credence in the old aphorism that among friends a constitution is not necessary and among enemies it is of no avail. The area of practicability lies in between.

Integration is a matter of fact, not of time. If people on both sides do not fear war and do not prepare for it, it matters little how long it took them to reach this stage. But once integration has been reached, the length of time over which it persists may contribute to its consolidation.

It should be noted that integration and amalgamation overlap, but not completely. This means that there can be amalgamation without integration, and that there can be integration without amalgamation. When we use the term "integration or amalgamation" in this book, we are taking a short form to express an alternative between integration (by the route of either pluralism or amalgamation) and amalgamation short of integration. We have done this because unification movements in the past have often aimed at both of these goals, with some of the supporters of the movements preferring one or the other goal at different times. To encourage this profitable ambiguity, leaders of such movements have often used broader symbols such as "union," which would cover both possibilities and could be made to mean different things to different men.

.   .   .

The Integrative Process: Some General Characteristics

For purposes of exposition, we have divided our findings into two parts: first, general changes in our way of thinking about political integration; and second, specific findings about the background conditions and the dynamic characteristics of the integrative process. . . . [W]e shall first discuss our general findings. Our more specific findings will follow in later sections. . . .

Reexamining Some Popular Beliefs

To begin with, our findings have tended to make us increasingly doubtful of several widespread beliefs about political integration. The first of these beliefs is that modern life, with rapid transportation, mass communications, and literacy, tends to be more international than life in past decades or centuries, and hence more conducive to the growth of international or supranational institutions. Neither the study of our cases, nor a survey of more limited data from a larger number of countries, has yielded any clear-cut evidence to support this view. Nor do these results suggest that there has been inherent in modern economic and social development any unequivocal trend toward more internationalism and world community.

. . .

Another popular belief that our findings make more doubtful is that the growth of a state, or the expansion of its territory, resembles a snowballing process, or that it is characterized by some sort of bandwagon effect, such that successful growth in the past would accelerate the rate of growth or expansion of the amalgamated political community in the future. In this view, as villages in the past have joined to make provinces, and provinces to make kingdoms, so contemporary states are expected to join into ever-larger states or federations. If this were true, ever larger political units would appear to be the necessary result of historical and technological development. Our findings do not support this view. While the successful unification of England facilitated the later amalgamation of England and Wales, and this in turn facilitated the subsequent amalgamation of England and Wales with Scotland in the union of the two kingdoms, the united kingdom of Britain did not succeed in carrying through a successful and lasting amalgamation with Ireland. Nor could it retain its political amalgamation with the American colonies. These seceded from the British Empire in 1776 to form the United States; and Ireland seceded in effect in the course of the Anglo-Irish civil war of 1918–1921. The unity of the Habsburg monarchy became increasingly strained in the course of the nineteenth century and was followed by disintegration in the twentieth; and so was the more limited union of the crowns of Norway and Sweden.

. . .

Another popular notion is that a principal motive for the political integration of states has been the fear of anarchy, as well as of warfare among them. According to this view, men not only came to look upon war among the units concerned as unpromising and unattractive, but also as highly probable. For they came to fear it acutely while believing it to be all but inevitable in the absence of any strong superior power to restrain all participants. Consequently, according to this theory, one of the first and most important features of a newly-amalgamated security-community was the establishment of strong federal or community-wide laws, courts, police forces, and armies for their enforcement against potentially aggressive member states and member populations. Beliefs of this kind parallel closely the classic reasoning of Thomas Hobbes and John Locke; and some writers on federalism, or on international organization, have implied a stress on legal institutions and on the problem of coercing member states. Our findings suggest strong qualifications for these views. The questions of larger-community police forces and law enforcement, and of the coercion of member states, turned out to be of minor importance in the early stages of most of the amalgamated security-communities we studied.

.   .   .

This stress on the supposed importance of the early establishment of common laws, courts, and police forces is related to the suggestion that it is necessary to maintain a balance of power among the member states of a larger union or federation, in order to prevent any one state from becoming much stronger than the others. There is much to be said for this point of view: if a member state is far stronger than all the rest together, its political elite may well come to neglect or ignore the messages and needs of the population of the smaller member units, and the resulting loss of responsiveness may prevent integration or destroy it. The evidence from our cases suggests, however, that not merely amalgamation, but also responsiveness and integration can all be achieved and maintained successfully without any such balance of power among the participating states or political units. Neither England within the United Kingdom, nor Prussia in Germany after 1871, nor Piedmont in Italy for some time after 1860, was balanced in power by any other member or group of members, yet each of the larger political communities achieved integration.

.   .   .

General Findings

Among our positive general findings, the most important seems to us that both amalgamated security-communities and pluralistic security-communities are practicable pathways toward integration. In the course of our research, we found ourselves led by the evidence to attribute a greater potential significance to pluralistic security-communities than we had originally expected. Pluralistic security-communities turned out to be somewhat easier to attain and easier to preserve than their amalgamated counterparts. . . .

The strengths of pluralism. The somewhat smaller risk of breakdown in the case of pluralistic security-communities seems indicated by an examination of the relative numbers of successes and failures of each type of security-community. We can readily list a dozen instances of success for each type. . . .

On the other hand, we find a sharp contrast in the number of failures for each type. We have found only one case of a pluralistic security-community which failed in the sense that it was followed by actual warfare between the participants, and it is doubtful whether a pluralistic security-community existed even in that case: this was the relationship of Austria and Prussia within the framework of the German Confederation since 1815. . . .

On balance, therefore, we found pluralistic security-communities to be a more promising approach to the elimination of war over large areas than we had thought at the outset of our inquiry.

But this relative superiority of a pluralistic security-community as a more easily attainable form of integration has limited applications. It worked only in those situations in which the keeping of the peace among the participating units was the main political goal overshadowing all others. This goal has been the main focus of our study. In our historical cases, however, we found that men have often wanted more: they have wanted a political community that would not merely keep the peace among its members but that would also be capable of acting as a unit in other ways and for other purposes. In respect to this capacity to act—and in particular, to act quickly and effectively for positive goals—amalgamated security-communities have usually been far superior to their pluralistic counterparts. In many historical cases, men have preferred to accept the somewhat greater risk of civil war, or of war among the participating units, in order to insure this greater promise of joint capacity for action. It is only today, in the new age of nuclear weapons, that these risks and gains must be reevaluated. Now a pluralistic security-community may appear a somewhat safer device than amalgamation for dealing with man's new weapons.

The thresholds of integration. Our second general finding concerns the nature of integration. In our earliest analytical scheme, we had envisaged this as an all-or-none process, analogous to the crossing of a narrow threshold. On the one side of this threshold, populations and policy-makers considered warfare among the states or political units concerned as still a serious possibility, and prepared for it; on the other side of the threshold they were supposed to do so no longer. . . .

Somewhat contrary to our expectations, however, some of our cases taught us that integration may involve a fairly broad zone of transition rather than a narrow threshold; that states might cross and recross this threshold or zone of transition several times in their relations with each other; and that they might spend decades or generations wavering uncertainly within it.

Thus we found that states could maintain armed forces which were potentially available for warfare against each other, but which were not specifically committed to this purpose. The American state militias from 1776 to 1865 and the forces of the Swiss cantons from the thirteenth to the nineteenth centuries seem to have been available for such purposes if the political temper of their respective communities had warranted such employment, as it did on a few occasions. It would thus be extraordinarily difficult to say just in which year warfare between the Protestant and Catholic cantons ceased to be a practical political possibility after 1712, or when it again became temporarily a practical possibility between 1815 and 1847; or just when integration within the United States was lost in the period between

1820 and 1861, and warfare between North and South became a substantial possibility.

. . .

The threshold of integration thus turned out to be far broader, and far less easy to discern, in our historical cases than we had envisaged at the outset. Not only the approach toward integration, but the very act of crossing the integration threshold, have turned out to be much lengthier and more uncertain processes than had been expected.

Communication and the sense of community. Integration has proved to be a more continuous process than our earliest analytical scheme had suggested; but it continues to be characterized by important thresholds. Within this framework of our revised general concept of integration, we have arrived at a somewhat deeper understanding of the meaning of "sense of community." It appears to rest primarily on something other than verbal assent to some or many explicit propositions. The populations of different territories might easily profess verbal attachment to the same set of values without having a sense of community that leads to political integration. The kind of sense of community that is relevant for integration, and therefore for our study, turned out to be rather a matter of mutual sympathy and loyalties; of "we-feeling," trust, and mutual consideration; of partial identification in terms of self-images and interests; of mutually successful predictions of behavior, and of cooperative action in accordance with it—in short, a matter of a perpetual dynamic process of mutual attention, communication, perception of needs, and responsiveness in the process of decision-making. "Peaceful change" could not be assured without this kind of relationship.

. . .

Growth around core areas. As such a process of integrative behavior, sense of community requires some particular habits of political behavior on the part of individuals and some particular traditions and institutions on the part of social groups and of political units, such as provinces or states.

These habits, in turn, are acquired by processes of social learning. People learn them in the face of background conditions which change only slowly, so that they appear at any moment as something given—as political, economic, social, or psychological facts that must be taken for granted for the purposes of short-range politics. The speed and extent of this learning of habits of integrative political behavior are then influenced in each situation by these background conditions, as well as by the dynamics of the particular political process—the particular movement toward integration. Some of our more specific findings deal with the importance of certain background conditions in each area studied, while others deal with the successive stages of the integrative political process that occurred.

The outcome, then, of the integrative process among any particular group of countries depends on the interplay of the effects of background conditions with moving political events. One aspect of this interplay deserves to be singled out for particular attention. It is the matter of political, economic, and social capabilities of the participating political units for integrative behavior.

Generally, we found that such integrative capabilities were closely related to the general capabilities of a given political unit for action in the fields of politics, administration, economic life, and social and cultural development. Larger, stronger, more politically, administratively, economically, and educationally advanced political units were found to form the cores of strength around which in most cases the integrative process developed.

Political amalgamation, in particular, usually turned out to be a nuclear process. It often occurred around single cores, as in the case of England, Piedmont, Prussia, and Sweden. Each of these came to form the core of a larger amalgamated political community (even though the Norwegian-Swedish union turned out to be transitory). . . .

The need for rising capabilities. The extent of integrative capabilities which already existed in the individual political units at the beginning of a major drive toward amalgamation thus turned out to be very important for the future development of the process. But another step was no less important: the further increase of these capabilities in the course of the movement toward amalgamation. The presence or absence of growth in such capabilities played a major role in every integrative process we studied, and particularly in every case of an amalgamation movement.

Generally, amalgamation did not come to pass because the government of the participating units had become weaker or more inefficient; nor did it come to pass because men had been forced to turn away from these increasingly incapable organizations to the building of a larger and less decrepit common government. Rather, amalgamation occurred after a substantial increase in the capabilities of at least some of the participating units, or sometimes of all of them. Examples are the increase in the capabilities of the American colonies before 1789, and in the capabilities of Prussia before 1871. The increase in the capabilities of the political organizations or governments of the individual states, cantons, principalities, and the like, formed a major element in the dynamic political process leading to amalgamation in each instance.

Such capabilities relevant to integration were of two broad kinds. One was related to the capacity to act of a political unit—such as its size, power, economic strength, administrative efficiency, and the like. The other kind was related to the ability of a unit to control its own behavior and to redirect its own attention. More accurately, this means the ability of its political decision-makers and relevant political elites to redirect and control their own attention and behavior so as to enable rulers to receive communications from other political units which were to be their prospective partners in the integrative process. It means, further, the ability to give these messages from other political units adequate weight in the making of their own decisions, to perceive the needs of the populations and elites of these other units, and to respond to them quickly and adequately in terms of political or economic action. The first kind of capabilities—those related to the capacity to act and to overcome external obstacles—are closely linked to what we often call power; the second kind are linked to what we propose to call responsiveness.

.   .   .

The race between capabilities and loads. Another set of data we found to be of crucial importance pertained to the burdens thrown upon the tangible and intangible resources of political units by the requirements of establishing or maintaining either an amalgamated or a pluralistic security-community. Such loads or burdens, as we have called them, were of many kinds. They included military or financial burdens, drains on manpower or wealth; the burden of risk from political or military commitments; costs of social and economic readjustments, such as at the establishment of a customs union; and similar burdens of a material kind. But they also included intangible burdens upon government, which could be visualized as somewhat similar to traffic loads of vehicles at a road intersection or of messages at a telephone exchange. In the cases of crossroads or switchboards, the flow of vehicles or messages requires more than a certain volume of material facilities for its accommodation; it also requires a certain number of decisions which must be made in a limited amount of time by the traffic officer who controls traffic at the intersection, or by the persons or apparatus that control the flow of calls through the telephone exchange.

It is this burden, imposed by the traffic load of messages and signals upon the attention-giving and decision-making capabilities of the persons or organizations in control, that has close parallels in the burden of government upon rulers. It is a burden upon the attention-giving, information-processing, and decision-making capabilities of administrators, political elites, legislatures, or electoral majorities. Thus the failure of the British Parliament to respond quickly and adequately to the disastrous Irish famine of 1846 was not caused primarily by any lack of material or financial resources to provide relief. Rather, the failure was one of adequate attention, perception, and decision-making to meet the burdens of responsibility which the Parliament had taken upon itself under the terms of Anglo-Irish union. It was nonetheless a failure that was to have far-reaching effects upon the future of Anglo-Irish relations.

Political amalgamation in general tended to increase the load of demands upon the material resources and the decision-making capabilities of governments, since decisions for larger areas and populations had to be made by fewer central institutions. The success or failure of amalgamation, then, depended in considerable part upon the relationship of two rates of change: the growing rate of claims and burdens upon central governments as against the growing—in some instances, the insufficiently growing—level of capabilities of the governmental institutions of the amalgamated political community. The load of communications, demands, and claims upon the capabilities of government was also growing from independent causes—such as the increasing complexity of economic life, the increasing level of popular expectations in terms of living standards, social opportunities, and political rights, and the increasing political activity of previously passive groups and strata. Hence the outcome of the race between the growth of loads and capabilities sometimes remained precarious for a longer period, or it changed from one period to another.

. . .

The Importance of Background Conditions

In general, our cases have left us impressed with the importance of certain background conditions for the success or failure of the integrative process. The influence of background conditions appears to be larger, and the opportunities for decisive action by political leaders or movements appear to be somewhat more limited, than we had thought at the beginning of our study.

To be sure, we found that the importance of a few background conditions had been somewhat overrated. Certain conditions which had often been considered as essential for the establishment of an amalgamated security-community turned out to be helpful to that end but not essential to it. Such helpful but nonessential conditions included previous administrative and/or dynastic union; ethnic or linguistic assimilation; strong economic ties; and foreign military threats. While all of these turned out to be helpful to integration, none of them appeared to be essential since each of them was absent in the successful establishment of at least one amalgamated security-community.

. . .

Some Essential Requirements for the
Establishment of Amalgamated Security-Communities

A number of conditions appear to be essential, so far as our evidence goes, for the success of amalgamated security-communities—that is, for their becoming integrated. None of these conditions, of course, seems to be by itself sufficient for success; and all of them together may not be sufficient either, for it is quite possible that we have overlooked some additional conditions that may also be essential. Nonetheless, it does seem plausible to us that any group of states or territories which fulfilled all the essential conditions for an amalgamated security-community which we have been able to identify should also be at least on a good part of the way to successful amalgamation.

Values and Expectations

The first group of essential conditions deals with motivations for political behavior, and in particular with the values and expectations held in the politically relevant strata of the political units concerned. In regard to values, we found in all our cases a compatibility of the main values held by the politically relevant strata of all participating units. Sometimes this was supplemented by a tacit agreement to deprive of political significance any incompatible values that might remain.

.   .   .

Values were most effective politically when they were not held merely in abstract terms, but when they were incorporated in political institutions and in habits of political behavior which permitted these values to be acted on in such a way as to strengthen people's attachment to them. This connection between values, institutions, and habits we call a "way of life," and it turned out to be crucial. In all our cases of successful amalgamation we found such a distinctive way of life—that is, a set of socially accepted values and of institutional means for their pursuit and attainment, and a set of established or emerging habits of behavior corresponding to them. To be distinctive, such a way of life has to include at least some major social or political values and institutions which are different from those which existed in the area during the recent past, or from those prevailing among important neighbors. In either case, such a way of life usually involved a significant measure of social innovation as against the recent past.

Putting the matter somewhat differently, we noted in our cases that the partial shift of political habits required in transferring political loyalties from the old, smaller political units, at least in part, to a new and larger political community has only occurred under conditions when also a great number of other political and social habits were in a state of change. Thus we find that the perception of an American people and an American political community, as distinct from the individual thirteen colonies, emerged between 1750 and 1790. This occurred at the same time as the emergence of a distinct American way of life clearly different from that of most of the people of Great Britain or French Canada. This way of life had been developing since the beginnings of colonial settlement in the seventeenth century, but had undergone accelerated change and development in the course of the American Revolution and its aftermath. . . .

In regard to expectations, we found that in all our cases amalgamation was preceded by widespread expectations of joint rewards for the participating units, through strong economic ties or gains envisaged for the future. By economic ties, we mean primarily close relations of trade permitting large-scale division of labor and almost always giving rise to vested interests. It was not necessary, however, for such strong economic ties to exist prior to amalgamation. . . . Only a part of such expectation had to be fulfilled. A "down payment" of tangible gains for a substantial part of the supporters of amalgamation soon after the event, if not earlier, seems almost necessary. . . .

Some noneconomic expectations also turned out to be essential. In all our cases of successful amalgamation we found widespread expectations of greater social or political equality, or of greater social or political rights or liberties, among important groups of the politically relevant strata—and often among parts of the underlying populations—in the political units concerned.

Capabilities and Communication Processes

Values and expectations not only motivate people to performance, but the results of this performance will in turn make the original values and expectations weaker or stronger. Accordingly, we found a number of essential conditions for amalgamation which were related to the capabilities of the participating units or to the processes of communication occurring among them. The most important of these conditions was an increase in the political and administrative capabilities of the main political units to be amalgamated. Thus the amalgamation of Germany was preceded by a marked increase in the political and administrative capabilities of Prussia from 1806 onward, and by a lesser but still significant increase in the corresponding capabilities of Bavaria and of other German states. . . .

Another essential condition for amalgamation, closely related to the increase in capabilities, is the presence of markedly superior economic growth, either as measured against the recent past of the territories to be amalgamated, or against neighboring areas. Such superior economic growth did not have to be present in all participating units prior to amalgamation, but it had to be present at least in the main partner or partners vis-à-vis the rest of the units to be included in the amalgamated security-community. . . .

Another essential requirement for successful amalgamation was the presence of unbroken links of social communication between the political units concerned, and between the politically relevant strata within them. By such unbroken links we mean social groups and institutions which provide effective channels of communication, both horizontally among the main units of the amalgamated security-community and vertically among the politically relevant strata within them. Such links thus involve always persons and organizations.

. . .

[A final] essential condition, related to the preceding one, is the broadening of the political, social, or economic elite, both in regard to its recruitment from broader social strata and to its continuing connections with them. An example of such a broadening of the elite was the emergence of a new type of political leader among the landowners of Virginia, such as George Washington, who retained the respect of his peers and at the same time also knew, well before the American Revolution, how to gain the votes of poorer farmers and frontiersmen at the county elections in Virginia. . . .

Mobility of Persons
Another condition present in all our cases of successful amalgamation was the mobility of persons among the main units, at least in the politically relevant strata. It is quite possible that this condition, too, may be essential for the success of amalgamation. In any event, our cases have persuaded us that the mobility of persons among the main political units of a prospective amalgamated security-community should be given far more serious consideration than has often been the case. Full-scale mobility of persons has followed every successful amalgamated security-community in modern times immediately upon its establishment. . . .

Multiplicity and Balance of Transactions
We also found that it was not enough for a high level of communications and transactions to exist only on one or two topics, or in one or two respects, among two or more political units if their amalgamation was to be successful. Rather it appeared that successfully amalgamated security-communities require a fairly wide range of different common functions and services, together with different institutions and organizations to carry them out. Further, they apparently require a multiplicity of ranges of common communications and transactions and their institutional counterparts. . . .

Two other conditions may well turn out to be essential for the success of amalgamation, but these will have to be investigated further. The first of them is concerned with the balance in the flow of communications and transactions between the political units that are to be amalgamated, and particularly with the balance of rewards between the different participating territories. It is also concerned with the balance of initiatives that originate in these territories or groups of population, and finally with the balance of respect—or of symbols standing for respect—between these partners. In the course of studying cases of successful amalgamation, we found that it was apparently important for each of the participating territories or populations to gain some valued services or opportunities. It also seemed important that each at least sometimes take the initiative in the process, or initiate some particular phase or contribution; and that some major symbol or representative of each territory or population should be accorded explicit respect by the others. . . .

The second condition follows from the preceding one. It was not essential that the flow of rewards, of initiatives, or of respect should balance at any one moment, but it seems essential that they should balance over some period of time. Sometimes this was accomplished by alternating flows or by an interchange of group roles. Territories which received particular prestige, or material benefits, at one time might become sources of benefits for their partners at another; or territories whose political elites found themselves ranged with a majority on one political issue might find themselves in a minority on another, without any one particular division between majorities and minorities becoming permanent. . . .

Mutual Predictability of Behavior

A final condition that may be essential for the success of amalgamation may be some minimum amount of mutual predictability of behavior. Members of an amalgamated security-community—and, to a lesser extent, of a pluralistic security-community—must be able to expect from one another some dependable interlocking, interchanging, or at least compatible behavior; and they must therefore be able, at least to that extent, to predict one another's actions. Such predictions may be based on mere familiarity. . . . While familiarity appears to have contributed successfully to the growth of mutual trust in some of our cases, such as that between Scottish Highlanders and Lowlanders, and later between Scots and Englishmen, or between German, French, and Swiss during much of the eighteenth century, we found in a number of our cases that mutual predictability of behavior was eventually established upon a firmer basis.

This firmer basis was the acquisition of a certain amount of common culture or of common group character or "national character." In this manner, an increasing number of Germans in the German states, of Italians in the Italian principalities, and of Americans in the American colonies, came to feel that they could understand their countrymen in the neighboring political units by expecting them, by and large, to behave much as they themselves would behave in similar situations; that is to say, they came to predict the behavior of their countrymen in neighboring political units on the basis of introspection: by looking into their own minds they could make a fairly good guess as to what their neighbors would do, so they could trust them or at least understand them, to some extent much as they would trust or understand themselves. The extent of mutual predictability of behavior, however, seems to have varied from case to case, and it also seems to have varied with the particular political elites or relevant strata concerned. That some mutual predictability of political behavior is an essential condition for an amalgamated security-community seems clear from our cases; but the extent of such predictability must remain a matter for further research.

Summary

Altogether we have found nine essential conditions for an amalgamated security-community: (1) mutual compatibility of main values; (2) a distinctive way of life; (3) expectations of stronger economic ties or gains; (4) a marked increase in political and administrative capabilities of at least some participating units; (5) superior economic growth on the part of at least some participating units; (6) unbroken links of social communication, both geographically between territories and sociologically between different social strata; (7) a broadening of the political elite; (8) mobility of persons, at least among the politically relevant strata; and, (9) a multiplicity of ranges of communication and transaction. And we have found indications that three other conditions may be essential: (10) a compensation of flows of communications and transactions; (11) a not too infrequent interchange of group roles; and (12) considerable mutual predictability of behavior.

.   .   .

Background Conditions Conducive to Disintegration

Several conditions were found present in all cases of disintegration of amalgamated political communities which we studied, and they appear likely to promote disintegration wherever they occur. This does not mean, however, that they are sufficient by themselves to produce disintegration. We have found these conditions also present in some cases where disintegration did not follow but where other factors favoring integration were present in particular strength. The establishment and preservation of amalgamated security-communities thus turned out to depend upon a balance of favorable and adverse conditions. Amalgamation does not seem likely to be established, or to persist, except in the presence of the nine essential conditions for amalgamation which we listed earlier in this chapter; but even in their presence, the disintegrative conditions which we shall discuss below could prevent, destroy, or at least endanger an amalgamated security-community.

In our earlier general discussion, we have described integration as a process depending upon a balance between political loads upon a government, and its capabilities for maintaining amalgamation, or its capabilities for maintaining integration within a pluralistic security-community. In accordance with this general view, we may group the disintegrative conditions in our cases under two headings: conditions that increased the burdens upon amalgamated governments, and conditions that reduced the capability of such governments to cope with the burdens put upon them.

One of the outstanding conditions that tended to destroy amalgamated security-communities by placing excessive burdens upon them was the effect of excessive military commitments. Common armies with light burdens and conspicuous gains in prestige or privileges, or short wars of similar character, were helpful, though not essential, to the deeper integration of a political community; but heavy military burdens with few conspicuous gains over the *status quo* tended to have the opposite effect.

. . .

Another condition which tended to increase greatly the load upon governments, and thus tended to disintegrate amalgamated security-communities, was a substantial increase in political participation on the part of populations, regions, or social strata which previously had been politically passive. Such a substantial increase in political participation meant in each case that the needs, wishes, and pressures of additional social strata or regions had to be accommodated within an old system of political decision-making that might be—and often was—ill-suited to respond to them adequately and in time. . . .

A further disintegrative condition related to this rise in political participation is the increase in ethnic or linguistic differentiation. Another aspect of the same condition is a rise in the political awareness of such differentiation as already may exist. Both of these are likely to be a consequence of the rise in political participation among groups that are already thus differentiated, in language and culture, from the predominant nationality or regional-cultural group within the political community in question. . . .

Another group of disintegrative conditions tends to weaken or destroy amalgamated security-communities by reducing the capabilities of their governments and political elites for adequate and timely action or response. One such condition in our cases appeared to be any prolonged economic decline or stagnation, leading to economic conditions comparing unfavorably with those in neighboring areas.

Another disintegrative condition of this kind was the relative closure of the established political elite. This tended to promote the rise of frustrated counter-elites, somewhat in Pareto's sense, among ethnic or cultural out-groups, or in outlying regions.

Another disintegrative condition, related to the foregoing, was the excessive delay in social, economic, or political reforms which had come to be expected by the population—reforms which sometimes had already been adopted in neighboring areas.

.   .   .

Special Features of Pluralistic Security-Communities

In regard to the problem of a pluralistic security-community, we found that its attainment would be favored by any conditions favorable to the success of an amalgamated security-community, and that it was sometimes hindered by conditions or processes harmful to the latter. Pluralistic security-communities sometimes succeeded, however, under far less favorable conditions than the success of an amalgamated government would have required; and they sometimes survived unfavorable or disintegrative processes which would have destroyed an amalgamated political community.

.   .   .

Of the twelve conditions that appeared to be essential for the success of an amalgamated security-community, or at least potentially so, only two or possibly three were found to be very important for a pluralistic security-community as well. The first of these was the compatibility of major values relevant to political decision-making. The second was the capacity of the participating political units or governments to respond to each other's needs, messages, and actions quickly, adequately, and without resort to violence. . . . A third essential condition for a pluralistic security-community may be mutual predictability of behavior; this appears closely related to the foregoing. But the member-states of a pluralistic security-community have to make joint decisions only about a more limited range of subject matters, and retain each a far wider range of problems for autonomous decision-making within their own borders. Consequently the range and extent of the mutual predictability of behavior required from members of a pluralistic security-community is considerably less than would be essential for the successful operation of an amalgamated one.

.   .   .

Altogether, our findings in the field of background conditions tend to bring out the great and potentially restrictive importance of these conditions for the establishment and preservation of amalgamated security-communities. Further, our findings tend to bring out the very considerable potentialities of pluralistic security-communities for overcoming even partially unfavorable background situations.

Political Integration as a Dynamic Process

The transition from background to process is fluid. The essential background conditions do not come into existence all at once; they are not established in any particular fixed sequence; nor do they all grow together like one organism from a seed. Rather, it appears to us from our cases that they may be assembled in almost any sequence, so long only as all of them come into being and take effect. Toward this end, almost any pathway will suffice. As each essential condition is fulfilled, it is added, one by one or a few at a time, as strands are added to a web, or as parts are put together on an assembly line.

So long as this assembling of conditions occurs very slowly, we may treat the status of each condition and the status of all of them together at any one time as a matter of stable, seemingly unchanging background. Indeed, in our historical cases they were so considered, as practically unchanged or slow-changing situations, by most of their contemporaries. But as the last of the conditions in each sequence are added to those whose attainment was assembled previously, the tempo of the process quickens. Background and process now become one. A multiplicity of ranges of social communication and transaction was a background condition for amalgamation, but the rapid adding of new ranges of such communications and transactions is a process. Moreover, it is a process that may become accelerated as a by-product of other processes of political and social change. A balance of flows of transactions between the different units eligible for amalgamation is another of the necessary background conditions for amalgamation. This is particularly true in regard to a balance of initiatives, of rewards, and of respect. But substantial progress toward the establishment of some such balance may be a matter of political process, or else a political process directed toward the attainment of amalgamation may produce a better balance of transaction flows as one of its by-products.

.   .   .

The Issue of Functionalism as a Pathway to Amalgamation

Our finding that the bringing together of the necessary background conditions for amalgamation in our cases resembled an assembly-line process suggests indirectly an answer to an old question: does merging of one or more governmental functions among two or more political units promote progress toward later over-all amalgamation of their governments? Or, on the contrary, does what we shall call functional amalgamation impede such over-all amalgamation by inadequate performance of the few already amalgamated functions? Does it take the wind from the sails of the movement for full-scale amalgamation by making the few already amalgamated functions serve adequately the main needs which had supplied most of the driving power for the over-all amalgamation movement?

Before we answer this question, we must say exactly what we mean by functionalism. As we are using the term here, it includes all cases of partial amalgamation, where some governmental functions are delegated by the participating units on a low or a high level of decision-making. Whether a particular function or institution is so important that its pooling with another government would have the effect of over-all amalgamation rather than partial—and thus take it out of the field of functionalism—depends on the importance of this particular function or institution in the domestic politics of the participating units.

.   .   .

How helpful, then, has functionalism been? We have found, first of all, that over-all amalgamation can be approached functionally and by steps, with successful over-all amalgamation at the end. This occurred in the cases of Germany with the Zollverein (of which, significantly, Austria was not a member); the United States with the common administration of Western lands under the Articles of Confederation; the Swiss cantons since the fourteenth century, and the common citizenship between Geneva, Bern, and Fribourg, and later other Swiss cantons from the sixteenth century onward; finally, between England and Wales and England and Scotland before the union of crowns preceding full amalgamation. In all these cases amalgamation eventually was successful. But functional amalgamation was also proposed and rejected among the Italian states in the 1840's, and eventually amalgamation was achieved without its aid. Moreover, functional amalgamation took place in at least three of our cases that were eventually unsuccessful: there was the union of crowns between Austria, Bohemia, and Hungary from 1526 onward; there was the union of crowns between Norway and Sweden in 1814; and there were various forms of partial amalgamation between England and Ireland before 1801.

These examples are taken from a sample collection of historical cases and situations in which instances of successful amalgamation outnumber the unsuccessful ones by more than two to one. From this it should be clear that the historical evidence in favor of functionalism is quite inconclusive.

It seems safest to conclude that the issue of functionalism has been greatly overrated. Functionalism, it appears, is a device that has been widely used both in successful and in unsuccessful movements toward amalgamation, somewhat as functional devolution and decentralization have been used in successful and in unsuccessful attempts at secession. The outcome in all such situations seems mostly to have been the result of other conditions and other processes—depending largely on whether functionalism mainly was associated with experiences of joint rewards or of joint deprivations—with functionalism in itself doing little to help or to harm. . . . Perhaps the most that can be said for functionalism as an approach to integration is that it seems less hazardous than any sudden attempt at over-all amalgamation.

.   .   .

17

The Uniting of Europe

Ernst B. Haas

Ernst B. Haas (1925–2003), an immigrant born in Frankfurt, was among the US social scientists applying behavioral methods to international relations in the 1950s. In 1958 he published a book entitled The Uniting of Europe: Political, Social, and Economic Forces, 1950–1957, *in which he used the European Coal and Steel Community as a case study in an attempt to dissect the "actual 'integration process' . . . to derive propositions about its nature." Haas recognized that functional integration was taking place in Europe, but that functionalism as a theory had failed to explain why decision-makers chose to integrate in some areas and not others. Functionalism needed a theory of politics, which Haas provided.*

Haas first defined political integration as "the process whereby political actors in several distinct national settings are persuaded to shift their loyalties, expectations, and political activities toward a new center, whose institutions possess or demand jurisdiction over the pre-existing national states." Then he drew on democratic theory, systems theory, group theory, and a number of other approaches to produce a scientifically rigorous explanation for European political integration that he also believed held predictive power. This neofunctionalist approach (here introduced by Haas in the preface to The Uniting of Europe *and described in greater detail by Alec Stone Sweet and Wayne Sandholtz in Chapter 24) views the integration process as group driven. Federal institutions are established because important political groups see tangible benefits from joint governance in specific areas. The integration process pushes forward when federal institutions affect the interests of groups that respond by organizing across national boundaries and pushing for more integration. Thus integration in one area spills over into another when groups perceive it to be in their interest.*

Haas wrote prolifically on integration in the 1960s and early 1970s as the acknowledged leader of the neofunctionalist school. Neofunctionalism remains influential, and Ernst Haas is still widely read.

Reprinted from *The Uniting of Europe: Political, Social, and Economic Forces, 1950–1957* (Stanford University Press, 1958). Copyright 1958, 1968 by Ernst B. Haas. Notes omitted. Used with permission of Peter M. Haas.

"United Europe" is a phrase meaning many things to many men. To some it implies the creation of a full-fledged federation of the independent states of Western Europe, either the Six of "Schumania" or the Fifteen of the Council of Europe. To others the phrase means no more than the desirability of creating a loose concert or confederation. Some see in it the guarantee for future greatness, a political, economic and cultural renaissance for the Old Continent, about to be eclipsed by the United States, the Soviet world, and perhaps the Arab-Asians. But others identify it with the death of cherished patterns of national uniqueness. Even government policy, on both sides of the Atlantic, sometimes hesitates between endorsing the creation of a new center of economic and political power and fearing the evolution of a high-tariff region or of institutionalized "third force" sentiments. One must add the still lively controversy over whether economic or military unification, or both, is possible without prior or simultaneous political federation. The arguments over the merits and types of unification have continued since the end of World War II; they are unlikely to be exhausted soon.

But for the political scientist the unification of Europe has a peculiar attraction quite irrespective of merits and types. He may see in it, as I do, an instance of voluntary "integration" taking place before his eyes, as it were under laboratory conditions. He will wish to study it primarily because it is one of the very few current situations in which the decomposition of old nations can be systematically analyzed within the framework of the evolution of a larger polity—a polity destined, perhaps, to develop into a nation of its own. Hence, my purpose is not the evaluation of the virtues and drawbacks of a United Europe in terms of European, American, national, international, free-enterprise, or welfare-state values. Nor is it an analysis of the advantages of federation over intergovernmental cooperation, economic over military unity. My aim is merely the dissection of the actual "integration process" in order to derive propositions about its nature. Hence, I focused my analysis on selected groups, institutions and ideologies which have already been demonstrated to act as unifying agents in political systems clearly "integrated" by any applicable standard. Further, I confined the analysis to the impact of the one organization whose powers, functions and composition make it *a priori* capable of redirecting the loyalties and expectations of political actors: the European Coal and Steel Community. My study, then, attempts to advance generalizations about the processes by which political communities are formed among sovereign states, and my method is to select specific political groups and institutions, to study their reactions to a new species of "federal" government, and to analyze the impact of that government in terms of the reactions caused. On the assumption that "integration" is a two-way process in which the central institutions affect and are affected by the subject groups, the Coal and Steel Community is to serve as a case study illustrating the effects on the totality of interactions.

. . .

The essential conclusions may be briefly summarized. The initiation of a deliberate scheme of political unification, to be accepted by the key groups that make up a pluralistic society, does not require absolute majority support, nor need it rest on identical aims on the part of all participants. The European Coal and Steel Community was initially accepted because it offered a multitude of different advantages to different groups. Acceptance of a federal scheme is facilitated if the participating state units are already fragmented ideologically and socially. Moreover, the acceptance of such a scheme is considerably eased if among the participating industrial, political, or labor groups there is a tradition, however vague, of mutual consultation and of rudimentary value sharing. A helpful, but by no means indispensable, condition is the existence of an external threat, real or imagined.

Once established, the central institution will affect political integration meaningfully only if it is willing to follow policies giving rise to expectations and demands for more—or fewer—federal measures. In either case, the groups concerned will organize across national state boundaries in order to be able to influence policy. If the central institution, however, fails to assert itself in any way so as to cause strong positive or negative expectations, its impact on unity will be as small as the integrative role of such technically powerful international administrative unions as the Danube Commissions or the Universal Postal Union. As far as the industrial groups—business and labor—are concerned, they tend to unite beyond their former national confines in an effort to make common policy and obtain common benefits. Thus perhaps the chief finding is that group pressure will spill over into the federal sphere and thereby add to the integrative impulse. Only industries convinced that they have nothing to gain from integration will hold out against such pressures. But industrial sectors initially opposed to integration for a variety of motives do change their attitude and develop strong positive expectations if they feel that certain common problems can be more easily met by a federal authority. More commonly still, groups are likely to turn to the federal authority for help in the solution of purely national problems if the local government proves uncooperative. Groups with strong initial positive expectations do not necessarily turn against the principle of integration if their hopes are disappointed: they merely intensify their efforts to obtain the desired advantages on the federal level, thus integrating themselves into organizations less and less dependent on and identified with the national state. Political parties, if allowance is made for their varying ideologies and constituencies, tend to fall into the same pattern. National governments, operating in the nexus of all these forces, may on occasion attempt to side-step, ignore, or sabotage the decisions of the federal authority. The study of the Coal and Steel Community shows, however, that governments also recognize a point beyond which such evasions are unprofitable, and that in the long run they tend to defer to federal decisions, lest the example of their recalcitrance set a precedent for other governments.

After five years of activity, the pattern of supranational pressure and counter-pressure has become apparent: groups, parties, and governments have reassessed and reformulated their aims in such a way that the drive for a United Europe has become the battle cry of the Left. The "sinistration" of federalism has been accomplished in the recognition of trade unions and Socialist parties that their version of the welfare state and of peace can rationally be achieved only in a federated Western Europe. Perhaps the most salient conclusion we can draw from the community-building experiment is the fact that major interest groups as well as politicians determine their support of, or opposition to, new central institutions and policies on the basis of a calculation of advantage. The "good Europeans" are not the main creators of the regional community that is growing up; the process of community formation is dominated by nationally constituted groups with specific interests and aims, willing and able to adjust their aspirations by turning to supranational means when this course appears profitable.

Our study thus substantiates the pluralistic thesis that a larger political community can be developed if the crucial expectations, ideologies, and behavior patterns of certain key groups can be successfully refocussed on a new set of central symbols and institutions. Yet this conclusion also begs the question of the generality of the process laid bare. Can larger political communities be created on this basis in all sections of the world, in all ages, irrespective of the specific powers initially given to the central authority? I suggest that the value of this case study is confined to the kind of setting which reproduces in essence the physical conditions, ideologies, class structure, group relations, and political traditions and institutions of contemporary Western Europe. In short, I maintain that these findings *are* sufficiently general in terms of the socio-political context to serve as propositions concerning the formation of political communities—*provided* we are dealing with (1) an industrialized economy deeply enmeshed in international trade and finance, (2) societies in which the masses are fully mobilized politically and tend to channel their aspirations through permanent interest groups and political parties, (3) societies in which these groups are habitually led by identifiable elites competing with one another for influence and in disagreement on many basic values, and (4) societies in which relations among these elites are governed by the traditions and assumptions of parliamentary (or presidential) democracy and constitutionalism. It may well be that the specific economic conditions under which the European coal and steel industries operate act as additional factors limiting the possibility of generalizing. Monopolistic competition and the prevalence of private ownership are such factors, though isolated pockets of nationalized industry exist in the total industrial complex. It may also be true that the impact of an overwhelmingly powerful external economic center acts as a limiting condition. Economic integration in Europe might have been much slower if the governments had been compelled to come to grips with investment, currency and trade questions—decisions which were in effect spared them by the direct and indirect role of United States economic policy. Hence, I would have little hesitation in applying the technique of analysis here used to the study of integration under NATO, the Scandinavian setting, the Organization for European Economic Co-operation, or Canadian-United States relations. I would hesitate to claim validity for it in the study of regional political integration in Latin America, the Middle East, or South-East Asia.

.   .   .

18

Obstinate or Obsolete?
The Fate of the Nation-State
and the Case of Western Europe

Stanley Hoffmann

The early 1960s were optimistic years for students of integration. The European Economic Community was pressing integration forward at a rapid pace and neofunctionalists seemed to have discovered the means by which advanced industrialized nations could push the international community beyond the sovereign state and dramatically reduce the possibility of war. But was this, in fact, the end of the nation-state? De Gaulle's precipitation of the "empty chair crisis" in 1965 indicated to many international observers that the nation-state was alive and well. One of them was Stanley Hoffmann of Harvard University.

Hoffmann—who was born in Vienna and raised in wartime France—argued in this very long 1966 Daedalus article (which bears close reading in its entirety) that the states of Europe were still self-interested entities with clear interests, despite their willingness to engage in closer cooperation in areas of "low politics," such as agriculture and trade. The members of the European Communities stubbornly hung on to the sovereignty that counts—control over foreign policy, national security, and the use of force ("high politics")—while only reluctantly bargaining away control over important aspects of their economies in exchange for clear material benefits. Thus functional integration, Hoffmann argued, reached its limits very quickly, failing to take Europe "beyond the nation-state."

Hoffmann's approach to international relations does not fit neatly into any single category.[1] At one level he is a "realist" who sees international politics as the interaction of self-interested states that protect their sovereignty in an anarchic world. At the same time, he admits the possibility of

Reprinted from *Daedalus*, from the issue entitled "Tradition and Change," vol. 95, no. 3 (Summer 1966). Reprinted with permission from MIT Press Journals. Copyright 1966 by the American Academy of Arts and Sciences. Notes omitted.

ɔeration among sovereign states, the development of norms govern-
...ɡ *international behavior, and the impact of domestic politics on state
interests. In this sense he is more of a "liberal." These two perspectives
come together in his view of European integration. Cooperation among
European states has changed the system of state interaction, but it has not
eliminated state sovereignty. Integration occurs, according to Hoffmann,
when sovereign states, pursuing their national interests, negotiate cooperative agreements—a view often labeled "intergovernmentalism." Intergovernmental bargaining can result in significant cooperation when the
interests of the negotiating states coincide. But when states disagree over
the best course of action, cooperation stalls, as it did in Europe in the 1960s.*

*Intergovernmentalism, with its emphasis on the strength of the nation-
state, provides a theoretical counter to neofunctionalism (Chapter 17) with
its accent on the erosion of sovereignty by supranational actors. Hoffmann
was one of the first intergovernmentalists to challenge the core assumptions
of the neofunctionalists and thus helped lay the foundation for the great
theoretical debate of the early 1990s.*

The critical issue for every student of world order is the fate of
the nation-state. In the nuclear age, the fragmentation of the world into
countless units, each of which has a claim to independence, is obviously
dangerous for peace and illogical for welfare. The dynamism which ani-
mates those units, when they are not merely city-states of limited expanse
or dynastic states manipulated by the Prince's calculations, but nation-states
that pour into their foreign policy the collective pride, ambitions, fears,
prejudices, and images of large masses of people, is particularly formidable. An abstract theorist could argue that any system of autonomous units
follows the same basic rules, whatever the nature of those units. But in
practice, that is, in history, their substance matters as much as their form;
the story of world affairs since the French Revolution is not merely one
more sequence in the ballet of sovereign states; it is the story of the fires
and upheavals propagated by nationalism. A claim to sovereignty based on
historical tradition and dynastic legitimacy alone has never had the fervor,
the self-righteous assertiveness which a similar claim based on the idea and
feelings of nationhood presents: in world politics, the dynastic function of
nationalism is the constitution of nation-states by amalgamation or by
splintering, and its emotional function is the supplying of a formidable
good conscience to leaders who see their task as the achievement of nationhood, the defense of the nation, or the expansion of a national mission.

This is where the drama lies. The nation-state is at the same time a
form of social organization and—in practice if not in every brand of
theory—a factor of international non-integration; but those who argue in
favor of a more integrated world, either under more centralized power or
through various networks of regional or functional agencies, tend to forget

Auguste Comte's old maxim that *on ne détruit que ce qu'on remplace*: the new "formula" will have to provide not only world order, but also the kind of social organization in which leaders, élites, and citizens feel at home. There is currently no agreement on what such a formula will be; as a result, nation-states—often inchoate, economically absurd, administratively ram-shackle, and impotent yet dangerous in international politics—remain the basic units in spite of all the remonstrations and exhortations. They go on *faute de mieux* despite their alleged obsolescence; indeed, not only do they profit from man's incapacity to bring about a better order, but their very existence is a formidable obstacle to their replacement.

If there was one part of the world in which men of goodwill thought that the nation-state could be superseded, it was Western Europe. One of France's most subtle commentators on international politics has recently reminded us of E. H. Carr's bold prediction of 1945: "we shall not see again a Europe of twenty, and a world of more than sixty independent sovereign states." Statesmen have invented original schemes for moving Western Europe "beyond the nation-state," and political scientists have studied their efforts with a care from which emotional involvement was not missing. The conditions seemed ideal. On the one hand, nationalism seemed at its lowest ebb; on the other, an adequate formula and method for building a substitute had apparently been devised. Twenty years after the end of World War II—a period as long as the whole interwar era—observers have had to revise their judgments. The most optimistic put their hope in the chances the future may still harbor, rather than in the propelling power of the present; the less optimistic ones, like myself, try simply to understand what went wrong.

My own conclusion is sad and simple. The nation-state is still here, and the new Jerusalem has been postponed because the nations in Western Europe have not been able to stop time and to fragment space. Political unification could have succeeded if, on the one hand, these nations had not been caught in the whirlpool of different concerns, as a result both of profoundly different internal circumstances and of outside legacies, and if, on the other hand, they had been able or obliged to concentrate on "community-building" to the exclusion of all problems situated either outside their area or within each one of them. Domestic differences and different world views obviously mean diverging foreign policies; the involvement of the policy-makers in issues among which "community-building" is merely one has meant a deepening, not a decrease, of those divergencies. The reasons follow: the unification movement has been the victim, and the survival of nation-states the outcome, of three factors, one of which characterizes every international system, and the other two only the present system. Every international system owes its inner logic and its unfolding to the diversity of domestic determinants, geo-historical situations, and outside aims among its units; any international system based on fragmentation tends, through the dynamics of unevenness (so well understood, if applied only to economic unevenness, by Lenin) to reproduce diversity. However, there is no inherent reason that the model of the fragmented international system should rule out by itself two developments in which the critics of the nation-state have put their bets or their hopes. Why must it be a diversity of nations? Could it not be a diversity of regions, of "federating" blocs, superseding the nation-state just as the dynastic state had replaced the feudal puzzle? Or else, why does the very logic of conflagrations fed by hostility not lead to the kind of catastrophic unification of exhausted yet interdependent nations, sketched out by Kant? Let us remember that the unity movement in Europe was precisely an attempt at creating a regional entity, and that its origins and its springs resembled, on the reduced scale of a half-continent, the process dreamed up by Kant in his *Idea of Universal History*.

The answers are not entirely provided by the two factors that come to mind immediately. One is the legitimacy of national self-determination, the only principle which transcends all blocs and ideologies, since all pay lip service to it, and provides the foundation for the only "universal actor" of the international system: the United Nations. The other is the newness of many of the states, which have wrested their independence by a nationalist upsurge and are therefore unlikely to throw or give away what they have obtained only too recently. However, the legitimacy of the nation-state does not by itself guarantee the nation-state's survival in the international state of nature, and the appeal of nationalism as an emancipating passion does not assure that the nation-state must everywhere remain the basic form of social organization, in a world in which many nations are old and settled and the shortcomings of the nation-state are obvious. The real answers are provided by two unique features of the present international system. One, it is the first truly global international system: the regional subsystems have only a reduced autonomy; the "relationships of major tension" blanket the whole planet; the domestic polities are dominated not so much by the region's problems as by purely local and purely global ones, which conspire to divert the region's members from the internal affairs of their area, and indeed would make an isolated treatment of those affairs impossible. As a result, each nation, new or old, finds itself placed in an orbit of its own, from which it is quite difficult to move away: for the attraction of the regional forces is offset by the pull of all the other forces. Or, to change the metaphor, those nations that coexist in the same apparently separate "home" of a geographical region find themselves both exposed to the smells and noises that come from outside through all their windows and doors, and looking at the outlying houses from which the interference issues. Coming from diverse pasts, moved by diverse tempers, living in different parts of the house, inescapably yet differently subjected and attracted to the outside world, those cohabitants react unevenly to their exposure and calculate conflictingly how they could either reduce the disturbance or affect in turn all those who live elsewhere. The adjustment of their own relations within the house becomes subordinated to their divergences about the outside world; the "regional subsystem" becomes a stake in the rivalry of its members about the system as a whole.

However, the coziness of the common home could still prevail if the inhabitants were forced to come to terms, either by one of them, or by the fear of a threatening neighbor. This is precisely where the second unique feature of the present situation intervenes. What tends to perpetuate the nation-states decisively in a system whose universality seems to sharpen rather than shrink their diversity is the new set of conditions that govern and restrict the rule of force: Damocles' sword has become a boomerang, the ideological legitimacy of the nation-state is protected by the relative and forced tameness of the world jungle. Force in the nuclear age is still the "midwife of societies" insofar as revolutionary war either breeds new nations or shapes regimes in existing nations; but the use of force along traditional lines, for conquest and expansion—the very use that made the "permeable" feudal units not only obsolete but collapse and replaced them with modem states often built on "blood and iron"—has become too dangerous. The legitimacy of the feudal unit could be undermined in two ways: brutally, by the rule of force—the big fish swallowing small fish by national might; subtly or legitimately, so to speak, through self-undermining—the logic of dynastic weddings or acquisitions that consolidated larger units. A system based on national self-determination rules out the latter; a system in which nations, once established, find force a much blunted weapon rules out the former. Thus agglomeration by conquest or out of a fear of conquest fails to take place. The new conditions of violence tend even to pay to national borders the tribute of vice to virtue: violence which dons the cloak of revolution rather than of interstate wars, or persists in the form of such wars only when they accompany revolutions or conflicts in divided countries, perversely respects borders by infiltrating under them rather than by crossing them overtly. Thus all that is left for unification is what one might call "national self-abdication" or self-abnegation, the eventual willingness of nations to try something else; but precisely global involvement hinders rather than helps, and the atrophy of war removes the most pressing incentive. What a nation-state cannot provide alone—in economics, or defense—it can still provide through means far less drastic than hara-kiri.

These two features give its solidity to the principle of national self-determination, as well as its resilience to the U.N. They also give its present, and quite unique, shape to the "relationship of major tension": the conflict between East and West. This conflict is both muted and universal—and both aspects contribute to the survival of the nation-state. As the superpowers find that what makes their power overwhelming also makes it less usable, or rather usable only to deter one another and to deny each other gains, the lesser states discover under the umbrella of the nuclear stalemate that they are not condemned to death, and that indeed their nuisance power is impressive—especially when the kind of violence that prevails in present circumstances favors the porcupine over the elephant. The superpowers experience in their own camps the backlash of a rebellion against domination that enjoys broad impunity, and cannot easily coax or coerce third parties into agglomeration under their tutelage. Yet they retain the means to prevent other powers from agglomerating away from their clutches. Thus, as the superpowers compete, with filed nails, all over the globe, the nation-state becomes the universal point of salience, to use the new language of strategy—the lowest common denominator in the competition.

Other international systems were merely conservative of diversity; the present system is profoundly conservative of the diversity of nation-states, despite all its revolutionary features. The dream of Rousseau, concerned both about the prevalence of the general will—that is, the nation-state—and about peace, was the creation of communities insulated from one another. In history, where "the essence and drama of nationalism is not to be alone in the world," the clash of non-insulated states has tended to breed both nation-states and wars. Today, Rousseau's ideals come closer to reality, but in the most un-Rousseauean way: the nation-states prevail in peace, they remain unsuperseded because a fragile peace keeps the Kantian doctor away, they are unreplaced because their very involvement in the world, their very inability to insulate themselves from one another, preserves their separateness. The "new Europe" dreamed by the Europeans could not be established by force. Left to the wills and calculations of its members, the new formula has not jelled because they could not agree on its role in the world. The failure (so far) of an experiment tried in apparently ideal conditions tells us a great deal about contemporary world politics, and about the functional approach to unification. For it shows that the movement can fail not only when there is a surge of nationalism in one important part but also when there are differences in assessments of the national interest that rule out agreement on the shape and on the world role of the new, supranational whole.

.   .   .

Since it is the process of European integration that is its [Western Europe's] most original feature, we must examine it also. We have been witnessing a kind of race, between the logic of integration set up by Monnet and analyzed by Haas, and the logic of diversity, analyzed above. According to the former, the double pressure of necessity (the interdependence of the social fabric, which will oblige statesmen to integrate even sectors originally left uncoordinated) and of men (the action of the supranational agents) will gradually restrict the freedom of movement of the national governments by turning the national situations into one of total enmeshing. In such a milieu, nationalism will be a futile exercise in anachronism, and the national consciousness itself will, so to speak, be impregnated by an awareness of the higher interest in union. The logic of diversity, by contrast, sets limits to the degree to which the "spill-over process" can limit the freedom of action of the governments; it restricts the domain in which the logic of functional integration operates to the area of welfare; indeed, to the extent that discrepancies over the other areas begin to prevail over the laborious harmonization in welfare, even issues belonging to the latter sphere may become infected by the disharmony which reigns in those other areas. The logic of integration is that of a blender which crunches the most diverse products, overcomes their different tastes and perfumes, and replaces them with one, presumably delicious juice. One lets each item be ground because one expects a finer synthesis: that is, ambiguity helps rather than hinders because each "ingredient" can hope that its taste will prevail at the end. The logic of diversity is the opposite: it suggests that, in areas of key importance to the national interest, nations prefer the certainty, or the self-controlled uncertainty, of national self-reliance, to the uncontrolled uncertainty of the untested blender; ambiguity carries one only a part of the way. The logic of integration assumes that it is possible to fool each one of the associates some of the time because his over-all gain will still exceed his occasional losses, even if his calculations turn out wrong here or there. The logic of diversity implies that, on a vital issue, losses are not compensated by gains on other (and especially not on other less vital) issues: nobody wants to be fooled. The logic of integration deems the uncertainties of the supranational function process creative; the logic of diversity sees them as destructive past a certain threshold; Russian roulette is fine only as long as the gun is filled with blanks. Ambiguity lures and lulls the national consciousness into integration as long as the benefits are high, the costs low, the expectations considerable. Ambiguity may arouse and stiffen national consciousness into nationalism if the benefits are slow, the losses high, the hopes dashed or deferred. Functional integration's gamble could be won only if the method had sufficient potency to promise a permanent excess of gains over losses, and of hopes over frustrations. Theoretically, this may be true of economic integration. It is not true of political integration (in the sense of "high politics").

The success of the approach symbolized by Jean Monnet depended, and depends still, on his winning a triple gamble: on goals, on methods, on results. As for goals, it is a gamble on the possibility of substituting motion as an end in itself, for agreement on ends. It is a fact that the transnational integrationist élites did not agree on whether the object of the community-building enterprise ought to be the construction of a new super-state—that is, a federal potential nation, *à la* U.S.A., more able because of its size and resources to play the traditional game of power than the dwarfed nations of Western Europe—or whether the object was to demonstrate that power politics could be overcome through cooperation and compromise, to build the first example of a radically new kind of unit, to achieve a change in the nature and not merely in the scale of the game. Monnet himself has been ambiguous on this score; Hallstein has been leaning in the first direction, many of Monnet's public relations men in the second. Nor did the integrationists agree on whether the main goal was the creation of a regional "security-community," that is, the pacification of a former hotbed of wars, or whether the main goal was the creation of an entity whose position and might could decisively affect the course of the cold war in particular, of international relations in general. Now, it is perfectly possible for a movement to feed on its harboring continental nationalists as well as anti-power idealists, inward-looking politicians and outward-looking politicians—but only as long as there is no need to make a choice. Decisions on tariffs did not require such choices. Decisions on agriculture already raise basic problems of orientation. Decisions on foreign policy and membership and defense cannot be reached unless the goals are clarified. One cannot be all things to all people all of the time.

As for methods, there was a gamble on the irresistible rise of supranational functionalism. It assumed, first, that national sovereignty, already devalued by events, could be chewed up leaf by leaf like an artichoke. It assumed, second, that the dilemma of governments having to choose between pursuing an integration that ties their hands and stopping a movement that benefits their people could be exploited in favor of integration by men representing the common good, endowed with the advantages of superior expertise, initiating proposals, propped against a set of deadlines, and using for their cause the technique of package deals. Finally, it was assumed that this approach would both take into account the interests of the greater powers and prevent the crushing of the smaller ones. The troubles with this gamble have been numerous. One, even an artichoke has a heart, which remains intact after the leaves have been eaten. It is of course true that a successful economic and social integration would considerably limit the freedom governments would still enjoy in theory for their diplomacy and strategy; but why should one assume that they would not be aware of it? As the artichoke's heart gets more and more denuded, the governments' vigilance gets more and more alerted. To be sure, the second assumption implies that the logic of the movement would prevent them from doing anything about it: they would be powerless to save the heart. But, two, this would be true only if governments never put what they consider essential interests of the nation above the particular interests of certain categories of national, if superior expertise were always either the Commission's monopoly or the solution of the issue at hand, if package deals were effective in every argument, and, above all, if the governments' representatives were always determined to behave as a "community organ" rather than as the agents of states that are not willing to accept a community under any conditions. Finally, functional integration may indeed give lasting satisfaction to the smaller powers, precisely because it is for them that the ratio of "welfare politics" to high politics is highest, and that the chance of gaining benefits through intergovernmental methods that reflect rather than correct the power differential between the big and the small is poorest; but this is also why the method is not likely *à la longue* to satisfy the bigger powers as much: facing them, the supranational civil servants, for all their skill and legal powers, are a bit like Jonases trying to turn whales into jellyfish. Of course, the idea—ultimately—is to move from an essentially administrative procedure in which supranational civil servants enter a dialogue with national ministers, to a truly federal one in which a federal cabinet is responsible to a federal parliament; but what is thus presented as linear progress may turn out to be a vicious circle, since the ministers hold the key to the transformation, and may refuse it unless the goals are defined and the results already achieved are satisfactory.

There was a gamble about results as well. The experience of integration would entail net benefits for all, and bring about clear progress toward community formation. Such progress could be measured by the following yardsticks: in the realm of interstate relations, an increasing transfer of power to the new common agencies, and the prevalence of solutions "upgrading the common interest" over other kinds of compromises; in the realm of transnational society, an increasing flow of communications; in the area of national consciousness—which is important both for interstate relations, because (as seen above) it may set limits to the statesmen's discretion, and for transnational society, because it affects the scope and meaning of communication flows—progress would be measured by increasing compatibility of views about external issues. The results achieved so far are mixed: negative on the last count (see below), limited on the second, and marked on the first by features that the enthusiasts of integration did not expect. On the one hand, there has been some strengthening of authority of the Commission, and in various areas there has been some "upgrading of common interests." On the other hand, the Commission's unfortunate attempt to consolidate those gains at de Gaulle's expense, in the spring of 1965, has brought about a startling setback for the whole enterprise; moreover, in their negotiations, the members have conspicuously failed to find a common interest in some vital areas (energy, England's entry), and sometimes succeed in reaching apparently "integrating" decisions only after the most ungainly, traditional kinds of bargaining, in such uncommunity-like methods as threats, ultimatums and retaliatory moves, were used. In other words, either the ideal was not reached, or it was reached in a way that was both the opposite of the ideal and ultimately its destroyer. If we look at the institutions of the Common Market as an incipient political system in Europe, we find that its authority remains limited, its structure weak, its popular base restricted and distant.

. . .

There are two important general lessons one can draw from a study of the process of integration. The first concerns the limits of the functional method: its very (if relative) success in the relatively painless area in which it works relatively well lifts the participants to the level of issues to which it does not apply well anymore—like swimmers whose skills at moving quickly away from the shore suddenly brings them to the point where the waters are stormiest and deepest, at a time when fatigue is setting in, and none of the questions about the ultimate goal, direction, and length of swim has been answered. The functional process was used in order to "make Europe"; once Europe began being made, the process collided with the question: "making Europe, what for?" The process is like a grinding machine that can work only if someone keeps giving it something to grind. When the users start quarreling and stop providing, the machine stops. For a while, the machine worked because the governments poured into it a common determination to integrate their economies in order to maximize wealth; but with their wealth increasing, the question of what to do with it was going to arise: a technique capable of supplying means does not *ipso facto* provide the ends, and it is about those ends that quarrels have broken out. They might have been avoided if the situation had been more compelling—if the Six had been so cooped up that each one's horizon would have been nothing other than his five partners. But this has never been their outlook, nor is it any more their necessity. Each one is willing to live with the others, but not on terms too different from his own; and the Six are not in the position of the three miserable prisoners of *No Exit*. Transforming a dependent "subsystem" proved to be one thing; defining its relations to all other subsystems and to the international system in general has turned out to be quite another—indeed, so formidable a matter as to keep the transformation of the subsystem in abeyance until those relations can be defined.

The model of functional integration, a substitute for the kind of instant federation which governments had not been prepared to accept, shows its origins in important respects. One, it is essentially an administrative model, which relies on bureaucratic expertise for the promotion of a policy defined by the policy authorities, and for the definition of a policy that political decision-makers are technically incapable of shaping—something like French planning under the Fourth Republic. The hope was that in the interstices of political bickering the administrators could build up a consensus; but the mistake was to believe that a formula that works well within certain limits is a panacea—and that even within the limits of "welfare politics" administrative skill can always overcome the disastrous effects of political paralysis or mismanagement (cf. the impact of inflation, or balance of payment troubles, on planning). Two, the model assumes that the basic political decisions, to be prepared and pursued by the civil servants but formally made by the governments, would be reached through the process of short-term bargaining, by politicians whose mode of operation is empirical muddling through, of the kind that puts immediate advantages above long-term pursuits: this model corresponds well to the nature of parliamentary politics with a weak Executive, for example, the politics of the Fourth Republic, but the mistake was to believe that all political regimes would conform to this rather sorry image, and also to ignore the disastrous results which the original example produced whenever conflicts over values and fundamental choices made mere empirical groping useless or worse than useless (cf. decolonization).

The second lesson is even more discouraging for the advocates of functionalism. To revert to the analogy of the grinder, what has happened is that the machine, piqued by the slowing down of supply, suddenly suggested to its users that in the future the supplying of grinding material be taken out of their hands and left to the machine. The institutional machinery tends to become an actor with a stake in its own survival and expansion. But here we deal not with one but with six political systems, and the reason for the ineffectiveness of the Council of Ministers of the Six may be the excessive toughness, not the weakness, of the national political systems involved. In other words, by trying to be a force, the bureaucracy here, inevitably, makes itself even more of a stake that the nations try to control or at least to affect. A new complication is thus added to all the substantive issues that divide the participants.

·   ·   ·

What are the prospects in Western Europe? What generalizations can one draw from the whole experience?

·   ·   ·

It has become possible for scholars to argue both that integration is proceeding and that the nation-state is more than ever the basic unit, without contradicting each other, for recent definitions of integration "beyond the nation-state" point not toward the emergence of a new kind of political community, but merely toward "an obscur[ing of] the boundaries between the system of international organizations and the environment provided by member states." There are two important implications.

The first one is, not so paradoxically, a vindication of the nation-state as the basic unit. So far, anything that is "beyond" is "less": that is, there are cooperative arrangements with a varying degree of autonomy, power, and legitimacy, but there has been no transfer of allegiance toward their institutions, and their authority remains limited, conditional, dependent, and reversible. There is more than a kernel of truth in the Federalist critique of functional integration: functionalism tends to become, at best, like a spiral that coils *ad infinitum*. So far, the "transferring [of] exclusive expectations of benefits from the nation-state to some larger entity" leaves the nation-state both as the main focus of expectations, and as the initiator, pace-setter, supervisor, and often destroyer of the larger entity: for in the international arena the state is still the highest possessor of power, and while not every state is a political community there is as yet no political community more inclusive than the state. To be sure, the military function of the nation-state is in crisis; but, insofar as the whole world is "permeable" to nuclear weapons, any new type of unit would face the same horror, and, insofar as the prospect of such horror makes war more subdued and conquest less likely, the decline of the state's capacity to defend its citizens is neither total nor sufficient to force the nation-state itself into decline. The resistance of the nation-state is proven not only by the frustrations of functionalism but also by both the promise and the failure of Federalism. On the one hand, Federalism offers a way of going "beyond the nation-state," but it consists in building a new and larger nation-state. The scale is new, not the story, the gauge not the game. Indeed, the Federalist model applies to the "making of Europe" the Rousseauistic scheme for the creation of a nation: it aims at establishing a unit marked by central power and based on the general will of a European people. The Federalists are right in insisting that Western Europe's best chance of being an effective entity would be not to go "beyond the nation-state," but to become a larger nation-state in the process of formation and in the business of world politics: that is, to become a sovereign political community in the formal sense at least. The success of Federalism would be a tribute to the durability of the nation-state; its failure so far is due to the irrelevance of the model. Not only is there no general will of a European people because there is as of now no European people, but the institutions that could gradually (and theoretically) shape the separate nations into one people are not the most likely to do so. For the domestic problems of Europe are matters for technical decisions by civil servants and ministers rather than for general wills and assemblies (a general will to prosperity is not very operational). The external problems of Europe are matters for executives and diplomats. As for the common organs set up by the national governments, when they try to act as a European executive and parliament, they are both condemned to operate in the fog maintained around them by the governments and slapped down if they try to dispel the fog and reach the people themselves. In other words, Europe cannot be what some nations have been: a people that creates its state; nor can it be what some of the oldest states are and many of the new ones aspire to be: a people created by the state. It has to wait until the separate states decide that their peoples are close enough to justify a European state whose task will be the welding of the many into one; and we have just examined why such a joint decision has been missing. The very obstacles which make the Federalist model irrelevant to nations too diverse and divided also make all forms of union short of Federalism precarious. Functionalism is too unstable for the task of complete political unification. It may integrate economies, but either the nations will then proceed to a full political merger (which economic integration does not guarantee)—in that case the federal model will be vindicated at the end, the new unit will be a state forging its own people by consent and through the abdication of the previous separate states, but the conditions for success described above will have to be met—or else the national situations will remain too divergent, and functionalism will be merely a way of tying together the preexisting nations in areas deemed of common interest. Between the cooperation of existing nations and the breaking in of a new one there is no stable middle ground. A federation that succeeds becomes a nation; one that fails leads to secession; half-way attempts like supranational functionalism must either snowball or roll back.

But the nation-state, preserved as the basic unit, survives transformed. Among the men who see in "national sovereignty" the Nemesis of mankind, those who put their hopes in the development of regional super-states are illogical, those who put their hopes in the establishment of a world state are utopian, those who put their hopes in the growth of functional political communities more inclusive than the nation-state are too optimistic. What has to be understood and studied now—far more than has been done, and certainly far more than this essay was able to do—is, rather than the creation of rival communities, the transformation of "national sovereignty": it has not been superseded, but to a large extent it has been emptied of its former sting; there is no supershrew, and yet the shrew has been somewhat tamed. The model of the nation-state derived from the international law and relations of the past, when there was a limited number of players on a stage that was less crowded and in which violence was less risky, applies only fitfully to the situation of today. The basic unit, having proliferated, has also become much more heterogeneous; the stage has shrunk, and is occupied by players whose very number forces each one to strut, but its combustibility nevertheless scares them from pushing their luck too hard. The nation-state today is a new wine in old bottles, or in bottles that are sometimes only a mediocre imitation of the old; it is not the same old wine. What must be examined is not just the legal capacity of the sovereign state, but the *de facto* capacity at its disposal; granted the scope of its authority, how much of it can be used, and with what results? There are many ways of going "beyond the nation-state," and some modify the substance without altering the form or creating new forms. To be sure, as long as the old form is there, as long as the nation-state is the supreme authority, there is a danger for peace and for welfare; Gullivers tied by Lilliputians rather than crushed by Titans can wake up and break their ties. But Gullivers tied are not the same as Gullivers untied. Wrestlers who slug it out with fists and knives, prisoners in a chain gang, are all men; yet their freedom of action is not the same. An examination of the international implications of "nation-statehood" today and yesterday is at least as important as the ritual attack on the nation-state.

.   .   .

Note

1. We have altered our view of Hoffmann in this edition based on his autobiographical article "A Retrospective," in *Journeys Through World Politics: Autobiographical Reflections of Thirty-four Academic Travelers,* ed. Joseph J. Kruzel and James N. Rosenau (Lexington, Mass.: Lexington Books, 1989), pp. 263–278.

19

The Theory of Economic
Integration: An Introduction

Bela Balassa

Federalists, functionalists, and neofunctionalists in the postwar period were largely concerned with the political results of integration, even if some of them (i.e., most federalists and functionalists) paid little attention to the political dimension of the integration process. They were, after all, chiefly interested in the peaceful resolution of international conflict. Postwar economists were also interested in the integration process in Europe but for different reasons. They were engaged in describing the process of economic integration and its impact on welfare. As war among West European nations became unthinkable in the years immediately following World War II, the economic gains of integration became the chief motive for continuing the process. Thus, the work of the economists took on added importance.

Bela Balassa (1928–1991), a professor of political economy at Johns Hopkins University, was one of the most productive students of economic integration. Drawing on the work of Jacob Viner and others, Balassa made a major contribution to our understanding of the effects of integration on trade and other economic activities in the 1960s and 1970s. In this introductory chapter to his important work, The Theory of Economic Integration *(1961), Balassa defines economic integration, identifies its stages, discusses political and ideological aspects of the integration process, and specifies what he means by "economic welfare." Finally, Balassa argues that functional integration, while perhaps politically expedient, is not as economically defensible as "the simultaneous integration of all sectors."*

The Concept and Forms of Integration

In everyday usage the word "integration" denotes the bringing together of parts into a whole. In the economic literature the term "economic integration"

Reprinted from *The Theory of Economic Integration* (R. D. Irwin, 1961). Notes omitted.

does not have such a clear-cut meaning. Some authors include social integration in the concept, others subsume different forms of international cooperation under this heading, and the argument has also been advanced that the mere existence of trade relations between independent national economies is a sign of integration. We propose to define economic integration as a process and as a state of affairs. Regarded as a process, it encompasses measures designed to abolish discrimination between economic units belonging to different national states; viewed as a state of affairs, it can be represented by the absence of various forms of discrimination between national economies.

In interpreting our definition, distinction should be made between integration and cooperation. The difference is qualitative as well as quantitative. Whereas cooperation includes actions aimed at lessening discrimination, the process of economic integration comprises measures that entail the suppression of some forms of discrimination. For example international agreements on trade policies belong to the area of international cooperation, while the removal of trade barriers is an act of economic integration. Distinguishing between cooperation and integration, we put the main characteristics of the latter—the abolition of discrimination within an area—into clearer focus and give the concept definite meaning without unnecessarily diluting it by the inclusion of diverse actions in the field of international cooperation.

Economic integration, as defined here, can take several forms that represent varying degrees of integration. These are a free-trade area, a customs union, a common market, an economic union, and complete economic integration. In a free-trade area, tariffs (and quantitative restrictions) between the participating countries are abolished, but each country retains its own tariffs against nonmembers. Establishing a customs union involves, besides the suppression of discrimination in the field of commodity movements within the union, the equalization of tariffs in trade with nonmember countries. A higher form of economic integration is attained in a common market, where not only trade restrictions but also restrictions on factor movements are abolished. An economic union, as distinct from a common market, combines the suppression of restrictions on commodity and factor policies, in order to remove discrimination that was due to disparities in these policies. Finally, total economic integration presupposes the unification of monetary, fiscal, social, and countercyclical policies and requires the setting-up of a supra-national authority whose decisions are binding for the member states.

Adopting the definition given above, the theory of economic integration will be concerned with the economic effects of integration in its various forms and with problems that arise from divergences in national monetary, fiscal, and other policies. The theory of economic integration can be regarded as a part of international economics, but it also enlarges the field of international trade theory by exploring the impact of a fusion of national markets on growth and examining the need for the coordination of economic policies in a union. Finally, the theory of economic integration should incorporate elements of location theory, too. The integration of adjacent countries amounts to the removal of artificial barriers that obstruct continuous economic activity through national frontiers, and the ensuing relocation of production and regional agglomerative and deglomerative tendencies cannot be adequately discussed without making use of the tools of locational analysis.

The Recent Interest in Economic Integration

In the twentieth century no significant customs unions were formed until the end of the Second World War, although several attempts had been made to integrate the economies of various European countries. Without going into a detailed analysis, political obstacles can be singled out as the main causes for the failure of these projects to materialize. A certain degree of integration was achieved during the Second World War via a different route, when—as part of the German *Grossraum* policy—the Hitlerites endeavored to integrate economically the satellite countries and the occupied territories with Germany. In the latter case, economic integration appeared as a form of imperialist expansion.

The post–Second World War period has seen an enormous increase in the interest in problems of economic integration. In Europe the customs union and later the economic union of the Benelux countries, the European Coal and Steel Community, the European Economic Community (Common Market), and the European Free Trade Association (the "Outer Seven") are manifestations of this movement. Plans have also been made for the establishment of a free-trade area encompassing the countries of the Common Market and the Outer Seven, but negotiations in the years 1957–60 did not meet with success. However, concessions offered in early 1961 by the United Kingdom with regard to the harmonization of tariffs on non-agricultural commodities give promise for the future enlargement of the Common Market in some modified form.

. . .

The interwar period has witnessed a considerable degree of disintegration of the European and the world economy. On the European scene the mounting trade-and-payments restrictions since 1913 deserve attention. Ingvar Svennilson has shown that, as a result of the increase in trade impediments, the import trade of the advanced industrial countries of Europe shifted from the developed to the less developed economies of this area, which did not specialize in manufactured products. This shift implies a decline in competition between the industrial products of the more advanced economies and a decrease in specialization among these countries. But lessening of specialization was characteristic not only among the more advanced European economies but also of the European economy as a whole. This development can be demonstrated by trade and production figures for the period of 1913–38. While the volume of commodity production in Europe increased by 32 per cent during those years, intra-European trade increased by 10 per cent. The formation of a European union can be regarded, then, as a possible solution for the reintegration of European economies.

Another factor responsible for the disintegration of the European economy has been the stepping-up of state intervention in economic affairs in order to counteract cyclical fluctuations, sustain full employment, correct income distribution, and influence growth. Plans for economic integration are designed partly to counteract the element of discrimination inherent in the increased scope of state intervention.

A related argument regards the establishment of customs unions as desirable for mitigating cyclical fluctuations transmitted through foreign-trade relations. The foreign-trade dependence of the European Common Market countries decreases, for example, by about 35 per cent if trade among the six countries is regarded as internal trade. The memory of the depression in the 1930s gives added weight to this argument. Note, however, that for this proposition to be valid, there is need for some degree of coordination in countercyclical policies among the participating countries.

Last but not least, it is expected that integration will foster the growth of the European economies. This outcome is assumed to be the result of various dynamic factors, such as large-scale economies on a wider market, lessening of uncertainty in intra-area trade, and a faster rate of technological change. In this regard, the increased interest in economic growth has further contributed to the attention given to possibilities of economic integration.

.   .   .

To summarize, economic integration in Europe serves to avoid discrimination caused by trade-and-payments restrictions and increased state intervention, and it is designed to mitigate cyclical fluctuations and to increase the growth of national income.

.   .   .

Integration and Politics

In examining the recent interest in economic integration, we have yet to comment on the role of political factors. There is no doubt that—especially in the case of Europe—political objectives are of great consequence. The avoidance of future wars between France and Germany, the creation of a third force in world politics, and the re-establishment of Western Europe as a world power are frequently mentioned as political goals that would be served by economic integration. Many regard these as primary objectives and relegate economic considerations to second place. No attempt will be made here to evaluate the relative importance of political economic considerations. This position is taken, partly because this relationship is not quantifiable, partly because a considerable degree of interdependence exists between these factors. Political motives may prompt the first step in economic integration, but economic integration also reacts on the political sphere; similarly, if the initial motives are economic, the need for political unity can arise at a later stage.

From the economic point of view, the basic question is not whether economic or political considerations gave the first impetus to the integration movement, but what the economic effects of integration are likely to be. In some political circles the economic aspects are deliberately minimized and the plan for economic integration is regarded merely as a pawn in the play of political forces. Such a view unduly neglects the economic expediency of the proposal. Even if political motives did have primary importance, this would not mean that the economist could not examine the relevant economic problems without investigating elusive political issues. By way of comparison, although the formation of the United States was primarily the result of political considerations, nobody would deny the economic importance of its establishment.

We shall not disregard the political factors, however. Political *ends* will not be considered, but at certain points of the argument we shall examine various economic problems the solution of which is connected with political *means* and political processes. We shall explore, for example, how the objective of exploiting the potential benefits of economic integration affects the decision-making process. Changes in the decision-making process, on the other hand, become a political problem. Nevertheless, we shall go no further than to state the need for coordinated action in certain fields and will leave it for the political scientist to determine the political implications of such developments.

The "Liberalist" and the "Dirigist" Ideal of Economic Integration

The recent interest in economic integration has prompted various proposals concerning the means and objectives of integration. Two extreme views—an all-out liberalist and a dirigist solution—will be contrasted here. The champions of economic liberalism regard regional integration as a return to the free-trade ideals of the pre–First World War period within the area in question and anticipate the relegation of national economic policy to its pre-1914 dimensions. If this approach is followed, integration simply means the abolition of impediments to commodity movements. At the other extreme, integration could also be achieved through state trading and through the coordination of national economic plans without the lifting of trade barriers. This alternative discards the use of market methods and relies solely on administrative, nonmarket means. It can be found in the integration projects of Soviet-type economies; the operation of the Council of Mutual Economic Assistance, comprising the Soviet Union and her European satellites, is based on the coordination of long-range plans and bilateral trade agreements. A similar method, but one which put more reliance on market means, was used by Germany during the last war. In this study we shall examine problems of economic integration in market economies and shall not deal with Nazi Germany and Soviet-type economies. Nevertheless, we shall see that dirigistic tendencies appear in the writings of some Western authors, too.

Among the proponents of the liberalist solution, Allais, Röpke, and Heilperin may be cited. They regard economic integration as identical with trade (and payments) liberalization. Allais asserts that "practically, the only mutually acceptable rule for close economic cooperation between democratic societies is the rule of the free market." Röpke is of the opinion that European economic integration is nothing else than an attempt to remedy the disintegration of the post-1914 period that destroyed the previous integration of national economies. A less extreme position is taken by Heilperin, who rejects the consideration of regional development plans and subsidies to industries for reconversion purposes but accepts state responsibility for investment decisions in certain areas. To the majority of observers, however, the liberalist ideal of integration is a relic from the past, and its application to present-day economic life appears rather anachronistic. As Jean Weiller put it, "It would be a great error to believe that the decision to create a regional union would re-establish the conditions of an economic liberalism, extirpating with one stroke all so-called dirigistic policies."

It can rightly be said that considerations such as the avoidance of depressions, the maintenance of full employment, the problems of regional development, the regulation of cartels and monopolies, and so forth, require state intervention in economic life, and any attempts to integrate national economies would necessarily lead to harmonization in various policy areas. This idea is not new. The need for the coordination of fiscal, monetary, social, and countercyclical policies was stressed in the League of Nations study on customs unions published immediately after the end of the Second World War. In fact, the question is not whether government intervention is needed or not in an integrated area, but whether economic integration results in a more intensive participation of the state in economic affairs or in a more intensive reliance on market methods.

Some authors advocate an intensification of state intervention in economic affairs. The need for economic planning in a union is emphasized, for example, by André Philip and by other French Socialists. In Philip's opinion, "there is no alternative to a directed economy," since "the market can be extended not by liberalizing but by organizing." Although not an advocate of centralized planning, the stepping-up of state intervention is also recommended by Maurice Byé, who contrasts his "integration theory" with Heilperin's "market theory." Considering the pronouncements of French economists and industrialists, it can be said that, by and large, the French view of economic integration contains more dirigistic elements than, for example, that of most German economists and entrepreneurs.

The defenders of dirigistic tendencies fail to consider, however, the lessening of planning and government intervention—and the beneficial effects thereof—in Europe since the end of the Second World War. Although this change does not indicate a return to the pre-1914 situation, it brought about an increased use of the market mechanism and contributed to the spectacular growth of the European economy during the 1950's. It appears, then, that a reintroduction of dirigistic methods would slow down, rather than accelerate, future growth. State intervention may be stepped up in some areas, such as regional development planning, and will also be required to deal with transitional problems, but it is expected that an enlargement of the economic area will intensify competition and lead to less interference with productive activities at the firm level. Therefore, those who regard the European Common Market as a *marché institué* err in the opposite direction from the holders of old-fashioned liberalist views.

.   .   .

Economic Integration and Welfare

It can be said that the ultimate objective of economic activity is an increase in welfare. Thus, in order to assess the desirability of integration, its contribution to welfare needs to be considered. But the concept of welfare is fraught with much obscurity. First, the noneconomic aspects present some ambiguity; second, even restricting the meaning of the concept to "economic welfare" in the Pigovian tradition, we are confronted with the well-known difficulties of interpersonal comparisons if we try to say anything over and above the Pareto condition: an increase in one man's welfare leads to an increase in social welfare only if there is no reduction in the welfare of any other members of the group. In the case of integration, economic welfare will be affected by (a) a change in the quantity of commodities produced, (b) a change in the degree of discrimination between domestic and foreign goods, (c) a redistribution of income between the nationals of different countries, and (d) income redistribution within individual countries. Accordingly, distinction is made between a real-income component and a distributional component of economic welfare. The former denotes a change in potential welfare (efficiency); the latter refers to the welfare effects of income redistribution (equity).

With regard to potential welfare, separate treatment is allotted to changes in the quantity of goods produced and changes in their distribution. First, there is an increase (decrease) in potential welfare if—owing to the reallocation of resources consequent upon integration—the quantity of goods and services produced with given inputs increases (decreases) or, alternatively, if the production of the same quantity of goods and services requires a smaller (larger) quantity of inputs. If we regard inputs as negative outputs, we may say that a rise in net output leads to an increase in potential welfare. A higher net output entails an increase in potential welfare in the sense that a larger quantity of goods and services can now be distributed among individuals so as to make some people better off without making others worse off. Second, potential welfare is also affected through the impact of economic integration on consumers' choice. Restrictions on commodity movements imply discrimination between domestic and foreign commodities; a tariff causes consumers to buy more of lower-valued domestic and less of higher-valued foreign goods. The removal of intra-union tariffs will do away with discrimination between the commodities of the member countries but will discriminate against foreign goods in favor of the commodities of partner countries. In short, economic efficiency means efficiency in production and efficiency in exchange, and an improvement in one or both constitutes an increase in potential welfare.

Given a change in potential welfare (the real-income component), we also have to consider the distributional component in order to determine changes in economic welfare. It can easily be seen that an evaluation of changes in income distribution would require interpersonal comparisons of welfare. The new welfare economics, however, does not admit the possibility of making interpersonal comparisons. As a possible solution, it has then been suggested that changes in welfare could be determined in terms of potential welfare; that is, the *possibility* of making everybody better off (or, at least, no one worse off) would be taken as equivalent to an increase in economic welfare. This proposition can be criticized primarily on the grounds that the hypothetical situation *after* compensation is irrelevant if compensation actually does not take place. Nevertheless, changes in the real-income component give a good approximation of changes in welfare *within a country,* since compensation is politically feasible, and in case of integration this would actually be carried out to some degree in the form of assistance to relocating workers or reconverting firms. In addition, a nation can be regarded as an entity, where a redistribution of income accompanying an increase in real income can be accepted—provided that the redistribution does not run counter to generally accepted ideals of equity.

The distribution component cannot be neglected if economic integration redistributes income between countries, especially between the member states of a union, on the one hand, and the nonparticipating economies, on the other. It is not possible to claim an increase in world welfare in every case when the increase in real income in the participating countries will be greater than the loss to third countries. This proposition would hold true only if international comparisons of welfare could be made or if we disregarded differences in the marginal utility of income between countries. The first possibility was ruled out above, and the equality of the marginal utility of income is no less implausible. According to some, the marginal utility of income in an underdeveloped economy might be two or three times as high as in the rest of the world. If such a view were accepted, a union of developed economies which would register gains in the real-income component might still reduce world welfare by redistributing income from "poor" to "rich" countries.

In the preceding discussion we have followed the customary exposition of welfare economics in using the concept of potential welfare in a static sense. Thus an increase in potential welfare was taken as equivalent to an improvement in the allocation of resources at a point of time. Static efficiency, however, is only one of the possible success criteria that can be used to appraise the effects of economic integration. Instead of limiting our investigation to a discussion of efficiency in resource allocation under static assumptions, greater attention should be paid to the impact of integration on dynamic efficiency. I have elsewhere defined dynamic efficiency as the hypothetical growth rate of national income achievable with given resource use and saving ratio. In technical terms, whereas static efficiency would require that the economy operate on its production-possibility frontier, dynamic efficiency can be represented by the movement of this frontier in the northeast direction. The concept of dynamic efficiency can be used in intercountry comparisons to indicate which economy is capable of faster growth under identical conditions with regard to resources and saving, or, alternatively, it can be applied for comparing the growth potentialities of an economy at different points of time. In the present context, we wish to compare the hypothetical growth rate attainable *before* and *after* integration, under the assumption of given initial resources and saving ratio.

Given the static efficiency of an economy, the main factors affecting its dynamic efficiency are technological progress, the allocation of investment, dynamic interindustry relationships in production and investment, and uncertainty and inconsistency in economic decisions. In addition to these factors, the actual growth of national income would also be affected by an increase in the proportion of national income saved and/or by interference with the individual's choice between work and leisure. Changes in the latter variables will be disregarded here, partly because we assume that they are but rarely affected by economic integration, partly because their effects cannot be evaluated in welfare terms, given the disutility of increased saving and/or work. Under these assumptions an increase in the rate of growth can be considered as equivalent to an improvement in dynamic efficiency and represents a rise in potential welfare.

In evaluating the effects of economic integration, we shall use dynamic efficiency as the primary success indicator, taking into account both changes in the efficiency of resource allocation in the static sense and the dynamic effects of integration. In addition, attention will be paid to the impact of integration on income distribution, on the regional pattern of production and income, and on the stability of the participating economies.

. . .

The Sectoral Approach to Integration
In this chapter, distinction has been made between various forms of economic integration. All these forms require concerted action in the entire field of economic activity, be it the abolition of customs barriers or the coordination of fiscal policies. Another approach to economic integration would be to move from sector to sector, integrating various industries successively. The application of this method had already been commended in the interwar period, and it found many champions in the period following the Second World War. Proposals were made to integrate various sectors such as the iron and steel industry, transportation, and agriculture. The Stikker Plan advocated the integration of national economies by removing barriers, industry by industry. Supporters of this view contended that national governments were more inclined to make limited commitments with reasonably clear implications than to integrate all sectors at the same time. The flexibility of this method was also extolled, and it was hoped that integration in one sector would encourage integration on a larger scale.

From the theoretical point of view, various objections can be raised against the sectoral approach. Whereas the simultaneous integration of all sectors allows for compensating changes, integration in one sector will lead to readjustment in this sector alone, the reallocation of resources in other sectors being impeded by the continued existence of tariffs and other trade barriers—hence the losses suffered by countries whose productive activity in the newly integrated sector contracts will not be compensated for until the next phase. More generally, under the sectoral approach every step in integration results in a new and temporary equilibrium of prices, costs, and resource allocation, and this "equilibrium" is disturbed at every further step. Production decisions will then be made on the basis of prices that are relevant only in a certain phase of integration, and shifts in resource allocation will take place which may later prove to be inappropriate. On the other hand, the adjustment of relative prices and the reallocation of resources proceed more smoothly if all sectors are integrated at the same time, since some industries are expanding, others contracting, and unnecessary resource shifts do not take place.

Integration sector by sector puts an additional burden on the external balance also. At various steps, pressures will be imposed on the balance of payments of countries where the newly integrated sector is a high-cost producer. In the absence of exchange-rate flexibility, this process unnecessarily burdens exchange reserves in some, and inflates reserves in other, participating countries. If, on the other hand, exchange rates are left to fluctuate freely, temporary variations in rates of exchange will bring about transitional and unnecessary changes in the international division of labor.

In addition, lack of coordination in monetary, fiscal, and other policies is likely to cause difficulties under the sectoral approach, since differences in economic policies can lead to perverse movements of commodities and factors. For example, if inflationary policies are followed in one country while deflationary policies are pursued in another, an overadjustment will take place in the integrated sector (or sectors), while trade barriers restrict adjustments in other industries. Finally, any joint decisions made with respect to the integrated sector will affect all other branches of the participating economies.

A noneconomic objection of considerable importance should also be mentioned here. The sectoral approach is bound to bring about a conflict between producer and user interests in individual countries. In countries with relatively high production costs, for example, users will welcome integration because of its price-reducing effect; high-cost producers, however, will object to it. Experience suggests that producer interests have greater influence on governmental decisionmaking; hence these pressures are likely to have a restrictive effect on integration if the sectoral approach is followed. The interests of exporting and importing countries being opposed, there can be no "give and take"—the necessary pre-condition for intercountry agreements in most practical instances.

These theoretical objections suggest the inadvisability of integration sector by sector. This conclusion does not mean, however, that integration in one sector may not be beneficial if political obstacles hinder integration in all areas. The European Coal and Steel Community is a case in point. At the time of its inception, the realization of a European Common Market was not yet possible, but the governments of the participating countries were prepared to accept a limited measure of integration. The establishment of the Coal and Steel Community has been conducive to the expansion of production and trade in the partaking industries, and the Community demonstrated the possibility of integration in Europe, thereby contributing to the establishment of the Common Market.

It has also been argued that the difficulties of adjustment in production and trade in the Coal and Steel Community have been less than expected because the considerable increase in the national incomes of every participating country has made adjustment easier. This does not, however, rule out the possibility of maladjustments in other industries which will not be corrected until trade barriers are removed in all sectors. In addition, the Coal and Steel Community has encountered serious difficulties with respect to transportation policies, fiscal and social problems, etc., which have been due—to a great degree—to the fact that integration extends over only one sector.

20

Of Blind Men, Elephants and International Integration

Donald J. Puchala

Numerous scholars in international relations and comparative politics in the 1960s applied their considerable energies to exploring the European integration process. Neofunctionalists, intergovernmentalists, and economists debated one another. But conflict also shook the neofunctionalist movement. By 1970 the theory was rigorously specified but very complex—hardly the elegant model of the early 1960s. Some scholars began to feel uneasy about the direction integration theory was headed and began to wonder if what was happening in Europe was actually part of something much broader.

One of the first scholars to raise serious questions about the state of integration theory was Donald Puchala (University of South Carolina). In 1971 he famously likened scholars in the field to a set of blind men each describing a separate part of an elephant. The image stuck.

Integration theorists often spoke past each other because they failed to agree first on what it was they were studying. They were also finding little "integration" in Europe: federalists saw scant movement toward the emergence of a central government in Europe; transactionalists and neofunctionalists saw no emerging regional nationalism; functionalists saw little authority gravitating to "technocrats, bureaucrats and non-governmental actors"; and intergovernmentalists saw nothing more than power politics in European relations. But Puchala believed that each school was missing important questions about the changing nature of international politics; scholars focused too much on what ought to be rather than what was "here and now." In his view, a new international system of cooperation was emerging; what was happening in Europe was part of a broader global transformation, not the emergence of a new regional state. Puchala believed it was time for theorists to look beyond Europe.

Reprinted with permission from *Journal of Common Market Studies* 10, no. 3 (1971): 267–284. Copyright 1971 by John Wiley and Sons.

Puchala was only slightly ahead of his time. Problems with integration theory continued to mount in the early 1970s. Then in 1975, in a rare act of academic humility, Ernst Haas declared regional integration theory "obsolescent" and abandoned the field. Most neofunctionalists took Haas's (and Puchala's) hints and moved on to other theories of international political economy, such as interdependence theory and regime theory. By the late 1970s, integration theory had gone dormant, much like the European Community itself.

The story of the blind men and the elephant is universally known. Several blind men approached an elephant and each touched the animal in an effort to discover what the beast looked like. Each blind man, however, touched a different part of the large animal, and each concluded that the elephant had the appearance of the part he had touched. Hence, the blind man who felt the animal's trunk concluded that an elephant must be tall and slender, while his fellow who touched the beast's ear concluded that an elephant must be oblong and flat. Others of course reached different conclusions. The total result was that no man arrived at a very accurate description of the elephant. Yet, each man had gained enough evidence from his own experience to disbelieve his fellows and to maintain a lively debate about the nature of the beast.

The experience of scholars who have been conceptually grappling with contemporary international integration is not unlike the episode of the blind men and the elephant. More than fifteen years of defining, redefining, refining, modeling and theorizing have failed to generate satisfactory conceptualizations of exactly what it is we are talking about when we refer to "international integration" and exactly what it is we are trying to learn when we study this phenomenon. Part of the problem stems from the fact that different researchers have been looking at different parts, dimensions or manifestations of the phenomenon.

Furthermore, different schools of researchers have exalted different parts of the integration "elephant." They have claimed either that their parts were in fact whole beasts, or that their parts were the most important ones, the others being of marginal interest. Added conceptual confusion has followed from the fact that the phenomenon under investigation—international integration and all it involves—has turned out to be more complex than anyone initially suspected. Consequently, uncertainty *within* schools of researchers currently compounds dissension *between* the schools. Alas, the "elephant" grew in size and changed in form at the very moment that the blind men sought to grasp it! Finally, many of those who have tried to describe and explain international integration have been influenced in their intellectual efforts by normative preferences. As a result we have all too often found international integration discussed in terms of what it *should be* and what it *should be leading toward* rather than in terms of what it really is and is actually leading toward. In light of the reigning conceptual confusion in the realm of integration studies it is difficult to see why the field has acquired a reputation for theoretical sophistication. Rather, I should think that those of us in the field would be rather embarrassed at the fact that after fifteen years of effort we are still uncertain about what it is we are studying.

This paper is about international integration, about what it is, and about what it is not. My problem: what is actually taking place "out there" in the empirical world when we say that something we call international integration is taking place? Since questions of definition and description continue to pose barriers to cumulative research and theoretical synthesis in integration studies, what I offer here is yet another tilt at the definitional windmill. My hope is that some youthful irreverence combined with new thinking about international relations in our world today will lend fresh meaning to the concept "international integration."

The reader will note that my effort in this paper leads to a call for new empirical research within the framework of a new descriptive model of the international integration phenomenon. Consequently the points that I make are much more in the nature of hypotheses and notions rather than assertions. . . .

The Inadequacies of Conventional Conceptualizations

One of the most difficult intellectual feats to accomplish is to confront an essentially new phenomenon, recognize its novelty, and then go on to describe and explain this novelty without destroying it with blunt and inappropriate analytical instruments. More specifically, I believe that I can make a fairly strong case for the assertion that those clusterings of events we label "international integration" are essentially new happenings peculiar to the post-World War II era. Contemporary international integration is a product of forces, interests and attitudes peculiarly prevalent in the post-1945 world. It consequently embodies structures and processes and thrives in an attitudinal environment characteristic of this new postwar world. Despite this, however, we in integration studies have continually insisted upon analyzing cases of this new phenomenon as if they were instances of more familiar and timetested patterns. That is, instead of asking "what is contemporary international integration?" and thereby opening our minds to its novelty, we have asked, "is it federalism?" "is it nationalism?" "is it functionalism?" or "is it old-fashioned power politics?" As it has turned out, after some fifteen years of research, contemporary international integration is none of these, nor any combination of them. Therefore, conventional analytical models reflecting traditional familiar phenomena do not accurately describe, do not satisfactorily explain, and do not even raise very productive questions about the new, unfamiliar, and rather unconventional phenomenon, contemporary international integration. For example:

1. *Contemporary international integration is not federalism.* At least it is not classical federalism. Thus far, the patterns of political-economic interaction in different regions of the world—Western Europe, Central America, East Africa, Eastern Europe—which have attracted the attentions of students of international integration, have not by and large resembled patterns suggested by the federalist model. For example, no new central governments have been established to assume functions traditionally allotted to federal governments. Not even in Western Europe are new central authorities representing groups of states in international relations. On the occasions when the Commission speaks for the Six internationally, as in the case of the Kennedy Round negotiations or with regard to association agreements, its positions symbolize multilateral diplomatic compromises among six governments much more than they represent the policies of any central or "federal" governments. In addition, even when the Commission intermittently speaks for the "Six" each member-state continues to speak for itself in world councils and capitals. Then, too, let us not forget that all international integration arrangements currently in existence, including the Western European system, are functionally limited mostly to economic concerns, and therefore poorly approximate the functionally diffuse systems implicit in the federalist model.

In fairness, it is true that analysts using federalist models as guides to inquiry have looked upon contemporary international integration as emergent rather than "mature" federalism. Nevertheless, the point is that they have been preoccupied (if not obsessed) with questions about the degree of central authority present, the degree of state sovereignty relinquished, and the parceling of prerogative, power and jurisdiction among national and international authorities. Moreover, these same analysts have tended to equate "progress" or "success" in international integration with movement toward central government.

Such analysis is of course legitimate. But it has not been very productive. Most obviously it has not turned up very much federalism in contemporary international integration. But more importantly, conceptualizing and conducting inquiry in terms of the federalist model has tended to blind analysts to a number of interesting questions. Most broadly, is it really true that no progress toward international integration in various parts of the world has been made simply because little movement in the direction of regional central government has been registered? More provocatively perhaps, to what extent does participation in an international integration arrangement actually enhance rather than undermine national sovereignty? Relatedly, to what extent does an international integration arrangement preserve rather than supersede an international state system? Clearly, the analyst in the federalist mode is not prompted to ask these latter sorts of questions. Is he missing something of significance?

2. *Neither is international integration actually "nationalism" at the regional level.* So ingrained has the nationalism model become in Western political thinking and analysis, that we find it difficult to conceive of a non-national international actor, or a political system uncomplemented by an underlying community of people or peoples. Naturally, then, when talk of and movement toward regional unity in different parts of the world attracted the attentions of scholars, a good many assumed that movement toward international integration had to be progress toward the social and cultural assimilation of nationalities—i.e., toward *nationalism* at the regional level. For example, cued by historical precedents we looked for evidence of integration in Western Europe in the "Europeanization" of Frenchmen, Germans and Italians, much in the way that historians sought and found evidence of national integration in the Frenchifying of Normans, the Germanization of Bavarians and the Italianization of Neopolitans. The nationalism model led us to focus upon the assimilatory impacts of interactions and transactions among diverse peoples manifested in enhanced familiarity, responsiveness, and mutual identification, as well as emergent in-group/out-group consciousness. But though we were guided by validated and operational theories of nationalism, and despite the fact that we wielded the most sophisticated methodological tools of modern social science, our research turned up few "Europeans," even fewer "Central Americans" and "East Africans" and no "East Europeans," at all. This lacking evidence of progress toward the social and cultural assimilation of nationalities led some analysts to conclude that contemporary international integration was more myth than reality—no nationalism, therefore no integration! Others, however, cherished evidence drawn from youth studies and concluded that regional nationalism, at least in Western Europe, was present after all, and that the heyday of European community would arrive as the current younger generation gained maturity and as its members acquired positions of influence and responsibility. Still others, convinced that assimilation simply had to be a component of contemporary international integration, worded and reworded survey questions until "regional nationality" did at last emerge in poll results, irrespective of whether it existed in respondents' attitudes.

Credit goes to the nationalism analysts for recognizing that contemporary international integration requires a particular kind of attitudinal environment. However, the environment they seek has failed to materialize. Problems in using the nationalism model as a guide to analyzing contemporary international integration are similar to those involved in using the federalism model. First, testing the model against reality in Western Europe, in

Central America and elsewhere produces negative results. Regional nationalism, as noted, turns out not to be a component of international integration. Second, as with the federalist case, asking the analytical questions suggested by the nationalism model, deters thinking about a range of interesting alternative questions. For example, the analyst guided by the nationalism model is directed toward asking questions about people-to-people interactions and transactions, about similarities and differences in peoples' life styles, value systems and cultural norms, and especially about their attitudes toward one another and attendant perceptions of "we-ness." But are these really the appropriate questions to ask about the attitudinal environments supportive of intergovernmental cooperation and international institutionalization? Does it really matter what peoples think about one another? Or, rather, does it perhaps matter more what these people think about international cooperation and about supranational decision-making? The point here is that while the analyst guided by the nationalism model has been primarily concerned with links and bonds among peoples, he has by and large ignored links and bonds between peoples and their governments and between peoples and international organizations and processes. Is he missing something of significance?

3. *Nor is contemporary international integration functionalism in the Mitrany tradition.* Functionalist analysts have achieved greater descriptive accuracy than others grappling with contemporary international integration. Part of this accuracy, of course, must be accounted for by the fact that architects of international integration in Western Europe and elsewhere were directly influenced by functionalist thinking and therefore constructed their systems from functionalist blueprints. Still, let us give credit where credit is due. Functionalist analysts have accurately located the origins of international cooperation in realms of functional interdependence; they have pinpointed the significance of sector approaches; they have grasped the importance of non-governmental transnational actors.

Yet, very little in contemporary international integration has actually "worked" the way the functionalist design said that it would. Most revealingly, national governments have remained conspicuous and pivotal in internationally integrating systems, quite in contrast to the functionalist model which shunts these to the periphery of action. Leadership, initiative and prerogative have by and large remained with national governments. They have not gravitated to technocrats, bureaucrats and non-governmental actors. Moreover, national governments participating in international integration schemes have proven far more interested in "welfare" pursuits and far more restrained in "power" pursuits than functionalist theorizing would have led us to believe. Equally significant, functional task-areas in international economics, communications, science and technology, which the functionalist model stipulates [are] immune from international politics, have in fact turned out to be the central issue-areas in the lively international politics of international integration. There are simply no non-political issues in relations among states!

Most important, the functionalist model misses the essence of the growth and expansion of international regimes during international integration. So concerned are functionalist analysts with sector-to-sector task expansion, that many have failed first to recognize that this sectoral "spillover" is but one possible variety of expansion or growth during international integration. It is also, incidentally, the variety of growth that is least in evidence in existing cases. But, at least two other varieties can be monitored. First, there is expansion in the volume of internationally coordinative activities within given functional sectors. In addition, and much more important, there is possible expansion in the *political system* brought into being when functional sectors are integrated internationally. Such systemic expansion is evidenced by the entrance of increasing numbers of actors and interests into international program planning and policy making.

Second, neither have functionalist analysts been fully cognizant of the fact that sector-to-sector task expansion, spillover or its variants index integrative progress only if one assumes that "functional federation" or multi-sector merger is the end product of international integration. Here again, we are evaluating the present in terms of a hypothetical future which may never come about. If multi-sector merger is not the end product of international integration, if integration does not really go very far beyond the nation-state, then other varieties of systemic growth which reflect activity and complexity rather than extension might be the more telling indicators of healthy and productive international integration.

In sum, the functionalist analyst too has been partially strait-jacketed by his framework for thinking about international integration. He asked how men may achieve international cooperation by circumventing politics among nations. But, he has not asked how international cooperation is in fact achieved during international integration in the very course of international politics. Then, he has asked how functional integration spreads or spills over in the direction of federal government. But, in light of what has actually come to pass in Western Europe, might it not have been more productive to ask how a program of transnational sectoral merger fits into and becomes an integral part of a broader pattern of intra-regional international relations? That is, what if the termination state for international integration in fact resembles Western Europe, *circa* 1970? Why do some sectors get merged and others do not? More significantly, what kind of international politics results in a system where some functional sectors are transnationally merged and others are not? Impressionistically speaking, it would seem that this "broader pattern of intraregional international relations," this complex of merged and unmerged sectors and the aggregation of associated governing authorities of one type or another begins to approximate what we are really talking about when we speak of contemporary international integration. Does the functionalist analyst really recognize this? Is he missing something if he does not?

4. *Nor, finally, is contemporary international integration simply power politics.* The school of analysts who have looked upon and thought about international integration within the framework of "Realist" or *Macht Politik* models have fallen short of understanding what the phenomenon is or involves. To these analysts, international integration is a process of mutual exploitation wherein governments attempt to mobilize and accumulate the resources of neighboring states in the interest of enhancing their own power. Power is to be enhanced so that traditional ends of politics among nations may be accomplished—i.e., international autonomy, military security, diplomatic influence and heightened prestige. In Realist thinking, international organizations created in the course of international integration are but instruments to be used by national governments pursuing self-interests. They are made at the convergent whims of these governments, and flounder or fossilize as their usefulness as instruments of foreign policy comes into question. Over all, the Realist analyst argues that what we are observing "out there" and calling international integration are really international marriages of convenience, comfortable for all partners as long as self-interests are satisfied, but destined for divorce the moment any partner's interests are seriously frustrated. Hence, international integration drives not toward federalism or nationalism or functionalism, but toward disintegration. It never gets beyond the nation-state.

The wisdom of the Realist model is that it conceives of international integration as a pattern of international relations and not as something above, beyond or aside from politics among nations. But the shortcoming in the model is that it conceives of international integration as *traditional international relations* played by traditional actors, using traditional means in pursuit of traditional ends. So convinced is the political Realist that "there is nothing new under the sun" in international relations that he never seriously asks whether international actors other than national governments may independently influence the allocation of international rewards. Nor does he ask whether actors committed to international integration may be pursuing any other than the traditional inventory of international goals—autonomy, military security, influence and prestige. Do these really remain important goals in contemporary international relations? Nor, finally, does the Realist ask how actors committed to integration agreements in fact define their self-interests. Could it be that actors engaged in international integration actually come to consider it in their own self-interest to see that their partners accomplish their goals? In sum, by assuming that international politics remains the "same old game" and that international integration is but a part of it, the Realist analyst is not prompted to ask what is new in contemporary international relations? Is he missing something of significance?

Toward a New Conceptualization

If there has been a central theme running through my review of analytical models, it is that our conventional frameworks have clouded more than they have illumined our understanding of contemporary international integration. No model describes the integration phenomenon with complete accuracy because all the models present images of what integration could be or should be rather than what it is here and now. Furthermore, attempts to juxtapose or combine the conventional frameworks for analytical purposes by and large yield no more than artificial, untidy results. Clearly, to surmount the conceptual confusion we must set aside the old models, and, beginning from the assumption that international integration could very well be something new that we have never before witnessed in international relations, we must create a new, more appropriate, more productive analytical framework. I contend that this new model must reflect and raise questions about what international integration *is* in Western Europe, Central America, East Africa, etc., *at present*. We must, in other words, stop testing the present in terms of progress toward or regression from hypothetical futures since we really have no way of knowing where or how contemporary international integration is going to end up. . . .

Is It Really an "Elephant" After All?

Complexity of structure. I will hypothesize, though I cannot argue the case as convincingly as I would like to at this moment, that *contemporary international integration can best be thought of as a set of processes that produce and sustain a Concordance System at the international level.* "Concordance," according to dictionaries I have consulted, means "agreement" or "harmony," and "concord," its root, refers to "peaceful relations among nations." A "Concordance System" by my definition is an international system wherein actors find it possible consistently to harmonize their interests, compromise their differences and reap mutual rewards from their interactions. I selected the term "Concordance System" primarily because I found it necessary to have a name for what I believe I see coming into being "out there" in the empirical world.

. . . .

Part 3
Europe Relaunched

21

The European Community and Nation-State: A Case for a Neofederalism?

John Pinder

The apparent stagnation of the European Community in the 1970s and early 1980s and the consequent abandonment of neofunctionalism after 1975 had a chilling effect on integration theory. Most scholars (at least in the United States) migrated to other areas; those who remained interested in the EC (primarily Europeans) focused on how the Community actually worked, steering far clear of grand theory. Studies of EC decisionmaking in specific policy areas proliferated. These studies often relied on the theoretical concepts developed during the halcyon days of neofunctionalism and quietly laid the groundwork for later theoretical advances.

Overshadowed by this scientific examination of the inner workings of the EC were the European federalists, the idealistic "true believers" in a United States of Europe. They still believed that the most democratic and just way to prevent war and promote prosperity in Europe was to create a European super-state with full federal powers. Most maintained that functional integration had failed to dent national sovereignty. They continued to argue quietly for a great leap to federalism.

John Pinder (College of Europe) for several decades was and continues to be a prolific student of federalism. He has consistently supported the development of federal institutions for Europe, but he has been critical of many federalists for failing to think practically about how to achieve a federal goal. Federalism, in his view, needs to "refer both to a federalizing process and to a federal end." In the 1986 International Affairs article reprinted here, Pinder argued that while the EC had engaged in "incremental federalism," no one had examined the exact circumstances under which

Reprinted from *International Affairs* (London), 62, no. 1 (Winter 1985–1986): 50–54. Copyright 1985–1986 by John Wiley and Sons. Reproduced with permission of Blackwell Publishing Ltd. Notes omitted.

federalist advances were taking place. Pinder suggested that the background conditions outlined by Deutsch (Chapter 16) had all been met in Europe, but that political leadership was missing. He asserted that with leadership from the member states the prospects were good for "taking further steps in a federal direction." His specific policy suggestions, such as majority voting in the Council of Ministers, increased power for the European Parliament, and monetary union, sounded much like the Maastricht treaty, signed five years later. It also sounds today like some version of functionalism, albeit with a clear federal goal.

Pinder's early neofederalist call to think theoretically and practically about how to achieve a European Union was an indication that integration theory was making a comeback in the late 1980s.

. . .

Thinking other than that of the federalists has had relevance to the Community experience. But the "realist" and the "regime" and "system" schools have been too reductionist about the possibilities of movement in the direction of federal institutions with substantial competences. The neofunctionalists took, on the contrary, too facile a view of such possibilities, without clarity about the conditions under which integrative steps would be possible and without appreciating the strength of the nation-state. Federalists are less inclined to err in either of these directions. But, although they have acted in support of the Community's step-by-step development, they have not thought deeply enough about "the intermediary stage between normal interstate relations and normal intrastate relations" or about the concept of constitution-building as not just a single act, but also "an evolutionary development." If it is to help us assess the prospects for development of the Community, federalist theory needs to refer both to a federalizing process and to a federal end which implies substantial transfers of sovereignty. Its scope needs to incorporate steps in the development of European institutions and in their assumption of functions and competences; the resistance of member states to this process and the pressures that may induce them to accept it; and the perspective of possible "qualitative breaks" involving a "constitutional redistribution of powers." Existing theories do not seem to deal adequately with these things.

The neofunctionalists appeared strangely uninterested in evaluating how far any particular functions needed to be performed by supranational institutions. The assumption that such institutions would come to assume all important functions begged the critical question of the circumstances in which states would establish institutions with federal characteristics, or transfer competences to them, as they did when they launched the ECSC [European Coal and Steel Community], the Treaties of Rome and, to some extent, the EMS [European Monetary System]. . . . Nor did the neofunctionalists seem much concerned about the form of democratic control by European institutions that can be seen as a corollary of the more far-reaching transfers of competence. The classic federalists were clearer about this, proposing democratic federal institutions to accompany the transfer of the more basic competences such as money, taxation or armed forces. But because they did not consider any process of establishing federations other than through a single act transferring to them coercive and security powers, their thinking was not directly applicable to the transfer of less fundamental competences. Thus the political problem of transferring particular competences or instruments from the member states to the Community has been neglected by the various schools of thought, and much the same can be said of the political problem of securing the Community's institutional development, from the original addition of the Parliament, Court and Council to the High Authority mentioned in the Schuman declaration, through the establishment of the European Council, the European Parliament's budgetary powers and the direct elections, to the point where the Draft Treaty had only to propose majority voting and legislative codecision to convert the Community institutions into a federal form. A useful contribution to evaluating the prospects for the main elements in European Union proposals would be greater understanding of the circumstances which have enabled such increments of federal institutions or competences to be decided in the Community up to now.

One circumstance which stood in the way of such increments in the 1960s was . . . de Gaulle's leadership of France. He was doubtless unusual in the consistency with which his "supreme value" remained the nation-state. On the other hand, the British have been quite variable, from their loss of confidence in the nation-state in the late 1930s through the reassertion of confidence after the war to the rearguard action in its defense by contemporary "pragmatists." While the smaller member states harbor few illusions about the reality of national independence, the middle powers are still pulled in one direction by their attachment to the nation-state and in the other by their worries about the technological challenge from America and Japan, the power of the dollar, and security in the period of superpower tensions and the American Strategic Defense Initiative.

The background conditions which favor steps towards community or integration have been fairly extensively studied. Prominent among them are the degree of similarity or difference in certain attributes among members of the group. Economic and political systems and culture are usually regarded as sufficiently similar among West European countries to facilitate a substantial degree of integration. . . . In politics, it has been observed that like-mindedness between Adenauer, de Gasperi and Schuman facilitated the establishment of the ECSC, whereas different orientations among the political leaders of member countries can impede integration.

The intensity of interdependence and communication among the member countries is also held to condition the prospects for integration. There has, however, been surprisingly little effort to link measures of economic interdependence with constraints on national policies and with readiness for policy integration, in view of their potential significance for European integration. The MacDougall report showed that between 40 and 80 percent of regional gross domestic product was traded across the boundaries of each British region and of Brittany, compared with about 50 percent for Belgium and the Netherlands. Thus Belgium and the Netherlands appear to be as trade-dependent as at least a number of British and French regions. The larger EC [European Community] countries are about half as trade-dependent as Belgium and the Netherlands; and the trade-dependence of the great economies of the United States, Japan and the EC as a whole is about half that again. Thus the smaller countries' lack of illusions regarding national independence finds some statistical confirmation, and the larger EC member states, although their trade-dependence has greatly increased since the 1960s, may still feel themselves to be at a half-way house. But gross trade-dependence is only one measure of constraint on national policies; the influence of international capital markets and, hence, of American interest rates may, for example, be more important.

The conclusion of a study of various transnational links between the (then) six member countries in the late 1960s was that "if . . . India is seen as a nation, then Europe may well be described as an emergent nation." Some writers have tried to encapsulate the conditions that make federal institutions feasible in the formula that there must first be a single "people" or "nation." Yet this remains too vague an assertion unless the concept of a "people" or "nation" is defined and related to the characteristics of the population of the countries in question. It has indeed been observed that, in the field of theory, "no positive definition of the nation exists," and that national behavior is linked with "the situation of power, and probably depends on it." Is the assertion that a European nation is a precondition of a "fully democratic European Union" perhaps either tautological (a European nation being defined as a population which can uphold a European federal system), or merely another way of saying that we need to study the similarities, links, differences and divergences between member states in order to judge how far they can move towards federation?

One empirical way to judge the capacity of European peoples to sustain common institutions is observation of their behavior in relation to the institutions they already sustain together. The existence of prior association has long been seen as a condition that favors federalism. The experience of working the EC institutions, with their various federal attributes, may help us to judge whether member countries could support such reforms as co-decision and a considerable expansion of the scope for majority votes. However favorable the conditions may be for steps towards federal institutions and competences, such steps are not likely to be taken without adequate political leadership. The neofunctionalists were too little concerned about the political efforts required to secure such steps; and they were justifiably criticized for concentrating on the Commission as the political motor for integration. The European Parliament has the electoral base that the Commission lacks; but the political leadership which the Parliament has shown with its Draft Treaty could hardly secure major reforms, as distinct from public support for such reforms, without corresponding leadership from among the member states. The roles of Monnet and of Schuman, Adenauer and de Gasperi in relation to the ECSC have been noted . . . ; Monnet and Spaak were outstanding among the promoters of the Rome Treaties; understanding between Heath and Pompidou was crucial to the first enlargement of the EC and that between Giscard and Schmidt to the creation of the European Monetary System. The American federalists and Washington only come first to mind among a number of historical examples. Theories which understate the need for political efforts and leadership will, like neofunctionalism, separate themselves to that extent from reality.

The argument of this article suggests that the British, in order to play a more constructive and successful role in future discussions and negotiations on European Union, will need to take more seriously the possibility of developing the Community's institutions, as well as its competences, thus continuing a process which, thanks mainly to the initiatives of the founder members, is already fairly far advanced in the form of the Community as it exists today. The tendency to identify federalism with a great leap to a federation with military and coercive power inhibits practical thought about the prospects for taking further steps in a federal direction, whether in the form of a system of majority voting to complete the internal market, developing the EMS in the direction of monetary union, an increase in the powers of the European Parliament, or a package of such reforms that could deserve to be called European Union. Such thought would be helped by systematic study of the specific steps that could be taken and of the conditions that favor or impede them. If the term "neofederalism" would help the British to come to terms with the process of incremental federalism, the neologism would be a small price to pay for a major advance in our capacity to play our proper part in contemporary European and international politics.

22

1992: Recasting the European Bargain

Wayne Sandholtz and John Zysman

The adoption of the 1992 Program (1985) and the passage of the Single European Act (1986) revitalized the European Community and marked a new stage in the integration process. The new enthusiasm in the Community awoke grand integration theory from a long slumber as scholars—some new, some veterans of former debates—attempted once again to explain what was happening in Europe. They initially focused their attention on the decision to create a single market and to revise the Treaty of Rome to expedite the process. Ultimately, they were trying to explain why, after years of stagnation, the integration process was suddenly moving forward again. These scholars drew on neofunctionalism and a number of other approaches derived from international relations and EC decisionmaking to provide answers to their theoretical questions.

Wayne Sandholtz (University of Southern California) and John Zysman (University of California–Berkeley) opened the theoretical debate in 1989 with an attempt to explain the "1992 process" by focusing on supranational institutions. They argued first that changes in the international structure—specifically the decline of the United States and the rise of Japan—"triggered the 1992 process." They then coupled this idea with neofunctionalist and domestic politics notions to explain the timing and specific nature of recent integrative behavior. From neofunctionalism, they drew out the importance of supranational institutions (primarily the Commission) and European interest groups (organized European industrialists); from theories of domestic politics, they emphasized the effect of the domestic political context on the receptiveness of national governmental elites to initiatives from the Commission and European business. Thus in their view, recent integration was best viewed as a bargain between elites in EC institutions, European industry, and member governments, with the Commission supplying most of the policy leadership.

Reprinted with permission from *World Politics* 41, no. 1 (1989): 95–128. Copyright 1989 by Cambridge University Press. Notes omitted.

The focus for Sandholtz and Zysman was primarily, although not exclusively, on the actors working in the realm above the member states. For this reason, other scholars often labeled their view as supranationalist.

Under the banner of "1992," the European Communities are putting in place a series of political and business bargains that will recast, if not unify, the European market. This initiative is a disjunction, a dramatic new start, rather than the fulfillment of the original effort to construct Europe. It is not merely the culmination of the integration begun in the 1950s, the "completion" of the internal market. The removal of all barriers to the movement of persons, capital, and goods among the twelve member states (the formal goal of the 1992 process) is expected to increase economies of scale and decrease transaction costs. But these one-time economic benefits do not capture the full range of purposes and consequences of 1992. Dynamic effects will emerge in the form of restructured competition and changed expectations. Nineteen ninety-two is a vision as much as a program—a vision of Europe's place in the world. The vision is already producing a new awareness of European strengths and a seemingly sudden assertion of the will to exploit these strengths in competition with the United States and Japan. It is affecting companies as well as governments. A senior executive of Fiat recently declared, "The final goal of the European 'dream' is to transform Europe into an integrated economic continent with its specific role, weight and ability on the international scenario vis-à-vis the U.S. and Japan."

But why has this process begun, or begun again, now? In this article, we propose that changes in the international structure triggered the 1992 process. More precisely, the trigger has been a real shift in the distribution of economic power resources (crudely put, relative American decline and Japanese ascent). What is just as important is that European elites perceive that the changes in the international setting require that they rethink their roles and interests in the world. The United States is no longer the unique source of forefront technologies; in crucial electronics sectors, for example, Japanese firms lead the world. Moreover, Japanese innovations in organizing production and in manufacturing technologies mean that the United States is no longer the most attractive model of industrial development. In monetary affairs, some Europeans argue that Frankfurt and Tokyo, not Washington, are now in control. In short, shifts in relative technological, industrial, and economic capabilities are forcing Europeans to rethink their economic goals and interests as well as the means appropriate for achieving them. American coattails, they seem to have concluded, are not a safe place when the giant falters and threatens to sit down.

While economic changes have triggered the 1992 process, security issues may shape its outcomes. Europe's economic relationship with the United States has been embedded in a security bargain that is being reevaluated. This is not the first reassessment of the alliance, but it is the first time that it takes place against the backdrop of Soviet internal reform and external overtures to dismantle the symbols of the cold war. The point is that the security ties that underpinned U.S.-European economic relations are being reconsidered in Europe. But we need not look deeply into the security issues to understand the origins of the 1992 movement, though some believe that the nuclear horsetrading at Reykjavik accelerated the 1992 process. Eventually, the economic and security discussions will shape each other.

We hypothesize that structural change was a necessary, though not a sufficient, condition for the renewal of the European project. It was a trigger. Other factors were equally necessary and, in combination, sufficient. First, 1992 emerged because the institutions of the European Communities, especially the Commission, were able to exercise effective policy leadership. International structural shifts and a favorable domestic setting provided a motive and an opportunity for restarting the Communities. The Commission played the role of policy entrepreneur. The renewed drive for market unification can be explained only if theory takes into account the policy leadership of the Commission. To be sure, the Commission did not act alone; a transnational industry coalition also perceived the need for European-level action and supported the Commission's efforts. The Commission, aided by business, was able to mobilize a coalition of governmental elites that favored the overall objective of market unification. Member governments were receptive to the 1992 initiatives because of the domestic political context in the member states, which had altered in ways that made European-level, market-oriented initiatives viable. The most important elements of the domestic political setting were the failure of existing, purely national economic strategies, the decline (or transformation) of the left, and the presence of vigorously market-oriented governments on the right. Without these shifts, an EC-based response to the changing international structure would have been politically impossible.

We therefore propose to analyze 1992 in terms of elite bargains formulated in response to international structural change and the Commission's policy entrepreneurship. In the sections immediately following, we lay out an analytical framework and examine the origins of the 1992 movement and its constituent bargains.

The 1992 process has so far been limited to the Community institutions, the governments, and leaders of major companies. National parliaments, political parties, and trade unions have not yet become centrally involved. That will change. How and when the 1992 process will draw in other political actors (like labor) is one of the many uncertainties.

.   .   .

Explaining 1992: Alternative Approaches

Analysis of the 1992 project in Western Europe could follow any one of three broad approaches, each with a different focus. One approach would look to the internal dynamics of the integration process itself, as in integration theory. A second would concentrate on the domestic politics behind the regional agreements. The third approach, for which we argue, focuses on elite bargains in response to the challenges and opportunities posed by international and domestic changes. The analysis of elite bargains incorporates the strengths of the other two approaches while avoiding their major weaknesses. Although we have no intention of elaborating three different theoretical frameworks, we will briefly describe what appear to be the chief shortcomings of the integration theory and domestic politics approaches.

Consider integration theory. Instead of a single theory, there were numerous permutations, each employing different concepts and definitions. But what distinguished integration theory from other, traditional analyses of international politics was that it assigned causal significance to the process of integration itself. Indeed, a genuine integration theory would have to posit some specific political effects stemming from the internal logic of integration. This was the contribution of neofunctionalist integration theories, which were in turn partly inspired by the functionalist theory of David Mitrany.

Integration begins when governments perceive that certain economic policy problems cannot be solved by national means alone and agree to joint policymaking in supranational institutions. Initially, therefore, experts in the supranational organization apply technical solutions to (primarily) economic problems. Integration proceeds through the "expansive logic" of spillovers. Spillovers occur when experience gained by one integrative step reveals the need for integration in functionally related areas. That is, in order to accomplish the original objectives, participants realize that they must take further integrative steps. Creating a common market, for example, might reveal the need for a regional fund to manage short-term current accounts imbalances among the members. That would constitute a spillover. In the long term, according to the formulations of Ernst Haas, as more technical functions shift to the integrated institutions, the loyalties and expectations of the populations transfer from the historical nation states to the larger supranational entity.

Haas and other scholars later modified these initial neofunctionalist conceptions. Nye noted that integration could progress by means of deliberate linkages that created "package deals." He also argued that functional links among tasks did not always lead to spillovers, but could have a negative impact on integration. Others further refined the kinds of internal dynamics of integration to include "spill-back," "spill-around," and "forward linkage." Haas recognized that spillovers could be limited by the "autonomy of functional contexts" and that integration turned out not to be the steady, incremental process originally envisioned.

For a number of reasons, we do not believe that integration theories are well suited for analyzing the 1992 movement. The major weaknesses were recognized by the integration theorists themselves; two of their criticisms are most relevant to the concerns of this paper. (1) The internal logic of integration cannot account for the stop-go nature of the European project. One possibility is that the Community attained many of its objectives, which led to "the disappearance of many of the original incentives to integrate." The question then becomes, why did the renewed drive for the single internal market emerge in the mid-1980s and why did it rapidly acquire broad support among governments and business elites? (2) Even where the Community did not meet expectations or where integration in one area pointed out problems in functionally related areas, national leaders could frequently opt for national means rather than more integration. That is, even in issue areas where the pressure for spillovers should have been strong, national means appeared sufficient and were preferred. In the 1960s, efforts to establish a common transport policy fell flat because national policies appeared adequate to interested parties. During the 1970s, the Commission's efforts on behalf of broad Community science and technology planning (the Spinelli and Dahrendorf plans) got nowhere because governments perceived science and technology as areas in which national policies could and should be pursued. The national option always stands against the EC option and frequently wins.

An explanation rooted in the domestic politics of the various European countries is a second possible approach to explaining 1992. Certainly the shift of the socialist governments in France and Spain toward market-oriented economic policies (including privatization and deregulation) was essential for acceptance of the 1992 movement. The Thatcher government in the U.K. could also support measures that dealt primarily with reducing regulations and freeing markets. Thus, the favorable domestic political context was one of the necessary conditions that produced 1992.

But domestic politics cannot carry the full analytical burden, for three main reasons. (1) An argument based on domestic politics cannot answer the question, why now? Such an argument would have to account for the simultaneity of domestic developments that would induce states to act jointly. Attention to changes in the international context solves the problem. International changes posed challenges and choices to all the EC countries at the same time. (2) The political actors that figure in analyses of European domestic politics have not yet been mobilized in the 1992 project, though perhaps that is now beginning. Although the political parties and the trade unions now talk about 1992, they were not involved in the discussions and bargains that started the process. Governments (specifically, the national executives) and business elites initiated and defined 1992 and have moved it along. (3) An argument based on domestic politics cannot explain why domestic political change produced the 1992 movement. The project did not bubble up spontaneously from the various national political contexts. On the contrary: leadership for 1992 came from outside the national settings; it came from the Commission.

The third approach to analyzing 1992 is the one we advance in this paper. It focuses on elite bargains formed in response to changes in the international structure and in the domestic political context. The postwar order of security and economic systems founded upon American leadership is beginning to evolve after a period of relative U.S. decline and Japanese ascent. These developments have led Europeans to reconsider their relations with the United States and within the European Communities. The international and domestic situations provided a setting in which the Commission could exercise policy entrepreneurship, mobilizing a transnational coalition in favor of the unified internal market.

The 1992 movement (as well as the integration of the 1950s) can be fruitfully analyzed as a hierarchy of bargains. Political elites reach agreement on fundamental bargains embodying basic objectives; subsidiary bargains are required to implement these objectives. The fundamental bargains agreed upon for 1992 are embodied in the Single European Act and in the Commission's White Paper which outlined specific steps toward the unified internal market. The Single European Act extended majority voting in the Council and cleared the way politically for progress toward unifying the internal market. Endorsement of the Commission's proposals in the White Paper represents agreement on the fundamental objective of eliminating barriers to the movement of persons, goods, and capital. The specific measures proposed by the Commission (some 300 of them) can be thought of as implementing bargains.

. . .

The original European movement can be seen in terms of this framework. The integration movement was triggered by the wrenching structural changes brought about by World War II; after the war, Europe was no longer the center of the international system, but rather a frontier and cushion between the two new superpowers. Political entrepreneurship came initially from the group surrounding Robert Schuman and Jean Monnet. The early advocates of integration succeeded in mobilizing a transnational coalition supportive of integration; the core of that coalition eventually included the Christian Democratic parties of the original Six, plus many of the Socialist parties.

The fundamental objectives of the bargains underlying the European Coal and Steel Community (ECSC) and the expanded European Communities were primarily two: (1) the binding of German industry to the rest of Europe so as to make another war impossible, and (2) the restarting of economic growth in the region. These objectives may have been largely implicit, but they were carried out by means of a number of implementing bargains that were agreed upon over the years. The chief implementing bargains after the ECSC included the Common Market, the Common Agricultural Program, the regional development funds, and, most recently, the European Monetary System (EMS).

The fundamental external bargain made in establishing the Community was with the United States; it called for (certainly as remembered now in the U.S.) national treatment for the subsidiaries of foreign firms in the Common Market. That is, foreign (principally American) firms that set up in the Community could operate as if they were European. American policy makers saw themselves as willing to tolerate the discrimination and potential trade diversion of a united Europe because the internal bargain of the EEC would contribute to foreign policy objectives. Not only was part of Germany tied to the West, but sustained economic growth promised political stability. All of this was framed by the security ties seen as necessary on both sides of the Atlantic to counter the Soviet Union.

The European bargains—internal and external—were made at the moment of American political and economic domination. A bipolar security world and an American-directed Western economy set the context in which the European bargain appeared necessary. Many expected the original Community to generate ever more extensive integration. But the pressures for spillover were not that great. Economics could not drive political integration. The building of nation states remains a matter of political projects. Padoa-Schioppa has put it simply and well: "The cement of a political community is provided by indivisible public goods such as 'defence and security'. The cement of an economic community inevitably lies in the economic benefits it confers upon its members." The basic political objectives sought by the original internal bargain had been achieved: the threat of Germany was diminished and growth had been ignited. When problems arose from the initial integrative steps, the instruments of national policy sufficed to deal with them. Indeed, the Community could accommodate quite distinct national social, regulatory, and tax policies. National strategies for growth, development, and employment sufficed.

Several fundamental attributes of the economic community that emerged merit emphasis, as they prove important in the reignition of the European project in the mid-1980s. First, the initial effort was the product

This is not a story of mass movements, of pressure groups, or of legislatures. In the 1950s, the European project became a matter of party and group politics. In the 1980s, the EC institutions were not the object of debate; they were a political actor. Indeed, the Commission exercised leadership in proposing technical measures for the internal market that grabbed the attention of business and government elites, but were (in the initial stages at least) of little interest to the organs of mass politics. The governments and business elites had already been challenged by the international changes in ways that the parties and unions had not been. Some business and government leaders involved in 1992 are, in fact, trying to sidestep normal coalition politics in order to bring about domestic changes.

Consequently, any explanation of the choice of Europe and its evolution must focus on the actors—the leadership in the institutions of the European Community, in segments of the executive branch of the national governments, and in the business community (principally the heads of the largest companies)—and what they have achieved. These are the people who confronted the changes in the international environment and initiated the 1992 process. Each of these actors was indispensable, and each was involved with the actions of the others. The Community remains a bargain among governments. National governments—particularly the French—have begun to approach old problems in new ways and to make choices that are often unexpected. The Commission itself is an entrenched, self-interested advocate of further integration, so its position is no surprise. The multinationals are faced with sharply changed market conditions, and their concerns and reactions are not unexpected. The initiatives came from the EC, but they caught hold because the nature of the domestic political context had shifted. The interconnections and interactions among them will almost certainly defy an effort to assign primacy, weight, or relative influence.

In this section, we first address the domestic political context that prepared the ground for the Commission's plans. We then look at the Commission's initiatives, and finally at the role of the business elite in supporting the 1992 project.

The question is why national government policies and perspectives have altered. Why, in the decade between the mid-1970s and the mid-1980s, did European governments become open to European-level, market-oriented solutions? The answer has two parts: the failure of national strategies for economic growth and the transformation of the left in European politics. First, the traditional models of growth and economic management broke down. The old political strategies for the economy seemed to have run out. After the growth of the 1960s, the world economy entered a period of stagflation in the 1970s. As extensive industrialization reached its limits, the existing formulas for national economic development and the political bargains underpinning them had to be revised. Social critics and analysts in fact defined the crisis as the failure of established formulas to provide even plausible guides for action. It was not simply that the price of commodities rose, but that the dynamics of growth and trade changed.

Growth had been based on the shift of resources out of agriculture into industry; industrial development had been based on borrowing from abroad the most advanced technologies that could be obtained and absorbed. Suddenly, many old industrial sectors had to be closed, as in the case of shipbuilding. Others had to be transformed and reorganized, factories continuously upgraded, new machines designed and introduced, and work reorganized. The arguments that eventually emerged held that the old corporate strategies based on mass production were being forced to give way to strategies of flexibility and adaptability. Despite rising unemployment, the steady pace of improvement in productivity, coupled with the maintenance and sometimes reestablishment of a strong position in production equipment in vital sectors, suggested that Europe's often distinctive and innovative approaches to production were working. However, that was only to come toward the end of the decade. In short, during the 1970s, national executive and administrative elites found themselves facing new economic problems without adequate models for addressing them.

The 1970s were therefore the era of Europessimism. Europe seemed unable to adjust to the changed circumstances of international growth and competition after the oil shock. At first, the advanced countries stumbled, but then the United States and Japan seemed to pick themselves back up and to proceed. Japan's growth, which had originally been sustained by expansion within domestic markets, was bolstered by the competitive export orientation of major firms in consumer durables. New approaches to manufacturing created substantial advantages. In the United States, flexibility of the labor market—meaning the ability to fire workers and reduce real wages—seemed to assure jobs, albeit in services and often at lower wages, despite a deteriorating industrial position in global markets. Japan experienced productivity growth; the United States created jobs. Europe seemed to be doing neither and feared being left behind by the U.S.-Japanese competition in high technology.

For Europe, the critical domestic political issue was jobs, and the problem was said to be labor market rigidity. In some sense that was true, but the rigidities did not lie exclusively or even primarily with the workers' attitudes. They were embedded in government policy and industrial practice. In most of Western Europe, the basic postwar political bargain involved governmental responsibility for full employment and a welfare net. Consequently, many European companies had neither the flexibility of their American counterparts to fire workers or reduce wages, nor, broadly across Europe, the flexibility Japan displayed in redeploying its labor force. As unemployment rose, the old growth model built on a political settlement in each country was challenged—initially from the left by strategies of nationalization with state investment, and then from the right by strategies of deregulation with privatization. The political basis, in attitude and party coalition, for a more market-oriented approach was being put in place.

For a decade beginning with the oil shocks, the external environment for Europe was unstable, or turbulent, but its basic structure remained unchanged. While the United States was unwilling or unable to assure a system of fixed exchange rates, it remained the center of the financial system even as it changed the rules. The European Monetary System was an effort to create a zone of currency stability so that the expansion of trade inside Europe could continue. In the 1960s and 1970s, a long debate on technology gaps and the radical extension of American multinational power had not provoked joint European responses. During the 1970s, the mandate for the European Community was not altered; it was stretched to preserve its original objectives in the original context. The international economic turbulence and fears of a relative decline in competitive position did not provoke a full-blown European response. The extent of the shifts in relative economic power was not yet apparent. National strategies in many arenas had not yet failed, or at least were not yet perceived as having failed. In other arenas, the challenges could be dealt with by accommodations within the realm of domestic politics.

The question remains: Why did national policy change, why did the perceptions of choice evolve, the range of options shift? Policy failure must be interpreted; it can be assigned many meanings. National perceptions of position are filtered through parties and bureaucracies, shaped and flavored by factions, interests, and lobbies. In 1983, the French Socialist party was divided between those led by Laurent Fabius, who concluded that pressure on the franc was a reason to reverse policy direction and to stay within the European Community, and those like Chevènement, who felt the proper choice was to withdraw from the EMS, even if that resulted in an effective weakening of the Community. The choice, to stay in the EMS, was by no means a foregone matter. The French response to the currency crisis was a political choice made in the end by the president.

Thus, the second aspect of the changed domestic political context was the shift in government coalitions in a number of EC member states. Certainly the weakening of the left in some countries and a shift from the communist to the market-socialist left in others helped to make possible a debate about market solutions (including unified European markets) to Europe's dilemma. In Latin Europe, the communist parties weakened as the era of Eurocommunism waned. Spain saw the triumph of Gonzalez's socialists, and their unexpected emergence as advocates of market-led development and entry into the Common Market. Italy experienced a weakening of the position of the communists in the complex mosaic of party positioning.

In France, Mitterrand's victory displaced the communists from their primacy on the left. The first two years of the French socialist government proved crucial in turning France away from the quest for economic autonomy. After 1983, Mitterrand embraced a more market-oriented approach and became a vigorous advocate of increased European cooperation. This had the unexpected consequence of engendering independence for the state-named managers of nationalized companies. When the conservative government of Jacques Chirac adopted deregulation as a central policy approach, a second blow was dealt to the authority of the French state in industry. In Britain and Germany, the Labour and Social Democratic parties lost power as well as influence on the national debate.

Throughout Europe the corporatist temptation waned; that is, management of the macroeconomy by direct negotiations among social groups and the government no longer seemed to work. In many union and left circles an understanding grew that adaptation to market processes would be required. (As the 1992 movement progressed, unions in most countries became wary that the European "competitive imperative" might be used to justify policies that would restrict their influence and unwind their positions and gains. As a counterpoint on the right, Thatcher began to fear a bureaucratized and socialized Europe.)

In an era when deregulation—the freeing of the market—became the fad, it made intuitive sense to extend the European internal market as a response to all ailments. Moreover, some governments, or some elites within nations, can achieve purely domestic goals by using European agreements to limit or constrain national policy choices. The EMS is not only a means of stabilizing exchange rates to facilitate trade, but also a constraint on domestic politics that pushes toward more restrictive macroeconomic policies than would otherwise have been adopted. There is little doubt that the course of the social experiment in 1981 would have been different if France had not been a member of the EMS, which required formal withdrawal from commitments if a country wanted to pursue independent expansionary policies. In a different vein, some Italians use the threat of competitive pressures as a reason to reform the administration. As one Italian commentator put it, "Europe for us will be providential. . . . The French and Germans love 1992 because each thinks it can be the key country in Europe. The most we can hope for is that 1992 straightens us out."

In any case, in Europe we are watching the creation of like-minded elites and alliances that at first blush appear improbable—such as Mitterrand and Thatcher committed to some sort of European strategy. These elites are similar in political function (though not in political basis) to the cross-national Christian Democratic alliance that emerged in support of the original Community after World War II in Germany, France, and elsewhere. European-level, market-oriented solutions have become acceptable.

This was the domestic political soil into which the Commission's initiatives fell. Traditional models of economic growth appeared to have played themselves out, and the left had been transformed in such a way that socialist parties began to seek market-oriented solutions to economic ills. In this setting, the European Community provided more than the mechanisms of intergovernmental negotiation. The Eurocracy was a standing constituency and a permanent advocate of European solutions and greater unity. Proposals from the European Commission transformed this new orientation into policy, and, more importantly, into a policy perspective and direction. The Commission perceived the international structural changes and the failure of existing national strategies, and seized the initiative.

To understand how the Commission's initiatives led governments to step beyond failed national policy, let us examine the case of telematics, the economically crucial sector combining microelectronics, computers, and telecommunications. By 1980, European policy makers were beginning to realize that the national champion strategies of the past decade or so had failed to reverse the steady international decline of European telematics industries. Throughout the 1970s, each national government in Europe had sought to build up domestic firms capable of competing with the American giants. The state encouraged or engineered mergers and provided research-and-development subsidies; state procurement heavily favored the domestic firms. By 1980, none of these approaches had paid off. Europe's champions were losing market shares both in Europe and worldwide, and most of them were operating in the red. Even Europe's traditional electronics stronghold, telecommunications equipment, was showing signs of weakness: the telecommunications trade surplus was declining annually while U.S. and Japanese imports were accounting for ever larger shares of the most technologically advanced market segments.

In telematics, European collaboration emerged when the Commission, under the leadership of Etienne Davignon, struck an alliance with the twelve major electronics companies in the EC. Because of the mounting costs and complexity of R&D, rapid technological and market changes, and the convergence of hitherto separate technologies (e.g., computing and telecommunications), these twelve companies were motivated to seek interfirm partnerships. Although such partnerships were common with American firms, the possibilities within Europe had not been explored. The twelve firms designed the European Strategic Programme for Research and Development in Information Technology (ESPRIT) and then sold it to their governments. The RACE program (Research in Advanced Communications for Europe) emerged via a similar process. In short, the Community's high-technology programs of the early 1980s took shape in a setting in which previous national policies had been discredited, the Commission advanced concrete proposals, and industry lent essential support. In a sense, the telematics cases prefigure the 1992 movement and display the same configuration of political actors: the Commission, certain political leaders and specific agencies within the national governments, and senior business leaders.

The Commission again took the initiative with the publication of its "White Paper" in June 1985. The initiative should be seen as a response to the stagnation of the Community enterprise as a result of, among other things, the budget stalemates. When Jacques Delors took office as president of the European Commission in 1985, he consciously sought an undertaking, a vision, that would reignite the European idea. The notion of a single market by 1992 caught the imagination because the need for a broader Europe was perceived outside the Commission. Helen Wallace and Wolfgang Wessels suggest that if the EEC and the European Free Trade Association (EFTA) had not existed by the late 1980s, they would have had to be invented. Or, as was the case, reinvented.

The White Paper set out a program and a timetable for the completion of the fully unified internal market. The now famous set of three hundred legislative proposals to eliminate obstacles to the free functioning of the market, as well as the analyses that led up to and followed it, expressed a clear perception of Europe's position. European decline or the necessities of international competitiveness (choose your own phrasing) require—in this view—the creation of a continental market.

The White Paper's program had the political advantage of setting forth concrete steps and a deadline. The difficult political questions could be obscured by focusing on the mission and by reducing the issues to a series of apparently technical steps. Advocates of market unification could emphasize highly specific, concrete, seemingly innocuous, and long overdue objectives rather than their consequences. In a sense, the tactic is to move above and below the level of controversy. The broad mission is agreed to; the technical steps are unobjectionable. Of course, there is a middle ground where the questions of the precise form of Europe, the allocation of gain and pain in the process, become evident. A small change in, say, health and safety rules may appear unimportant, but may prove to be the shelter behind which a national firm is hiding from European and global competitors. Here we find the disputes about outcomes, both in terms of market results and of social values. Obscuring the issues and interests was crucial in developing Europe the first time, one might note, and has been instrumental once again.

Implementation of the White Paper required a separate initiative: the limitation, expressed in the Single European Act, of national vetoes over Community decisions. At its core, the Community has always been a mechanism for governments to bargain. It has certainly not been a nation state, and only a peculiar kind of federalism. Real decisions have been made in the Council by representatives of national governments. The Commissioners, the department heads, are drawn from a pool nominated by the governments. Broader representative institutions have played only a fictive (or, more generously, a secondary) role. Moreover, decisions taken by the Council on major issues had to be unanimous, providing each government with a veto. For this reason, it has been painfully difficult to extend the Community's authority, to change the rules of finance, or to proceed with the creation of a unified market and change the rules of business in Europe. The most reluctant state prevailed. Furthermore, domestic groups could block Community action by persuading their government to exercise their veto.

Many see the Single European Act as the most important amendment to the Treaty of Rome since the latter was adopted in 1957. This act has replaced the Luxembourg Compromise (which required decisions to be taken by unanimity) with a qualified majority requirement in the case of certain measures that have as their object the establishment and functioning of the internal market. The national veto still exists in other domains, but most of the three hundred directives for 1992 can be adopted by qualified majority. As a result, disgruntled domestic interest groups have lost a source of leverage on their governments; the national veto no longer carries the clout it once did. Perhaps equally important, the Single European Act embodies a new strategy toward national standards that were an obstacle to trade within the Community. Previously, the EEC pinned its hopes on "harmonization," a process by which national governments would adopt "Euronorms" prepared by the Commission. The Single European Act instead adopts the principle affirmed in the famous Cassis de Dijon case. That principle holds that standards (for foodstuffs, safety, health, and so on) that prevail in one country must be recognized by the others as sufficient.

The third actor in the story, besides the governments and the Commission, is the leadership of the European multinational corporations. In a number of ways, they have experienced most directly some of the consequences of the international economic changes. They have acted both politically and in the market. The White Paper and the Single European Act gave the appearance that changes in the EC market were irreversible and politically unstoppable. Businesses have been acting on that belief. Politically, they have taken up the banner of 1992, collaborating with the Commission and exerting substantial influence on their governments. The significance of the role of business, and of its collaboration with the Commission, must not be underestimated. European business and the Commission may be said to have together bypassed national governmental processes and shaped an agenda that compelled attention and action.

Substantial support for the Commission's initiatives has come from the Roundtable of European Industrialists, an association of some of Europe's largest and most influential corporations, including Philips, Siemens, Olivetti, GEC, Daimler Benz, Volvo, Fiat, Bosch, ASEA and Ciba-Geigy.

Indeed, when Jacques Delors, prior to assuming the presidency of the Commission in 1985, began campaigning for the unified internal market, European industrialists were ahead of him. Wisse Dekker of Philips and Jacques
Solvay of Belgium's Solvay chemical company in particular were vigorously arguing for unification of the EC's fragmented markets. In the early
1980s, a booklet published by Philips proposed urgent action on the internal market. "There is really no choice," it argued, "and the only option left
for the Community is to achieve the goals laid down in the Treaty of Rome.
Only in this way can industry compete globally, by exploiting economies of
scale, for what will then be the biggest home market in the world today: *the
European Community home market.*"

It is hard, though, to judge whether the business community influenced
Europe to pursue an internal market strategy or was itself constituted as a
political interest group by Community action. Business began to organize
in 1983, when the Roundtable of European Industrialists was formed under
the chairmanship of Pehr Gyllenhammer, of Volvo. Many of the original
business discussions included senior Community bureaucrats; in fact, Etienne Davignon reportedly recruited most of the members of the original
group. The executives constituting the Roundtable (numbering 29 by mid-
1987) were among the most powerful industrialists in Europe, including the
non-EEC countries. The group initially published three reports: one on the
need for development of a Europe-wide traffic infrastructure, one containing proposals for Europe's unemployment crisis, and one, *Changing Scales,*
describing the economies of scale that would benefit European businesses
in a truly unified market.

The European Roundtable became a powerful lobby vis-à-vis the
national governments. One member of the Delors cabinet in Brussels has
declared, "These men are very powerful and dynamic . . . when necessary
they can ring up their own prime ministers and make their case." Delors
himself has said, "We count on business leaders for support." Local and
regional chambers of commerce have helped to establish about fifty European Information Centers to handle queries and publicize 1992. In short,
the 1992 process is repeating the pattern established by ESPRIT: major
businesses have allied with the Commission to persuade governments,
which were already seeking to adapt to the changed international structure.

At the same time that the business community has supported the political initiatives behind the 1992 movement, it has been acting in the market
place. A series of business deals, ventures, and mergers form a critical part
of the 1992 movement. Even if nothing more happens in the 1992 process,
the face of business competition in Europe is being changed. The structure
of competition is being altered.

There has been a huge surge in joint ventures, share-swapping, and
mergers in Europe. Many are justified on the grounds of preparing for a

unified market, some for reasons of production and marketing strategies, and some as a means of defense against takeovers. But much of the movement is a response to business problems that would exist in any case. Still, the process has taken on a life of its own. The mergers provoke responses in the form of other business alliances; the responding alliances appear more urgent because of the political rhetoric. As the Europeans join together, American and Japanese firms scurry to put their own alliances in place and to rearrange their activities.

The meaning of the process is far from evident. Are we watching the creation of European competition, or the cartelization of industry at a European level? In some sectors, such as textiles and apparel, there already is an effective European market. In others, such as telecommunications, the terms of competition—whatever the corporate reshufflings—will turn on government regulation and choice. Since U.S. firms are already entrenched, the real newcomers are the Japanese. A surge of Japanese investment is taking place in Europe.

.   .   .

Conclusion

Europe is throwing the dice. It is confronted with a change in the structure of the international economy, with emerging Japanese and dwindling American power and position. It feels the shift in Asian competitive pressure in industry and finance. The problems are no longer those of American production in Europe, but of Japanese imports and production displacing European production. More importantly perhaps, Europe also feels the shift in rising Japanese influence in the monetary and technology domains. The industrial and governmental presumptions and deals with which Europe has operated are changing or will change. Indeed, Europeans may have to construct a coherent political presence on the global stage in order to achieve the most attractive accommodation to the new order.

We hypothesize that change in the international economic structure was necessary for the revival of the European project. A full-fledged test of this proposition will require detailed analysis of the perceptions and beliefs of those who participated in launching the 1992 movement. We have mentioned other analytical approaches—based on integration theory and domestic politics—that appear logically unsuited to explaining 1992. Of course, these approaches are not really alternatives. There are functional links among some of the bargains being struck, and domestic factors clearly shaped governmental responses to the international changes. But tests of alternative explanations often create a false sense of scientism by setting individually weak explanations against each other and finding "confirmation" by denying the worst of them. Competing explanations often represent different types of explanation, different levels of analysis. In the end, it is not a matter of which one is better, but of whether the right questions are being asked. This article is an effort to frame the proper questions and propose analytical links among them.

We argue that structural situations create the context of choice and cast up problems to be resolved, but they do not dictate the decisions and strategies. In other words, the global setting can be understood in neorealist terms, but the political processes triggered by changes in the system must be analyzed in other than structural terms. The choices result from political processes and have political explanations. In this case, the process is one of bargains among nations and elites within the region. The political process for implementing these bargains is labeled "Europe 1992," a complex web of intergovernmental bargains and accommodations among the various national business elites.

In this essay, we showed why 1992 has so far been a project of elites. The commitment of the governments to the process, the fundamental bargain, is expressed by the end of the single-nation veto system, which changed the logic of Community decisionmaking. Europe's states have thrown themselves into the drive for a unified market, unleashing business processes that in themselves are recasting the terms of competition within Europe. The terms of the final bargains are open.

The effort to reshape the European Communities has so far been guided by three groups: Community institutions, industrial elites, and governments. The Commission proposes and persuades. Important business coalitions exercise indispensable influence on governments. Governments are receptive because of changes in the world economy and shifts in the domestic political context. The domestic context has changed in two key ways: (1) with the failure of traditional models of growth and purely national strategies for economic management; and (2) with the defeat of the left in some countries, and with its transformation because of the weakening of communist parties in others. These changes opened the way for an unlikely set of elite alliances. In this context, EC initiatives began to demonstrate that there were joint European alternatives to failed national strategies. The telematics programs were one precursor. Delors built on the budding sense of optimism and gave energy and leadership to the notion of a genuine single market. Whether a broader range of political groups will become involved is an open issue, one that may determine both whether the process continues and what form it takes.

The outcomes are quite unknowable, dependent on the timing and dynamics of a long series of contingent decisions. But the story, and consequently the analysis, concerns political leadership in creating a common European interest and then constructing a set of bargains that embody that understanding. Many of the choices are simply calculated risks, or perhaps explorations that will be entrenched if they work and refashioned if they don't. Even if we could predict the outcomes of any single choice with a high degree of confidence, the sequencing of diverse decisions and their cumulative effects would be impossible to foresee. It would be ironic if 1992 succeeded formally but economic rejuvenation did not follow. In any case, Europe's choices—particularly the possibility of a coherent Western Europe emerging as an actor on the global stage—will powerfully influence the world economic system, and perhaps the security system as well.

23

The Choice for Europe

Andrew Moravcsik

The revival of supranationalism in the 1980s and 1990s did not go unchallenged. Andrew Moravcsik (Princeton University)—a former student of Stanley Hoffmann's and undoubtedly the most controversial theorist of the "relaunched" period—wrote a series of closely argued, sometimes polemical articles that forced students of the European Union to take seriously his "liberal intergovernmental" perspective. While most scholars in the field assumed member states were losing sovereignty to increasingly independent supranational institutions, Moravcsik argued that, on the contrary, European governments were still very much in charge of the integration process. Thus many of the theoretical debates in the 1990s took an "us-versus-them" tone: supranationalists v. intergovernmentalists—or more often than not, the world v. Andrew Moravcsik.

In reality, Moravcsik and the rest of the field were not worlds apart. Moravcsik, like most of his opponents, was a rationalist and an institutionalist, meaning that he believed human beings generally acted rationally to further their material interests and that the institutions they established had real effects on behavior. But his view of international relations was more like Hoffmann's than Haas's: cooperation was possible among sovereign states, but only when it was in each state's particular interest; member states were quick to halt or reverse integration when it no longer met their needs. Moravcsik's basic argument with the field was that most theorists failed to rigorously test their supranational view against the obvious alternative that the EU serves the interests of its member states.

The Choice for Europe was Moravcsik's monumental attempt "to explain why sovereign governments in Europe have chosen repeatedly to coordinate their core economic policies and surrender sovereign prerogatives within an international institution." His focus was not on the day-to-day operations of the EU, but on the major turning points—the big bargains—in the history of

European integration. ~~He argued that European countries in establishing the~~ ~~Community had not engaged in~~ extraordinary behavior but had responded ~~rationally to their changing economic and technological environment.~~ The cooperative agreements they reached, he argued, reflected ~~their drive for commercial advantage, the distribution of power among them,~~ and their decision ~~to rely on supranational institutions to enforce their commitments.~~ Each of these explanatory factors rested on additional theories of political economy, interdependence, bargaining, international regimes, and so on. In the end, Moravcsik claimed not to be articulating a grand theory but rather ~~a multicausal explanation of one aspect of integration, the big bargain.~~ His emphasis on the decisions of national governments, however, continued to set him apart from the majority of EU scholars who preferred to highlight the independence of supranational actors.

> The study of regional integration should be both included in and
> subordinated to the study of changing patterns of interdependence.
> —*Ernst Haas,* The Obsolescence of Regional Integration Theory, *1975*

The construction of the European Community (EC) ranks among the most extraordinary achievements in modern world politics, yet there is little agreement about its causes.[1] EC rules influence most aspects of European political life, from the regulation of the habitat of wild birds to voting within the World Trade Organization. The EC's complex institutions include a semi-autonomous legal system, parliament, and bureaucracy as well as detailed norms, principles, rules, and practices governing direct relations among national governments. These institutions resemble those of a modern nation-state as much as those of a conventional international regime. Today the EC is a unique, multileveled, transnational political system.

The Question: Explaining Major Turning Points

This book addresses the most fundamental puzzle confronting those who seek to understand European integration, namely to explain why sovereign governments in Europe have chosen repeatedly to coordinate their core economic policies and surrender sovereign prerogatives within an international institution. In the history of the EC, the most important such choices are five treaty-amending sets of agreements that propelled integration forward[: the Treaty of Rome, the consolidation of the Common Market in the 1960s, the European Monetary System, the Single European Act, and the Treaty on European Union]. Variously termed constitutive, constitutional, history-making, or grand bargains, they punctuate EC history at a rate of roughly once per decade. Each grand bargain, three aimed at trade liberalization and two at monetary cooperation, set the agenda for a period of consolidation, helping to define the focus and pace of subsequent decision-making. The

EC has evolved, as some have said of global economic institutions more generally, as a "sequence of irregular big bangs." At the core of this book is a series of structured narratives of these decisions or, more properly, bundles of decisions. The account focuses primarily on German, French, and British policies.

. . .

The Argument: Economic Interest, Relative Power, Credible Commitments

My central claim is that the broad lines of European integration since 1955 reflect three factors: patterns of commercial advantage, the relative bargaining power of important governments, and the incentives to enhance the credibility of interstate commitments. Most fundamental of these was commercial interest. European integration resulted from a series of rational choices made by national leaders who consistently pursued economic interests—primarily the commercial interests of powerful economic producers and secondarily the macroeconomic preferences of ruling governmental coalitions—that evolved slowly in response to structural incentives in the global economy.

When such interests converged, integration advanced. The fact that economic interests did consistently converge reflected fundamental trends in post-war international political economy—in particular, a fifty-year boom in trade and investment among industrialized countries. The resulting expansion of intra-industry trade both predated the EC and induced policy changes regardless of whether the countries in question were EC members. Similarly, rising capital mobility undermined the autonomy of national macroeconomic policies, creating greater pressures for monetary cooperation. At its core, I argue, European integration has been dictated by the need to adapt through policy coordination to these trends in technology and in economic policy.

This explanation of national preferences for integration is grounded in political economy, not economics. Despite the importance of economic benefits, economists themselves were skeptical of, if not outright opposed to, many of the major steps in European integration. Construction of a customs union, a common agricultural policy, monetary union—almost all were, from the perspective of an economist, "second best" policies. Preferences for such policies emerged from a process of domestic political conflict in which specific sectoral interests, adjustment costs and, sometimes, geopolitical concerns played an important role. Consistent with modern theories of foreign economic policy, I argue that the specific conditions under which governments were willing to liberalize trade reflected their international economic competitiveness; the conditions under which they accepted monetary integration reflected prevailing macroeconomic policies and preferences.

Yet the EC was shaped by more than the convergence of national preferences in the face of economic change. There were important distributional conflicts not just within states but among them. These interstate conflicts were resolved only through hard interstate bargaining, in which credible threats to veto proposals, to withhold financial side-payments, and to form alternative alliances excluding recalcitrant governments carried the day. The outcomes reflected relative power of states—more precisely, patterns of asymmetrical interdependence. Those who gained the most economically from integration compromised the most on the margin to realize it, whereas those who gained the least or for whom the costs of adaptation were highest imposed conditions. To secure the substantive bargains they had made, finally, governments delegated and pooled sovereignty in international institutions for the express purpose of committing one another to cooperate. Where joint gains were large, but each government faced a strong temptation to defect from agreements—as was the case for the Common Agricultural Policy and for Economic and Monetary Union—governments tended to establish qualified majority voting and delegate tasks to the Commission.

In short, I argue that a tripartite explanation of integration—economic interest, relative power, credible commitments—accounts for the form, substance, and timing of major steps toward European integration. . . .

This explanation of integration breaks with the bulk of existing scholarship on the EC. It rejects the view that integration has been driven primarily—as Jean Monnet [Chapter 5] and his social-scientific counterparts, the neofunctionalists, long maintained—by a technocratic process reflecting the imperatives of modern economic planning, the unintended consequences of previous decisions, and the entrepreneurship of disinterested supranational experts. The integration process did not supercede or circumvent the political will of national leaders; it reflected their will. Nor—as the most prominent critics of neofunctionalism contend—can we account for integration primarily as the result of a coincidental postwar link between the "low politics" of foreign economic policy and geopolitical "high politics." The primary motivation of those who chose to integrate was not to prevent another Franco-German war, bolster global prestige and power, or balance against the superpowers. Nor—as numerous historians, political scientists, and members of the European movement continue to maintain—does integration represent a victory over nationalistic opposition by proponents of a widely shared, idealistic vision of a united Europe, an interpretation known in the classical lexicon as the "federalist" theory of integration. To be sure, technocratic imperatives, geopolitical concerns, and European idealism each played a role at the margin, but none has consistently been the decisive force behind major decisions. Nor, finally—although this book shares much with recent studies of European integration in the 1950's by economic historians such as Alan Milward—was integration primarily an effort to preserve a system of social welfare provision unique to postwar Western Europe or any of its member-states.

All such explanations treat the EC as unique, an exception in world politics that requires a *sui generis* theory. This assumption led the study of regional integration to develop over the past forty years as a discipline apart, one divorced from general studies of international cooperation. The paradoxical result: today no claim appears more radical than the claim that the behavior of EC member governments is *normal*. The revisionist quality of the argument in this book lies precisely in its effort to normalize the actions of European governments—to treat them as a subset of general tendencies among democratic states in modern world politics. Governments cooperated when induced or constrained to do so by economic self-interest, relative power, and strategically imposed commitments. Far from demonstrating the triumph of technocracy, the power of idealism, and the impotence or irrelevance of the modern nation-state, European integration exemplifies a distinctly modern form of power politics, peacefully pursued by democratic states for largely economic reasons through the exploitation of asymmetrical interdependence and the manipulation of institutional commitments. If the motivations of postwar European leaders were distinctive, it was because their countries were touched more intensely by economic trends common to all advanced industrial democracies, most notably the rapidly increasing potential for industrial trade among industrialized nations since World War II, disorder in the international monetary system after 1970, and widespread pressures for liberalization and disinflation in recent decades.

Through an analysis of EC history, this book also seeks to advance a distinctive theoretical position in current debates in international relations theory. The explanation of European integration sketched above is formulated as a distinct series of answers to three questions central to modern theories of comparative and international political economy. In a world in which governments are, broadly speaking, rational and instrumental, integration can be seen as a process in which they define a series of underlying objectives or preferences, bargain to substantive agreements concerning cooperation, and finally select appropriate international institutions in which to embed them. Any explanation of rational state choices to coordinate policy through international institutions must therefore address three questions. First, what best explains national preferences, the fundamental motivations underlying support for or opposition to economic integration? Second, given a set of national preferences, what best explains outcomes of interstate bargaining within the EC? Third, given a set of substantive bargains, what best explains state choices to construct European institutions and transfer sovereignty to them? This book suggests a distinct answer to each question. Let us consider each in turn.

Patterns of national preferences, the focus of the first stage, vary greatly over EC history. France, Germany, and Britain promoted and opposed integration in different substantive areas and to different ends. Their respective positions also shifted, if usually only in incremental fashion, over time. In explaining foreign economic policy, international relations theorists concerned with national preference formation have long debated the relative weight of security and political economic motivations.

One theory holds that world politics contains a hierarchy of issues headed by security concerns. Foreign economic policy is driven, therefore, not by its direct economic consequences but by its indirect consequences for national security, termed "security externalities." This is the dominant view in the study of the EC where diplomatic historians, European foreign policy specialists, and those who study the role of ideas in foreign policy have long argued that European economic integration has been pursued not primarily for its own sake but to counter geopolitical threats and realize geopolitical goals. Postwar European leaders who constructed and extended the EC sought to tie down the Germans, balance the Russians, establish a third force against the Americans, overcome right-wing and Communist extremism at home, or suppress nationalism to realize a distinctive vision of European federalism. Geopolitical interest and ideology explain traditional British semi-detachment from Europe, German federalist sympathies, and French vacillation between the two poles.

I conclude instead in favor of an alternative theory of foreign economic policy that holds that there is no hierarchy of interests; national interests tend instead to reflect direct, issue-specific consequences. National preferences concerning international trade and monetary policy can therefore be understood as a reflection of the economic incentives generated by patterns of international economic interdependence—the core of so-called "endogenous" theories of tariff and exchange-rate policy. The dominant motivations of governments in the EC decisions studied here reflected not geopolitical threats or ideals but pressures to coordinate policy responses to rising opportunities for profitable economic exchange, in particular growing intra-industry trade and capital movements. While more strictly commercial in its focus, this view is consistent with those of economic historians who have studied EC history. Trade liberalization followed export opportunities. In monetary policy, preferences for integration reflected the relative macroeconomic performance and preference of national governments alongside commercial considerations.

The primacy of economic interests does not relegate geopolitical ideology to insignificance. Taken by themselves, naked economic preferences would probably have led to a highly institutionalized pan-European free trade area with flanking policies of regulatory harmonization and monetary stabilization—somewhat more intensive arrangements than those pursued by the

European Free Trade Area (EFTA) and European Monetary System (EMS). These activities would have been embedded in weaker, less overtly constitutional, but still autonomous international institutions, such as those found in EFTA, the World Trade Organization (WTO), and the North Atlantic Free Trade Area (NAFTA). Explaining the emergence and expansion of a geographically more limited, institutionally more developed, and substantively more diverse institution required attention to geopolitical ideology.

Yet economic interests remained primary. Pressures from economic interest groups generally imposed tighter constraints on policy than did security concerns and the ideological visions of politicians and public opinion. When one factor had to give way, it tended to be geopolitics. Economic interests, moreover, determined the circumstances under which geopolitical ideology could influence policy. Only where economic interests were weak, diffuse, or indeterminate could national politicians indulge the temptation to consider geopolitical goals. Political economic interests predominated even where we would least expect them to. For example, the vital interest behind General de Gaulle's opposition to British membership in the EC, I argue, was not the pursuit of French *grandeur* but the price of French wheat.

The second question concerns the outcomes of interstate bargaining. Of particular theoretical interest are the extent to which negotiated outcomes are efficient, exploiting all possible joint gains, and the extent to which resolution of distributive conflict over the division of gains in specific cases has favored one or another country. EC bargaining, I argue, is generally Pareto-efficient, but its distributive outcomes vary greatly. Some bargains, such as the one struck over the institutions governing a single currency, favored Germany; others, such as the creation of the Common Agricultural Policy, favored France; and still others, such as the establishment of regional policy, favored Britain. How is this variation best explained?

International relations theorists have long debated the relative importance of various factors for the outcomes of noncoercive interstate bargaining. Theoretical debates divide those who hold that international institutions—in particular, autonomous supranational officials empowered by them—decisively influence interstate bargaining from those who believe that bargaining outcomes reflect the relative power of states.

The first theory, as applied to the EC, focuses on the essential role of "supra-national" entrepreneurs in overcoming the high transaction costs of interstate bargaining, which prevent governments from negotiating efficiently. This view, which dominates the study of the EC to this day, follows from neofunctionalist theory, which views the EC as a novel institutionalized realm, but it is also consistent with distinct theoretical approaches to the study of international regimes, negotiation, and law. Many scholars stress the role of international officials, who initiate, mediate, and mobilize societal groups around international agreements. The EC Commission,

Court, and Parliament are said to have empowered a particular breed of supranational political entrepreneurs, from Jean Monnet in the 1950s to Jacques Delors in the 1990s. Their interventions, it is argued, have repeatedly increased the efficiency of negotiations and shifted the distributional outcomes in directions favored by international technocrats. I conclude, by contrast, in favor of a second theory, which maintains that interstate bargaining outcomes are decisively shaped by the relative power of nation-states. This view termed "intergovernmental" in the EC literature, draws on general theories of bargaining and negotiation to argue that relative power among states is shaped above all by asymmetrical interdependence, which dictates the relative value of agreement to different governments. These distributive results can be predicted to a first approximation through the use of Nash bargaining theory: the governments that benefit most from the core agreement, relative to their best unilateral and coalitional alternatives to agreement, tend to offer greater compromises in order to achieve it. Where the threat to form an alternative coalition is credible, governments have exploited threats to exclude one another. Bargaining tends to be issue-specific with cross-issue linkages restricted to balancing out benefits among governments and generally taking the form of cash payments or institutional concessions.

The entrepreneurship of supranational officials, by contrast, tends to be futile and redundant, even sometimes counterproductive. Governments generally find it easy to act as their own entrepreneurs and to impose distributional bargains through the use of traditional nonmilitary instruments of power politics, including credible unilateral vetoes, threats of exclusion, and financial side-payments. The distributive outcomes of negotiations have reflected not the preferences of supranational actors but the pattern of asymmetrical interdependence among policy preferences. This is not to deny the influence of supranational entrepreneurs altogether, but their influence has been limited to helping improve the efficiency of one of five agreements, namely the Single European Act (SEA) of 1986. This account reverses the focus of recent EC scholarship. While most analysts generalize from a single case, namely the Commission under Jacques Delors in the mid-1980s, and ask why the Commission was so effective, a comparative analysis invites us to pose the opposite puzzle: Why is the SEA the only major EC bargain about which a serious empirical debate about supranational entrepreneurship can be conducted?

The final step is to explain the choices of governments to delegate and pool sovereignty in international institutions. While the formal powers of supranational officials and qualified majority voting do not extend to major treaty-amending negotiations—hence the skepticism about their influence over the bargains studied in this book [*The Choice for Europe*]—the everyday legislative process *within* the Treaty involves pooling of sovereignty in majority voting arrangements and substantial delegation directly to supranational officials. Here there is much variation. In some areas extensive powers of implementation and proposal have been delegated to central authorities. In others, qualified majority voting governs interstate decision-making. In still others, national vetoes and unanimity voting have been retained. How are the varied choices of governments to delegate and pool sovereignty to be explained?

General theories of international relations and institutional delegation suggest three reasons why governments might pool and delegate sovereignty. First is commitment to the ideology of European federalism. Recent writings on international cooperation stress the independent role of ideas in shaping institutional preferences. Numerous historians and social scientists attribute the EC's quasi-constitutional institutions to pressure from federalists, particularly in Germany and the Benelux countries, who favored them for ideological reasons.

Second is the need to economize on the generation and analysis of information by centralizing technocratic functions in an international organization. Some international lawyers, regime theorists, and economists maintain that international institutions are often more efficient than decentralized governments at processing information; the need for centralized economic planning was a central element in the neofunctionalist conception of integration. The historical record suggests that the role of ideological commitment to Europe was limited to cases where little *de facto* sovereignty was pooled or delegated, or where the substantive implications of doing so remained unclear and relatively modest, such as transfers of agenda setting power from the Commission to the European Parliament. The role of technocratic information was negligible.

I conclude, therefore, in favor of a third explanation. Choices to pool and delegate sovereignty to international institutions are best explained as efforts by governments to constrain and control one another—in game-theoretical language, by their effort to enhance the credibility of commitments. Governments transfer sovereignty to international institutions where potential joint gains are large, but efforts to secure compliance by foreign governments through decentralized or domestic means are likely to be ineffective. This general explanation lies at the heart of functional theories of international regimes, the central strand of which views international institutions as devices to manipulate information in order to promote compliance with common rules. Significant pooling and delegation tend to occur, I find, not where ideological conceptions of Europe converge or where governments agree on the need to centralize policy-making in the hands of technocratic planners, but where governments seek to compel compliance by foreign governments (or, in some cases, future domestic governments) with a strong temptation to defect. It was in fact often the countries least committed in principle to supranational institutions, such as Gaullist France, that imposed them on purportedly federalist governments.

Viewed, then, from the perspective of modern theories of international political economy, this explanation of integration is distinctive in two ways. First, rather than assess competing unicausal explanations or present an amalgam of factors as necessary conditions, this explanation distinguishes clearly between theories that are complements and theories that are substitutes—thereby grounding a multicausal explanation in an explicit framework consistent with rational state behavior. Such a framework must contain distinct explanations of national preferences, substantive bargaining outcomes, and decisions to delegate and pool sovereignty in international institutions. This framework stresses the priority of state preferences, which define not only the goals states seek but to a very substantial degree—via asymmetries in the intensity of preferences—their relative power. This framework is generalizable to any international negotiation. Second, within this framework, the explanation weighs in on the side of economic interests rather than security externalities as fundamental sources of state preferences, the structure of asymmetrical interdependence rather than the process-level intervention of institutional entrepreneurs as a determinant of bargaining outcomes, and the desire for more credible commitments, rather than ideology or technocratic information management, as a motivation to delegate and pool sovereignty.

. . .

The Literature Beyond "Grand Theory"

. . . [L]et us take a final moment to consider the relationship of this [theoretical perspective] to existing theory. In doing so, one turns inevitably to "classical" theories of regional integration, the most influential of which is neofunctionalism [Chapters 17 and 24]. Developed by Ernst Haas and others in the 1950s and 1960s, neofunctionalism remains a touchstone for scholarship on European integration. Neofunctionalists initially maintained that the unintended consequences of integration, once launched, would be self-reinforcing. This, they argued, assures the continuance of integration—though this teleology was later heavily qualified. Such feedback takes two forms. Initial steps toward cooperation bolster a technocratic consensus in favor of further integration by expanding, empowering, and encouraging societal groups supportive of further state intervention in the economy. The establishment of international institutions also centralizes power in the hands of supranational officials whose political entrepreneurship promotes further integration.

[The Choice for Europe] should not be read as an evaluation of—let alone a wholesale rejection of—neofunctionalism or any other classical theory. To be sure, this book tests (and for the most part disconfirms) some narrower propositions advanced by neofunctionalists—the claims, for example, that national interests are technocratic rather than reflect fundamental domestic conflict, that supranational entrepreneurship decisively alters interstate bargaining outcomes, and that delegation to international institutions reflects the need for centralized, expert planners. In other ways, such as its recognition of the primacy of economic interests, the book supports traditional neofunctionalist claims. In still other ways, such as the extent to which some national preferences for integration may be endogenous to a path-dependent process of prior integration, it does not directly address neofunctionalist concerns. . . .

This book is thus not yet another confrontation with neofunctionalism but an acknowledgement and response to criticisms of the style of "grand theory" neofunctionalism represents—criticisms that emerged in large part from the neofunctionalists themselves. By the early 1970s it was evident even to its creators that neofunctionalism required fundamental revision.

At one level the failure of neofunctionalism was empirical. European integration had not expanded steadily but by stops and starts. Significant domestic conflict remained. Integration had focused not on areas of state intervention and planning, such as atomic energy and public transport, but on areas of market liberalization, such as tariff policy. It had not generated uniformly stronger centralized institutions but a curious hybrid still heavily dependent on unanimous consensus among governments. And governments did not always privilege regional over global multilateral cooperation. These events seemed to disconfirm early, teleological variants of neofunctionalism.

Yet the most important weakness of neofunctionalism was not empirical but theoretical. For once the simple teleology toward integration was abandoned, neofunctionalism and other grand theories lacked the resources to construct a positive response. Neofunctionalism proved at once too ambitious, too vague and too incoherent to generate precise predictions suitable for empirical evaluation. To see why, we need only turn to theoretical lessons neofunctionalists themselves drew from these failures. Three stand out.

The neofunctionalists concluded that an explanation of integration must be imbedded in a multi-causal framework comprised of numerous narrower theories. Scholars came to realize in the 1970s that any single unified theory of American or comparative politics—say, "structural-functionalism"—was too abstract and undifferentiated to permit concrete theory testing and development. Most neofunctionalists concluded that no single theory could satisfactorily account for a phenomenon as complex as European integration; more concrete theories were required. However, their response, namely to construct amalgams of variables, failed to overcome, as Haas observed, the "nonadditive character of theories [that] coexist on different levels of abstraction." In an influential critique, Donald Puchala invoked the metaphor of the blind men and the elephant: different theories seemed to explain different aspects of the (elephantine) integration process. It follows that any general explanation of integration cannot rest on a single theory, neofunctionalist or otherwise, but must rest on a multi-causal framework that orders a series of more narrowly focused theories—a conclusion echoed to the present day.

Variables in the multi-causal framework must each be grounded in a general theory of political behavior. Theories that treat regional integration as a *sui generis* phenomenon, Haas argued, could be little better than "pre-theories." They breed theoretical insularity. With the EC as the sole major success, regional integration theory in practice became an ideal-typical summary of factors that appear to have influenced the European case. This focus on a *sui generis* Europe-centered theory cut the study of European integration off from revolutionary theoretical currents in comparative and international political economy over the three decades that followed. Sensing this, Haas proposed that "the study of regional integration should be both included in and subordinated to the study of changing patterns of interdependence." Consistent with this analysis, Stanley Hoffmann, Robert Keohane, Joseph Nye, Henry Nau, and many others drew the conclusion that the EC should be viewed as an international regime designed to manage interdependence.

Finally, each theory should be actor-oriented, that is, it should highlight the purposive choices of states and social actors within constraints rather than the unintended dynamics of broad structural processes. A fundamental weakness of neofunctionalism lay in its aspiration to trace dynamic endogenous effects (incremental feedback, unintended consequences, and the resulting change over time) without a baseline theory of exogenous constraints (state economic interests, political constraints, and delegation) through which dynamic change must take place. For example, neofunctionalists maintained (as I do . . .) that the pursuit of economic interest is the fundamental force underlying integration, but they offered only a vague understanding of precisely what those interests are, how conflicts among them are resolved, by what means they are translated into policy, and when they require political integration. This in turn reflected the lack of a generalizable micro-foundational basis necessary to support predictions about variation in support for integration across issues, countries, and time.

Without such micro-foundations, the predictions of neofunctionalism were indeterminate. Feedback, Haas conceded in his later self-criticism, "may transform the system" but need not do so. An entire taxonomy of alternative outcomes consistent with the underlying theory arose: "spillover," "spillback," "spill-around," "encapsulation." Once neofunctionalism dropped the optimistic notion that integration was automatically self-reinforcing and would evolve smoothly to federal union without triggering fundamental distributive or ideological conflicts, it could say "little about *basic causes*" of national demands for integration or interstate agreements to achieve it. . . . More concretely, neofunctionalism lacked explicit theories of interest-group politics, interstate bargaining, and international institutions. With few outcomes theoretically excluded, a rule of thumb emerged in the literature on the European Community: when integration stagnated, scholars criticized neofunctionalism; when integration progressed, they rediscovered it.

By the mid-1970s these three criticisms had inspired a degree of consensus concerning the proper theoretical direction forward. Unintended consequences and feedback, the initial core of neofunctionalism, should take a role secondary to the concrete beliefs, preferences, and strategies of political actors. As Haas said, "all political action is purposively linked with individual and group perception of interest." Greater attention should be focused on purposive behavior and strategic interaction: "the type of demands that are made, the variety of concessions . . . exchanged, and the degree of delegation of authority to new central institutions." Hoffmann, Keohane, and even, if to a lesser degree, Haas himself proposed studying the EC as an international regime constructed through a series of purposive decisions by governments with varying preferences and power. Hoffmann proposed a synthetic approach that examined first "the domestic priorities and foreign policy goals of the member states, then . . . the impact of the environment [and] finally the institutional interplay between the states and the Community." Keohane and Hoffmann concluded that spillover and unintended consequences required a prior intergovernmental bargain among member-states, thereby refocusing our attention on the exogenous determinants of major decisions.

Yet most scholarship on European integration over the past two decades has ignored these self-criticisms. Few scholars test general theories or employ a multi-causal framework. Nearly all continue instead either to structure research around a single variable (e.g., supranational influence, domestic politics, public opinion), often linked to an ideal-typical "grand theory" of integration or international relations, or to invoke a theoretically unstructured amalgam of causes. As a result, decades of analysis of the EC have multiplied conjectures about integration but generated few reliable empirical conclusions about the relative importance of forces that have made the EC what it is today. "Confirmed" determinants of integration and "necessary" conditions for its success proliferate unchecked. Some scholars go further, defending this tendency on the ground that integration is the result of an indeterminate, path-dependent process.

The proper measure of our understanding of integration is not the multiplication of intuitively plausible claims; it is the development, evaluation, and ultimately rejection of testable hypotheses. Where hypotheses are rarely discarded, they are rarely confirmed. Thus the basic thrust of this book runs contrary to the current literature on European integration. Rather than employ neofunctionalism and other grand theories as interpretive lenses, it seeks to move beyond them by employing narrower and concrete hypotheses drawn from general theories of economic interest, interstate bargaining, and international regimes to support rigorous testing. . . .

Note

1. Since the ratification of the Maastricht Treaty, the organization has been referred to as the European Union (EU). This [chapter] deals with major interstate bargains up to and including Maastricht, so the older term European Community is used throughout.

Integration, Supranational Governance, and the Institutionalization of the European Polity

Alec Stone Sweet and Wayne Sandholtz

Supranationalists responded to Andrew Moravcsik's intergovernmentalist challenge in the 1990s. Scholars who believed that European states had lost some control over integration to supranational EU institutions, however, took several different theoretical routes. One route was to revisit neofunctionalism as the grand theory best able—with some modifications—to explain European integration.

Alec Stone Sweet (Yale Law School) and Wayne Sandholtz (University of Southern California), in the selection below, moved beyond a vague supranationalism and explicitly developed a modern neofunctionalist account of the institutional development of the EU. In their view, the increase in cross-border exchanges in Europe created political pressures on governments to regulate international transactions. Governments responded—just as Haas predicted—by creating supranational institutions that met some needs but revealed others, which were subsequently met by granting the supranational institutions even more authority in repeated demonstrations of classic neofunctionalist "spillover." Thus, following Deutsch (Chapter 16), observers should be able to account for the development and speed of integration in particular policy areas by examining the rates of transactions in corresponding sectors.

Reprinted from *European Integration and Supranational Governance*, by Wayne Sandholtz and Alec Stone Sweet, eds. (1998), pp. 1–26. Reprinted by permission of Oxford University Press. Notes omitted.

Six governments, moved by a hope for enduring peace in a prosperous Europe, in 1957 signed the Treaty of Rome establishing the European Community.[1] The EC thus began its life as an agreement among independent nation-states. Forty years later, the European Community has developed into something more than a pact among governments. In fact, it is now commonplace to compare the Treaty of Rome to a constitution, and to refer to the European Community in terms that imply an analogy with nation-states. In this [chapter] we theorize, and assess empirically, the institutionalization of the European Community, that is, its remarkable transformation from an interstate bargain into a multidimensional, quasi-federal polity. We propose a theory of European integration, focusing on the process through which supranational governance—the competence of the European Community to make binding rules in any given policy domain—has developed.

We therefore confront some of the most puzzling questions posed by the evolution of the Community. Why does policymaking sometimes migrate from the nation-state level to the European Community? Why has integration proceeded more rapidly in some policy domains than it has in others? To what extent is the Community governed by "intergovernmental" or "supranational" modes of decision-making? What accounts for the relative dominance of the neoliberal project, and for the relative failure of social democratic visions of Europe to gain influence? We do not claim to have definitively settled all controversies. But our theory yields responses to these questions in the form of testable propositions. . . .

We do not explain the founding of the EC, but rather its institutional development. Our starting point, therefore, is the Treaty of Rome. The Treaty established a cluster of organizations (Council, Commission, Court, and Parliament) and a set of rules whose central purpose was to promote exchange across national borders. The founders of the European Community reasoned that a "common market," linking their diverse national economies, would both accelerate the generation of wealth and make war among the member states unthinkable. The Treaty of Rome thus created a social and political space that intentionally privileged transnational economic interests. That is, the point of the EC was to facilitate exchange among its member countries. Because the Community was designed to promote intra-EC exchange, its rules and organizations have favored economic actors with a stake in cross-border transactions (trade, investment, production, distribution). Rising levels of transnational exchange trigger processes that generate movement toward increased supranational governance. We do not claim to explain policy processes, or their substantive outcomes, in terms of increasing cross-border exchange; specific policies are the product of complex political interactions. Rather, increasing exchange provokes behaviors and processes that are decisively shaped by the institutional context of the EC, and these processes tend to produce or reinforce supranational rule-making.

In other words, we emphasize the role of transnational exchange (e.g. trade, investment, the development of Euro-groups, networks, and associations) in pushing the EC's organizations to construct new policy and new arenas for policy-relevant behavior. Once constituted, these arenas sustain integration in predictable ways, not least, by promoting additional transnational exchange. . . .

Our analytical goals, and thus our theory, differentiate us from existing approaches. "Intergovernmentalism" [Chapter 23] denies the significance of supranational governance, arguing instead that the member states control policy processes and outcomes. Institutionalization is not an issue because the EC remains as it began, a set of bargains among independent nation-states. Scholars who analyze the EC in terms of "multilevel governance" [Chapter 26] or "policy networks" focus on the processes by which the contemporary EC produces policy outcomes. That is, they take a certain amount of supranational governance for granted. But the policy-centered approaches do not take as part of their task the explanation of how the EC developed from an interstate treaty to a system of governance, or why some policy domains have become more integrated than others.

This chapter proceeds as follows. In Section 1, we briefly contrast our theory with the main features of neofunctionalism and intergovernmentalism. Some urge that the neofunctionalist-intergovernmentalist debate be abandoned. We would respond that there has been no genuine debate; since the mid-1970s, very few have claimed the neofunctionalist banner, much less offered a systematic, full-fledged neofunctionalist argument on European integration. Instead, theoretical discussions tend to involve a ritual dismissal of neofunctionalism followed by either a critique or an endorsement of intergovernmentalism. That hardly constitutes a debate. Sometimes the impatience with the neofunctionalist-intergovernmentalist debate simply amounts to the claim that no general theory of European integration is possible (often tied to a preference for analyses of individual policies or sectors). In reply, we are placing on the table a general theory along with supportive empirical evidence. . . . The onus is on those who reject the possibility of broad theories to show why our results should not be taken seriously.

In Sections 2 and 3 of this chapter, we elaborate a theory that offers a positive alternative to intergovernmentalism. We define key concepts, discuss causal relationships between variables, and derive hypotheses about how European integration proceeds. In the concluding section we clarify our differences with intergovernmentalist theories of integration.

Theoretical Context

The primary theoretical divide in EC studies has been between intergovernmentalism and neofunctionalism. Endless nuance and distinction exist within each approach, but in the end most theorizing on integration endorses either the following statement or its opposite: the distribution of preferences and the conduct of bargaining among the governments of the member states broadly explain the nature, pace, and scope of integration, and neither supranational organization nor transnational actors generate political processes or outcomes of seminal importance. In recent decades, intergovernmentalists have worked to refine their framework, and some have aggressively proclaimed its superiority. At the same time, neofunctionalism has gradually been abandoned. Its original adherents have moved away from integration studies, and critics of intergovernmentalism have not developed their own general theory, least of all by refining neofunctionalism.

We set ourselves the task of developing and testing a theory of how supranational governance evolves over time. What we are seeking to explain, the nature and extent of supranational governance, varies along a number of dimensions. In some sectors, the competence to govern is held exclusively by the Community; in others, national institutions are the primary sites of policymaking; and in many domains, the transfer of power from the national to the supranational level has been only partial. Within the same policy sector, the answer to the question, "who governs?" has changed over time. And in those areas in which EC institutions have become sites of policy innovation and change, one finds variation in the relative capacity of the member-state governments, acting in summits and in the Council of Ministers, to control that policy. In specifying the research problem in this way, we commit ourselves to theorizing integration as a dynamic process that yields divergent outcomes. We therefore problematize the notion, strongly implied by neofunctionalist theories, that integration is the process by which the EC gradually but comprehensively replaces the nation-state in all of its functions. And we reject the comparative statics of intergovernmentalists as a mode of analysis incapable of capturing crucial temporal elements of European integration.

Our theory, set out in Sections 2 and 3 below, privileges the expansion of transnational exchange, the capacities of supranational organizations to respond to the needs of those who exchange, and the role of supranational rules in shaping subsequent integration. We argue that supranational governance serves the interests of 1) those individuals, groups, and firms who transact across borders, and 2) those who are advantaged by European rules, and disadvantaged by national rules, in specific policy domains. The expansion of transnational exchange, and the associated push to substitute supranational for national rules, generates pressure on the EC's organizations to act. Generally, EC organizations, such as the Commission and the Court, respond to this pressure by working to extend the domain of supranational rules, in order to achieve collective (transnational) gains and to accomplish the purposes of the Treaties, broadly interpreted. A first hypothesis, then, is that the relative intensity of transnational activity, measured across time and policy sectors, broadly determines variation on the dependent variable (supranational governance).

We claim that transnational activity has been the catalyst of European integration; but transnational exchange can not, in and of itself, determine the specific details, or the precise timing, of Community rule-making. Instead it provokes, or activates, the Community's decision-making bodies, including the Council of Ministers. Member-state governments often possess (but not always) the means to facilitate or to obstruct rule-making, and they use these powers frequently. Nevertheless, we argue, among other things, that as transnational exchange rises in any specific domain (or cluster of related domains), so do the costs, for governments, of maintaining disparate national rules. As these costs rise, so do incentives for governments to adjust their policy positions in ways that favor the expansion of supranational governance. Once fixed in a given domain, European rules—such as relevant treaty provisions, secondary legislation, and the ECJ's case law—generate a self sustaining dynamic, that leads to the gradual deepening of integration in that sector and, not uncommonly, to spillovers into other sectors. Thus, we view intergovernmental bargaining and decision-making as embedded in processes that are provoked and sustained by the expansion of transnational society, the pro-integrative activities of supranational organizations, and the growing density of supranational rules. And, we will argue, these processes gradually, but inevitably, reduce the capacity of the member states to control outcomes.

Our theory has important affinities with neofunctionalism. We acknowledge the insights of two of the founders of integration theory, Karl Deutsch [Chapter 16] and Ernst Haas [Chapter 17]. On crucial questions, we believe, they got it right. What we find complementary are Deutsch's emphasis on social exchange, communication, and transactions, and Haas's attention to the relationship between global interdependence, political choice, and the development of supranational institutions.

Deutsch and his collaborators held that increasing density of social exchange among individuals over prolonged periods of time would lead to the development of new communities (shared identity) and, ultimately, to the creation of a super-state with centralized institutions. We agree that social exchange across borders drives integration processes, generating social demands for supranational rules, and for higher levels of organizational capacity to respond to further demands. If this demand is not supplied, the development of higher levels of exchange will be stunted. We set aside Deutsch's concern with the formation of communities and identities per se, and the issue of whether or not identity formation precedes state-building. Our dependent variable remains mode of governance, not the construction of a pan-European identity or of a super-state.

Haas conceived of integration as the product of growing international interdependence and pluralist, interest-driven politics. Mitrany [Chapter 15] had theorized what would happen in a world increasingly beset by policy problems that transcended national borders: governmental functions would steadily migrate from national governments, who would act on the basis of "politics," to global technocrats, who would act on the basis of expertise. Haas recognized that the transfer of functions to supranational bodies would always be intensely contested, as some groups foresaw gains while others feared losses. He consequently saw the initial construction of supranational authority as the crucial political hurdle. Stripped down, Haas's neofunctionalist argument runs something like this. Some elite groups (leadership of political parties, industry associations, and labor federations) begin to recognize that problems of substantial interest cannot be solved at the national level. These groups push for the transfer of policy competence to a supranational body, finding each other and establishing cross-national coalitions along the way. If the problem is important enough and pro-integration elites are able to mount sufficient political leverage, governments establish supranational institutions.

Once supranational institutions are born, a new dynamic emerges. Haas pioneered in theorizing the logic of institutionalization at the supranational level. He suggested a dynamic process. The creation of supranational authority leads to changes in social expectations and behavior, which feed back onto supranational policymaking, and so on. As supranational bodies begin to deliver the coordinative solutions that pro-integrationists hoped for, they become the locus of a new kind of politics. Groups increasingly seek influence over supranational policies, opening up new political channels, but also helping supranational organizations acquire expertise, information, and legitimacy, thus bolstering their authority. The dynamic is reinforced by the potential, inherent in integration processes, for functional "spillover." Spillover is achieved when it becomes evident that initial policy objectives can not be adequately attained without such an extension. Neofunctionalists—especially Philippe Schmitter—also attended to the role of bargaining among member governments. But they at least implicitly argued (and we argue explicitly) that, as integration proceeds, member-state governments become less and less proactive, and more and more reactive to changes in the supranational environment to which they belong.

The three constituent elements of our theory are prefigured in neofunctionalism: the development of transnational society, the role of supranational organizations with meaningful autonomous capacity to pursue integrative agendas, and the focus on European rule-making to resolve international policy externalities. Further, we appreciate Haas's insight that supranational policymaking (governance) generates a dynamic process of institutionalization. We do not, however, embrace all of Haas's neofunctionalism. Haas defined integration as "the process whereby political actors . . . are persuaded to shift their national loyalties, expectations, and political activities to a new and larger center." Again, we leave as an open question the extent to which the loyalties and identities of actors will shift from the national to the European level. There is substantial room for supranational governance without an ultimate shift in identification. And we will specify somewhat differently the causal mechanisms by which integration is provoked and sustained, tying both to the development of transnational society and to contemporary theories of institutions and institutionalization.

Intergovernmentalists conceptualize EC politics as a subset of international relations, namely as an example of interstate cooperation sustained by an international regime. Successful regimes facilitate the ongoing coordination of policy among member states, by reducing the costs of information, policy innovation, and negotiation. In Andrew Moravcsik's "liberal intergovernmentalism," regime theory has been supplemented to take account of domestic politics. At times, Moravcsik conceives European politics as a two-level game. The crucial actors are national executives, who continuously mediate between domestic interests and the activities of the international regime. At other times, Moravcsik sequences, for analytical purposes, national preference formation (domestic politics) and intergovernmental bargaining (regime politics). National executives are constrained by, but also aggregate, domestic interests as national preferences; once fixed, the distribution of preferences among, and the "relative bargaining power" of member-state governments determine outcomes.

European integration is a product of these outcomes. As Moravcsik puts it: "the EC has developed through a series of celebrated intergovernmental bargains, each of which sets the agenda for an intervening period of consolidation." In order to consolidate these bargains efficiently, member-state governments establish and delegate powers to the EC's organizations, like the Commission and the Court of Justice (ECJ). Although intergovernmentalists rarely focus empirical attention on the process of consolidation, they claim that the EC's organizations broadly pursue goals previously determined by the member-state governments, or are called to order if they pursue divergent agendas.

National executives construct the EC's capacity to govern, Moravcsik argues, for two main reasons. First, for electoral reasons executives may find it in their interest to respond to international policy externalities by pooling their sovereignty at the supranational level. Such externalities are generated by international interdependence. Second, in order to enhance their own autonomy *vis-à-vis* domestic actors, national executives may shift competence to govern to an arena (such as the Council of Ministers) that operates with fewer constraints on executive authority than national arenas. Why executives do so in some policy domains, but not in others, appears to be indeterminate.

For Moravcsik, the following sequence encompasses virtually all that is important: rising interdependence > delegation to supranational authorities > intergovernmental bargaining > delegation to supranational authorities > consolidation. Integration proceeds, but the sequence never varies in any meaningful way. In this imagery, transnational actors and society do not exist; instead, he notices domestic groups impact integration processes in autonomous and decisive ways; instead, in accordance with their place in the sequence, they behave as rather faithful agents of intergovernmental bargains. By our reading, rising interdependence constitutes the only important causal factor that both provokes integration and is not decisively determined by intergovernmental bargaining. On this point, intergovernmentalism hardly displaces neofunctionalism, but rather relies on a causal argument developed by the neofunctionalists.

We will return to our differences with intergovernmentalists in the concluding section.

A Transaction-Based Theory of Integration

As most students of EC policymaking have observed, simple characterizations of the Community, as either "intergovernmental" or "supranational," will not do. The brute fact is that integration has proceeded unevenly, and theories of integration have failed to explain this unevenness. Most recent research on EC politics has focused either on the grand bargains (the Single European Act or the Maastricht Treaty, for instance), or on how day-to-day policy is made in specific sectors. Neither emphasis has provided an adequate basis for theorizing the dynamic nature of integration over time across policy domains. . . .

From Intergovernmental to Supranational Politics

We thus propose a continuum [Figure 24.1] that stretches between two ideal-typical modes of governance: the intergovernmental (the left-hand pole), and the supranational (the right-hand pole). One pole is constituted by intergovernmental politics. The central players in intergovernmental politics are the national executives of the member states, who bargain with each other to produce common policies. Bargaining is shaped by the relative powers of the member states, but also by state preferences, which emerge from the pulling and hauling among domestic groups. These preferences are then given agency, as negotiating positions, by national executives in EC organizations such as the Council of Ministers. The EC level of governance operates as an international regime in the functional, transaction-costs mode: it is a "passive structure" that enhances the efficiency of interstate bargaining.

The other pole is constituted by supranational politics. A "supranational" mode of governance is one in which centralized governmental structures (those organizations constituted at the supranational level) possess jurisdiction over specific policy domains within the territory comprised by the member states. In exercising jurisdiction, supranational organizations

Figure 24.1 Governance in the European Union

Note: From left to right, the continuum measures the increasing influence of three factors on policy-making processes and outcomes within any given policy sector. These factors are: (1) supranational organizations, (2) supranational rules, and (3) transnational society.

are capable of constraining the behavior of all actors, including the member states, within those domains. Many would argue that "federal politics" would be the appropriate label. We use the term "supranational" to emphasize that the EC is an international organization, and that EC politics is a form of international politics. And we have avoided using the term "federal" here in order to avoid an argument about the precise nature of the EC polity and how it compares with other federal polities. Movement from left to right along the continuum indicates that a shift away from intergovernmentalism, and toward supranationalism, has taken place.

In principle, the continuum is capable of situating—and therefore of characterizing—all international regime forms as sites (more or less) of intergovernmental or sites (more or less) of supranational politics. Unlike most regimes, which tend to organize interstate cooperation in one or a few closely related sectors, the EC possesses differing degrees of competence across a diverse range of policy areas. In principle, one could use the continuum to characterize the development of the EC as a whole, in terms of the composite picture of all policy areas. One could also use the continuum to chart the comparative development or lack of development of different policy sectors comparatively. Thus, policy sector A may be located at point 2, shading toward intergovernmental politics, while policy sector B may be located at point 4, exhibiting strong features of supranationalism. Used in this way, the continuum asserts that there are potentially many ECs. As discussed in the next section, we hope that by disaggregating EC governing processes by policy sector, we will be able to learn more about the nature of European integration than we can by working to characterize, in a blanket fashion, the EC as an "intergovernmental" or "supranational" regime.

Dimensions of Institutionalization
The continuum measures the movement from intergovernmental to supranational governance in three interrelated dimensions:

- *EC rules:* the legal, and less informal, constraints on behavior produced by interactions among political actors operating at the European level;
- *EC organizations*: those governmental structures, operating at the European level, that produce, execute, and interpret EC rules; and
- *transnational society*: those non-governmental actors who engage in intra-EC exchanges—social, economic, political—and thereby influence, directly or indirectly, policymaking processes and outcomes at the European level.

For any given policy area or process, movement from left to right along the continuum therefore measures the growing presence and intensity of each of these factors.

We understand these dimensions to be crucial indicators of levels of integration in the EC. By "integration," we mean the process by which the horizontal and vertical linkages between social, economic, and political actors emerge and evolve. Vertical linkages are the stable relationships, or patterned interaction, between actors organized at the EC level and actors organized at or below the member-state level. Horizontal linkages are the stable relationships, or patterned interaction, between actors organized in one member-state with actors organized in another. We understand these linkages to be "institutionalized" to the extent that they are constructed and sustained by EC rules.

The three dimensions are analytically distinct, although we expect them to covary, as integration proceeds, in predictable ways. As we move from left to right along the continuum the influence of EC (or supranational) organizations on policymaking processes and outcomes increases. Supranational EC organizations include the Commission, the Court of Justice, the Parliament, and even at times the Council of Ministers. At the left-hand pole, the regime's organizations exhibit little if any meaningful autonomy from the most powerful member states. By autonomy, we mean an organization's capacity to define and pursue, on an ongoing basis, a politically relevant agenda. In intergovernmental politics, organizations facilitate intergovernmental bargaining and logistical coordination (they lower the transaction costs for governments). At point 3 on the continuum, supranational organizations may often be the source of successful policy innovation, a form of "relative"—but meaningful—autonomy. At the supranational pole, institutions may exercise substantial autonomy, as when they are able to innovate, in policy-relevant ways, at times even in the face of member-state indifference or hostility.

The second dimension built into the continuum is legal-normative. As we move from left to right along the continuum, EC rules achieve higher degrees of clarity and formalization. Consider those rules that govern the production, application, and interpretation of all other rules, such as secondary legislation, within the Community. At the far left of the continuum, rules are few and weak; they do not trump individual governmental interests that conflict with them. As we move along the continuum, rules stabilize state bargaining, delegitimize exit, and—at the level of law—lay down binding standards of conduct enforceable by courts. Many of the rules governing EC policymaking are behavioral, that is, they have resulted from many years of constant interaction between state and supranational officials in a myriad of settings. But many of these rules are also highly formal, codified in treaty law, secondary legislation, and the ECJ's jurisprudence. Within any given policy domain, as we move leftward the rules governing the interactions of all actors, public and private, grow more dense and elaborate.

The third dimension captured by the continuum is the presence and influence of transnational actors—interest groups, business, knowledge-based elites—on policy processes and outcomes. In intergovernmental politics, national executives mediate between domestic actors and supranational organizations and rules. In supranational politics, transnational actors have a choice of fora in which to exert their influence. They may target national governmental structures—executive, legislative, or judicial—as well as supranational bodies, and they may play one level off against the other.

Taken together, these dimensions are constitutive of supranational politics. If this is so . . . these three factors must move together, and the disjunctures that do occur in movement are short-lived. Organizations, rules, and social exchange are closely linked in the development of society and systems of governance; they are similarly connected in supranational politics. Organizations produce and transmit the rules that guide social interaction. They structure access to policy processes, defining political power and privileging some parts of society more than others. As supranational organizations acquire and wield autonomy, they are able to shape not only specific policy outcomes but also the rules that channel policymaking behaviors. As supranational organizations and rules emerge and solidify, they constitute transnational society by establishing bases for interaction and access points for influencing policy. As transnational society endures and expands, the organizations and rules that structure behaviors become more deeply rooted as "givens," taken for granted as defining political life. Growth in one element of the supranational trio (organizations, rules, transnational society) creates conditions that favor growth in the other two. An expansion of the tasks or autonomy of supranational organizations creates opportunities for political action, which actors and groups will seek to exploit, thus expanding transnational society. As societal actors adjust their behaviors in response to new supranational rules, these rules can gradually be locked in. If broader, global trends promote the growth of transnational society, there will be a corresponding demand for increased organizational capacity and rules to coordinate and to guide interactions.

Why Movement Occurs

The continuum gives us tools with which to describe EC governance. We have also offered a proposition that would account for some of the dynamics of integration, namely that movement in any one of the dimensions will tend to produce movement in the other two. In other words, there is an internal dynamic of institutionalization. But important questions remain to be theorized. Why does movement on any of the dimensions occur in the first place? Why do some policy domains move farther and faster toward the supranational pole than others? In this section we offer a theoretical account that can generate answers to such questions.

Our starting point is society, in particular, non-state actors who engage in transactions and communications across national borders, within Europe. These are the people who need European standards, rules, and dispute resolution mechanisms—who need supranational governance. In the beginning, the causal mechanism is quite simple: increasing levels of cross-border transactions and communications by societal actors will increase the perceived need for European-level rules coordination, and regulation. In fact, the absence of European rules will come to be seen as an obstacle to the generation of wealth and the achievement of other collective gains. Separate national legal regimes constitute the crucial source of transaction costs for those who wish to engage in exchanges across borders: customs and other border controls, differing technical standards, divergent health and environmental regulations, distinct systems of commercial law, diverse national currencies, and so on. Further, the costs of transacting across borders are higher than those involved in contracting within a single member-state, to the extent that there exists no secure common legal framework at the supranational level, comparable in its efficacy to that of national legal systems. As transnational exchanges rise, so does the societal demand for supranational rules and organizational capacity to regulate. Transactors can exert pro-integration pressure on their own governments, but when these are reticent, transactors can access supranational arenas dominated by the Commission and the European Court of Justice.

Governmental actors clearly have their own interests, which may include maximizing their autonomy and control over resources. They may resist the shift toward supranational policymaking. But as they do so, they inhibit the generation of wealth within their territory by those actors that depend on European transactions. Such resistance is therefore sustainable only at a cost in prosperity. They can also attempt to slow integration or push it in directions favorable to their perceived interests, but they do not drive the process or fully control it. In a fundamental sense, governments are reactive, constantly adjusting to the integration that is going on all around them.

On this point, the contrast between our theory and intergovernmental approaches to the EC could hardly be greater, but we have not written national governments out of the story. In fact, intergovernmental decision-making is ubiquitous in the EC, present even at the far right-hand pole of our continuum (as it is in Canada and other federal systems). EC summits, intergovernmental conferences, and meetings of the Council of Ministers are practically defined by tough, interest-driven negotiation. But that is part of the problem with intergovernmental approaches to integration. Adherents of these approaches always begin by announcing that the "grand bargains" are the defining moments of European integration, and then these historic agreements become the object of empirical research. But the grand bargains are, by definition, intergovernmental. The research results are quite predictable when one looks to intergovernmental bargains for evidence of intergovernmental bargaining. Thus the observation that bargaining among governments is ubiquitous in the EC does not settle theoretical controversy. Put differently, the term "intergovernmental" is useful as a description of a specific mode of decision-making within the EC policy process. But to attend to what is intergovernmental about the construction of supranational governance does not require us to adopt, or to accept the validity of, "intergovernmentalism-as-theory."

Indeed, we argue that intergovernmental bargaining in the EC more often than not is responsive to the interests of a nascent, always developing, transnational society. Indeed, the demand for EC rules and regulation provides the subject matter for the bargaining. With very few exceptions, EC legislation concerns, directly or indirectly, the creation of rules that facilitate or regulate intra-EC exchange and communications. The configuration of social interests that will be affected by European policy innovation may vary from state to state, which creates the differences over which governments must negotiate. But rather than being the generator of integration, intergovernmental bargaining is more often its product.

The exclusive focus on grand intergovernmental bargains can also lead to serious distortions of the historical record. The 1970s have generally been regarded as disconfirmation of neofunctionalism; intergovernmentalists typically note that member-state preferences diverged during those years and that few of the EC's ambitious plans at the beginning of the decade bore fruit. We do not read the story of European integration as one of stop-and-go, at least not in any general or comprehensive sense. At the height of de Gaulle's power in the 1960s, the ECJ moved aggressively to "constitutionalize" the treaties. In the worst days of "Eurosclerosis" in the 1970s, levels of intra-EC trade and other forms of exchange soared. And, as we would expect, both the amount of legislation and the number of organized EC pressure groups grew steadily through the 1970s. Integration always proceeded, in some sectors and from some vantage points, despite the Luxembourg compromise and despite the divergence of state preferences.

.   .   .

The transactions-based theory implies a coherent answer to the question, why does integration proceed faster or farther in some policy areas than in others? We would look to variation in the levels of cross-border interactions and in the consequent need for supranational coordination and rules. In sectors where the intensity and value of cross-national transactions are relatively low, the demand for EC-level coordination of rules and dispute resolution will be correspondingly low. Conversely, in domains where the number and value of cross-border transactions are rising, there will be increasing demand on the part of the transactors for EC-level rules and dispute-resolution mechanisms. It makes sense, then, that the EC has moved farthest toward the supranational pole with respect to managing the internal market. Intra-EC trade and investment have grown steadily since the founding of the EEC [European Economic Community], creating the need for greater degrees of supranational governance in issue areas closely linked to expanding the common market. Naturally, the EC rules for the single market have in turn encouraged increases in the cross-border transactions they were meant to facilitate. In contrast, there are few societal transactions that are impeded by the absence of a common foreign and security policy. Or, put differently, though some argue for the political benefits that CFSP [Common Foreign and Security Policy] would bring, few societal transactors find its absence costly. There is therefore minimal social demand for integration in that policy domain.

Furthermore, the capacity of supranational organizations to make rules in a given policy domain appears to vary as a function of the level of transnational activity. . . . [L]itigation of free movement of goods disputes dominates the work of the European Court of Justice, and legal principles developed by the ECJ in the domain have animated the Court's decision-making in other areas. Mark Pollack finds that the Commission exercises greater autonomy in some policy sectors than in others. The Commission's authority is greatest when it is supported by EC rules, pro-integrative Court decisions, and transnational interests. We would argue that variation in these factors is not random: higher levels of transactions push the EC to legislate, the Court to clarify the rules, and interests to organize. It is therefore not surprising that . . . the Commission's powers are greater in competition policy than in structural funds or external trade. Even within competition policy, the Commission acts with greater authority where transaction levels are high (telecommunications) relative to where they are low (electricity).

The theory also allows us to explain the general direction of integration in the common market. Business is likely to be the segment for which the material stake in cross-border transactions is greatest and most obvious. Indeed, the Treaty of Rome created rules whose purpose was to promote cross-national economic activities. Companies with an interest in cross-national sales or investment will press for the reduction of national barriers, and for the establishment of regional rules and standards. By the same token, the consequences of integration for people in their roles as workers and consumers are less transparent. This would explain why European companies have had a greater impact on integration than have labor or consumers. We can thus account for the decisively neo-liberal (pro-market) character of recent events like the 1992 program and the Maastricht provisions on EMU. If integration is driven fundamentally by private transactors, and if capital is the group with the clearest immediate stake in intra-EC transactions (not to mention the resources required for political influence), it is not surprising that the major steps in integration should be congenial to those segments of business.

We can now also respecify the spillover mechanism. As the most obvious hindrances to cross-national exchange are removed, or their effects reduced by the transaction-cost-reducing behavior of supranational organizations and rules, new obstacles to such transactions are revealed and become salient. With the removal of tariffs and quotas, for example, differences in national regulatory standards—for the environment, health and safety, technical compatibility, and so on—become more apparent as obstacles to exchange. Economic actors seeking to benefit from intra-Community exchange will then target these obstacles, both by attacking regulatory barriers through litigation and by pressuring EC legislative institutions to widen the jurisdiction of the EC into new domains. Transactors will always prefer, other things being equal, to live under (or adapt to) one set of rules rather than six, or twelve, or fifteen. As governments and EC institutions respond, spillover occurs.

Globalization, which is integration of a broader geographic scope, can also stimulate movement toward increased supranational governance within Europe. The integration of national markets (for goods, services, and capital) and multilateral approaches to global problems (ozone, climate change, weapons proliferation) can create pressures for integration from above the nation-state. Transnational actors are sometimes the conduit through which globalization stimulates advances in European integration. For instance, with the goal of increasing their competitiveness in world markets, European multinationals pressed for active EC high-technology programs (ESPRIT, RACE) as well as the creation of a genuine internal market. But globalization can also exert pressure directly on EC organizations. For example, the involvement of the EC in global environmental negotiations has strengthened Commission competencies and roles.

Institutionalization

Once movement toward the supranational pole begins, European rules generate a dynamic of [their] own, which we call institutionalization. In lay-

complete the common market, was sustained by private actors desiring the elimination of national practices that limited intra-EC trade.

.   .   .

Thus, though the Treaty is the indispensable starting point, over time supranational rules and rule-making processes evolve in ways that are not predictable from the *ex ante* perspective of those who establish them. The new rules create legal rights and open new arenas for politics; in this fashion they structure political processes thereafter. Actors—including governments, private entities, and EC bodies—adapt to the new rules and arenas. This dynamic is wholly absent in the intergovernmentalist account. Intergovernmentalists see governments as the sole mediators between non-state actors and EC policymaking. In contrast, our theory leads us to expect (and we do observe) private actors successfully employing the EC judicial process against member governments and pursuing political strategies directly at the Commission. Intergovernmentalists depict governments as directing the process of integration and establishing its limits. Our approach, in contrast, views governments as powerful actors that cannot always impose their preferred outcomes on other players in the EC political system (transnational actors, the Commission and the ECJ), who also possess substantial legal and political powers.

Finally, governments are ultimately constrained by rules whose production they do not control. National courts, guided by ECJ decisions, can compel their governments to comply with EC rules they have opposed. For example, though the UK has taken the most anti-integration position in the Council with respect to social provisions, British courts responding to private litigants and ECJ rulings have forced the government to change domestic policies so that they align with EC laws that Britain opposed. Similarly, though member governments bargained with each other with respect to telecommunications liberalization, that bargaining took place during the crucial phase under the shadow of the Commission's newfound capacity, affirmed by the Court, to enact its preferred policies via Art. 90 directives.

The rule-centered logic of institutionalization also suggests why it is difficult, and sometimes impossible, for governments to reverse the shifts toward supranational governance that have occurred. The Treaty—the constitution of the European polity—fixes the rule-making processes of the EC and the ECJ is authoritative interpreter of this constitution. As substantive rules, such as secondary legislation, evolve, actors (including governments, as well as EC bodies and non-state entities) adjust their behaviors. The rules, since the impetus behind them is to facilitate cross-border transactions and communications, lead to new kinds and higher levels of transactions. The new transactions entrench interests. The result is a high degree of "stickiness" in movement along the continuum.

Two logics, or languages, capture the essence of that stickiness. The first has to do with path dependence, the second with principal-agent relations. Paul Pierson makes two interrelated points: first, that significant gaps emerge between member-state preferences and the functioning of EC policies and institutions; and second, that once such gaps develop states cannot simply close them. The latter point is the crucial one with respect to the difficulty of reversing shifts toward supranational governance. Pierson argues that institutional change is a "path-dependent" process; once institutional and policy changes are in place, social actors adapt to those changes, frequently making substantial investments in the process. A policy turnabout would entail the loss of these sunk costs, thus raising the costs for governments seeking to unwind supranational governance. Furthermore, decision rules often constitute major obstacles to reversing course. The process of adaptation to change in complex social settings also produces unintended consequences that are difficult to unwind. Thus institutional and policy outcomes become "locked in," channeling politics down specific paths and closing previously plausible alternatives.

Mark Pollack assesses the conditions under which the EC Commission can act autonomously, recognizing that the Commission is the most constrained of the EC's supranational bodies (as compared to the Parliament and the ECJ). He employs principal-agent imagery to argue that the administrative and oversight mechanisms that principals (member governments) use to rein in agents (the Commission) can be costly and of limited effectiveness. Furthermore, agents can exploit divergent preferences among multiple principals, especially under more demanding decision rules, like unanimity.

The path-dependence and principal-agent logics reinforce our argument that institutionalization in the EC is not reducible to the preferences of, or bargaining among, member governments. The expansion of transnational society pushes for supranational governance, which is exercised to facilitate and regulate that society. Once in place, supranational rules alter the context for subsequent transactions and policymaking. Actors—governments, supranational organizations, and non-state entities alike—adapt their preferences, strategies, and behaviors to the new rules. These adaptations, plus the importance of rules in shaping preferences and behaviors, are what make shifts toward supranational governance sticky and difficult to undo. Finally, because specific policies and organizational forms emerge through a path-dependent process, in which numerous social systems interact in quite contingent ways, those outcomes can only be analyzed through historical, process-tracing case studies. Thus, whereas broad aggregate data reflect the casual link between cross-border transactions and EC rule-making, case studies are essential for explaining the specific content and form of EC rules and policies.

Conclusion

We have proposed a theory of integration that relies on three causal factors: exchange, organization, and rules. Transnational exchange provokes supranational organizations to make rules designed to facilitate and to regulate the development of transnational society. To the extent that supranational organizations are successful at doing so, specific causal connections between our three factors will be constructed. These connections sustain an inherently expansionary process, not least, by means of policy feedback. As the structure of European rules becomes more dense and articulated, this structure itself will encourage private and public actors at all levels of the Community to forge new, or intensify existing, linkages (vertical and horizontal). Member-state governments are important actors in this process. Nevertheless, we argue that the integration-relevant behavior of governments, whether acting individually or collectively, is best explained in terms of the embeddedness of governments in integration processes, that is, in terms of the development of transnational society and its system of governance.

We do not want to be misunderstood on this last point. No one denies that certain elements, or stages, of the European policy-making process are intergovernmental. Governments are repositories of immense resources, both material (e.g. financial) and non-material (e.g. legitimacy). In the EC, national executives pursue what they take to be their own interests, which they express as constituting the national interest. And in the bargaining process, executives from the larger states command greater resources and tend to wield greater influence on EC policy outcomes than those from the smaller states. But noticing governments and power does not entail accepting intergovernmentalism as a body of causal propositions about how integration has proceeded. Although we dismiss as untenable Moravcsik's proclamation that his version of intergovernmentalism is the "indispensable and fundamental point of departure for any general explanation of regional integration," we have no trouble recognizing that intergovernmental bargaining is an ubiquitous feature of supranational governance (as it is in many federal polities). Indeed, in our research we constantly attend to the question of whether and how integration shapes the preferences of governments over time, and the extent to which it casts (and recasts) the nature and content of intergovernmental bargaining. In our opinion, Moravcsik has developed a theory of intergovernmental bargaining within a specific institutional context, that of the EC, but not a satisfying general theory of integration.

Our theory accounts for causal relationships between variables that are systematically downplayed or de-emphasized by intergovernmentalism and, we argue, these relationships will regularly produce outcomes that significantly impact the trajectory of integration. Intergovernmentalism is rigid; integration proceeds, but nothing essential in European politics ever changes. In contrast, we expect that integration produces new political arenas; that the politics in these arenas will qualitatively differ from purely intergovernmental politics; and that this difference will have an impact downstream, on subsequent policy processes and outcomes. In Moravcsik's view, supranational organizations, like the Commission, are virtually always "perfectly reactive agents," responding only to the "delegation" of tasks pursuant to the "pooling" of state sovereignty. In contrast, we expect supranational bodies to work to enhance their own autonomy and influence within the European polity, so as to promote the interests of transnational society and the construction of supranational governance. In Moravcsik's view, "Only where the action of supranational leaders *systematically* bias outcomes away from the long term self-interest of member states can we speak of a serious challenge to an intergovernmentalist view" (emphasis in original). In response, we expect what intergovernmentalism is not capable of explaining, namely that, as integration proceeds, the Court and the Commission will routinely produce rules (policy outcomes) that would not have been adopted by governments in the Council of Ministers, or in summitry. And we argue that the long-term interests of member-state governments will be increasingly biased toward the long-term interest of transnational society, those who have the most to gain from supranational governments.

Note

1. We recognize the important distinctions between "European Community" and "European Union." However, since most of the activities we refer to in this chapter occur under the aegis of the European Community, in this chapter we consistently use "EC" and "European Community."

25

The Study of the European Community: The Challenge to Comparative Politics

Simon Hix

The revival of integration in the 1980s and 1990s inspired some scholars to start thinking of the EU as a single polity. These scholars not only rejected intergovernmentalism as an explanation for post-Maastricht developments, they also began to question the applicability of theories of international relations to the European Union. In their view, politics in the EU had moved beyond relations between states into the realm of politics within a single state.

Simon Hix (London School of Economics and Political Science) did not think the European Union (he uses "Community") constituted a single state, but he did believe it had developed to the point where comparative politics approaches had become more appropriate for studying its "politics." In this 1994 article, Hix discussed each of the important international relations theories used to explain integration (not reprinted here), then he compared them with approaches aimed at understanding politics in single states. He concluded that international relations approaches were still appropriate for explaining behavior in areas where "member states remain sovereign," but that comparative politics approaches would yield greater insights in most issue areas.

The article was a bold call to treat the European Union as though it were a domestic polity that could be compared to other national political systems, most particularly the United States. Reactions to Hix largely depended on perceptions of the nature of the EU. Was it an international organization composed of sovereign states, a federal state with a domestic polity, or was it sui generis—like no other polity in history? Each answer required entirely different explanatory and methodological approaches.

Reprinted from *West European Politics* 17, no. 1 (1994): 1–30. Copyright 1994 by Frank Cass. Reprinted by permission of the publisher, Taylor and Francis Ltd., www.tandfonline.com. Notes omitted.

Although the political system of the European Community (EC) may only be "part formed" and largely *sui generis*, politics in the EC is not inherently different to the practice of government in any democratic system. As in all modern polities, EC "politics" is dominated by questions of representation and participation, the distribution and allocation of resources, and political and administrative efficiency. To study the connection between political "inputs" and "outputs" on these issues, one would naturally use the discourse of "comparative politics"—the subfield of political science concerned with the study of the "internal" politics of "political systems."

Since its birth in the 1950s, however, the EC has mainly been studied as an example of the supranational integration of, or intergovernmental cooperation between, (previously) sovereign nation-states. It was thus appropriate that the traditional analysis of the EC used the discourse of International Relations (IR). However, now that the EC is more than an "international organization," theories of international politics are of limited use for studying the "internal" politics of the Community. For example, from an IR perspective political conflict in the EC is primarily along a single dimension; where actors (be they nation-states in the Realist approach, or interest groups in the Pluralist approach) either support or oppose further supranational integration. As the "political" nature of the EC develops, however, there is also conflict over questions of allocation and distribution of resources. On these socioeconomic issues, political competition is along a fundamentally different dimension, which in comparative political terms is classically referred to as the "Left-Right." However, this limitation of the IR approach is not by itself sufficient to claim the superiority of a "comparative" approach to the EC. A more rigorous investigation needs to be undertaken.

. . .

Comparative Politics Paradigms and EC Politics

The field of comparative politics has only recently woken up to the possibility of applying its theories and principles to political behavior and action in the Community. . . . However, direct applications of comparative politics to the EC remain few and far between. Hence, although this section will involve an analysis of these recent approaches, it will also include a discussion of possible further applications within the comparative politics paradigms for the study of EC politics.

Pluralist Approaches

Like pluralist theories in international relations, pluralism in comparative politics is an agent-biased paradigm, which assumes that political outcomes in a democratic system are shaped by competing economic and social interests. Evolving from the "group theories" of the 1950s, the interest group process is a main component of pluralist approaches in both fields. Politics for most citizens is believed to be a "remote, alien and unrewarding activity." Hence, issues must be of great personal importance when individuals group together in an attempt to influence the political process. Moreover, the pluralist "ideal type" is when interest groups are multiple, voluntary, competitive, non-hierarchically ordered, self-determined, not recognized or subsidized by the state, not monopolistic, and internally democratic. Although there are few explicit pluralist approaches to the EC in the field of comparative politics, several authors claim that interest aggregation and articulation in the Community is close to this ideal type.

Comparative pluralist interpretations of the EC argue that the decision-making process in the Community is more like the United States in the 1960s than the (neocorporatist) European tradition. The understaffing of most Commission Directorates and the multiple channels of access to EC decision making—because the same draft directive is dealt with in several divisions in the Commission, in several committees of the European Parliament (EP), as well as in COREPER and the Council of Ministers—give organized interests at the European level more opportunity to be heard than in the more corporatist national systems where decision making is traditionally controlled by the governing parties and the "coopted" peak organizations of business and labor. Moreover, business groups, who are primarily interested in the regulation of their products or services in the market place, have been motivated to organize at the European level by the Single Market program which passed such market regulation from the national governments to the EC. Consequently, since the mid-1980s there has been a rapid growth of "lobbying" in the Community, and the number of officially recognized interest groups [European Interest Groups (EIGs)] has risen from approximately 500 in 1985 to over 1,500 by 1990.

However, this vision of the EC as a pluralist dream is slightly misleading. As with the criticism of the pluralist analysis of US politics, there is little "countervailing power" in the Community. The decision-making process is fragmented into specific interest areas, and each area is controlled by "special interest coalitions." The access of all interest groups to EC policy channels is far from equal, despite the Commission policy of subsidizing non-economic interests. Moreover, because of the high organizational costs of establishing a pan-European group, the larger economic interests (such as in the agriculture and petrochemicals sectors) are able to lobby the Commission far more effectively than the "counter" interests (such as consumer or environment groups). Hence, although there is multiple and open access for organized interests in the Community, the EC is perhaps closer to American "Post-pluralism," where decision makers are no longer neutral arbiters but proactively take account of countervailing interests; or even "neocorporatism," where there is a combination of pluralist articulation and special representation for the "two sides of industry" (as in the special status of UNICE [Union of Industrial and Employers' Confederation of Europe] and the ETUC [European Trade Union Confederation] in the development of legislation under the Social Charter).

However, although the comparative politics pluralist approaches to the EC may be at a primitive stage, they have begun to make an important contribution to the analysis of the political process in the Community. Moreover, from the same ontological and methodological assumptions as the international relations pluralist theories, the comparative politics approaches shed light on the nature of decision making at the European level, rather than on the importance of organized interests for the development of national positions towards integration. If the Community is treated as a system of government decision making, the substantial comparative literature on interest organization and representation can be applied to politics in the EC. In contrast, in analyzing the power of interest groups in the EC, the international relations pluralist approaches, such as neofunctionalism, are constrained by their discourse which does not use such theoretical tools as "countervailing power," "interest group stasis," "the theory of plural elites," or "corporatist tripartitism."

Rational Choice Approaches

As with the realist theories in international relations, rational choice approaches treat actors as fundamentally self-interested. Rational choice also assumes, however, a logical connection between rationally ordered preferences (ends) and rationally evaluated behavior (means). By assuming rationality, the observer can use techniques, such as decision-theory or game theory, to understand individual behavior when faced with uncertainty. This can either be "natural" uncertainty, arising from environmental factors, or "strategic" uncertainty, when facing other actors. The rational choice modeler does not claim that when making a decision an actor actually goes through the same methodological (and often mathematical) processes as the observer, but simply that the actor behaves "as if" she is following the same procedures. Unlike the realist approaches in international relations, however, there have been relatively few rational choice applications to the EC.

Consciously attempting to "move beyond the approaches prevalent in the international relations literature on cooperation," Garrett employs a game-theoretical framework for understanding the EC decision to adopt the internal market program. Apart from arguing that his approach is more rigorous, Garrett also criticizes the realist approaches to the EC for wrongly assuming "that the institutions associated with international cooperation have little impact on the political structure of the international system and represent little or no challenge to the sovereignty of the nation-states." Using techniques from spatial theories of competition, Garrett's two main conclusions are that: first, rather than the internal market being a simple question of transactions costs economics, a specific set of political and economic principles were chosen from many possible "Pareto-nearing outcomes" because of "institutional and ideological constraints"; and, second, despite the final agreement being by unanimity, the outcome accorded closely to the wishes of the more powerful member states.

Other rational choice approaches appear to confirm this second conclusion. Utilizing the Shapley-Shubik and Banzhaf indices of voting power, Herne and Nurmi find that the larger member states are clearly dominant in the Council of Ministers, regardless of whether simple majority, qualified majority or unanimity voting procedures are used; and in negotiations with the European Parliament, Tsebelis also finds that the outcome is closer to the preferences of the larger member states. However, although these findings appear to confirm the qualitative findings of the realist approaches in international relations, rational choice approaches to the EC have suggested some interesting developments that have not been highlighted by the IR theories. For example, rational choice approaches have also illustrated the importance of ideology in the internal market negotiations, that the EP is a "conditional agenda setter," and that there is an integral link between party competition in the national and EC arenas.

Hence, from the same basic assumptions as the realist approaches in international relations, the few rational choice approaches to the EC have already begun to discover some important features of EC decision making. As with all the comparative politics approaches, the rational choice theorists accept the EC system as a "given" and ask questions about the nature of political behavior "within," and between, the EC's institutional settings. However, even the rational choice approaches have their limitations. First, like the realists, the rational choice applications tend to regard the member states as unitary actors, with "hierarchically-ordered" and "single-peaked" preferences. Second, and also like the realist approaches, they tend to view political conflict in the EC as single-dimensional, with the actors (be they the member states, the EC institutions themselves, or the parties in the European Parliament) positioned on a single continuum between "more" and "less" integration. Even though Garrett highlights the importance of economic ideology, he bases his spatial analysis of the internal market negotiations on the single "integration" continuum. . . .

Hence, although rational choice approaches to the EC have produced fruitful observations . . . they fail to formally integrate internal national competition or institutional and ideological considerations into their models. As the number of rational choice approaches to the EC increases, however, more complex models of decision making in the EC are likely to evolve. We may thus see a rational choice analysis of EC politics which is multi-dimensional, structurally constrained, and ideological oriented. At present, however, and without the technical ability of the public choice theorists, these issues may also be incorporated into non-rational choice comparative approaches to the EC—within the sociological and institutional paradigms.

Sociological Approaches

As with the structural approaches in international relations, there are few (if any!) direct sociological approaches to the EC. By treating the EC as a "political system," however, one is implicitly making reference to the sociologically derived "systems theories" of politics. Developing his approach from Parsons' and Easton's theories, Almond states, "the sociological approach . . . suggests how the application of certain sociological and anthropological concepts may facilitate systematic comparison among the major types of political systems." This sociological approach thus laid the foundations for the study of the different elements and the development of political systems, much of which can be used in the analysis of the EC. For example, an approach derived from Parsons and Almond, which can be applied to the dimensions of political conflict in the EC, is the Lipset and Rokkan theory of nation-building. First, however, there is one theory which explicitly applies a sociological approach to EC politics.

Starting from the assumption that the EC has "developed beyond the role of a traditional international organization," Shackleton asks: "What kind of institution or set of institutions is the European Community?" Using "cultural theory," from political sociology, there are two dimensions of the relationship between the individual and the political system: "group," the extent to which an individual is incorporated into bounded units; and "grid," the degree to which an individual's life is circumscribed by externally imposed restrictions. Hence, in the EC, "group" refers to the degree of supranational integration, whereas "grid" refers to the degree of central regulation. The interaction of these two dimensions thus produces four possible "ways of life": hierarchical, fatalistic, egalitarian, and individualistic. Shackleton hence concludes that the present sociological and institutional structure of the EC means that it is closest to the "egalitarian" (low regulation and high integration) way of life; but there is also an inherent tension between two other ways of life—the "hierarchical" and "individualistic." More relevant to this research, however, cultural theory also suggests that there are inherently two types of political conflict in the EC: "group conflict," between supranational centralization and national independence (a pro- and anti-integration dimension); and "grid conflict," between economic and social regulation and deregulation (an ideological dimension).

The existence of these two fundamental dimensions of conflict in the EC is also implied by the application of the sociological theories of nation-building to the development of the EC. From the sociological assumptions of Talcott Parsons' "theory of action," Lipset and Rokkan proposed a model of nation-building to explain the matrix of social and political "cleavages" in contemporary political systems. The cleavages arise from dichotomous conflicts created by "critical junctures" in the historical development of each system. For example, the National Revolution produced Church versus State and center versus periphery conflicts, and the Industrial Revolution produced landed versus urban and middle-class versus working-class conflicts. However, whereas center-periphery and church-state conflicts do not exist in every system because of different national revolution experiences, socioeconomic conflicts are prevalent in all Western nations because of the common experience of industrialization and the prevalence of the capitalist system of economic exchange.

Applying cultural theory and the Lipset-Rokkan thesis to the EC system, therefore, there are two fundamental lines of conflict produced by two separate critical junctures. Moreover, because cultural theory and Lipset and Rokkan both derive their models from the Parsonian theory of socialization, it is not a coincidence that Lipset and Rokkan's "territorial-cultural" and "functional" cleavage dimensions correspond closely to cultural theory's "group" and "grid" conflicts, respectively. Hence, first, as with the process of national integration, supranational integration produces a center versus periphery cleavage, between national-interest and European-interest. This cleavage is thus manifest in the conflict between pressures for further supranational integration and the desire to preserve national sovereignty. Second, the industrial revolution produces a socioeconomic or Left-Right cleavage. The movement from an agrarian to an industrial economy introduces conflicts between more or less state intervention in the market and more or less redistribution. Hence, this Left-Right cleavage is manifest at the European level with the "politicization" of the EC, as decisions on questions of market regulation (such as in the Single Market program) and redistribution (social and regional policies) begin to be taken at the supranational level.

.   .   .

"Old" and "New" Institutional Approaches

The study of political institutions has always been a central pillar of comparative politics. Although the traditional legal-formal institutional approaches were abandoned for more sophisticated sociological and behavioral methods in the 1950s, 60s and 70s, there has recently been a re-emphasis of the importance of institutions for structuring individual behavior. In the comparative analysis of the EC one also finds these "old" and "new" institutional approaches.

Although contemporary, most analyses of the EC within comparative constitutional law and comparative public law are "old" institutional approaches because of their emphasis on formality and objectivity. Illustrating "the difference between the political (traditional IR perspective) and legal assessment of the Community," juridical approaches make a distinction between the conventional international treaty elements of EC law and the novel and unprecedented "supranational" elements of the Community System. Moreover, scholars of EC law point out that the European Court of Justice (ECJ) has contributed significantly to the integration process, and illustrate how the Community has begun to develop a "constitution." Thus, the main elements of the EC's constitution are "the undisputed supremacy clause," which places EC law above national law in a similar fashion to a federal constitution; the direct effect of EC regulations and the immediate enforceability of certain directives; the growing case law rights of EC "citizens"; and the EC's powers of judicial review of all other organs of the Community. As a result, the political system of the EC already rests on a fairly firm legal base which contains elements of administrative and judicial review and a division of competences similar to those in a federal constitution.

However, there are also "new" institutional approaches to the EC, which use contemporary decision-making theories, and compare the EC's institutional rules and environment to classic models of government. Like the legal approaches, one group of these neoinstitutionalists argues that the EC can be analyzed using the concept of federalism. However, in this approach, "federalism" does not have to imply that the EC is an explicit federation of states. Furthermore, the Community does not fit comfortably into the traditional Anglo-American typologies of federal systems where the clarity of the division of authority between the central government and the constituent units is regarded as a crucial indicator of the degree of federalism. The complexity of the EC system of "mixed" and "shared" competences implies that tasks do not simply have to be *either* in the hands of the central organs *or* in the hands of the constituent governments in perpetuity. Thus, the new institutionalists prefer to use the concepts of "subsidiarity" and "cooperative federalism," where the majority of competences are "concurrent," to describe decision making in the EC. For example, in the EC, as in Germany and Switzerland, the majority of (concurrent) decisions display elements of both intergovernmentalism and supranationalism; hence, "a mixed national/community system . . . in which the emphasis is placed on the 'pooling of sovereignties.'"

A second new institutionalist approach to the EC suggests that the Community is a "consociational" democracy. The concept of consociational democ-

racy was first proposed to illustrate how, in contradiction of Almond's sociological typology of comparative systems, deeply divided (segmented) societies
can remain stable as a result of behavior and rules that produce "elite accommodation." Consequently, there are features of a consociational democracy: a
pillarized society, elite predominance, a "cartel of elites," segmental autonomy,
proportionality, minority veto, and oversized coalitions—all of which exist in
the EC. First, the EC is a "territorially" pillarized system because individual
interaction and loyalty is primarily focused within the EC nation-states. Second, elites predominate within their "pillars" because the national governments
control the allocation of resources and maintain a monopoly over the forces of
coercion within the national territory. Third, there is a "cartel of elites" at the
European level because of the elite/governmental nature of EC decision making and because of the rules to ensure elite accommodation. Fourth, in the EC
the desire of governments to protect their national sovereignty is the equivalent
of segmental autonomy within territorially pillarized federal states. Fifth, proportionality is ensured in the EC in the systems of representation in the Council of Ministers and the European Parliament, in the allocation of jobs in the
institutions' administrations, and in the allocation of EC resources. Sixth,
mutual veto is guaranteed in the EC by the Luxembourg Compromise, which
allows a member state to exercise a veto if there is a threat to a "vital national
interest." Finally, oversized coalitions exist because of the qualified majority
voting in the Council of Ministers and the majority requirements in the EP,
which facilitates a *de jure* Socialist-Christian Democrat coalition.

As a result, the institutional approaches to the EC have illustrated how
comparative politics types can be beneficially used to analyze the institutional features of the Community system. In contrast to the international
relations institutional approaches, the comparative approaches thus seek
less to *prescribe* an institutional structure than to *describe* the decision-
making environment as it stands at the present time. Moreover, the observation that the EC displays elements of "cooperative federalism" and
"consociational democracy" has important implications for the analysis of
political conflict in the Community. It is these institutional features that
organize the behavior of the actors, and structure the conflict. Describing
the EC in these terms thus allows further comparisons to be drawn from
politics in other federally organized and territorially pillarized systems.

In contrast to IR approaches to EC politics, a comparative analysis thus
suggests that there are two fundamental dimensions of politics in the Community. First, there is the national-supranational dimension highlighted by
the pluralist and realist approaches in international relations, and which is
used in rational choice approaches to the EC. However, sociological
approaches to the Community illustrate that there is also a socioeconomic
conflict, which is present ("latent") in all European systems because of the
common problems involved in governing a capitalist economy. The Lipset-
Rokkan model also suggests, however, that the Left-Right dimension

emerges (is "manifest") in the EC only when basic socioeconomic issues are tackled at the European level. This thus reinforces the intuitive argument that "party-political divisions" will only exist at the EC level as a result of the "politicization" of the Community.

However, the interaction between these two dimensions is also dependent upon the institutional environment in the EC—the constraints inherent in "cooperative federalism" and "consociationalism." In consociational systems where the "pillars" are not based on class divisions, the Left-Right conflict is often subsidiary (or only equal) to the conflict between the pillars, which may be a territorial, linguistic or religious cleavage. Furthermore, the institution of elite accommodation works to "control" the development of conflicts that cut across (and thus undermine) the internal cohesion of the pillars. In a similar way, the institution of federalism limits the salience of ideological conflicts, and restricts the evolution of party structures. Nevertheless, in the "European" tradition of federalism, the ideological tradition of the *Parteienstaat* is often stronger than the institution of the *Bundestaat*. Despite these constraints, therefore, on Left-Right issues (such as the Social Charter) party-political positions may be better indicators of EC policy-outcomes than the "national interests" of the governments.

Conclusion—A Call for Comparativist Research

Consequently, comparing the comparative politics and international relations approaches derived from the same ontological and methodological assumptions suggests that the comparative politics paradigms often produce more profitable insights for the study of EC "politics." Whereas IR pluralist theories concentrate on the attitudes of actors towards "integration," "comparative" pluralist approaches describe the nature of interest representation and intermediation in the Community. Furthermore, whereas realist and rational choice approaches both regard actors as aligned on a single "independence-integration" continuum, rational choice models also determine the relative strength of each actor and illustrate the importance of the institutional mechanisms. Moreover, whereas structuralist theories simply regard EC politics as the interaction of the West European states' attempts to come to terms with global changes, sociological theories provide a framework for understanding the EC as a "political system." Finally, whereas IR institutional approaches prescribe a "politics-free" supranational system, the comparative institutional approaches use traditional concepts to describe the shape of the EC's institutional structures and environment.

The international relations approaches may be appropriate for the study of European *integration*. However, comparative politics approaches are more appropriate for the analysis of European Community *politics*. As sub-fields of the same discipline (political science), international relations and comparative politics have a certain amount of literature in common. However, because they have focused on diametrically opposed areas of the discipline—the politics "among" against the politics "within" nations—the academic discourse of IR scholars and comparativists has grown apart as the fields have matured. Consequently, in their application to the EC, it is natural that international relations and comparative politics theories are applicable for different aspects of the EC system. Hence in areas where the EC member states remain sovereign, international relations theories of "cooperation" may still produce accurate and parsimonious explanations. However, where decisions are taken which involve crosscutting party-political and national interests, decision and coalition theories from comparative politics are likely to have a higher explanatory value. Moreover, because of the focus of the comparative literature, this will probably be true for most areas of EC politics: from general questions such as the connection between political inputs and outputs, or the relationship between the EC institutions, to specific matters such as the representation of territorial and functional interests, or the choice of voting procedures.

Only recently, however, has a textbook on EC politics appeared which attempts to claim the study of the "internal" politics of the Community for the field of comparative politics. In the introduction to this groundbreaking collection of essays, Sbragia argues that "thinking about the Community comparatively will prove to be more fruitful analytically than simply describing the Community as 'unique' and consequently analyzing it exclusively on its own terms. Theories, concepts, and knowledge drawn from the study of other polities can in fact be illuminating when applied to the study of the Community." The above discussion appears to support this argument. As more academics and students become interested in the significance and functioning of the European Community the time is right for "comparativists" to take up their pens and challenge the dominance of the international approaches.

26

Multi-Level Governance
in the European Union

Liesbet Hooghe and Gary Marks

For some in the late 1990s, the European Union at the end of the century looked less and less like a system of cooperating nation-states and more and more like a "domestic" political system, albeit with some rather unique characteristics (see Chapter 25). Many students of the EU began to speak of European "governance" as a special political phenomenon that the stale supranational-versus-intergovernmental debate could not address.

Liesbet Hooghe and Gary Marks (both of the University of North Carolina at Chapel Hill) were two early advocates of a governance approach. They did not wholly abandon the supranational-intergovernmental debate because to proceed they had to first prove that the EU was not the result of normal international relations, as Moravcsik maintained (see Chapter 23), but was in fact a new domestic polity. They drew a very stark contrast between "state-centric" (intergovernmentalist) and "multilevel governance" models of EU decisionmaking and marshaled considerable evidence to demonstrate that member states had lost individual and collective control over the European decisionmaking process. Other supranationalists had covered much of this ground in the 1990s, but the unique contribution made by Hooghe and Marks was their description of what had taken the place of state-centric decisionmaking. In their view, European governance was now dominated by a complex web of interconnected institutions at the supranational, national, and subnational levels of government. National governments could no longer automatically get their way; they could now be outvoted in the Council of Ministers, stymied by their electorates, or bypassed by their own local governments, interest groups, and executive bureaucracies. "Multilevel governance" had opened up opportunities for public and private interests of all kinds to enter the policymaking process, thus gently, almost imperceptibly, undermining state sovereignty.

Reprinted with permission from *Multi-Level Governance and European Integration* by Liesbet Hooghe and Gary Marks (Lanham, MD: Rowman and Littlefield Publishers, 2001), pp. 1–29. Notes omitted.

The multilevel governance approach was more descriptive than theoretical, but it changed the way many scholars looked at the EU and it encouraged new lines of inquiry, which have matured in the contemporary period.

Developments in the European Union (EU) over the last two decades have revived debate about the consequences of European integration for the autonomy and authority of the state in Europe. The scope and depth of policy making at the EU level have increased immensely. The European Union completed the internal market on schedule in 1993, and eleven of the fifteen member states formed an economic and monetary union (EMU) in 1999, with a European central bank and a single currency, the euro. These policy-making reforms have been accompanied by basic changes in European decision making. The Single European Act (1986), which reduced nontariff barriers, also established qualified majority voting in the Council of Ministers and significantly increased the power of the European Parliament. The Maastricht Treaty (1993) increased the scope of qualified majority voting in the Council and introduced a codecision procedure giving the European Parliament a veto on certain types of legislation. The Treaty of Amsterdam (1999) extended codecision to most areas of policy making in the European Community, except for EMU.

Our aim in this chapter is to take stock of these developments. What do they mean for the political architecture of Europe? Do these developments consolidate national states or do they weaken them? If they weaken them, what kind of political order is emerging? These are large and complex questions, and we do not imagine that we can settle them once and for all. Our strategy is to pose two basic alternative conceptions—state-centric governance and multi-level governance—as distinctly as possible and then evaluate their validity by examining the European policy process.

The core presumption of state-centric governance is that European integration does not challenge the autonomy of national states. State-centrists contend that state sovereignty is preserved or even strengthened through EU governments. No government has to integrate more than it wishes because bargains rest on the lowest common denominator of the participating member states. In this model, supranational actors exist to aid member states, to facilitate agreements by providing information that would not otherwise be so readily available. Policy outcomes reflect the interests and relative power of national governments. Supranational actors exercise little independent effect.

An alternative view is that European integration is a polity-creating process in which authority and policy making influence are shared across multiple levels of government—subnational, national, and supranational. While national governments are formidable participants in EU policy making, control has slipped away from them to supranational institutions. States have lost some of their former authoritative control over individuals in their respective territories. In short, the locus of political control has changed. Individual state sovereignty is diluted in the EU by collective decision making among national governments and by the autonomous role of the European Parliament, the European Commission, the European Court of Justice, and the European Central Bank.

We make this argument in this chapter along two tracks. First, we analyze the variety of conditions under which national governments will voluntarily or involuntarily lose their grip on power. Second, we examine policy making in the EU across its different stages, evaluating the validity of contending state-centric and multi-level models of European governance.

Two Models of the European Union

The models that we outline below are drawn from a large and diverse body of work on the European Union, though they are elaborated in different ways by different authors. Our aim here is not to replicate the ideas of any particular writer, but to set out the basic elements that underlie contending views of the EU so that we may evaluate their validity.

The core ideas of the *state-centric model* are put forward by several authors, most of whom call themselves intergovernmentalists [Chapter 23]. This model poses states (or, more precisely, national governments) as ultimate decision makers, devolving limited authority to supranational institutions to achieve specific policy goals. Decision making in the EU is determined by bargaining among national governments. To the extent that supranational institutions arise, they serve the ultimate goals of national governments. The state-centric model does not maintain that policy making is determined by national governments in every detail, only that the overall direction of policy making is consistent with state control. States may be well served by creating a judiciary, for example, that allows them to enforce collective agreements, or a bureaucracy that implements those agreements, but such institutions are not autonomous supranational agents. Rather, they have limited powers to achieve state-oriented collective goods.

EU decisions, according to the state-centric model, reflect the lowest common denominator among national government positions. Although national governments decide jointly, they are not compelled to swallow policies they find unacceptable because decision making on important issues operates on the basis of unanimity. This allows states to maintain individual as well as collective control over outcomes. While some governments are not able to integrate as much as they would wish, none is forced into deeper collaboration than it really wants.

State decision making in this model does not exist in a political vacuum. In this respect, the state-centric model takes issue with realist conceptions of international relations, which focus on relations among unitary state actors. National governments are located in the domestic political arena, and their negotiating positions are influenced by domestic political interests. But—and this is an important assumption—those arenas are discrete. That is to say, national decision makers respond to political pressures that are *nested* within each state. The fifteen national governments bargaining in the European arena are complemented by fifteen separate national arenas that provide the sole channel for domestic political interests at the European level. The core claim of the state-centric model is that policy making in the EU is determined primarily by national governments constrained by political interests nested within autonomous national arenas.

One can envision several alternative models to this one. The one we present here, which we describe as *multi-level governance*, is drawn from several sources. Once again, our aim is not to reiterate any one scholar's perspective, but to elaborate essential elements of a model drawn from several strands of writing, which makes the case that European integration has weakened the state.

The multi-level governance model does not reject the view that national governments and national arenas are important, or that these remain the most important pieces of the European puzzle. However, when one asserts that the state no longer monopolizes European-level policy making or the aggregation of domestic interests, a very different polity comes into focus. First, according to the multi-level governance model, decision-making competencies are shared by actors at different levels rather than monopolized by national governments. That is to say, supranational institutions—above all, the European Parliament, the European Commission, and the European Court—have independent influence in policy making that cannot be derived from their role as agents of national executives. National governments play an important role but, according to the multi-level governance model, one must analyze the independent role of European-level actors to explain European policy making.

Second, collective decision making among states involves a significant loss of control for individual national governments. Lowest common denominator outcomes are available only on a subset of EU decisions, mainly those concerning the scope of integration. Decisions concerning rules to be enforced across the EU (e.g., harmonizing regulation of product standards, labor conditions, etc.) have a zero-sum character and necessarily involve gains or losses for individual states.

Third, political arenas are interconnected rather than nested. While national arenas remain important arenas for the formation of national government preferences, the multi-level governance model rejects the view that subnational actors are nested exclusively within them. Instead, subnational actors operate in both national and supranational arenas, creating transnational associations in the process. National governments do not monopolize links between domestic and European actors. In this perspective, complex interrelationships in domestic politics do not stop at the national state but extend to the European level. The separation between domestic and international politics, which lies at the heart of the state-centric model, is rejected by the multi-level governance model. National governments are an integral and powerful part of the EU, but they no longer provide the sole interface between supranational and subnational arenas, and they share, rather than monopolize, control over many activities that take place in their respective territories.

From State-Centric to Multi-Level Governance

Has national government control over EU decision making been compromised by European integration? In this section we argue that state sovereignty has been diminished by restrictions on the ability of individual governments to veto EU decisions and by the erosion of collective government control through the Council of Ministers.

Limits on Individual National Government Control

The most obvious constraint on the capacity of a national government to determine outcomes in the EU is the decision rule of qualified majority voting in the Council of Ministers for a range of issues from the internal market to trade, research policy, and the environment. In this respect, the European Union is clearly different from international regimes, such as the UN or World Trade Organization, in which majoritarian principles of decision making are confined to symbolic issues.

State-centrists have sought to blunt the theoretical implications of collective decision making in the Council of Ministers by making two arguments.

The first is that while national governments sacrifice some independent control by participating in collective decision making, they more than compensate for this by their increased ability to achieve the policy outcomes they want. Andrew Moravcsik has argued that collective decision making actually enhances state control because national governments will only agree to participate insofar as "policy coordination increases their control over domestic policy outcomes, permitting them to achieve goals that would not otherwise be possible." By participating in the European Union, national governments are able to provide policy outcomes, such as a cleaner environment, higher levels of economic growth, and so forth, that they could not provide on their own. But two entirely different conceptions of power are involved here, and it would be well to keep them separate.

On the one hand, power or political control may be conceptualized as control over persons. *A* has power over *B* to the extent that she can get *B* to do something he would not otherwise do. This is a zero-sum conception: if one actor gains power, another loses it. By contrast, power conceived as the ability to achieve desired outcomes entails power over nature in the broadest sense. According to this conception, I have power to the extent that I can do what I wish to do. A government that can achieve its goal of low inflation and high economic growth is, from this standpoint, more "powerful" than one that cannot.

The latter way of conceiving power is not "wrong," for concepts can be used in any way one wishes to use them. But it does confuse two things that are sensibly regarded as separate: who controls whom, and the ability of actors to achieve their goals. . . .

A second line of argument adopted by state-centrists is that majoritarianism in the Council of Ministers camouflages, rather than undermines, state sovereignty. They argue that treaty revisions and new policy initiatives remain subject to unanimity, and that the Luxembourg compromise gives national governments the power to veto any policy that contravenes their vital national interests. Ultimately, they emphasize a national government could pull out of the EU if it so wished.

However, the Luxembourg veto is available to national governments only under limited conditions, and even then, it is a relatively blunt weapon. As we detail below, the Luxembourg veto is restricted by the willingness of other national governments to tolerate its use.

From the standpoint of physical force, member states retain ultimate sovereignty by virtue of their continuing monopoly of the means of legitimate coercion within their respective territories. If a national government breaks its treaty commitments and pulls out of the EU, the EU itself has no armed forces with which to contest that decision. In this respect, the contrast between the European Union and a federal system, such as the United States, seems perfectly clear. In the last analysis, national states retain ultimate coercive control over their populations.

But monopoly of legitimate coercion tells us less and less about the realities of political, legal, and normative control in contemporary capitalist societies. A Weberian approach, focusing on the extent to which states are able to monopolize legitimate coercion, appears more useful for conceptualizing the emergence and consolidation of states from the twelfth century than for understanding changes in state sovereignty from the second half of the twentieth century. Although the EU does not possess supranational armed forces, a member state is constrained by the economic and political sanctions—and consequent political/economic dislocation—that it would almost certainly face if it revoked its treaty commitments and pulled out of the European Union.

Limits on Collective National Government Control

We have argued that national governments do not exert individual control over decision making in the Council of Ministers. State-centrists may counter that states still retain collective control over EU decision making through the Council of Ministers and the treaties.

In this section, we argue that neither the Council of Ministers nor the treaties give national governments full control over EU decision making. The Council is the most powerful institution in EU decision making, but it exists alongside a directly elected European Parliament (EP) that has a veto on legislation relating to a third of all treaty provisions. The power of the EP in the European political process has grown by leaps and bounds over the past twenty years, and collective national control of decision making has declined as a result.

The treaties are the main expression of national authority in the process of European integration. Because representatives of national governments are the only legally recognized signatories of the treaties, one may argue that state authority is enhanced in the process of treaty making. If a domestic group wishes to influence a clause of a formal EU treaty, it must adopt a state-centric strategy and focus its pressure on its national government.

To evaluate treaties as a vehicle for national government control, one needs to ask two questions: first, to what extent do national governments control the process of treaty negotiation and ratification; and second, to what extent do treaties determine European policy making?

National governments are the key actors in negotiating treaties, but since the tumultuous reception of the Maastricht Treaty in 1993, they have had to contend with the participation of many kinds of domestic actors. In Britain, opposition and back-bench Members of Parliament almost derailed the Treaty in the House of Commons. Just at a time when some observers were claiming that treaty making was strengthening national governments at the expense of parliaments, events in the United Kingdom were proving exactly the opposite. A Conservative government was held ransom by back-benchers, and a split developed within the party on the issue of European integration that fatally weakened the government during the remainder of its term and in the subsequent general election of 1997. In Germany, ratification of the Maastricht Treaty mobilized German regional governments who tried to block the Treaty in the constitutional court. In France, ratification was fought out in a popular referendum in September 1992, and the result was a hair's-breadth win for the government (51 percent in favor; 49 percent opposed). In each of these countries, and across the EU, public opinion was mobilized in ways that placed national governments on the defensive.

Tensions, and sometime outright splits, have arisen within major parties. The British Conservative party is deeply divided on the question of European monetary integration, as revealed in public squabbles and in a survey of MPs. In France, the Gaullist party split into two independent factions in the European election of 1999. In Germany, fissures are evident within the Christian Democratic party, and between the Christian Democrats and their Bavarian sister party, the Christian Social Union. These tensions are not random, but can be explained systematically in reference to party ideologies. . . .

So while it is true that national governments have a formal monopoly in making treaties, it is not at all clear that treaty making, or the process of European integration in general, has strengthened national governments against parliaments, regional governments, or public pressures.

To what extent do treaties allow national governments to determine institution building? The treaties are the ultimate legal documents of the European Union, so it may seem strange to pose the question. But a moment's thought suggests that the question is worth asking after all. To what extent are American, French, or German political institutions determined by their respective constitutions? Treaties, like constitutions, are frameworks that constrain, but do not determine, institutional outcomes. We would regard a study of American politics that focused exclusively on the development of the U.S. Constitution as strangely skewed. Treaties, like constitutions, are sensibly regarded as points of departure, not final destinations, in understanding the workings of a regime because they do not capture the way in which actors adapt to—and exploit—formal rules.

EU treaties have been reformed more frequently than most constitutions, and they lie closer to the ground of policy making. However, national government control is, to some extent, handcuffed by unanimity. Treaties have to surmount the highest conceivable decisional barrier: unanimous agreement among the principals. This not only makes innovation difficult but also makes it difficult for national governments to rein in institutions, as we discuss below.

The extent to which treaties constrain EU institutions is diminished because the treaties themselves tend to be vaguely written. The treaty-making process is heavily biased towards diffuse agreements that avoid contentious issues and allow politicians from all countries and of all ideological stripes to claim success at the bargaining table. The principals in treaty negotiations are not simply representatives of national preferences but are flesh and blood politicians who have private preferences that include a desire to perform well at the next general election. In this respect, the principals sitting around the European bargaining table, no matter how zero-sum their preferences, have a collective desire to agree to something so that the negotiation itself is not perceived as a failure. Ambiguity can serve rational political purposes. When individual or collective national control bumps up against electoral considerations, we expect that electoral considerations will usually emerge the winner.

These considerations suggest that the control of national governments over EU policies and institutions is highly imperfect. National governments no longer monopolize EU decision making, partly because the European

Parliament has become a co-legislator over much EU policy; increased public scrutiny of EU decision making increases the weight of public opinion on government policy; and national governments have limited control over supranational agents, such as the European Commission and the European Court of Justice. We examine these in turn.

European Parliament. The empowerment of an autonomous and directly elected Parliament over the past two decades presents a fundamental problem for accounts that conceive authority as delegated or pooled by member states. It seems forced to conceive the Parliament as an agent designed by national governments to realize their preferences. The EP increases, rather than reduces, transaction costs of decision making in the EU. The development of the EP cannot be explained as a functional response on the part of national governments to problems of intergovernmental bargaining. On the contrary, the EP is better explained in terms of the response of national governments to domestic pressures for greater democratic accountability in the European Union.

The EP does not fit well into an intergovernmental account of European integration. One line of response is that while Parliament has been strengthened, this has not been at the expense of other institutions. Andrew Moravcsik writes that the cooperation procedure "increased the participation of the Parliament without infringing on the formal powers of either the Commission or the Council." As we have noted above, the notion that power can be supplied as a normal good, so some people can have a bit more without anyone having less, confuses political power with ability. The rules comprising the basic governing institutions of the EU are interwoven, as we explain in the following section, so that a reform of one involves change for all. In the case of the cooperation procedure adopted in 1986, the increase in the formal power of the European Parliament came mainly at the expense of the Council of Ministers. The EP could offer amendments to certain legislation that could only be rejected by the Council if it did so unanimously. Formal theorists of EU rules agree with almost all participants and observers that this was an important increase in the EP's authority. While there has been disagreement about the relative consequences of cooperation and codecision (adopted in 1993), it is plain that the combined effect of these reforms has been to significantly strengthen the Parliament.

It is true that the European Parliament is elected nationally and can be conceived as a forum "in which national representatives, generally organized in political parties, can influence the legislative process." Members of the European Parliament, like those in the United States and most other democracies, represent those living in particular territories, but they do not represent the governments of those territories. Most members have interests and ideologies that may or may not lead them to preserve the authority of central governments, and these preferences are usually consistent with the political party to which they owe their election. Party membership is often a more powerful influence on parliamentarians' behavior and attitudes than country of origin.

The emergence of the European Parliament as a powerful European player has altered the institutional balance in the European Union, as we argue in detail below. The authoritative competences of the European Parliament are more narrowly circumscribed than those of the Council, but the Parliament is nonetheless a weighty player. As a result, national governments cannot impose their collective will in many areas of policy making.

Public scrutiny. EU decision making has come under greater public scrutiny. Prior to the Single European Act, European integration was essentially a technocratic process in which national governments coordinated around limited policy goals. European integration was pragmatically oriented, rather than politicized, and national governments dominated decision making to the virtual exclusion of other domestic actors. On the occasions when conflict did flare up—usually in the form of collective protest by farmers, coal miners, or steelworkers—national governments sought to buy off opposition through sectorial deals. EU bargaining was largely insulated from public pressures.

This changed with the introduction of the single market in the mid-1980s. As the reach of European policy making broadened, and as the stakes in most issue areas grew, so domestic groups were drawn directly into the European arena. Such mobilization has created new linkages between supranational institutions and subnational groups, and it has induced citizens with similar interests or ideological convictions to organize transnationally. EU decision making is no longer insulated from the kind of political competition that has characterized democratic politics in the member states.

In the pre-Maastricht era, treaty ratification was dominated by national governments through party control of their national legislatures. Not only did they determine the content of treaties but they could be reasonably confident that those treaties would be accepted in their respective domestic arenas. The Maastricht Treaty would change all that. The rejection of the Maastricht Treaty in June 1992 by Danish citizens sent a shock wave through European elites, and their anxiety was enhanced by a near-replay in the French referendum of September 1992. Moreover, public opinion polls indicated that German and British voters too might have rejected the Treaty if they had been given the opportunity. The fact that the Danes reversed their decision a year later did not put to rest fears that the process was out of control. Public scrutiny has changed the rules of the game of treaty negotiation. The action has shifted from national governments and technocrats in semi-isolation to domestic politics in the broad and usual sense: party programs, electoral competition, parliamentary debates and votes, public opinion polls, and public referenda.

Principal-agent dynamics. Even if national governments operated in a world without a European Parliament and without public pressures, it is likely that EU decisions would only imperfectly reflect the preferences of national governments. As governments have agreed to collaborate on more and more issues in the EU arena, so they have turned to supranational agents, particularly the European Commission and the European Court of Justice, to make collaboration work, and by so doing they risk diluting their control over decision making.

Principal-agent theory builds on the insight that principals—national governments, in this case—are not able to plan for all possible future ambiguities and sources of contention, and so they create agents—such as the European Commission and the European Court of Justice—to ensure compliance to interstate agreements and adapt them to changing circumstances. According to this line of theorizing, principals exert control over agents by creating the necessary incentives. If a principal discovers that an agent is not acting in the desired way, the principal can fire the agent or change the incentives.

Scholars who have applied principal-agent theory to American political institutions have found that the incentives available to principals are often ineffective. There are grounds for believing that limits on principal control in the EU are particularly severe.

Multiple principals. In the European Union there are as many principals as there are member states. Each has a veto over basic institutional change. This vastly complicates principal control. The more hands there are on the steering wheel, the less control any driver will have. The consequences of this in the EU are particularly severe because national governments have had widely different preferences concerning supranational agents.

As noted earlier, one consequence of multiple contending principals in the EU is that the treaties provide ample room for interpretation. The treaties are hammered out in interstate negotiations, in which there is a powerful incentive to allow ambiguity on points of contention so that each government can claim success in representing national interests.

The basic treaties of the EU have legitimated Commission initiatives in several policy areas, yet they are vague enough to give the Commission wide latitude in designing institutions. This has been described as a "treaty base game" in which the Commission legitimates its preferences by referring to a prior treaty commitment. This was the case in structural (or cohesion) policy, which, in the wake of the Single European Act, was transformed by the

Commission from a straightforward side payment transferring money from richer to poorer countries to an interventionist instrument of regional policy.

The European Court of Justice (ECJ) does not merely act as an agent in adapting member state agreements to new contingencies. Through its rulings, it has engineered institutional changes that escape, and transcend, treaty norms. Supranational authority in the ECJ deepened from the 1960s, with the establishment of principles of supremacy and direct effect, as a result of Court rulings, not because of treaty language. The constitutionalization of EU treaties is the product of Court activism, not of national government preferences.

Hurdles to change. Unanimity is a double-edged sword for supranational institutions in the EU. It raises the bar for any kind of major institutional change in the EU, whether it empowers supranational institutions or reins them in. A supranational actor need only dent a united front of national governments in order to block change. For example, the Commission sidestepped an attempt by a powerful coalition of national governments, including the U.K., Germany, and France, to renationalize cohesion policy in 1993 because it managed to gain the support of just three small member states: Ireland, Portugal, and Belgium.

Informational symmetries. Principal control may be weakened if an agent has access to information or skills that are not available to the principal. As a small and thinly staffed organization, the Commission has only a fraction of the financial and human resources available to national governments, but its position at the center of a wide-ranging network including national governments, subnational governments, and interest groups gives it a unique informational base for independent influence on policy making.

Mutual distrust. It is the collective interest of national governments to enact certain common regulations, but each may be better off if others adhere to them while it defects. One response is to establish a court that can contain defection. Another is to have very detailed legislation. The reverse side of ambiguity in the treaties has been a willingness on the part of national governments to allow the Commission to formulate precise regulations on specific policies so as to straitjacket principals and reduce their scope for evasion. The Commission likes to legitimate its role in technocratic terms, as the hub of numerous specialized policy networks of technical experts designing detailed regulations.

.   .   .

Conclusion

Multi-level governance does not confront the sovereignty of states directly. Instead of being explicitly challenged, states in the European Union are being melded into a multi-level polity by their leaders and the actions of numerous subnational and supranational actors. State-centric theorists are right when they argue that national states are extremely powerful institutions that are capable of crushing direct threats to their existence. The institutional form of the state emerged because it proved a particularly effective means of systematically wielding violence, and it is difficult to imagine any generalized challenge along these lines. But this is not the only, or even the most important, issue facing the state. One does not have to argue that states are on the verge of political extinction to believe that their control of those living in their territories has significantly weakened.

It is not necessary to look far beyond the state itself to find reasons that might explain such an outcome. When we disaggregate the state into the people and organizations that shape its diverse institutions, it is clear that key decision makers, above all those directing the national government, may have goals that do not coincide with projecting national sovereignty into the future. The state is a means to a variety of ends, which are structured by party competition and interest group politics in a liberal democratic setting.

Even if national governments want to maintain national sovereignty, they are often not able to do so. A government can be outvoted because most decisions in the Council are now taken by qualified majority. Moreover, the national veto, the ultimate instrument of sovereignty, is constrained by the willingness of other national governments to tolerate its use. But the limits on sovereignty run deeper. Even collectively, national governments do not determine the European agenda because they are unable to control the supranational institutions they have created. The growing diversity of issues on the Council's agenda, the sheer number of national principals, the mistrust that exists among them, and the increased specialization of policy making have made the Council of Ministers reliant upon the Commission to set the agenda, forge compromises, and supervise compliance.

The most obvious blow to Council predominance has been dealt by the European Parliament, which has gained significant legislative power since the Single European Act. Indeed, the Parliament has become a principal in its own right. The Council, Commission, and Parliament interact within a legal order, which has been transformed into a supranational one through the innovative jurisprudence of the European Court of Justice.

Since the 1980s, these changes in EU decision making have crystallized into a multi-level polity. With its dispersed competencies, contending but interlocked institutions, and shifting agendas, multi-level governance opens multiple points of access for interests. In this process of mobilization and counter-mobilization, national governments no longer serve as the exclusive nexus between domestic politics and international relations. Direct connections are being forged among political actors in diverse political arenas.

Multi-level governance may not be a stable equilibrium. There is no explicit constitutional framework. There is little consensus on the goals of integration. As a result, the allocation of competencies between national and supranational actors is contested. It is worth noting that the European polity has made two U-turns in its short history. Overt supranationalist features of the original structure were overshadowed by the imposition of intergovernmental institutions in the 1960s and 1970s. From the 1980s, a system of multi-level governance arose, in which national governmental control became diluted by the activities of supranational and subnational actors. The surreptitious development of a multi-level polity has engendered strong reactions. The EU-wide debates unleashed by the Maastricht Accord have forced the issue of national sovereignty onto the public agenda. Where governing parties themselves have shied away from the issue, opposition parties, particularly those of the extreme right, have raised it. States and state sovereignty have become objects of popular contention—the outcome of which is as yet uncertain.

Part 4

Current Debates
in Integration Theory

27

The Next Europe:
Toward a Federal Union

Nicolas Berggruen and Nathan Gardels

Federalism in the contemporary period remains for many scholars and policy-makers a strategy for solving Europe's economic and political problems. For these ideologically committed individuals, the cry for "more Europe" must be met by transforming the EU into a federal nation-state with democratically legitimate institutions. For some others, federalism describes a type of polity that opens the possibility of comparison. Students of federalism thus characterize the EU as a loose federation and usefully compare it to other federations, such as the United States, Canada, or Australia. Nicolas Berggruen and Nathan Gardels (both of the Berggruen Institute on Governance) are both committed European federalists and students of comparative federalism.

In this piece, previously published in Foreign Affairs, *Berggruen and Gardels advocate the transformation of the EU "into a real federal union, with common fiscal and economic policies to complement its single currency" so that it can meet the demands "of an ever more competitive global economy." They do not envision the EU with a robust central government such as that found in the United States. Rather, they see the EU developing "a strong but limited European government, one that resembles today's Swiss federation." To achieve such a decentralized end, they suggest several reforms of the EU institutions that would provide the Union with a directly elected president, upper and lower chambers of parliament, and a "European Chamber" to represent national parliaments. Such a structure, in their view, would preserve much national autonomy following the principle of subsidiarity. And like Spinelli (see Chapter 14), they believe the best way to accomplish a federalist end would be to call a "full-scale European convention."*

Toward a Federal Union

The European Union was born out of the ashes of World War II and the anguish of the early Cold War, as a project to build and sustain peace and prosperity across the continent. To accomplish its mission in the twenty-first century, however—to become more than simply "a defensive reaction to horror," in the French philosopher Andre Glucksmann's words—it needs to move forward now toward greater integration.

When the heads of the EU's three major institutions—the European Commission, the European Council, and the European Parliament—collected the Nobel Peace Prize together in Oslo last December [2012], they spotlighted the vague mandate and lack of institutional clarity that are at the core of the organization's current problems. Unless these institutions can garner legitimacy among European citizens and transform the EU into a real federal union, with common fiscal and economic policies to complement its single currency, Europe will be worried by its future as much as its past and continue to find its social model battered by the gales of an ever more competitive global economy.

The first step forward has to be developing an economic growth strategy, to escape the union's current debt trap and to create breathing space for the tough reforms that can make Europe as a whole competitive again. As former German Chancellor Gerhard Schroeder has said, "Structural reforms can only work in conjunction with a growth trajectory." Then, to sustain reform, the union needs a clear path to legitimacy for a strong but limited European government, one that resembles today's Swiss federation. This will entail creating an executive body that is directly accountable to Europe's citizens (emerging from the current commission), strengthening the parliament as a lower legislative house, and turning the council (a committee of the leaders of the member states) into an upper legislative house. Along the way, France will have to yield more sovereignty than its historic comfort zone has so far allowed, and Germany will have to realize that its own self-interest calls for it to bear the burden of resolving the current account imbalances within the eurozone.

The key to creating a federal Europe with legitimate governing institutions is appropriate implementation of the principle that Europeans already know as "subsidiarity," with higher levels of government taking on only those functions and responsibilities that cannot be fulfilled at a lower level. . . .

The German Problem

Proponents of a federal Europe need to make their case to an increasingly skeptical European public by stressing not only the benefits of a united continent, with the world's largest market and free mobility of labor and capital, but also the inadequacies of Europe's existing structures as a basis for success in an increasingly globalized world. German Chancellor Angela Merkel has put the issue squarely: Europe today has seven percent of the world's population, produces 25 percent of the world's products, and accounts for 50 percent of its social spending. Without reform, in an ever more competitive international economic environment, it will be difficult to finance the generous welfare state that Europeans are used to. The European public, notes former Polish Prime Minister Marek Belka, has come to see the common currency as "amplifying the dislocations of globalization," instead of shielding Europe from them, as if the advent of the euro helped hand Europeans' economic fate over to global financial markets and their jobs to distant low-wage countries, such as China. In fact, he points out, the reverse is true: the only way to make Europe competitive again and reap the benefits from globalization is to embark on a political union.

The failure of the euro would harm Europe's core every bit as much as its periphery, and Germany's middle class could well pay the highest price. Germany's success as Europe's most competitive trading nation today can be traced back to the structural reforms it enacted several years ago, including increasing the pensionable age and trimming labor costs while spurring investment in training and research and development. These have helped manufacturing to continue to account for a healthy 24 percent of the German economy. What never seems to be debated in Germany, however, is how this industrial foundation of German prosperity would be threatened if the euro failed. In that case, Germany would be forced to return to the deutsch mark, the value of its currency would skyrocket, and the competitiveness of its manufacturing sector would plummet. German multinational companies would waste little time before shifting their production out of Germany to take advantage of lower foreign labor costs, the global spread of technology, and the web of supply chains that enables quality production elsewhere. Research and design might remain at home, but the production and assembly associated with plentiful middle-income jobs would move away. The big losers in such a scenario would be the members of the German middle class—and so, properly understood, for Germany, the euro is a class issue.

Yet precisely because of its historically strong manufacturing economy, Germany has become less oriented to financial markets than other states, which has led to a certain deafness among German political elites to the effect of Germany's prescribed fiscal policies for Europe on global bond markets. Today, however, the reality is that those bond markets will dictate not only whether the euro will survive but also the costs that the German middle class will pay. If Germany wants to remain a broadly prosperous and fair society in a globalized world, it can do so only within a stable eurozone and all that that entails—to start with, a banking union, then fiscal union, and, ultimately, a federal political union.

If the euro were to fail, moreover, the German financial sector would also take a hit and further damage the economy. The domino effect of default in the European periphery would ultimately end up hitting German banks and savers alike, since they are among the major creditors owning those troubled debts (with outstanding loans in 2012 of more than 300 billion euros to Greece, Ireland, Italy, Portugal, and Spain). And failure of the eurozone due to hesitation in Berlin would place the blame for the ruin of Europe on Germany, something neither the public nor elites there want.

Germany has multiple strong reasons to want to maintain the euro, therefore, but to do so, it must help correct today's destabilizing current account imbalances by accepting a diminished external surplus. Indeed, with a diminished surplus, the so-called transfer union that so many Germans oppose—a permanent subsidy for the weaker peripheral states—would be unnecessary. But with continued large external surpluses, it would become indispensable, since only that would allow other Europeans to finance the purchase of German goods. The real issue for Germany today is thus not about bailing out the rest but about saving itself before it is too late.

Union Now

History offers few notable examples of successful political federations. At its moment of federation, in the 1780s, the United States was a sparsely populated handful of young states with a common culture and common language, and so it does not provide many relevant lessons for Europe today. Switzerland's experience, however, offers more, one of which is about slow gestation. "Federation needs time," says the former Swiss diplomat Jakob Kellenberger. "It took centuries for people living in Swiss cantons to get to know each other, then a long period of confederation before the move toward full federation in 1848. That transition was made only following an historical moment of great tensions between liberals and conservatives, Protestants and Catholics." The Swiss federation has worked, he notes, because the center has been respectful of the autonomy of the cantons (which were never anxious to hand over their authority) and careful not to abuse its powers. All powers not specifically delegated to the federal government by the Swiss constitution, moreover, continue to be held by the cantons. With decades of step-by-step integration already behind it and an accelerating world ahead, Europe must accomplish its shift to full political union in years and decades, not centuries, but this shift can nonetheless usefully follow much of the Swiss model.

Asked once how he would account for the prosperity of the Scandinavian nations despite their high tax rates, the economist Milton Friedman responded that it was because their common identity and homogenous culture had enabled consensus to emerge. Free markets, he pointed out, were important precisely because they allowed people without a common iden-tity to work together, even if they hated one another. Such a process of inte-gration has worked well in Europe so far, but in order to lock in the gains and connections, institutions need to follow where markets have already gone. These institutions must be limited to providing public goods that are in the common interest, even as they avoid unnecessary interventions in the autonomous lives of the union's national units. Like Switzerland, in other words, Europe needs a strong but limited central government that accom-modates as much local diversity as possible. As is the case everywhere, it is a matter of balancing priorities. Governance works best—because it is more legitimate and accountable—when the scale is small; markets are most prosperous when the scale is large.

One area that certainly needs centralized regulation and institutional guidance is finance. As former Spanish Prime Minister Felipe Gonzalez has argued, "It is ridiculous for member states to maintain different rules in this common and integrated space where financial institutions operate freely. The absence of homogenous regulation will only sow the seeds of the next financial crisis and hobble Europe in the decades ahead as it faces new competitive challenges in the global economy." European countries also need to agree to common balance-of-payments requirements and a harmo-nized minimum taxation in order to fund a European budget. Such moves would help drive deep structural reforms in individual countries, such as increasing flexibility in labor markets, that would promote competitiveness.

Some argue that aligning European states more closely on issues such as wage levels, the social contract, and tax rates should be the task of the European Commission—which represents all 27 member states—rather than of intergovernmental treaties whose negotiation is inevitably domi-nated by France and, particularly, Germany. This makes sense, but for the commission to take on such a role, it will need to acquire much more pop-ular legitimacy. This means that the commission's president will have to be elected directly by European citizens at large, in order to give a face to the political unity of Europe. The parliament and the council, meanwhile, need to be able to initiate legislation (a power only the commission has now). It would also make sense to allocate seats in the parliament in a way that more accurately reflected the populations of the member states and to cre-ate the office of a commissioner for savings, who could help see to it that the member states met their various financial and budgetary commitments and obligations.

Former German Foreign Minister Joschka Fischer, meanwhile, has sug-gested leveraging the current legitimacy of the nation-state to forge a more effective common European budget policy. "Because there can be no fiscal union without a common budget policy," he has argued, "nothing can be decided without national parliaments. This means that a 'European Chamber'

—comprising national parliament leaders—is indispensable. Such a chamber could [start out as] an advisory body, with the national parliaments maintaining their competencies; later, on the basis of an intergovernmental treaty, it must become a real parliamentary control and decision-making body, made up of national parliaments' delegated members." (In a similar vein, the German philosopher Jürgen Habermas has suggested bridging national and European sovereignty by having "certain members of the European Parliament at the same time hold seats in their respective national parliaments.")

Although a federal Europe must be open to all EU member states, forward movement toward it should not be blocked because some are not yet willing to go there, but nor should it be imposed from on high. The democratic public of each state will have to decide whether it is in its long-term interest to join the federation or opt out. It is an illusion to believe that a strong political union can be built on the weak allegiance that results from tweaking treaties. Its foundation must be a popular mandate. The appropriate venue for these discussions, as Schroeder and others have suggested, would be a full-scale European convention. Former Belgian Prime Minister Guy Verhofstadt, the German politician Daniel Cohn-Bendit (both members of the European Parliament), and others have proposed turning the 2014 elections for the European Parliament into the election of a constituent assembly to draft a new constitution for Europe that would incorporate these sorts of ideas.

How, specifically, might a political union in Europe work? The European Parliament could elect the chief executive of the European Commission, who would then form a cabinet of ministers out of the larger parties in the parliament—including a finance minister with the capacity to levy taxes and formulate a substantial budget on a Europe-wide basis. The finance minister's focus would be macroeconomic coordination, not microeconomic management. Other cabinet positions would cover the provision of supranational European public goods (defense, foreign policy, energy, infrastructure, and so forth), leaving as many decisions on other matters as possible in the hands of the national governments within the federation. The European Court of Justice would arbitrate any issues of disputed sovereignty arising between the commission and the member states.

Because the parliament would have enhanced power, selecting a chief executive for the union, it would make sense to have parliamentary elections based on Europe-wide lists instead of national party lists. Having more at stake in the elections would lead to more discussion and higher rates of voting, which would mean more legitimacy for the results and the institutions in general. Parties that obtained less than ten or 15 percent of the vote in Europe-wide elections would be present in debate but could not vote. Such a rule would tend to push politics toward centrist compromise and avoid gridlock that might arise from the veto power of small parties in a coalition.

The current European Council, in this scheme, would be transformed into the upper house of the union's legislature. Members would be selected by nation-states for staggered terms longer than the shorter electoral cycle of the lower house of the parliament, thus encouraging a longer-term perspective on governance. Unlike the lower house, which would focus primarily on the short-term interests of its national constituents, the upper house would be a more deliberative body, focused on broader and longer-term questions. Representation would be based on a proportional system according to the member states' populations.

In order to preserve some of the nonpartisan, meritocratic quality of the current commission, each cabinet minister in the commission would be paired with a permanent secretary from the European civil service in his or her area of competence. As in an ideal "Westminster system," the formulation of budgets would rest with the commission, not with the parliament. The commission's budget would be presented for an up-or-down vote in the parliament; a vote of "constructive no confidence" by the parliament might reject the policy direction set by the commission, in which case a new government would be formed. (A constructive no-confidence vote is a consensus-forging mechanism whereby a no-confidence vote can take place only if majority support for a new, alternative governing coalition has already been secured.) Taxes and legislation would have to be approved by a majority of both legislative houses.

If Not Now, When?

Any move toward such a political union would obviously raise myriad thorny issues. The new institutions and their rules would ideally be established from the bottom up through a constituent assembly, rather than by a treaty change—but how could a truly ground-up process ever get traction? The large parties that would win the most seats in the European Parliament would need to hash out a compromise or a common agenda robust enough to make governing possible—but what if they did not? And what is most fundamental, could a political union ever really cohere if not preceded by continent-wide nation building aimed at forging a forward-looking common identity? What is crucial now, however, is recognition that the current system is not working and that closer, rather than looser, integration is the more sensible and attractive option.

In 1789, Alexander Hamilton, then the U.S. secretary of the treasury, proposed a strong federal system of government that would assume the states' debts from the American Revolution while guaranteeing a steady future revenue stream, further integrating fiscal policy while preserving a large swath of local sovereignty on nonfederal issues. This was the first step in making the United States a continental and, ultimately, global power. So, too, in Europe, debt resolution can be the midwife of a political union that could make Europe a powerful pillar in the geopolitical order of the twenty-first century. The only way to answer Europe's current challenge in the face of the many uncertainties is for Europe's leaders, and its public, to at last commit to this transformation instead of remaining paralyzed with hesitancy.

28

The Institutional Construction of Interests

Craig Parsons

The increasingly sterile debates of the "relaunch" period between supranationalists (sometimes termed "institutionalists"), who believed EU institutions acted at some level independently of member-state governments, and intergovernmentalists, who argued that states remained in control of the integration process, began to peter out at the turn of the century. Fresh thinking arrived in the late 1990s with the introduction of "constructivism" to the debate.

Constructivism, like neofunctionalism and intergovernmentalism, had its roots in international relations theory. Unlike competing perspectives, however, constructivism contained an explicit critique of "rationalist" social science as overly obsessed with structural causes and material costs and benefits. Constructivists maintained that political actors—including nation-states—did not always make decisions based on calculations of material benefit. In their view, decisionmakers formulated their opinions and took action in a social and ideological context. These groups operated according to certain norms of behavior; they considered some ideas more acceptable than others; and they agreed on certain "facts" about the world. Constructivists, in sum, explored the ways group norms, ideas, and even cultures shaped, and sometimes changed, the identities and interests of political actors.

The European Union, with its levels of government and many formal and informal institutions, provided an ideal arena for constructivist exploration. But constructivists were hardly united in their approach to the EU. Some constructivists took a radical, postmodern perspective, arguing that the EU was a linguistic construct that masked and perpetuated power relations *(e.g., capital over labor; men over women). Other constructivists did not reject the scientific method but wished to bring social variables into explanations of integration.*

Craig Parsons is a constructivist who challenges some but not all elements of rationalist social science. In the introduction to his book, A Certain Idea of Europe, *Parsons argues that "ideas matter" to the development of institutions: "Ideas are autonomous factors in politics, and certain institutions arise because of the ideas actors hold." His objective is to demonstrate that ideas have had an independent impact on the evolution of French elite support for European integration and on the subsequent development of supranational institutions and policies. Parsons, while careful to employ a rigorous scientific research design, is not, however, committed to developing a general "theory of ideas" applicable beyond his single historical case. In his view, demonstrating that we may live in a socially constructed world makes it "illogical" to demand a general theory of politics when, in fact, every political phenomenon may be socially contingent. In other words, an ideational explanation of integration in Europe may have no relevance beyond the European case—which is no less scientific in Parson's view than any general theory of integration.*

> Force them to build a tower together and you will
> transform them into brothers. —*Antoine de Saint-Exupéry*

The European Union is, by all accounts, a remarkable creation. Its authority and scope resemble those of a weak federal state. Globally, it stands out as the major exception in the thinly institutionalized world of international politics. Something has led Europeans—and arguably only Europeans—beyond the political framework of the nation-state.

This book argues that this "something" was a particular set of ideas that appeared in Western Europe after the Second World War. Confronted by the two great wars and a fundamentally reconfigured environment, many Europeans began to reconsider long-held assumptions about the costs, benefits, and appropriate form of international cooperation. The new environment did not dictate their response, however. By the 1950s, a debate had emerged between advocates of several different views of Europeans' interests. One, the "community" model, connected a wide range of national problems to solutions in "supranational" European institutions, like those of today's EU. Others (the "traditional" and "confederal" models) defended solutions within the existing nation-state system, or in less radical departures from it. All were technically and politically viable ways to conceptualize Europeans' various "national interests." Only because certain leaders repeatedly chose "community" projects—and because these divisive debates gave leaders the autonomy to choose—did the EU gradually arise.

This story is not just about the assertion of certain ideas by an elite minority. It is also about how those ideas ruled out others as active options, making their victory permanent. A key aspect of this process was inherent in community ideas themselves. Since they focused on building new institutions, "pro-community" leaders left a legacy of new institutional constraints to their successors. When advocates of other ideas came to power, they found themselves pressed to adapt their own strategies to this legacy. Such adaptation was far from complete; confederalist or traditionalist leaders were able to block further community steps, and could partly reorient European relations toward their favored models. But since their competing ideas did not focus on major new institutions, their periods of rule left few new constraints to their successors. When community champions regained power, they were free to restart their project. Over time, the accumulation of community initiatives recast the framework for all of European politics. Once-powerful alternative ideas were crowded out as active possibilities.

This causal process of the institutionalization of ideas is the heart of the EU story. The community model became embedded as the constitutive "rules of the game" in contemporary Europe, effectively defining the interests even of actors who long advocated other ideas. This process caused and concretized one outcome from a very wide range of otherwise viable options. Those other options—the paths suggested by the other historically active ideas—differed not just institutionally from today's EU but substantively as well. I argue that only community ideas led to the EU's three most prominent policy elements: the Common Agricultural Policy, the Single Market, and the single currency. Without the causal drive of these ideas and their institutional consequences, Europe would have nothing close to these arrangements. Rather than standing out as exceptional in international politics, Europe would reflect the thinly institutionalized rule.

I demonstrate this argument in a detailed study of French policy-making in European integration from 1947 to 1997. The victory of the community project was not determined solely in France, but the key battle of European ideas occurred there. All accounts agree that Europe's other governments were willing to strike less institutionally ambitious bargains at each major step in the EU's construction; French insistence on the community model repeatedly decided the outcome. In the 1950s, France's partners generally preferred broad, weak cooperation to the institutionally strong, geographically limited European Economic Community (EEC) that Paris demanded. In the 1970s, the French increasingly championed delegations of monetary sovereignty over British and German reticence. In the 1980s, the French led the charge to strengthen the EEC institutions over British opposition and German hesitation. In the 1990s, the French wrested monetary union from a skeptical Germany while the British stood aside. Rather than reflecting a consensual national strategy, however, these French initiatives all emerged from a deep internal policy battle. Debate between community, confederal, and traditional European strategies consistently cut across the main right-left lines in French politics. These fragmented demands meant coalitions could be crafted to support any of several strategies. When pro-community leaders achieved power on other issues, they gained the autonomy—never the mandate—to assemble support behind their personal ideas on Europe. The institutional consequences of their initiatives progressively bound their compatriots, and all of Europe, into the community architecture.

The clarity and extent of this crosscutting battle of ideas in France also provide foundations for a much broader theoretical argument. My larger contribution does not take the form of a general "theory of ideas"; I suggest only a way to show that ideas matter, not a logic about when they do. (I suspect they always matter a great deal.) I argue, however, that my ability to nail down the wide impact of ideas in this case creates an unprecedented challenge to the prevailing standards for theorizing across the social sciences. These standards prioritize generality above all else. They suggest that my historical claims have little value without a general theory of ideas, or of institution building, or of some putatively general phenomenon. The problem with such standards is that they assume, quite unscientifically, that the world of human action is a highly general one. This study is constructed to convince even hard-nosed skeptics that the generality of the political world is an open question. Massive elements of contemporary Europe that mainstream scholars (and actors) now take as necessities in fact reflect the implications of a particular ideology. If this claim is plausible, all social science theorizing must at least allow that the same may be true elsewhere: that variation in any set of sociopolitical outcomes occurs for particular reasons (reflecting nonnecessary, historically situated, creative inventions of certain human beings) rather than for general ones. The mere possibility of a deeply particular, "socially constructed" world makes it illogical to accept generality as a standard a priori for theoretical value. Thus the kind of argument advanced in this book—a falsifiable set of historical claims about wide variation in important outcomes, assembled in a coherent theoretical logic—constitutes a more appropriate model of theoretical contribution in the social sciences.

Three Views of Institution Building

Explanations of institution building take three broad forms. For "structuralists," institution building responds to direct environmental pressures. Human beings are assumed to have similar, constant preferences for material concerns like security or economic welfare. They choose the actions that most rationally realize these goals given objectively available options. Actors' choices are thus explained as functions of their environmental constraints. Certain structural circumstances explain why certain institutions arise and persist.

This view dominates scholarship on institution building in comparative and international politics, as well as the specific literature on European integration. For Andrew Moravcsik, today's EU is the result of "normal politics." It reflects the straightforward aggregation of the objective economic interests of domestic groups, through government policies, into a series of European level intergovernmental bargains. If the EU is exceptional in international politics, this is because postwar Europe felt a particularly acute version of global trends to economic and political interdependence. Many leading EU historians make broadly similar arguments. . . .

This view of institution building as driven by the "constant causes" of structural constraints has been challenged most frequently by arguments privileging "historical causes." They constitute the "institutionalist" view of institution building. Here manmade organizations, conventions, and rules are held to intervene between environmental pressures and actors' choices. Institutionalists do not necessarily contest that institution building projects originate from structurally dictated material interests. But once institution building begins, they suggest, it can lead to feedback on the context for subsequent interaction. Organizations and rules advantage or disadvantage certain actors in ways independent from underlying structural conditions. Thus institutions may reflect actors' objective interests at their genesis, but do not necessarily adjust when structural conditions change. Instead, they constrain choices in a "pathdependent" process that can strongly skew political dynamics and outcomes over time.

Claims that institution building shapes subsequent action are now very common. One such argument provided the foundations of the EU literature. In the late 1950s, Ernst Haas constructed his "neofunctionalist" account of European integration around an institutional concept he called "spillover." Though Haas implicitly accepted structural causes of the first European institutions, he argued that their innovative creation of "supranational" European agents could feed back to affect Europe's future. This institutional change altered "normal politics" in Europe, opening up new possibilities. Driven by interests in increasing their own power, European agents might construct new European-level policies that promised domestic groups more welfare than those on offer by national governments. If this occurred, integration would spill over to new policy areas. Society-state relationships would be gradually supplanted by "society-Europe" ties. Political loyalties would shift to the supranational political unit. Though Haas's heady predictions for Europe were falsified by the early 1970s, his theoretical mechanism prefigured a wave of similar arguments in the 1980s and 1990s. "Constant cause" approaches, they assert, must be supplemented by "historical cause" analysis. The exceptional EU outcome resulted above all because early postwar Europe set itself on a self-reinforcing institutional path.

The third view makes a more fundamental critique of structuralist explanation and a partial critique of institutionalism as well. An "ideational" approach suggests that structural circumstances rarely dictate a specific course of action, and even institutional constraints may admit of multiple interpretations. The cognitive lenses through which actors interpret their surroundings shape how they respond to structural or institutional pressures. Any choice is predicated on assumptions about causal relationships, the prioritization of costs and benefits, and the normative legitimacy of various actions. Thus ideas (or "norms" or "identities" or "culture") affect action in two ways. On the one hand they constitute particular actors and their frameworks of action; the idea of sovereignty constitutes the state. More prosaically, ideas cause actions in a normal chronological sense; holding certain ideas at time t leads an actor to choose a certain action at time $t + 1$ that she would not have chosen otherwise. Though structural or institutional pressures may affect actors' beliefs, in neither their constitutive nor their causal capacities do ideas reduce to such pressures. Ideas are autonomous factors in politics, and certain institutions arise because of the ideas actors hold.

Like structuralism and institutionalism, such arguments have a long pedigree. They have also received growing attention in international and comparative politics since the 1980s. Most prominent among international relations (IR) theorists is the "constructivist" school, which draws upon a sociological tradition to argue that all interests are socially constructed. Constructivists tend to emphasize constitutiveness, highlighting the presence and evolution of intersubjective norms that shape states and their interaction. Comparativists and other IR scholars in the so-called ideas literature tend to focus on the causal impact of more discrete policy beliefs. Recently, both literatures have converged on the EU. Constructivists argue that national positions and policies in the EU reflect national "identities" reconstituted in the process of integration. Comparative political economists focus on how certain ideas about monetary policies and liberalization set the stage for the EU's acceleration since the mid-1980s.

This book is thus part of a growing ideational literature on the EU. It attempts, however, to turn it in two new directions. First, in theoretical terms, ideational work (on the EU and elsewhere) has generally emphasized either the structuring presence of constitutive norms or the immediate causal impact of certain ideas, without tracing the process by which certain ideas become embedded as constitutive norms or identities. I focus on this link, showing how ideas about Europe that were once hotly contested came to define the interests of all European actors. In so doing I incorporate elements of both causal and constitutive ideational approaches. Since much of my story concerns fairly discrete ideas before they became embedded norms, my vocabulary largely follows from the causal "ideas" literature. For reasons of tactical argumentation . . . I also often write as if I accept the more modest, "residual cause" view of ideas suggested by much of the "ideas" school. Yet my ultimate sympathies and ambitions lie with the constitutive focus of constructivists. I argue not only that ideas cause actors to make certain choices, but that the institutionalization of certain ideas gradually reconstructs the interests of powerful actors.

Second, this book takes ideational work on the EU in a new direction in focusing directly on the ideology of European integration. To date, ideational scholarship in this context has highlighted changing economic ideas or particular national identities, but has basically ignored ideas about "Europe" itself. This seems odd, at least superficially. Since the early postwar period, many European leaders have loudly proclaimed their commitment to various kinds of "European Union." Nontheoretical observers have uniformly described the champions of Europe's major institutional steps as ideological devotees of "supranational" integration. Their political opponents have often denounced them in similar terms. Yet academically, only a few vague works give any attention to European ideology. Scholars seem to have quickly become and remained highly skeptical of the rhetoric of European unification.

This skepticism is a healthy reflex, of course. Cheap talk about European integration has never been in short supply. Still, my contention is that not all such rhetoric is disingenuous. I show that certain ideas about Europe have shaped the French pursuit of European institutions, and by extension European outcomes themselves. At each step forward in institution building, ideas have provided a measurable "constant cause" directing the process along. In addition, I connect this argument to "historical causes" of an institutionalist logic of path dependence, showing that these ideas have been progressively embedded to constitute the "interests" perceived by all French leaders (whatever their ideas). The result is a striking contrast to either structuralist or pure institutionalist accounts. Europe's institutions do not reflect a simple aggregation of structurally determined interests. Nor are they merely an incremental institutional evolution from their founders' intentions. They are the product of a supremely political project that has bound all Europeans into a certain ideological agenda.

The Institutional Construction of Interests

My basic understanding of the institutionalization of ideas draws on several complementary literatures. My view of ideas rests on Ann Swidler's broader discussion of culture. Culture is a "tool kit" or "repertoire" of ways to organize behavior. Members of a culture share a restricted set of ways of dealing with any situation; this limits and channels their strategic choices. Ideas are the semidiscrete tools within such a kit. They are packages of related causal and normative assumptions that assign costs and benefits to possible actions. Like culture in general, shared ideas concern the means more than the ends of action. People who share certain ideas agree on ways of diagnosing problems and organizing action, though the ultimate ends they attach to those actions may vary more widely. We will see, for example, that French politicians on the right and the left with quite different values shared a certain analysis and vocabulary in advocating supranational institution building as the appropriate shape for European cooperation.

Additionally, ideas themselves can occupy various levels of generality and precedence, such that actors may attach different minor ideas to the same major idea. In other terms, actors who share one idea as the "master frame" for their action in an arena do not necessarily agree on more detailed actions therein. The French politicians of right and left who championed the master frame of a "community" Europe often disagreed over lesser (but still significant) arrangements within it. In the vocabulary of John Searle, pro-community politicians have advocated similar "constitutive rules" for the construction of a certain European arena, while not always favoring the same "regulative rules" for policies within that arena.

Many semirelated ideas compose a culture, but on any given issue cultures often contain several competing ideas. Choosing one ideational tool from the kit to frame or set the agenda for group action thus often occasions major political conflict. Such conflicts are particularly common in times of major structural change, when previously framed ideas or set agendas are reopened. During these "epochal moments," new problems can provoke the creation of new ideational tools. Innovations do not necessarily respond functionally to the new situation; adaptation of older ideas, or other new ideas, may suggest other solutions. The result is a "battle of ideas" in which groups or organizations debate several viable strategies. In such battles, when group positions are contested and coalitions are unclear, the personal views of top leaders can decide between very different alternatives. My story displays the emergence and consequences of such a battle between community, confederal, and traditional ideas about French interests in European institution building.

Battles of ideas are never separate from battles over the distribution of material gains. The former are important precisely because they can set the lines, dynamics, and results of the latter. Thus if I present my ideational argument as a competitor to structuralist or pure institutionalist approaches, this is not because these basic logics are mutually exclusive. Material reality, organizational arrangements, and ideas all play roles in politics. The interesting debate is not between them as incompatible concepts; it concerns how much we need ideational factors—ideas and their institutionalization—to explain how actors define their interests. In my argument, I allow that structural and institutional pressures may have given postwar Europeans broad interests in developing international cooperation but assert that they did not dictate the shape or extent of that cooperation. Within this structural and institutional environment, leaders' ideas led them to select in particular ways from several alternatives with very different institutional and distributional consequences. In other words, my focus on the "autonomous" role of ideas does not imply a monocausal account. To paraphrase Richard Biernacki, I show that ideas exercise an influence of their own but not completely by themselves.

My view of institutionalization is consistent with a variety of institutionalist vocabularies (elaborated below). I focus on formal institutions: explicit agreements that specify the rights and obligations of governments and other actors. The fundamental stuff of institutions is cognitive, consisting of actors' expectations; people negotiate new agreements to establish new expectations about rights and obligations. But institutions also often assume physical, organizational manifestations in the location of people and resources. Both aspects of institutions inform my logic on the institutionalization of ideas. Ideas are institutionalized if earlier advocates of other ideas come to act in accordance with them. This happens through the pressures of expectations and organizations engendered when certain ideas lead to certain institutional arrangements. The expectations of an actor's interlocutors can constrain it; promises made to powerful partners are hard to ignore. Organizational arrangements, once in place, can also make it costly to change strategies. For both reasons, institution building puts new constraints on subsequent action. Dissidents within groups that make new institutional commitments are pressed, to some degree, to alter their choices. This book is about how a new master frame idea became, through institutionalization, the "constitutive rules" of the European political game. The task of the following sections is to develop these abstract views on ideas and institutionalization into an empirically demonstrable argument. I do so in four steps. First I describe the challenge of specifying the causal impact of ideas. Next I suggest how, under certain conditions, this challenge can be overcome. Third, I discuss how (and how to show that) ideas become institutionalized. Fourth, I consider why certain ideas and not others may engage this process, becoming embedded as the framework of a political arena.

Ideas and the "How Much?" Problem

For students of politics, the basic problem for ideational argument is to separate the causal effects of actors' beliefs from direct structural or institutional pressures. This problem occurs at two levels. First, ideas are by their nature Janus-faced. In some cases actors' beliefs may guide their actions; in others their apparent beliefs simply rationalize strategies chosen for other reasons. Telling the difference between the two situations is difficult. Second, even assuming ideas do have causal impact, they do so as interpretations or "filters" of the objective environment. Wherever ideas have causal effect—in Max Weber's famous phrase, acting as "switchmen" among various material possibilities—so too does the objective context they interpret. Causal ideational argument must separate the ideational filter from its context, isolating the subjective components of actors' "interests" from their direct responses to the environment.

At the postmodern extreme of the ideational literature, this challenge is met by denying it. The very notion of an accessible objective context is rejected, making interpretation of ideas the entire exercise, without attempts to relate ideas to objective pressures. More mainstream ideational arguments, however, use fairly standard social science methods to suggest the need for similar kinds of interpretation. Most common in the constructivist and comparative literatures is reliance on some kind of "process tracing." The observer traces the objective pressures impinging on certain decisions and concludes that they did not fully determine a choice. Thus we need to interpret the beliefs that did. Cross-case comparisons are also often used to set up interpretation of ideas. In contexts ranging from the early Industrial Revolution to interwar military strategizing, scholars have shown that actors in objectively similar situations can adopt different strategies due to different ideas. Other studies show the need for interpretation in the proliferation of similar policies across structurally different cases.

Especially when combined, these methods produce strong claims that ideas can affect politics to some degree. Their main weakness, however, is their apparent inability to show how much ideas cause certain outcomes. These scholars offer qualitative assessments of the indeterminacy left by objective pressures, and interpretations of how certain ideas resolved it. Yet skeptics can always question the former assessment, suggesting (for example) that the objective economic pressures toward a strategy have been underestimated, meaning ideas caused it less than has been claimed. A process-tracing focus on a single course of action also offers little counterfactual leverage: what was the range of possibilities without these ideas? Cross-case comparisons help in this respect, suggesting alternatives in similar situations. But cross-national comparisons are rarely similar enough to ascribe all their variation to ideas. Critics may suspect that unnoticed differences in structures or institutions account for part of the divergence.

Overall, laments one sympathetic reviewer, ideas in today's literature are "simply another rather than the causal factor." For skeptics, these "how much" questions make all the difference. If variation in ideas alone cannot be tied to specific variation in historical outcomes, concludes a less sympathetic reviewer, ideas can still be dismissed as "a valuable supplement to [objective-] interest-based, rational actor models." Moravcsik defends the same view, quite powerfully, on the rhetoric of European unity. The "how much" challenge is the greatest barrier to my argument—and the largest remaining obstacle to the broad acceptance of ideas as major causes in politics.

One Way to Tie Ideas to Historical Outcomes

An unfortunate result of this "how much" challenge is that some scholars of ideas have stopped trying to make causal arguments altogether, asserting instead that the "constitutive" nature of ideas relieves them of the need to make clear causal claims. Others do the same thing implicitly, making causal claims but failing to engage seriously with nonideational alternative explanations. Yet there are some settings where ideational arguments can do more than preach to the choir. Where ideas strongly crosscut prevailing lines of organization in a political arena, we can display their autonomous impact in robust, methodologically conservative ways that should convince even the staunchest skeptics. Such cases will not prove that ideas matter everywhere, but they will establish that ideas can be major causes in politics.

This subsection elaborates the logic and methods behind this claim. Readers who already accept that ideas matter may find my approach exceedingly restrictive: I attribute causal effects to ideas only where their impact is most clearly demonstrable, and in so doing may miss their more subtle influence. Such tactical concessions are necessary, however, to achieve the larger goals of this book. To establish the broad plausibility of social construction and restructure our disciplinary criteria for theoretical progress, we must confine ourselves to strict, conservative, empirically demonstrable assertions.

Crosscutting Ideas and Individual Variation

Crosscutting ideas have particularly clear effects because they offer the sharpest possible contrast to the expectations of objective-interest theories. All such theories define actors' interests in terms of objective conditions at some level of organization. For realists, individuals in a state share interests defined by the distribution of power; political party theorists trace members' interests to electoral or coalitional constraints; bureaucratic theorists highlight units' interests within organizational rivalries; and liberals or Marxists derive group interests from economic constraints (in different ways). Ideational approaches posit, in contrast, that actors interpret their interests through ideas that can vary independently from their objective positions. Their greatest divergence from objective-interest theories thus occurs where ideas vary as independently as possible from organizational lines, strongly crosscutting the potential channels of interest aggregation in an arena. This does not mean that ideas have stronger causal effects where they crosscut groups; ideas shared within powerful groups may be equally (or more) significant for important outcomes. It simply means that ideas' autonomous effects should be particularly demonstrable in these cases.

To see this assertion in more detail, consider how it responds to the "how much" problem. We could isolate ideas precisely if we found an extremely close comparison, contrasting actors in near-identical places in the objective world to highlight the purely ideational variations in their behavior. Such comparisons are available at the individual level, within groups. Close organizational peers share positions in the objective world; comparing their views of their groups' interests can separate variation in their ideas from variation in objective pressures. Take two French diplomats, with similar social backgrounds and party sympathies, in the same office of the Foreign Ministry in 1950. One insists on French interests in a new "supranational" Franco-German federation; his colleague sees French interests in policies based on an informal partnership with Britain. These similarly placed individuals face all the same objective pressures but seem to interpret them differently.

If other similarly placed individuals across France also disagree with respect to similar strategic choices (in a pattern that crosscuts parties, bureaucracies, economic groups), this suggests that objective pressures leave French interests more broadly indeterminate across these alternatives. Two further kinds of evidence are necessary to draw this conclusion with confidence, however. First, debate within groups must persist to and past important collective decisions. Otherwise initial debates may simply reflect a vetting of options, from which a consensual group position coalesces as the need for a decision approaches. Second, to show that crosscutting debates reflect competing ideas rather than simple chaos, we need the kind of "interpretive" evidence typically offered by ideational accounts: that actors consistently say and write that they believe certain things, and that their peers think differently. Given a deeply crosscutting pattern of debate across a range of options, persistent divisions, and good rhetorical evidence, we can conclude that ideas alone are causing individual variation across that range.

This conclusion does not rule out that historical or psychological factors other than simple "ideas" (like past socialization, psychological dispositions, or individual experiences) may have led to this pattern of debate. But as long as current patterns of mobilization do not trace to current objective conditions (and do trace to differences in rhetoric), we have evidence that ideational factors are currently influencing action. Psychological or historical factors may help explain why actors came to hold certain ideas, but neither invalidates the claim that ideas are now causing variation in behavior. In other words, explaining the distribution of ideas as dependent variables is legitimately separate from showing their presence and effects as independent variables.

Far from exaggerating the range of purely ideational variation in individuals' views, this approach minimizes interpretive biases. It differs from most ideational arguments in that it is the actors, not the observer, who are defining the range across which ideas matter. . . . One actor wants to pursue option X; one of her close peers, in the same objective position, wants to pursue option Y. Given good evidence of differing preferences, and careful verification that they face identical objective constraints, this control for objective causes is as free from bias as qualitative observations can be.

Furthermore, this finding should tend to systematically underestimate the overall impact of ideas on individuals' views. Open disagreements may well be narrow debates within a consensus built on other ideas. French elites in the 1950s, for example, may share ideas about the legitimacy of the state, democracy, capitalism, and so on that greatly limit their debate over European policies. Nor may individuals voice the full range and strength of their views in internal debates, especially in hierarchical organizations like governments. Even when they do, obtaining evidence of internal dissent after the fact is often difficult. This approach highlights ideas' effects only where they separate most demonstrably from objective factors, without making claims about their less visible impact. Personally, I suspect the impact of ideas to be considerably more pervasive than this approach will ever suggest. But my goal here is to advance the most minimal, conservative, robust causal claims about ideas I can, based on a direct competition with nonideational explanations.

Leaders' Ideas and Entrepreneurial Coalition Building

Variation in individuals' ideas does not mean ideas matter in government strategies. Objective pressures in coalition building might ultimately impose one view on policy choices irrespective of individual views. Under certain conditions, however, they may not. Many scholars suggest that given fragmented demands on a given issue, several coalitions for various policies may be available. Entrepreneurial leadership may then determine which coalitions take shape. Strongly crosscutting cleavages maximize this possibility. A leader selected and supported in office on one cleavage may enjoy considerable autonomy to mobilize one of many potential coalitions on other issues.

There is nothing inherently ideational about such entrepreneurial leadership. When connected to ideational variation at the individual level, however, this mechanism can tie variation in ideas alone to variation in strategies and outcomes. If coalition building continues to operate along existing organizational lines as crosscutting ideas emerge, leaders' views in the new debate will disconnect from their main coalitional support. The concomitant fragmentation of demands may allow leaders to assert their personal views in policy choices, assembling scattered support across majority and opposition after the fact. In this case, we can say that leaders' ideas cause one choice across the range of debate. Other leaders in the same coalition (and party, bureaucracy, economic position) who differ only in holding different ideas would pursue a different strategy were the final choice theirs. By elaborating the alternatives and their counterfactual consequences, we can thus specify variation in outcomes caused by variation in ideas alone.

This dynamic requires that the crosscutting debate not overwhelm "normal" coalition building. Nonetheless, it is not limited to issues of secondary importance. In modern democracies, voters may be less informed or concerned (or both) about certain debates (especially new developments) than are policy-makers and interest groups. This seems particularly common in the domain of foreign policy. Electoral coalition building may continue along the "normal" issues resonant with voters, even though policy-makers perceive a new debate as extremely important. This disconnect opens the door to the ideas of entrepreneurial leaders.

French policy-making in early European institution building displays this process. Amid demands fragmented by crosscutting ideas, leaders followed their own ideas among several viable alternatives. In so doing, they chose not just an ambitious strategy for France, but a remarkable future for all of Europe.

The Institutionalization of Ideas

Crosscutting debate displays a wide battle of ideas over French strategies in early European institution building, but this battle narrowed to what looks like a fairly robust consensus by the late 1990s. On the surface, this evolution could seem to support standard structuralist views. Structuralists might admit that structural signals were somewhat blurred in the 1950s, but would argue that they have clarified over time. In the 1960s, even the antisupranational Charles de Gaulle recognized interests in a supranational Common Agricultural Policy. In the 1980s, even the Socialist François Mitterrand rallied to a deeply liberal "Single Market." In the 1990s, politically reluctant Gaullists and economically skeptical Socialists endorsed a supranational, monetarist project for a single currency. Whatever their early hesitations, French elites recognized the tightening imperatives to something like the EU.

But we will see that structuralism cannot survive a closer encounter with history. Were it correct, we would expect that the earlier dissidents' adjustments traced to identifiable structural shifts (economic, geopolitical, or electoral); that French groups or parties displayed greater internal agreement before deciding on later institutional steps (the imperatives forward now being clear); and that dissidents pointed to exogenous pressures to justify their alignment. The actual development of the French consensus on Europe exhibits a very different logic. Broader elite agreement on European strategies arose in discrete steps that followed institutional initiatives by pro-community leaders, not clear structural shifts. Only after advocates of that agenda successfully asserted it in a new European deal did proponents of other views reluctantly adjust their strategies to a revised institutional status quo. In so doing, they consistently referred to pressures from the new institutions themselves. In a short period of time after each deal, they changed their strategies and rhetoric to present the institutional steps they had opposed as "in French interests." In other words, the French battle of ideas over Europe did not simply resolve itself. Certain political actors resolved it by building French policies into an institutional structure.

How exactly new institutional deals led their opponents to alter their strategies is a complex question. Institutionalists differ over the mechanisms by which institution building affects subsequent action. "Rationalist institutionalists"—the scholars closest to rationalist structuralism—employ terms of constraint and incentive. Institutional deals bring new access to information or resources, or create organizational "sunk costs"; rational actors factor these changes into their choices alongside structural constraints. "Historical institutionalists" see the process as less completely objective. In addition to channeling actors' strategies through an organizational obstacle course, institutions enshrine principles or standards of legitimacy that actors come to accept. Actors are both objectively constrained and ideationally converted by institutions; "not just the strategies but the goals actors pursue are shaped by the institutional context." "Sociological institutionalists" focus more directly on conversion. Actors accept institutional rules due to the rules' legitimate authority rather than to objective costs or benefits.

My approach can be phrased as consistent with either constraint or conversion logics. I take this position because distinguishing between the two mechanisms empirically is very difficult where both may be operating, and because this distinction is ultimately unnecessary to my argument. Even where dissidents show clear reluctance in respecting new institutional rules (implying they feel constrained), we can rarely tell if they are objectively constrained by institutions or just converted to believing that they are. For example, before Charles de Gaulle came to power in France in 1958, he saw geopolitical and economic reasons to oppose the recently negotiated European Economic Community (EEC) treaty. Once in power, however, he largely went along with it because of various institutional pressures. I cannot tell if the EEC's institutional pressures should rationally have outweighed de Gaulle's prior concerns, or if his adjustment meant he had changed his ideas slightly (de Gaulle himself could not have told the difference). I can say, however, that consequences of the EEC deal did outweigh his prior concerns. To what extent this overall pattern of action reflected rational constraint or irrational conversion is practically impossible to judge. Either way, institutional pressures caused his strategic adjustment. De Gaulle's changed behavior reflected the institutionalization of an ideological agenda he had opposed.

Over the longer scope of my story, I believe that the cumulative adjustments of dissidents to community strategies fit a conversion vocabulary much better than one of rational constraint. [Former] French president Jacques Chirac, for example, opposed every major step in European institution building at the time of its negotiation but [later he presented] himself as a champion of the supranational EU. His views of desirable and legitimate European institutions seem to have changed fundamentally. Still, if the overall story stretches a vocabulary of fixed-preference rationality very uncomfortably, I do not insist that any step of this adjustment cannot be cast in those terms. Regardless of rationality, I show that certain ideas inform certain institutions, creating a new context that shapes the subsequent action of actors with other ideas.

Since historical institutionalists straddle the constraint-conversion divide as well, I adopt their vocabulary. As introduced above, institutions consist of expectations and organizational arrangements. An institutional arrangement defines each actor's "responsibilities and relationship to other actors" and thereby "creates a distinct pattern of constraints and incentives" that presses actors to act within it. Organizational constraints and incentives are straightforward; they make resources more easily available for certain strategies. How expectations constrain is more complicated. They affect actors' choices through the demands made on them by other actors. Once a new institutional arrangement is created, the parties make new demands on one another; actions (or failure to act) previously seen as legitimate become violations. (This is the whole point of creating formal institutions.) To the extent one actor needs support or cooperation from others to accomplish its own goals (whatever they may be), it must try to meet their new expectations. In other words, institutional deals are cognitive constructs that structure expectations, but they constrain subsequent action because those expectations are upheld by physical actors. Thus dissidents who opposed an institutional deal can find that their own separate ambitions depend on respecting it; their interlocutors will resist a return to the status quo ante. Dissidents will not necessarily be pressed to extend the deal—institutions prevent backward movement from the status quo more than they compel specific steps forward—but they will be unable to return fully to the alternative arrangement they preferred.

We will see, for example, that Charles de Gaulle's strategies in Europe were considerably altered by the EEC deal he inherited in 1958. A variety of viable bargaining solutions in European economic relations were on the table prior to the EEC negotiations in 1956-57. The deal de Gaulle's pro-community French predecessors were willing to strike was for gradual liberalization within supranational institutions. Though France's main partners (the Germans and Benelux) had actually preferred geographically broader, institutionally looser arrangements, the EEC thus set the terms they could demand from the unpredictable de Gaulle when he took power. De Gaulle, meanwhile, was focused on the separate goal of creating a French-led "third way" for Europe between the superpowers. He thought the EEC's economic provisions of little importance and detested its institutions, and wanted above all to establish a European mechanism for foreign policy cooperation. Yet since he needed German and Benelux cooperation to pursue his own agenda, he met their demands to maintain an EEC deal that he would never have struck (as he said himself). He did not become an EEC enthusiast; once his foreign policy plans failed, he tried to force changes in the EEC's institutions. But he soon backed down, and an only partly hobbled EEC ended up as his major institutional legacy. The demands de Gaulle faced, and the policy choices he made, were hugely reconfigured by his predecessors' institutional project. He did not simply extend his predecessors' path, but he could not move to the viable alternative path he had preferred in the 1950s. By the late 1960s, that alternative was history. The Gaullists defended the EEC as the foundation of French interests in Europe.

Institutional deals can thus narrow a battle of ideas in a government. Such deals will promote new expectations among its interlocutors. To the extent that operation with these interlocutors, even dissident policy-makers will be pushed to choose strategies in line with these expectations. Dissidents' alignment on the new status quo will rarely imply wholesale endorsement of the ideas they contested; in accepting adjustments, they will not necessarily adopt their competitors' views on steps beyond this status quo. Further steps in a similar direction may require a new infusion of leadership by its ideational champions. If such opportunities arise, a series of similar institution-building steps can progressively narrow the range of strategies debated in the government. Viable historical options will be crowded out at each step, eventually reducing a battle of ideas to an uneasy consensus on policies. Some will endorse the consensus enthusiastically because they share the ideas of the initial agenda; others will endorse it reluctantly because they see it as imposed by institutional pressures. But they will agree, ultimately, on their "interests." It is this process that I call the *institutional construction of interests.*

This argument is falsifiable. Failing a crosscutting battle of ideas, the argument does not apply. If a policy choice involving significant institutional change cannot be shown to constrain subsequent choices in significant ways, the argument is wrong. The less debates are narrowed by institution-building episodes, the less causal power the argument can claim. This approach is causal but nondeterministic; it explains but does not strongly predict. Institutionalized expectations are not concrete constraints like physical obstacles. They orient actors toward certain courses of action but do not physically prevent a resolute actor from ignoring this orientation. If individuals who opposed recently created institutional arrangements take power, they will feel pressure to align on them, but nothing existentially bars them from rejecting them. Thus strong new ideas and leadership—

agency, in general terms—can upset this causal mechanism. Structural unpredictability can do the same. Major environmental shifts may loosen or render indeterminate the dicta of existing institutions. My approach can show that the institutional construction of interests did happen in a given case of decision making over time, and can suggest how it may happen in others, but does not claim that it will happen as an uninterrupted process.

Which Ideas Win?

Ideas may inform strategies of institution building, and their institutional consequences may shape the context for subsequent action. But why do certain ideas and not others engage the institutionalization process? Particularly in a situation of crosscutting debates, where leadership may shift back and forth between advocates of competing ideas, what favors one agenda in the long term? In France, even if "confederal" or "traditional" leaders were pressured by community institutions, why did they not strike their own deals to reconfigure the institutional status quo, or at least to prevent the steady victory of the community model?

Given an even battle of ideas, certain ideas become institutionalized because they inherently lend themselves to institutionalization better than competitors, or because they "fit" better with elements of the environment. Some ideas crowd out competing ideas more actively than others. This is particularly true of ideas that center on formal institutional change. French champions of the community model consistently interpreted material problems as pointing to major European institution-building projects. Confederal or traditional leaders, in contrast, generally saw their material interests within the institutional status quo or in marginal modifications of it. Whenever the former were in power, they pursued institution building and left a further set of changed constraints to their successors. When the latter were in power, they defended the status quo or sought to decrease the constraints on subsequent French actions. Even though advocates of these perspectives alternated fairly regularly in leadership, French policies were increasingly embedded in the more institutionally activist community agenda. This was not necessarily because pro-community elites had more foresight. They simply connected their immediate problems to serious institutional change. Nor were confederal and traditional leaders passive in intra-European relations; we will see that Europe is littered with the husks of their weak projects (the Council of Europe, the OECD, the Western European Union, the Franco-German Treaty, the Luxembourg Compromise). Their strategies were perfectly viable while they held power but did little to crowd out alternatives thereafter. In a world where institutions matter, ceteris paribus, ideas that change them matter more.

Certain ideas are also favored in institutionalization if they connect to established elements of their environment. I do not see this "fit" in terms of functional results or instrumental payoffs to actors; such a view down-grades ideas to noncausal intermediaries between a set of objective conditions and actors' decisions. For new ideas to retain their causal autonomy, their "fit" must be to other ideas, norms, or agendas that support the new ideas without directly requiring them. Research on institutionalization suggests two abstract mechanisms along these lines. A central notion of sociological institutionalism is that new ideas survive and spread if they can connect in some way to already established norms. In a more contingent vein, historical institutionalists add that new policies may survive when they have consequences that appeal to their earlier critics in unforeseen ways. Both mechanisms, I argue, are important in explaining the long-term victory of the community model.

Two connections between community institution-building projects and broad norms have attracted the attention of EU scholars. The first concerns law in modern Europe. Some of the best work in EU studies shows that law has helped defend (and even expand) the scope of Europe's institutional deals. Community ideas, in contrast to confederal or traditional plans, called for elaborate institutions based in detailed legal treaties. They also included the early creation of "European" law itself, in the European Court of Justice. Law per se in no way implied supranational institutions, but basing such institutions in law protected them from their critics. Even in the early, open contested years of integration, calls for simply ignoring legal treaty deals were extremely rare. (In some cases governments ignored aspects of treaties but underlined legal norms in doing so quietly or in offering legal justifications). We will see that the notion that a treaty "can't be torn up" arose explicitly in internal French discussions after the EEC, the Single European Act, and the Maastricht Treaty. Leaders' reluctance to openly flaunt legal agreements extends to populations as well; Europe's citizens have accepted otherwise unimaginable policies in the name of the treaty engagements leading to EMU.

The second connection between community projects and broader norms is more recent. Since the late 1970s, argues Kathleen McNamara, European monetary integration has been greatly facilitated by the growing legitimacy of monetarist economic doctrine. Monetarism itself does not necessarily point to a European Central Bank (ECB) and single currency; experts agree that their economic logic is ambiguous at best. As a political program, however, this project drew considerable support from the simplified version of monetarist thought that is accessible in public debates. The basic monetarist notions of central bank independence and a priority on inflation fighting are easily connected to the ECB plan. The reasons why monetarism might better support less centralized traditional or confederal options are more complex. Overall, champions of monetary union found it particularly easy to present the euro as the logical (and even necessary) consequence of the move to monetarist policies.

Unforeseen consequences have also aided the institutionalization of community ideas. Once a policy decision has been made, its critics may find that it creates unforeseen opportunities to pursue their own (distinct) agendas. One illustration extends the de Gaulle example above. If the expectations engendered by the EEC were a major pressure behind de Gaulle's rally to it, he was also attracted to the opportunity the EEC presented for excluding the pro-American British from French-led Europe (since the British had already decided not to participate). Most of the EEC's French negotiators had not intended this result. Similarly, when President François Mitterrand began his push to the Single European Act (SEA) in 1984, he was not seeking the major deregulatory initiative that the SEA produced. At the outset, many of Mitterrand's conservative opponents— who had recently recast themselves as champions of deregulation—opposed his pursuit of European reforms. When deregulation became the SEA's main focus, however, conservatives found it difficult to disavow. The unintended consequences of a push for European institutional reform helped rally its opponents to it.

For these reasons, among the three views of French interests that were politically and technically viable at any given point, the community model had a long-term advantage. In an ongoing policy debate where control cycled among advocates of different views, community ideas assumed an increasingly dominant position. They aggressively crowded out their competitors, drew protection from deeply ingrained norms, and fortuitously benefited from unintended consequences that connected them to other (and previously antagonistic) agendas. These were diffuse advantages; I do not suggest that they are strong, predictive mechanisms. To the contrary, my central claim is that confederal and traditional strategies were real, viable alternatives to the community path in postwar Europe. The French elites who favored these alternatives were not being irrational, pursuing impossible courses of action. The victory of the community model was not overdetermined; it is a deeply contingent story. But these mechanisms suggest important reasons why contingency was resolved as it was.

This section has offered a way to understand theoretically and show methodologically how groups' interests can be defined, and political arenas structured, through the institutionalization of ideas. It boils down to two main claims. First, under conditions of crosscutting ideas, we can solve the difficult "how much" problem in ideational causality. Furthermore . . . such conditions should not be terribly rare; and even if they are, this demonstration of one major, distinct causal impact of ideas has important implications for the credibility of ideational argument more broadly. Second, given the presence of competing ideas, one idea may crowd out others through institutional consequences of constraint or conversion. This process—the institutional construction of interests—offers a novel perspective on broad

issues of the construction of interests in politics. . . . . [T]he existing literature on this subject tends to privilege structure over agency, consensus over
conflict, and persuasion over political maneuvering. While preserving that
literature's central insight—that the intersubjective construction of political
relations defines actors' interests—I bring agency, conflict, and politics
back in.

. . .

Theorizing in a (Potentially) Socially Constructed World

This book's ambitions extend beyond a fundamental revision of the EU histories offered by Haas, Milward, or Moravcsik. They reach past the several
lessons for ideational arguments elaborated in the concluding chapter. In
light of this argument, I submit, we must revise the prevailing standards for
social science theorizing.

Those standards are borrowed from the "hard" sciences. They mainly
reflect positivism, the nineteenth-century epistemology that portrayed the
discovery of objective general laws of everything as the clear and feasible
goal of scholarly work. In principle, most social scientists espouse something like the more nuanced epistemology of "sophisticated methodological
falsificationism" developed by Imre Lakatos. This still prioritizes general
theorizing above all, but surrounds the search for laws in intelligent caveats
that recognize our ultimate inability to access objective Truth. Although
real proof or falsification of any theory is thus impossible, Lakatos argues
that science still advances through pragmatic falsification (reasonable rejection rather than airtight disproof) and increasingly general theories. "Progressive" scholarship occurs either when an existing theory is extended to
account for new empirical facts, or when a new, broader theory accounts for
the empirically corroborated aspects of previous theories and new facts as
well. Advancing knowledge requires ever more general theory: "There is no
falsification before the emergence of a better theory."

Though Lakatos seemed to doubt the viability of such cumulative theorizing in historical explanations of human action, his writings largely
define progress in the "soft" sciences today. In codifying the current standards of political science, Gary King, Robert Keohane, and Sidney Verba
emphasize generality as the single most important measure of progress:
"The question is less whether, in some general sense, a theory is false or not
. . . than how much of the world the theory can help us explain." In practice, this often seems close to assigning value to generality irrespective of
empirical support. Embedding an argument in a highly general theory
makes it valuable, even if both the particular historical argument and
broader applications of the theory suffer from substantial empirical problems. Moravcsik's highly regarded application of economic-structuralist

theory to EU history is a good example. On my reading, the empirical evidence he offers is substantially incomplete at practically every step (and sometimes simply wrong). Nor am I aware of serious empirical studies showing the power of his kind of theory across any other major set of outcomes. But by embedding a poorly supported argument in a largely untested general theory, he has dominated EU studies. Behind his success lies a Lakatosian defense: whatever empirical objections may arise, only a better general theory represents progress over his own.

Crucially, this defense requires the assumption that the theories in question address highly general phenomena (since general theories are little use in explaining unrelated things). For the physical and mathematical sciences Lakatos studied, this is probably a good assumption. For the social sciences, however, this assumption hinges on rejecting even the possibility that ideas and social construction cause major variation in human behavior.

As long as most political scientists dismiss ideas as secondary, residual, derivative aspects of politics, they might reasonably assume to be studying an objectively general world. In such a world, most political outcomes presumably reflect regular, rational reactions of similar human beings to varying structural or institutional conditions. Yet if ideas can have major causal effects—if political outcomes can vary widely with the nonnecessary, historically situated inventions of certain human beings—the value of general theories becomes an open question. Much variation in politics may reflect particular social constructions rather than general conditions. Even very widespread phenomena may reflect the proliferation of particular ideas or norms rather than regular reactions to objective factors. There might be some general things to say about political processes in such a world—illustrating common mechanisms of social construction—but the content of preferences, patterns of behavior, and institutions might not follow from any general framework. In a deeply socially constructed world, then, the theoretical accounts that explain the most potential variation in important outcomes might not be very general at all. They would explain how certain ideas or norms rather than others came to dominate a major political arena.

This book speaks directly to the juncture between these alternative worlds. Its main point is to use a fortuitously clear pattern of crosscutting ideas in a self-evidently important case to convince skeptics that ideas can cause major variation in politics—and to thereby undercut the prevailing assumption that the political world is a general one. I do not claim to have shown that we live in a deeply socially constructed world in general (though I suspect we do). But by showing with new rigor that the EU is deeply socially constructed, I cut away the remaining room for skeptics to deny the plausibility (or demonstrability) of social construction in general. In other words, I use an important example to establish that we live in a potentially deeply socially constructed world.

How should we judge theoretical contributions in such a world? If the generality of politics is an open question, generality cannot be the standard a priori for theoretical contributions. Embedding arguments about particular cases in general propositions about human action may be a complete waste of time. Only documented generality deserves respect: where non-ideational arguments show, in direct competition with ideational alternatives, that there are reasons to attribute causality to objective conditions across a specific range of outcomes in a specific range of cases. In all cases such documentation will require qualitative process-tracing evidence in addition to correlation of explanatory logics and outcomes, since an objective theory that correlates well to outcomes may be accessing particular widespread ideas, being "right for the wrong reasons." On the other hand, documented particularity deserves the same respect: where ideational arguments show, in direct competition with nonideational alternatives, that social constructions generate "local" dynamics in important cases. The ultimate criterion of theoretical value is the ability to explain the widest range of potential variation in important outcomes, whether that variation occurs for general or particular reasons.

These revised standards recast the theoretical terrain for the debate between my account of EU history and its competitors, above all Moravcsik's influential book. Relying on existing standards, readers might see this as a debate between an ad hoc, inductive narrative and a deductive, carefully specified general theory. Whatever my empirical strength, Moravcsik would still hold the high theoretical ground. If undocumented generality is not a virtue, however, it is irrelevant that his account drags a general theory behind it. We are then left with two competing claims about concrete patterns of mobilization and interpretive evidence. Moravcsik expects support for EU institution building to trace to economic positioning and looks for interpretive evidence that actors perceived clear economic interests as paramount. I expect support for these deals to cut across economic and other objective positions, and offer interpretive evidence that actors followed one of three ideational models. Despite appearances, neither account is more concrete or parsimonious than the other. Few real people would agree that a story about narrow *homo economicus* is more "concrete" than one where actors consider a wider range of issues. Furthermore, only the familiarity of the notion of "economic interest" in contemporary social science allows it to seem parsimonious. Were Moravcsik to elaborate the assumptions behind such motivations as I do for my ideational models, his account would be no simpler than mine.

Some general theorists solve these problems by renouncing the goal of causal explanation, justifying general models purely on their ability to correlate to outcomes. This is not unreasonable for some practical purposes (especially, perhaps, in the narrow world of economics), but it effectively quits the field that interests me. Like most political scientists, I want to know why certain things happen and others do not. Documented claims about the impact of either general or particular causes help us take the first step to establishing such knowledge: to assess the objective generality or socially constructed particularity of the phenomena we study.

.   .   .

29

A Postfunctionalist Theory of European Integration: From Permissive Consensus to Constraining Dissensus

Liesbet Hooghe and Gary Marks

Craig Parsons (Chapter 28) was unwilling to offer his constructivist theory as a general explanation for European integration. Not all constructivists, however, were so reticent to draw general conclusions from their empirical and theoretical investigations. Some argued that a proper accounting of the social and cultural factors that shaped attitudes toward integration could deepen our understanding of the general integration process and help solve several empirical puzzles that eluded neofunctionalism and intergovernmentalism.

Liesbet Hooghe and Gary Marks (both of the University of North Carolina–Chapel Hill) attempt to explain integration by going beyond functionalism, with its reliance on the actions of economic and political elites pursuing material benefits, to postfunctionalism, which takes into account the powerful influence of communal identity. Taking their own multilevel governance approach as their starting place (see Chapter 26), Hooghe and Marks point out that the expansion of authority across traditional jurisdictions has created opportunities for domestic economic interest groups to connect with Europe-wide authorities. Further intertwining of domestic and supranational politics has occurred in the post-Maastricht era, as EU policies have reached deeper into member states, Brussels institutions have become more transparent and accountable, and member states have held more referenda on treaty revisions. The result has been a complex public debate over the economic benefits of integration and, increasingly, the impact of European unity on national identity. The conflict between effi-

Reprinted with permission from *British Journal of Political Science* 39 (2008): 1–23. Copyright by Cambridge University Press. Notes omitted.

ciency and identity (which must be constructed and mobilized by elites and political parties) has undermined a pro-Europe consensus among elites and electorates, dangerously divided some political parties, and boosted the fortunes of several Euroskeptical political parties from the "tan" (traditionalism/authority/nationalism) fringe of the identity spectrum.

According to Hooghe and Marks, domestic politics, which elites once walled off from decisionmaking in Brussels, has now been Europeanized in ways that can be explained using theories of interest mobilization and party competition. Integration can no longer be explained without accounting for the construction of identities in Europe and the use of "identity" for political purposes by party elites. But according to Hooghe and Marks, these explanations, far from being unique to specific situations, are rational and lead to generalizable conclusions.

At certain times in the history of a discipline, theories extend beyond the empirical facts that have been discovered to test them; at other times, new facts come to light that cannot be comprehended in terms of the theories available. For the past decade or more, European integration has thrown up a series of facts that escape the theories on offer. How can one explain the outcomes of referendums which shape the course of European integration? What explains public opinion, competition among political parties and the populist pressures that have thrust Europe into domestic politics? Why has the process of decision making over Europe changed? These questions have drawn comparativists to examine the European Union, but this research has rarely been guided by theories of regional integration.

The purpose of theory is to frame research agendas—to direct empirical research to interesting developments, to find and solve empirical puzzles, as well as to generalize. In this article we outline a research programme that seeks to make sense of new developments in the politics of the European Union (EU) and the middle-range theories that account for them.

We do so by using the building blocks of the multi-level governance approach to European integration. Multi-level governance conceives regional integration as part of a more general phenomenon, the articulation of authority across jurisdictions at diverse scales. In earlier work we detected direct connections between domestic groups and European actors that contradicted the claim that states monopolize the representation of their citizens in international relations. Here we extend this line of argument by analysing how domestic patterns of conflict across the European Union constrain the course of European integration. Domestic and European politics have become more tightly coupled as governments have become responsive to public pressures on European integration.

A theory of regional integration should tell us about the political choices that determine its course. In order to explain the level and scope of integration, we need to understand the underlying conflicts: who is involved, on what issues and with what consequences. We therefore pay detailed attention to the substantive character of the debate over regional integration. What do key actors strive for?

The debate on Europe is complex, but recent research has shown it has structure. It is coherent, not chaotic. It is connected to domestic political conflict, not sui generis. And, while some have tried, no one has succeeded in reducing the debate to rational economic interest. For reasons that we turn to next, we believe that it is impossible to do so.

Every theory is grounded on a set of assumptions—intellectual short cuts—that reduce complexity and direct our attention to causally powerful factors. We claim that identity is decisive for multi-level governance in general, and for regional integration in particular. The reason for this derives from the nature of governance.

Governance has two entirely different purposes. Governance is a means to achieve collective benefits by co-ordinating human activity. Given the variety of public goods and their varying externalities, efficient governance will be multi-level. But governance is also an expression of community. Citizens care—passionately—about who exercises authority over them. The challenge for a theory of multi-level governance is that the functional need for human co-operation rarely coincides with the territorial scope of community. Communities demand self rule, and the preference for self-rule is almost always inconsistent with the functional demand for regional authority. To understand European integration we need, therefore, to understand how, and when, identity is mobilized.

We describe the research programme as postfunctionalist because the term reflects an agnostic detachment about whether the jurisdictions that humans create are, or are not, efficient. While we share with neofunctionalism and intergovernmentalism the view that regional integration is triggered by a mismatch between efficiency and the existing structure of authority, we make no presumption that the outcome will reflect functional pressures, or even that the outcome will reflect these pressures mediated by their distributional consequences. Political conflict makes all the difference, and that conflict, we argue, engages communal identities.

Our argument can be broken down into three logical steps. First, we theorize public and party preferences over European integration. Secondly, we theorize the conditions under which public and party preferences matter, i.e. the conditions under which European integration is politicized in high profile debate. Thirdly, we conclude by hypothesizing the consequences of politicization for the substantive character of European integration.

Before we lay out this argument we suggest why neofunctionalism and intergovernmentalism have become less useful guides for research on the European Union.

Neofunctionalism and Intergovernmentalism

Both neofunctionalism and intergovernmentalism refine a prior and simpler theory—functionalism—which shaped thinking about political integration among scholars and policy makers from the end of the First World War until the 1950s. Functionalism assumed that the sheer existence of a mismatch between the territorial scale of human problems and of political authority generates pressures for jurisdictional reform. David Mitrany, the principal functionalist thinker after the Second World War, believed that the welfare benefits of supranationalism would impel reform.

Later, scholars elaborated explanations from a more detached scientific standpoint. They retained the functionalist insight that regional integration is a response to the collective benefits of extending the territorial scope of jurisdictions, but they were well aware that the mismatch between collective welfare and the structure of authority does not speak for itself.

Neofunctionalists were puzzled by the speed and breadth of regional integration in Europe in the 1950s and 1960s. How, they asked, could rapid jurisdictional reform take place among embedded national states? They identified several political processes that intervened between functionality and the structure of authority. Jurisdictional reform had to be initiated and driven by transnational interest groups demanding supranational authority to reap (mainly economic) benefits. Once set in motion, the process was self-reinforcing. As integration deepened and supranational institutions gained power, so more transnational interests would be drawn to the supranational level. Supranational actors would themselves demand more authority. Progress in one area would give rise to pressures for integration in other areas. Transnational mobilization, supranational activism and policy spillover would intervene between sectoral pressures for jurisdictional reform and institutional outcomes.

After the debacle of Charles de Gaulle's opposition to supranationalism and the empty chair crisis of 1965–66, neofunctionalist predictions appeared too rosy. The most influential alternative approach—intergovernmentalism—describes a family of theories that conceive regional integration as an outcome of bargaining among national states. The puzzle was not the speed or breadth of regional integration, but the decision of national states to create an international regime in the first place. Given their power and resources, why should states pool authority? Robert Keohane's answer was that international regimes provide states with the functional benefit of facilitating mutually advantageous co-ordination.

Neofunctionalists and intergovernmentalists engaged in a decades-long debate about whether the impetus for regional integration comes from national governments or from supranational or transnational actors, whether supranational institutions such as the European Commission are autonomous from national governments, and whether regional integration transforms national states. To a considerable extent, neofunctionalists and intergovernmentalists talked past each other. Neofunctionalists were most concerned with day-to-day policy making, while intergovernmentalists were concerned with the major treaties. But we should not be dismayed that facts did not settle the issue. Facts do not stand up for themselves in validating or invalidating a theory, but are deployed and debated. Such debate rarely yields a clear winner. What distinguishes positive from negative research agendas is the ability of a theory to shed light on new facts without adopting ad hoc hypotheses.

Disagreements between neofunctionalists and liberal intergovernmentalists should not obscure two commonalities. First, both conceived preferences as economic. Neofunctionalists argued that Pareto-improving economic gains lie behind demands for regional integration. Transnational interest groups and supranational actors pursue incremental economic reform along the line of least resistance. This would eventually transform the national state, and even identities, in a European direction. Liberal intergovernmentalists stressed that preferences over European integration reflected the distribution of economic gains among states or business groups.

Secondly, both neofunctionalism and liberal intergovernmentalism focus on distributional bargaining among (economic) interest groups. Neofunctionalists hypothesized that such groups would operate at the supranational, as well as at the national level. Intergovernmentalists conceived interest-group pressures within discrete national arenas. Business groups lobby national governments because this is the most direct way to exert political influence over EU decision making.

A central claim of this article is that one must probe beyond the economic preferences of interest groups to understand the course of European integration. An approach stressing interest-group calculation is more appropriate for European integration in the late 1950s to the late 1980s than either before or since. Only after the defeat of a European Defence Community in the French National Assembly in 1954 by 319 to 264 votes did proponents of regional integration turn to the market. Market making was considered by many as a second-best solution. Jean Monnet considered it third best—after the failure of political union, he devoted his efforts to integration in nuclear energy. Historically, the turn to market integration was preceded by conflict among, and within, political parties on the merits of German rearmament and pooling sovereignty over defence.

In the 1990s, partisan conflict intensified as market integration was extended to monetary union, and as political union once again came on the agenda. According to Stefano Bartolini, European integration reverses a centuries-long process of national boundary construction by providing exit options for individuals who had previously been nationally bounded. Hanspeter Kriesi, Edgar Grande and colleagues argue that European integration and globalization constitute a critical juncture for conflict in

Europe. The issue has spilled beyond interest group bargaining into the public sphere. Hence, it does not make sense to regard functional economic interest groups as inherently decisive for European integration, but as decisive only under certain conditions. Neofunctionalism and liberal intergovernmentalism generalize from the first three decades of integration, when the creation of a European legal system was driven by the demand for adjudication of economic disputes between firms. The implications for most people (except perhaps for farmers) were limited or not transparent. Public opinion was quiescent. These were years of permissive consensus, of deals cut by insulated elites. The period since 1991 might be described, by contrast, as one of constraining dissensus. Elites, that is, party leaders in positions of authority, must look over their shoulders when negotiating European issues. What they see does not reassure them.

Writing in 1958, Haas defended an elite perspective on the grounds that the general public was indifferent or impotent: "The emphasis on elites in the study of integration derives its justification from the bureaucratized nature of European organizations of long standing, in which basic decisions are made by the leadership, sometimes over the opposition and usually over the indifference of the general membership." Neofunctionalism had the profound insight that this was a temporary state of affairs. As more issues shifted to the European level, elite decision making would eventually give way to a process of politicization in which European issues would engage mass publics. However, neofunctionalists believed that politicization would lead national governments towards further integration. The assumption was that European polity building would follow the logic of state building where popular pressures for welfare contributed to centralization. Intergovernmentalism, for its part, had little to say on the topic: public contestation was placed outside the theory on grounds of parsimony.

The Structure of Debate over Europe

The elite-centred view of European integration survived the creation of a European Parliament and even direct elections from 1979. European elections were popularity tests for national governments. European integration, as several researchers found, was largely a non-issue for the public.

This view rests on three assumptions, none of which now hold. First, the public's attitudes towards European integration are superficial, and therefore incapable of providing a stable structure of electoral incentives for party positioning. Secondly, European integration is a low salience issue for the general public (in contrast to its high salience for business groups), and therefore has little influence on party competition. And, thirdly, the issues raised by European integration are sui generis, and therefore unrelated to the basic conflicts that structure political competition.

The experience of the past fifteen years—and the research it generated—has dismantled each of these assumptions. Public opinion on European integration, as we discuss below, is rather well structured, affects national voting and is connected to the basic dimensions that structure contestation in European societies.

With the Maastricht Accord of 1991, decision making on European integration entered the contentious world of party competition, elections and referendums. Content analysis of media in France, the Netherlands, Germany, Britain, Switzerland and Austria reveals that the proportion of statements devoted to European issues in national electoral campaigns increased from 2.5 per cent in the 1970s to 7 per cent in the 1990s. In the 1990s, between a tenth and an eighth of all policy statements in a sample of British and Swiss media contained references to Europe.

Analysing a dataset of 9,872 protests from 1984 through 1997, Doug Imig and Sidney Tarrow conclude that "European integration is highly salient to a growing range of citizens across the continent." On conservative assumptions, they find that the proportion of social movement protest oriented to Europe has risen from the 5–10 per cent range in the 1980s to between 20 and 30 per cent in the second half of the 1990s.

An expert survey conducted by Kenneth Benoit and Michael Laver finds that European integration was the third most important issue in national party competition in Western Europe in 2003, behind taxes v. spending and deregulation/privatization, but ahead of immigration. European integration topped the list in Britain, France, Cyprus and Malta. In Eastern Europe, joining the European Union was typically the most salient issue. At the same time—no coincidence—conflict over Europe within national parties has intensified in almost all EU countries. . . .

Figure [29.1] provides a schematic overview of our argument concerning domestic politicization. The key variable is the arena in which decision making takes place, which we represent as a barbell from mass politics to interest group politics. We conceive the arena both as a dependent variable and as an independent variable. The process begins on the left-hand side with a reform impetus (1) arising from a mismatch between functional efficiency and jurisdictional form, leading to issue creation (2) as political parties respond to public opinion and interest groups. Political parties frame arena choice (4)—whether an issue enters the arena of mass politics or is contained in the interest group arena—but they are constrained by arena rules (3), the formal rules in a polity concerning arena choice (for example, rules mandating or prohibiting referendums). Arena choice, in turn, shapes whether the conflict structure (5) on the issue is biased towards identity or distribution.

We claim that politicization of European integration has changed the content, as well as the process of decision making. This argument does not require that the public has become significantly more Eurosceptical. . . .

Figure 29.1   A Model of Domestic Politicization

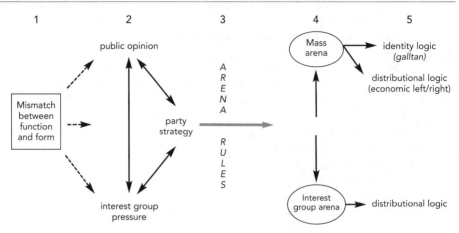

Notes: 1. Reform impetus: mismatch between jurisdictional architecture and functional pressures, which provokes tensions in prevailing interest constellation;

2. Issue creation: response (or non-response) by public opinion and interest groups to reform impetus, as framed and cued by political parties;

3. Arena rules: formal rules that constrain in which arena a decision about reform (or non-reform) will be taken;

4. Arena choice: selection of decision arena, which is mediated by political parties;

5. Conflict structure: extent to which an identity logic or distributional logic shape contestation about reform, bias to one or the other logic is affected by arena choice.

[Public opinion data] reveal that the level of public support in 2005 is not much lower than in 1985. The decisive change is that the elite has had to make room for a more Eurosceptical public. . . . The gap varies from large in Ireland (12 per cent), Luxembourg (17 per cent) and the Netherlands (18 per cent) . . . to extremely large in Sweden (57 per cent) and Germany (54 per cent). . . . In 1985 the public could be ignored; in 2005 this was no longer an option.

Closed shops of government leaders, interest groups and Commission officials have been bypassed as European issues have entered party competition. On major issues, governments, i.e. party leaders in positions of executive authority, try to anticipate the effect of their decisions on domestic publics. Public opinion on European integration has become a field of strategic interaction among party elites in their contest for political power.

Public Opinion

Not until the 1980s did researchers begin to take EU public opinion seriously. The point of departure was to hypothesize the objective consequences of market integration for individual economic well-being, using data on income, occupation and education. Later models extended economic theorizing to socio-tropic effects (for example, country-level indicators of inflation or growth), subjective effects (such as, "Will 2007 be better, worse or the same as it comes to the financial situation of your household?"), and subjective socio-tropic effects (for instance, "Will the economic situation in our country be better, worse, or the same in 2007?"). Such models explain about a fifth of the variance in public opinion on Europe. But could researchers assume that the economic calculations driving their models capture attitudes among unsophisticated respondents?

If individuals have neither the knowledge nor the time to figure out their economic interests in relation to European integration, perhaps they rely on cues. These cues could be ideological, deriving from an individual's position on left/right distributional conflict, or they could come from the media, intermediary institutions such as trade unions or churches, or from political parties. In fact, there is evidence for each of these. However, when one examines the content of such cues, it is clear that they engage identity as well as economic interest.

The reason for this is that the European Union is more than a means to lower economic transaction costs. It is part of a system of multi-level governance which facilitates social interaction across national boundaries, increases immigration and undermines national sovereignty. Economic losers are more prone than economic winners to feel culturally threatened, but the fit is loose.

Since 2002, researchers have probed how national identity shapes attitudes over Europe. This work draws on social identity theory which posits that group identifications shape individual self-conception. Humans have an "innate ethnocentric tendency," which leads a person to favour his or her own group over others. But favouritism for one's own group does not automatically lead to conflict or hostility towards others. Individuals typically have multiple identities. They identify with territorial communities on vastly different scales, from the local to the regional, to the national and beyond. What appears decisive is not the group with which one identifies, but how different group identities relate to each other, and whether and how they are mobilized in elite debate.

To explain how identity affects public opinion on Europe we must apply generalizations to specific circumstances. Three generalizations are particularly relevant:

- Identity has greater weight in public opinion than for elites or interest groups.
- Identity does not speak for itself in relation to most political objects, but must be politically constructed.

• The more exclusively an individual identifies with an ingroup, the less that individual is predisposed to support a jurisdiction encompassing outgroups.

The jurisdictional shape of Europe has been transformed, but the way in which citizens conceive their identities has not. Since 1992, when the European Union's public opinion instrument, Eurobarometer, began to ask questions about identity, the proportion of EU citizens who describe themselves as exclusively national, for example, British, French or Czech only, rather than national and European, European and national, or European only, has varied between 33 and 46 per cent, with no discernible trend. Neil Fligstein argues cogently that the experience of mobility and transnational social interaction spurs European identity, but the pace of such change is much slower than that of jurisdictional reform. Younger people tend to interact across national borders more than older people and, on average, they attest stronger European identity, but there is no evidence of an aggregate shift towards less exclusive national identities since the early 1990s, the period for which we have reasonably good data. Until generational change kicks in, Europe is faced with a tension between rapid jurisdictional change and relatively stable identities.

Two things would have to happen to activate such a tension politically, and both have happened. First, the tension must be salient. The scope and depth of European integration have perceptibly increased, and their effects have been magnified because they are part of a broader breakdown of national barriers giving rise to mass immigration and intensified economic competition.

Secondly, political entrepreneurs must mobilize the tension. Connections between national identity, cultural and economic insecurity and issues such as EU enlargement cannot be induced directly from experience, but have to be constructed. Such construction is most influential for individuals who do not have strong prior attitudes and for attitudes towards distant, abstract or new political objects. Hence, public opinion on Europe is particularly susceptible to construction: i.e. priming (making a consideration salient), framing (connecting a particular consideration to a political object) and cueing (instilling a bias).

It is not unusual for an individual to have a strong national attachment and yet be positively oriented to European integration. What matters is whether a person conceives of her national identity as exclusive or inclusive of other territorial identities. Individuals with exclusive national identities are predisposed to Euroscepticism if they are cued to believe that love of their country and its institutions is incompatible with European integration. Recent research by Catherine de Vries and Erica Edwards suggests that populist right parties are decisive in this regard. The stronger the party, the more likely it is that individuals with an exclusive national identity are Eurosceptics. The association indicates the limits as well as the power of framing, for individuals with inclusive identities are apparently not affected by either the existence or strength of a populist right party.

The claim that identity as well as economic interest underlies preferences over jurisdictional architecture sharply differentiates postfunctionalism from neofunctionalism and liberal intergovernmentalism. Identity is causally important to the extent that an issue has (a) opaque economic implications and (b) transparent communal implications that are (c) debated in public forums by (d) mass organizations rather than specialized interest groups.

A brake on European integration has been imposed not because people have changed their minds, but because, on a range of vital issues, legitimate decision making has shifted from an insulated elite to mass politics. This is the message of Figure [29.1]. Even if preferences have not changed much, the game has.

This has pushed Europe into national politics and national politics into decision making on Europe. In this sense the European system of multi-level governance has become more tightly coupled. But this has not led to homogenization. Public responses to Europe are refracted through national institutions and patterns of discourse that reflect distinct historical trajectories. Thomas Risse observes that "Europeanness or 'becoming European' is gradually being embedded in understandings of national identities." Public opinion researchers have hypothesized the effects of Catholic v. Protestant beliefs; of civic v. ethnic citizenship models; of co-ordinated v. market-liberal economic governance; of the communist legacy in Central and Eastern Europe, and of distinctive imperial experiences. National peculiarities are more pronounced among publics than elites because publics are more nationally rooted and are more dependent on information filtered by national media.

European politics has become multi-level in a way that few, if any, anticipated. The European Union is no longer insulated from domestic politics; domestic politics is no longer insulated from Europe. The result is greater divergence of politically relevant perceptions and a correspondingly constricted scope of agreement.

Political Parties

When researchers first tried to make sense of the politicization of European integration after the tumultuous response to the Maastricht Accord, they asked a simple question: how do European issues connect (or fail to connect) to the existing pattern of domestic conflict? An initial hunch was that contestation about the European Union would map on left v. right, which structures political conflict in most European countries. The logic of coalition building would then be distributional (as in Figure [29.1]), pitting parties representing economic factors (mainly labour v. capital) against each other. Coalitions would have to be broad to meet supermajoritarian hurdles within and across EU institutions. One coalition would encompass Christian democrats supporting social market capitalism and social democrats advocating market correcting measures at the European level, while seeking to preserve national spaces for redistribution. An opposing coalition would have conservatives and economic liberals as its core, and a Europe-wide (or wider) deregulated market as its goal. Labour and most social movements would undergird the first coalition, business and finance the second.

Evidence has accumulated for this conception of European politics. Left/right contestation structures competition on Europe among national political parties, roll-call voting in the European Parliament, social movement contention, media debates, the attitudes of European Commission officials, the positions adopted by member states in the Council of Ministers, and treaty bargaining.

However, left/right conflict over European issues is not the same as left/right conflict over national policies because the scope for economic redistribution is throttled in Europe. Convergence to a single European model would impose a dead-weight cost on diverse national welfare systems. Moreover, redistribution at the European level is not merely from the rich to the poor, but from the rich north and west to the poorer south and east. That is to say, redistribution at the individual level involves redistribution across member states—a large impediment to reform. If this were not enough, the left is faced with the challenge of cultural diversity which has increased considerably with enlargement to Central and Eastern Europe. Citizens are loath to redistribute income to individuals who are not perceived to belong to the same community. Currently, the European Union redistributes 0.75 per cent of its total economic product through agricultural and cohesion policies. This is a small proportion when compared to European states, though it is larger than that redistributed by any other international organization. Given the great and growing cultural diversity of the European Union, how much higher could this proportion go?

Consequently, left/right conflict at the European level is about social regulation, rather than redistribution. This alienates the radical left which regards the European Union as a one-sided capitalist project endangering social protection at the national level. Social democrats also wish to protect national welfare regimes from a European joint-decision trap, but see virtues in coordinating fiscal policy at the European level and in building a "citizens Europe." Social democratic parties, which formed governments or governing coalitions in thirteen of fifteen member states in 1997, pushed through the Amsterdam Treaty, which extended EU competence in employment, social regulation, women's rights, human rights and the environment.

In the second half of the twentieth century, politics in national states was oriented mainly to left/right conflict over policy outputs ("who gets what"), rather than the more combustible issue of the boundaries of the political community ("who is one of us"). European integration engages identity as well as distributional issues, but how would such pre-material issues be expressed?

In early 2000, the authors of this article were poring over newly collected data on the positioning of national political parties across the European Union. We expected to see a strong association between the left/right position of a party and its stance on European integration, but to our surprise, this was eclipsed when we substituted a non-economic left/right dimension, ranging from green/alternative/libertarian (or gal) to traditionalism/authority/nationalism (or tan). We came to realize that our analysis of politicization as a conflict between regulated capitalism and market liberalism was seriously incomplete.

Our hunch is that the statistical association between gal/tan and party positioning on European integration runs through something we do not measure directly: national identity. If this is correct, then the force that shapes public opinion on European integration also structures debate among political parties.

The association between gal/tan and support for European integration is particularly strong for parties located on the tan side of this dimension. Tan parties, such as the French Front National or the Austrian Freiheitliche Partei, reject European integration because they believe it weakens national sovereignty, diffuses self-rule and introduces foreign ideas. They oppose European integration for the same reasons that they oppose immigration: it undermines national community.

Conservative parties are also influenced by their location at the moderate tan side of the gal/tan dimension. They too defend national culture and national sovereignty against immigrants, against international regimes and against multiple territorial identities. In conservative parties, however, nationalism competes with neoliberalism. Nationalists resist dilution of national sovereignty in principle, while neoliberals are prepared to pool it to achieve economic integration. The clash between nationalism and neoliberalism has dominated the internal politics of the British Conservative party since the Maastricht Treaty, alienating the party from its traditional constituency—affluent, educated, middle-class voters—whose pragmatic Europeanism fits uncomfortably with the party's Euroscepticism. Similar disagreements in the Gaullist Rassemblement pour la Republique (RPR) propelled two anti-Europeanist factions to break away in the early 1990s. In

Germany, Angela Merkel, leader of the traditionally pro-European Christian democrats (CDU), has had her hands full with Eurosceptics in the Christlich Soziale-Union (CSU). In 2005 the CDU adopted the CSU's call for a petition against Turkey's membership of the European Union.

The result is that the line-up of supporters and opponents of European integration has changed. In 1984, two years before the single market, the main source of opposition was social-democratic and radical left. By the late 1990s, the largest reservoir of opposition was among radical tan parties.

The association between gal/tan attitudes and attitudes towards European integration is weaker on the gal side. However, the success of tan parties in connecting European integration to their core concerns has spurred their opponents. Green parties have come to consider European integration as part of their project for a multi-cultural European society—notwithstanding their misgivings about the European Union's democratic deficit and central bureaucracy. For left-gal parties, the European Union remains a difficult proposition because it combines gal policies with market liberalism. Les Verts and Groenlinks came out in favour of the Constitutional Treaty in the 2005 French and Dutch referendums, and they paid a price in terms of internal dissent and defection of their voters to the "No" camp.

Party conflict on European integration is simpler and more polarized in Central and Eastern Europe because gal/tan and left/right positions reinforce, rather than crosscut, each other. The axis of party competition that emerged after the collapse of communism runs from left-tan to right-gal, pitting market and cultural liberals against social protectionists and nationalists. Hence the two sources of Euroscepticism in Western Europe—tan and left—go together in the East. Left parties, including unreformed Communist parties, tend to be tan, and tan parties, including agrarian and populist parties, tend to be left. In Western Europe, the mobilization of national identity and of left concerns about the loss of national protection is expressed in different parties; in Eastern Europe, they are fused.

If we are right in arguing that jurisdictional issues are tapped by a gal/tan dimension of party competition, we can expect the following:

- European integration reinforces a previously subsidiary non-economic dimension. This non-economic dimension taps pre-material (rather than post-material) values arising from group (non)membership.
- This is bad news for mainstream political parties to the extent that it introduces salient concerns that cannot easily be accommodated in left/right contestation. A political party confronted by such an issue risks dividing its supporters.
- As the scope of European integration expands to non-economic issues, so Euroscepticism is likely to become more tan.
- Politicization is most pronounced in countries with populist tan parties.

Tan parties emphasize national values and this complicates transnational coalition-building. However, supermajoritarian decision rules (and unanimity on constitutional issues) magnify the influence of strategically located minorities with intense preferences. Opponents of reform are therefore less dependent on EU-wide coalition building than are supporters. A reform may be blocked if Eurosceptical parties gain control of government in one or two countries or if a simple majority of the public of one or two countries votes "No" in a referendum.

When Does an Issue Become Politicized?

To understand which issues are politicized we need to investigate strategic interaction among political parties. As European integration has grown in scope and depth, it has proved ripe for politicization. But there is nothing inevitable about this. Whether an issue enters mass politics depends not on its intrinsic importance, but on whether a political party picks it up. This is represented in Figure [29.1] as the interaction between public opinion, interest group pressures and party strategy. The consequence of party strategy for arena choice is mediated by the formal rules in a political system (for instance, on referendums) that facilitate or impede the shift of an issue from interest group politics to mass politics. Mass politics trumps interest group politics when both come into play. Interest groups are most effective when they have the field to themselves. When the spotlight of politicization is turned on an issue, when political parties and the public are focused on an issue, interest group lobbying may actually be counter-productive. As David Lowery summarizes: "the influence of organized interests—all other things equal—seems to be negatively associated with the scope of lobbying battles as measured by the number of organizations involved, the intensity of their lobbying, and how attentive the public is."

We assume that party leaders seek to politicize an issue when they see electoral advantage in doing so. We single out three (dis)incentives: a party's position on the issue in relation to other parties and the electorate; a party's ideological reputation; and the extent to which a party is united or divided on the issue.

• The greater a party's potential electoral popularity on an issue, the more it is induced to inject it into competition with other parties. The key term here is "potential," for party leaders strategize under uncertainty. How will opinion shift on an issue when it is debated? Will voters come to perceive the issue as salient, if they do not already? Elections are contests about what issues are important, and a party's decision to raise an issue in party competition rests on its strategic calculation that the issue will count, and will count in a particular direction.

• The ability of party leaders to chase votes by strategic positioning is constrained by reputational considerations and the ideological commitment of party activists. Political parties are not simply machines for aggregating the votes necessary to catapult ambitious individuals into government. Parties are membership organizations with durable programmatic commitments. These commitments constrain strategic positioning. Moreover, a party must strive to convince voters that it will actually do what it says it will do.

• Leaders are reluctant to raise the heat on an issue that threatens to divide their party. Disunity not only reduces a party's electoral popularity; it is the most frequent cause of party death.

This logic of party interaction and issue politicization appears consistent with what we know about the debate on European integration. Until the 1980s, most major parties steered clear of the issue. First, European integration was not salient among the public. The creation of a single European market was conceived as trade liberalization which had large and transparent effects on importers and exporters, but small and opaque effects for the general public. Secondly, to the extent that citizens had opinions on Europe, they were more sceptical than mainstream parties. Christian democratic and liberal parties had long staked out pro-integrationist positions. Until the 1980s, social democratic parties were dubious about economic integration, but once they came to realize that exit was not feasible, most campaigned for regulated capitalism, which would extend the scope of integration. Thirdly, internal dissent was the reward for mainstream parties that toyed with the issue. The identity concerns raised by European integration are orthogonal to left/right conflict which predominated in European party competition. When nationalist-oriented Gaullists or British conservatives campaigned against further integration, they were resisted by market liberals with harsh results for party unity.

Notwithstanding the general reluctance of elites to politicize European integration, some interesting exceptions arose when societies were confronted with basic decisions related to joining, enlarging or deepening the regime. The sheer existence of constitutional issues that cut against the axis of party competition is both a constant irritation and a standing temptation for party leaders. The flash point is the referendum. Referendums are elite-initiated events which can have elite-defying consequences. They are used for immediate effect, but their institutional impact has a considerable half-life. Referendums are not easily forgotten.

The process of legitimating the Maastricht Accord (1992) was a turning point in the causal underpinnings of European integration. It opened a complex elite bargain to public inspection, and precipitated referendums and a series of national debates that alerted publics to the fact that European integration was diluting national sovereignty. The rejection of the

Maastricht Accord in Denmark and its near rejection in France revealed an elite-public gap and sustained the populist notion that important EU decisions could no longer be legitimized by the executive and legislature operating in the normal way—direct popular approval was required.

Most mainstream parties continued to resist politicizing the issue. But a number of populist, non-governing, parties smelt blood. Their instinctive Euroscepticism was closer to the pulse of public opinion. On the far left, opposition to European integration expressed antipathy to capitalism; on the populist right, it expressed defence of national community.

European integration has been the project of mainstream parties of the centre right and centre left. For reasons we have spelled out, these parties have generally shied away from the issue. The debate on Europe has been framed by opponents of European integration, i.e. populist tan parties, nationalists in conservative parties, and radical left parties. Where the challenge comes from tan populists and national conservatives, the debate is conducted in terms of identity. Where the challenge comes from radical leftists, the debate is about distribution.

Conclusion

Our aim has been to draw on recent advances in the study of public opinion, political parties and identity in order to frame hypotheses about preferences, strategies and outcomes of regional integration. With respect to preferences over regional integration, we hypothesize sources of variation in the influence of identity across individuals, groups and countries. We argue that strong territorial identity is consistent with both support and opposition to regional integration; what matters is the extent to which identity is exclusive and whether it is cued by Eurosceptical political parties. We have reason to believe that identity is more influential (a) for the general public than for cognitively sophisticated individuals or functional interest groups, (b) for populist tan parties than for radical left parties, and (c) when regional integration is political as well as economic.

To explain when identity matters for the course of regional integration we theorize strategic competition among political parties. We have kept things simple by assuming that how an issue relates to the major conflicts in a society, and whether it is politicized or not, are determined by political parties seeking votes and avoiding internal conflict, while constrained by their ideology. Our account appears consistent with basic facts we observe: for example, that most mainstream parties are more Euro-supportive than voters, that mainstream parties have tried and failed to depoliticize the issue, that major EU issues are orthogonal to economic left/right competition, and that the heat has been raised mainly by oppositional parties or factions, particularly those on the populist right and radical left.

To the extent that exclusive identity infuses preferences and to the extent that European issues are politicized, so we expect to see downward pressure on the level and scope of integration. Domestic politics has become more tightly coupled with European outcomes. Treaty bargaining among national governments is mightily constrained by the fear of referendum defeat. Even when referendums are not on the agenda, party leaders in government worry about the electoral consequences of their European policies. A wide gap between public and elite, an increase in intra-party conflict, a series of referendum defeats and a deep reluctance on the part of governments to hazard public debate on further integration are consistent with the thrust of our argument.

Conflict over Europe is ideologically structured. Party government does not exist at the European level, but partisanship is influential in national responses to Europe and in European institutions. It is important to distinguish between rhetoric and reality when examining where national governments stand on Europe. Governments purport to represent all citizens living in their respective territories, and this leads them to frame their demands as expressions of national interest. When British Prime Minister John Major returned home from the Maastricht negotiations, he famously claimed "Game, set, and match" for the United Kingdom. But his chief victory, an opt-out from the Social Charter, was reversed as soon as a Labour government came to power.

Ideology may impede—or facilitate—the formation of supermajoritarian coalitions. Ideology may structure a negotiation, and thereby stabilize coalitions, reduce the number of effective actors and provide focal points for alternative agendas. However, the mobilization of exclusive national identity among mass publics is likely to raise the heat of debate, narrow the substantive ground of possible agreement and make key actors, including particularly national governments, less willing to compromise. Several observers have noted an intensification of national stubbornness in European negotiations. As European multi-level governance has become more closely coupled, so leaders have less room to manœuvre.

The problem with extrapolating this into the future is that people who can influence events may work around these constraints. We have endogenized politicization as an outcome of party strategy and public opinion. We consider treaties and referendums as instruments of human purpose, rather than fixed elements of political architecture, and this raises the question of how political leaders will respond.

First, and most obviously, controversial referendums are likely to be suppressed by repackaging reform into smaller, and therefore less referendum-prone, bundles. The challenge would then be to preserve the possibilities of log-rolling and side-payments across individual reforms. If this were not possible, then the scope for reform would narrow.

It is difficult to believe that politicization itself could be stuffed back in the bag. Institutional reforms could, however, lower the heat by providing greater flexibility for recalcitrant member states to opt out, or by making it easier for sub-sets of member states to co-operate, or by shifting decisions to non-majoritarian regulatory agencies. While we cannot predict which of these strategies will be tried out and which will work, we do predict that politicization will stimulate decisional reform.

The consequences of politicization would, of course, be transformed if the underlying preferences of citizens were to change. Identities change slowly, but they are far from fixed, and the way they constrain attitudes over European integration depends on party cues. Historically, identities were aligned with state jurisdictions because national rulers created the means to educate and socialize citizens, and reinforced national solidarity by impelling their populations into international conflicts. European integration, thankfully, is marked by absence of the coercion that has created states and nations. European integration can, therefore, be regarded as an experiment in identity formation in the absence of the chief force that has shaped identity in the past.

The research programme we present has several lacunae, the most important of which appear to us to be (a) an incomplete account of the construction of identity; (b) elegant (read simplistic) expectations about the relative causal weight of identity and distributional calculus; and (c) inadequate attention to geopolitics.

We have argued that the European Union is part of a system of multi-level governance which is driven by identity politics as well as by functional and distributional pressures. Conceptions of the political community are logically prior to decisions about regime form. In the European Union, the debate about who "we" are is politically charged and causally influential. Postfunctionalist theory does not expect jurisdictional design to be functionally efficient, or even to reflect functionality mediated by distributional bargaining. Functional pressures are one thing, regime outcomes are another. Community and self-governance, expressed in public opinion and mobilized by political parties, lie at the heart of jurisdictional design.

30

The Governance Approach to European Integration

Markus Jachtenfuchs

Hooghe and Marks (Chapter 26) introduced us to the governance approach to European Union politics. The "approach" is not a theory, but a perspective that opens the EU to a wide variety of theories of politics. Markus Jachtenfuchs (Hertie School of Governance) in this summary article attempts to make sense of the governance approach and its implications for the study of the EU.

Jachtenfuchs draws a distinction between classical theories of integration and the governance approach, arguing that the former attempts to explain the EU (the EU is the dependent variable) while the latter uses the EU to explain political phenomena (the EU is the independent variable). Thus, while neofunctionalism and intergovernmentalism attempt to identify the causes of European integration, the governance approach explores the ways the EU influences domestic "policies and politics" (Europeanization), explains the rise of the EU as a "regulatory state," and examines the intertwining of institutions and levels of government through network analysis.

While Jachtenfuchs is generally positive about the "achievements" of the governance approach, including its openness to other subdisciplines of political science, he is also aware of its weaknesses. In particular, he worries that the approach fails to take adequate account of "political power and rule," that it proliferates case studies, and that—most important—it has no clear theoretical focus. These "shortcomings," however, represent the maturation of the EU and EU scholarship. In Jachtenfuchs's view, a theory of European integration "is neither feasible nor desirable"; its time is past. Instead of looking for a theory to explain the EU, scholars should see the EU as "a unique laboratory for enhancing our understanding of politics in the twenty-first century"—and use it appropriately.

Reprinted with permission from *Journal of Common Market Studies* 39, no. 2 (2001): 245–264. Copyright 2001 by John Wiley and Sons. Notes omitted.

Introduction

In the last decade, the study of European integration has definitely come through the "dark ages" of the 1970s and early 1980s, a term that seems to be justified more with reference to the general mood prevailing at the time but which does not show up in time series of macro-quantitative data on the EU's development. In any case, since that period the quantity of scholarly work has increased considerably, theoretical issues rank high on the agenda of the sub-field and a number of substantive discoveries have been made. Still, the field is in rapid development and has a far from consolidated status with established theories, methods and a broadly consensual corpus of general knowledge and propositions. This article attempts to give an overview of the governance approach that has played an important role in the vitalization of European integration studies. Although it does not seek to discuss the concept of governance itself, governance can be understood as the intentional regulation of social relationships and the underlying conflicts by reliable and durable means and institutions instead of the direct use of power and violence. An even more straightforward definition of governance is to regard it as the ability to make collectively binding decisions, although in this case the definition of governance comes close to that of politics. The article is deliberately one-sided in that it looks only at the efficiency side of governance and for reasons of space entirely excludes the responsibility side, i.e. the question of democratic and legitimate governance. The argument proceeds in three steps. The first part traces the roots of this approach on the basis of sociology of knowledge perspective, the second presents a more general overview and synthesis of the approach, and the third contains a critical evaluation and an outlook for the future.

From Polity-Making to Governance

Conceptual Roots

The early phase of European integration studies was characterized by the search to understand the nature of the Euro-polity and the causes of its development. In this respect, the 1960s saw a lively debate between two theoretical orientations, neofunctionalism and intergovernmentalism. Whereas neofunctionalism saw the main dynamics of European integration in a broad social process of modernization, the rise of technocracy and what we today would call "globalization," intergovernmentalism while not denying the importance of these factors insisted that nation-states would not adapt smoothly to these social changes but that their reactions were shaped first and foremost by the competitive dynamics of the anarchical international system.

After its leading scholar [Haas] had declared its "obsolescence," regional integration theory vanished from scientific discussion. Students of regional integration directed their attention to other fields. The fundamental ideas of neofunctionalism proved to be extremely fruitful for other fields of research, symbolized by figures such as Joseph Nye for interdependence theory, John Gerard Ruggie for regime theory or Philippe Schmitter for neocorporatism. Others, such as Leon Lindberg, left the international realm and directed their attention towards domestic issues, such as the governance of the American economy or value change in western societies.

Hence, European integration studies appeared moribund in the mid-1970s. The emerging polity that had been so exciting both politically and scientifically seemed to have lost its momentum and its transformative power in the European state system. The standard rules of international relations seemed to apply and govern the relations between states in the European Union (EU) as well as elsewhere in the world. From this perspective, European integration was no more than a sub-field of the study of international relations and international organization.

However, research on European integration declined only if seen from the perspective of international relations theory. Scholars who were not interested in the possibility of a fundamental transformation of the international system but simply fascinated by the actual working of the new European institutions increasingly dominated the field. A major work from this perspective is *Policy-Making in the European Community* [by Helen Wallace and William Wallace], now in the fourth edition.

· · ·

The 1970s and the 1980s should not easily be dismissed as a lost era in the study of European integration just because grand theories in international relations had reached a dead end, and emphasis had moved to other issues. These two decades were full of empirical discoveries and yielded theoretical insights upon which present scholarship still builds. What may explain the bad reputation of this phase is its lack of theoretical focus—but not necessarily of theoretical interest. It did not have a common question that served as a focal point for competing theories and gave rise to substantive debates. Scholarship became fragmented and remained unconcerned with "big questions."

At the same time, normalization gained ground. Studies of party systems, electoral behavior or policy-making that are part of the established normal science of the study of domestic political systems were increasingly carried out with reference to the European Union. The same questions were asked that were asked elsewhere without ever turning to the fundamental issue of whether the basic categories of the sub-discipline of international relations—the nation-state and the anarchical international system—were still in place.

This started to change in the early 1990s. The internal market programme, launched in 1985, had given new political impetus to the stagnating integration process. This had two effects. On the one hand, it served as a stimulus for the question of classical integration theory and a renewed controversy surrounding the old issue of how the development of the Euro-polity could be explained.

On the other hand, a different question gained ground. As the Euro-polity grew more and more important, it became more interesting for researchers who were not genuinely interested in the European integration process as such, but had very different specializations such as comparative politics or policy analysis. In the latter field in particular, the development of the European Union seemed to abolish the conditions for an established division of labor within political science according to which students of domestic and comparative politics, on the one hand, and students of international relations on the other, dealt with rigidly separated fields of inquiry. Whereas the first had to do with matters within one or more states, the latter were concerned with what happened between states and remained largely unconcerned with domestic affairs.

True, there had been pioneering attempts to bridge the gap between the two camps of political science, raising questions about the impact of the international system on economic policy-making in different states. On the whole, however, they remained in a minority.

This was possible because, despite a growing literature on international interdependence, the assumption was that the external and internal relations of states were neatly separated. In other words, the idea that states were internally and externally sovereign remained at least a useful "as if" assumption on the basis of which a large body of substantive research could be produced. In the European Union after 1985, this assumption could no longer be upheld. The integration process blurred the distinction between domestic politics and international relations, and brought into question the assumption of the internally and externally sovereign nation-state. In the fast-growing literature on the impact of the European Union on domestic affairs of its member states, three major lines of thought emerged. These dealt with the Europeanization of the policies and politics, the rise of regulatory policy-making, and the emergence of a new mode of governance. Whereas the first two developed more or less simultaneously, the third joined in later.

At first sight, these lines of thought and the individual works that are part of them appear to deal with a highly diverging range of issues. They share, however, a common preoccupation which is entirely different from classic integration theory. Instead of asking how and why the Euro-polity came into existence, they take it as a given, and look at the impact of the Euro-polity on national and European policies and politics. To put it differently: in classic integration theory, the Euro-polity is the dependent variable, whereas in the governance literature it is the independent one.

Europeanization

The literature on the Europeanization of policies and politics started from the empirical observation that by no stretch of analytical imagination could political processes and policy-making in an EU member state now be adequately understood without taking into account the influence of the EU. From this starting point, a number of paths of inquiry developed that are not mutually exclusive and indeed are partly overlapping.

Two interrelated major concerns are characteristic of this type of literature. The first is an attempt to arrive at a broad empirical assessment of the degree of Europeanization of public policy across time and sectors. In this context, Europeanization is understood as the degree to which public policies are carried out either by the member state alone, jointly by member state and EU, or exclusively by the European Union. Several of these assessments are based on a scale originally developed by Lindberg and Scheingold. This scale ranges from 1 (exclusive domain of member state) to 5 (exclusive Union competence). The overall impression from this literature is, first, that over time and after an initial push of Europeanization most policy fields remain stuck somewhere between 3 and 4. Only in very few areas such as foreign trade policy has the EU achieved exclusive competence (i.e. a value of 5 on the Lindberg-Scheingold scale). This is not an indicator of the partial failure of integration, but on the contrary of its maturation. An average approximating a value of 5 would amount to a centralist state which is neither likely nor desirable. The present level is by and large comparable to that observed in federal systems but with a different distribution of individual scores, most notably in the field of foreign and security policy.

Second, variation between policy sectors is still huge. Hence, there is no uniform trend towards an ever-increasing Europeanization of policy-making as could be inferred from early neofunctionalist theorizing. Instead, we find joint policy-making in most fields with no signs of this being only a transitory stage towards complete Europeanization. On the contrary, joint policy-making seems to be both a general and a fairly stable pattern.

The second concern was with the substance of policies. Although this was often not set out explicitly, this type of literature had a distinct normative concern, namely the fear that national systems of regulation that were perceived as guaranteeing high standards of environmental, social or consumer protection or other valuable achievements were jeopardized by European integration. The reason for this assumption was the functioning of the EU's decision-making process. As most of the decisions were (and still are) taken by unanimity either *de jure* or *de facto,* it was reasonable to assume that outcomes reflected the lowest common denominator or the position of the least advanced member state. This becomes problematic in particular if seen in conjunction with the observation above. If an increasing number of policies are at least partly governed by the EU in addition to the member state *and* EU decisions are taken at the lowest common denominator level, it follows that in high-standard countries an increasing number of policies are in danger of harmonization towards the bottom.

Theoretical arguments and empirical observation lead to a complex picture with no clear tendency yet visible. Empirical studies have shown that the assumption of a *general* trend of harmonization towards the bottom is untenable. In the first place, the Europeanization of policy-making does not even lead to increasing uniformity, as one might perhaps expect. On the contrary, European policies present themselves as a "patchwork," a complex mixture of different policy-making styles, instruments and institutions. The process at work is less one of intentional and detailed harmonization but of "regulatory competition."

Second, if seen together European policies vary in terms of problem-solving capacity and effectiveness. In some fields, the EU was able to adopt policies even beyond those of the most advanced member states. At present, a number of partial theories seek to explain the observable empirical pattern of how the EU was able to escape from deadlock. They deal with negative *v.* positive integration, product *v.* process regulation, regulatory *v.* distributive policies, the availability of a credible exit option or the institutional transformation of conflicts and preferences. Even if one has no fundamental doubts about the possibility of achieving generalizable knowledge about policy processes, the available empirical evidence and the theoretical explanations to hand seem to indicate that there are no simple links between the EU's activity in a given policy area and the quality of policy outcomes.

The Rise of Regulatory Politics

This type of research can be traced back to the work of a single author: Giandomenico Majone. Starting in the early 1990s, Majone has systematically put forward theoretical arguments and empirical evidence that the European Union is what he calls a "regulatory state." Although his theory has been perceived largely as positive, it has a number of normative consequences that are probably more important than the analytical implications. In addition, Majone's conceptualization of the EU provided a fresh look at old institutions and opened up new possibilities for comparison.

In the first place, conceiving of the EU as a regulatory institution cuts across the dichotomies of the neofunctionalism *v.* intergovernmentalism debate in classic integration theory. It leaves aside the latter's concern with the driving forces of integration and looks at policy outcomes from a specific perspective. Regarding the EU as an instance of "regulatory federalism" thus provides a solution to the intriguing $n=1$ problem of integration theory by comparing it to other (federal) regulatory systems such as the US.

It also adopts the analytical perspective of the governance approach as outlined above by asking how the type of polity impacts on the policy adopted.

Majone's argument is that for a number of reasons, the EU is particularly well suited to regulatory policy-making, whereas at the same time it is ill equipped to deal with distributive or redistributive issues. The first reason is straightforward and simple; as the EU's budget is small compared to a federal state, policy-makers at the center (particularly in the European Commission) will propose regulatory policies out of their institutional self-interest in order to increase their power and influence. Regulatory policies do not require substantial financial commitment from public authorities because they put the financial burden of regulation on the addressees of regulation, i.e. mostly on private firms. Regulatory policy-making is by no means conflict-free because private actors may strongly oppose such regulation by referring to competitive pressures (as in the case of car emission standards). In general, however, the level of conflict to be expected is much lower than in the case of distributive or even redistributive policies where winners and losers are often easily visible and find themselves in a confrontational zero-sum game.

Second, the political goal of creating a European market requires a substantial degree of regulatory activity. In this view, markets are not self-constituting and self-stabilizing, but require constant regulation in order to constitute and maintain them. As a result, the Commission 1985 White Paper was by no means deregulatory in the sense of simply abolishing regulations but amounted to a massive re-regulation at the European level. Again, this is no accident but is rooted in the institutional structure of the European Union. In the EU, a unified economy co-exists with a fragmented political system in which each member state has an incentive to defect from European legislation in order to obtain benefits for its own population. In this situation, an institution insulated from political pressures, such as the European Commission, is particularly well suited to implement credible commitments for market preservation.

Third, the type of policy normally required in the European market is characterized by a high degree of specialized technical knowledge (e.g. in the field of medical drugs). Here, markets are best served by an efficiency-oriented policy that is best provided by experts independent of political pressure. Behind this is the idea that only in this case may policies achieve the optimal level of collective welfare, whereas political pressure typical of democratic institutions is likely to favor particular interests. Here, the EU institutions and in particular the Commission, the Court and most notably the newly established regulatory agencies are good examples of an "independent fourth branch of government" or of "non-majoritarian institutions." In addition, the structural problems of democracy at the European level and the somewhat weak legitimacy provided by the European Parliament make the EU an ideal candidate for efficiency-oriented regulatory policies. Efficiency-oriented policies, the argument says, require at best a weak degree of democratic control because they aim at Pareto-efficient solutions that are in the interest of everyone. Redistributive policies, on the other hand, are by definition not Pareto-efficient. As they make some people, groups or states better off at the expense of others, these policies require a high degree of democratic legitimacy that cannot be provided by the EU. Hence, the EU should concentrate on (efficiency-oriented) social regulation and leave (redistributive) social policy to the member states.

By this point at the latest, the normative implications of the theory become clear. The theory of the EU as a regulatory state not only seeks to understand regulatory growth in the European Union as a function of its institutional structure. At the same time it prescribes a particular institutional model for the EU as a response to the functional requirements of transnational markets, solutions to the problems of credible commitments and structural problems of democratic legitimacy. Contrary to most of the Europeanization literature, it does not confine itself to taking stock of the multitude of patterns, structures, ideas, and processes of European policy-making, but provides a yardstick for assessing the development of the Euro-polity beyond the old dichotomies of "federal state" and "intergovernmental organization."

Network Governance

In the policy-analytic literature of the last decade, "networks" is one of the most frequently used terms. With its emphasis on informal, loose structures that extend across and beyond hierarchies, the network concept appeared particularly well suited to grasp the essence of multi-level governance in the European Union. The network concept seemed to be the main opponent of intergovernmentalism which stressed clear hierarchies and privileged channels of access. In this respect, the network metaphor became a fruitful heuristic device for empirical analysis that considerably increased empirical knowledge about the actual working of EU policy-making at the micro-level, despite criticisms of its fuzziness.

In the first place, applying network analytic concepts to the study of the EU is another welcome attempt at seeing the EU in a comparative perspective. It appears that, on the whole, the fragmented and fluid institutional structure of the EU and the lack of a strong power center leads to an increase of channels of access and a larger variation of participants in the policy-making process as compared to governance systems in territorial states. But here, as in so many other fields of inquiry on the EU, we lack systematic and quantitative overall evidence.

A second branch of literature does not look at particular patterns of relationships between social actors in the tradition of socio-metric analysis, but regards networks as a particular mode of governance between hierarchy and anarchy or markets. Benz in particular has argued that networks are characterized by loose coupling of their constituent elements. Hierarchy, on the one hand, is characterized by rigid links between constituent elements, and markets, on the other hand, by no coupling at all. As a result, networks would be particularly well suited to the highly fragmented and decentralized institutional structure of the EU. As a prediction, it follows that networks should be more characteristic for the EU than for the average member state. In addition, the prevailing mode of network governance in the EU offers an explanation as to why the EU has managed to escape the "joint-decision trap." In essence, this is possible because in network governance, negotiators have relatively flexible mandates from their constituencies, whereas in more hierarchical systems such as German federalism, their negotiating position is much more rigid due to "narrow coupling" with their constituencies.

A variant of this literature has an even broader view of network governance: it is characterized by "consociation" as the organizing principle of political relations on the one hand, and the pursuit of individual interests (as opposed to the common good) as the constitutive logic of the polity. Thus, it is not only an analytical concept but also a political ideology, a kind of micro-constitutionalism of the European Union, because it starts from the assumption developed in modern systems theory that society is constituted by a number of sub-systems which largely function according to their own autonomous logic. For efficiency as well as for normative reasons, the autonomy of these sub-systems should be respected. Hierarchical governance in such a setting is not a very promising endeavor. If one adds territorial sub-systems to this perspective, one has an exact image of the European Union. Although this approach is still at an early stage—as is the case with most of the works reviewed above—it has the great advantage that it moves away from the proliferation of case studies on microscopic policy fields which only complicate our knowledge of the EU rather than simplifying it in order to discern characteristic features.

Critical Evaluation

Achievements
Much of the new dynamics in the study of European integration in the last decade is due to its governance orientation. This is not to deny that the question of classical integration theory (which forces and actors account for the development of the Euro-polity?) has not also seen a major development, driven notably by the controversy surrounding Andrew Moravcsik's liberal intergovernmentalist analysis of constitutional bargains [Chapter 23]. However, whereas the latter has a narrow focus, the former is much broader in orientation. This is both its strength and its weakness, as the following section claims.

The move in the analytical focus from polity development to governance has two important implications. First, it considerably broadens the field of inquiry and invites contributions from other sub-disciplines of political science, most notably from comparative politics, policy analysis and increasingly from political theory. As a result, the study of European integration diffuses into a number of sub-fields of political science with no particular interest in the EU as such. European integration has become a part of normal politics in a wide variety of issues and hence has to be taken account of by those working on these issues. With European integration becoming such a cross-cutting theme, its study hardly has any analytical core any longer. Political theory, electoral studies, interest group behavior and policy analysis all look at the EU from conceptual angles which are so different that the results are hard to communicate beyond the boundaries of the respective sub-discipline. As a result, European integration as a coherent field of study is disappearing. The old battles of the past between grand theories such as neofunctionalism and intergovernmentalism still continue, but they have lost their structuring force because they are of interest to only a small fraction of those studying the EU.

This is not a bad development. On the contrary, it is a sign of maturation and normalization, just as there is no theory of American, French or German politics and no sub-discipline for the study of one's own political system (at least in the eyes of some). It also alleviates the old $n=1$ problem that has plagued students of European integration for so long. As long as one takes into account the differences in the structure of the polity, there is no problem in comparing, say, patterns of interest intermediation or environmental policy-making in the US and the EU.

The second consequence is a certain disjuncture between American and European scholarship, with the former focusing more on classical integration theory and the latter more on the patterns and transformation of governance. This is easily explained by differing degrees of exposure to the object of inquiry. From a European perspective, the emergence of a supranational system that interferes in almost all aspects of political life is hard to deny. The consequences are also important not only for political scientists but for citizens. What from the outside may look like a rather obscure area interesting only to a handful of policy specialists (such as health and safety measures in the food sector) becomes an issue of public debate with constitutional implications if seen from inside.

To some degree, this is again a normal effect: interest in details decreases with distance from the object of study. Two points are, however, worth mentioning. First, there is no consensus as to whether health and safety measures in the food sector are a minor policy issue or a major constitutional question. Those who think it is such a question and who on the whole believe that the EU has developed into a political system with a constitution of its own are mostly located within Europe—but not all European scholars share this view. The health and safety example is one of a number of similar issues. Thus, it may seem that perhaps the most exciting and most important aspect of European integration—namely the transformation of traditional nation-states into constituent units of a new transnational political system that is not going to become a state—is largely overlooked from the outside. Second, this is not necessarily the sign of a comparative advancement of European scholars. There is also the risk of substantial parochialism.

On the whole, the governance approach to European integration has in the last three decades developed into a strong alternative to classical integration theory, both in terms of quantity and quality. The main growth period has been the 1990s because of the increasing intermingling of European and domestic affairs. Looking at governance in the European Union is not a competing approach to classical integration theory but a complement. Classical integration theory and the governance approach ask two different but complementary questions, the former on the causes and outcomes of polity development, the latter on forms, outcomes, problems and development paths of governance in the Euro-polity.

Like all dichotomies, this is a simplified image. Neofunctionalism, to take a prominent example from classical integration theory, has had a built-in feedback loop between polity development and governance: precisely because, under the conditions of internationalization and industrialization, governance by the EU was supposed to have a superior problem-solving capacity as compared to governance by the nation-states, [and] social actors were supposed to contribute to the further strengthening of the Euro-polity. Still, the basic research questions of the two branches of European integration studies are different. In the first case, the Euro-polity is the *explanandum;* in the second, it is the *explanans.*

The governance perspective considerably enlarges the perspective of looking at the EU as compared to classical integration theory with its strong international relations flavor. Simple as this may be, this is perhaps its most important effect. The fundamental concern of international relations theory is the question whether, to what degree and how international anarchy can be overcome. This is an extremely important question because it concerns the conditions for peaceful, non-violent relationships in a horizontally organized environment with no supreme authority and with no monopoly of the legitimate use of force.

Today, it is all too easily forgotten that classical integration theory began by trying to offer both a political and a scientific alternative to realism: regional integration in general and European integration in particular were seen as processes to overcome the anarchical structure of the international system, at least in limited geographical domains, and were supposed to create durable zones of peace beyond unstable balance-of-power arrangements. But this analytical perspective also has the disadvantage of elevating the question of the future of the sovereign nation-state to a fundamental issue of peace and war against which the problems of the European welfare state are just minor technical questions.

Again, this is a stark statement that does injustice to modern approaches of classical integration theory such as liberal intergovernmentalism or "multi-level governance." But the main issue remains: just because classical integration theory is engaged in a debate about the future of the sovereign state with respect to international institutions, it is less interested in a number of important questions that are at the core of the governance approach.

Most prominent in this respect is the question of the possibilities of democratic and legitimate governance beyond the nation-state (both in its analytical as well as its normative dimension) which has been neglected here because a fair treatment would require a separate paper. Second is the concern with the problem-solving capacity of national systems of governance and their transformation by Europeanization. Third is the question of political conflict as a result of the insertion of national systems of rules and regulations into a European political system.

Finally, by leaving aside the question of the future of the nation-state the governance approach is able to bridge the conceptual gap between the opposing ideal-typical worlds of the anarchical international system and hierarchical domestic systems. Both empirical research and theoretical arguments have pointed out for some time now that the idea of the modern state as externally sovereign and internally hierarchical is more an idealization of nineteenth-century political thought than a useful analytical concept for the reality of the twenty-first century. The state is increasingly faced with largely autonomous functional sub-systems and corporate actors. As a result, negotiating systems proliferate. This implies that the clear-cut distinction between the international system and domestic systems is increasingly blurred. A governance perspective has the potential to avoid a reification of this distinction by looking at the institutional forms of governance in negotiation systems.

Critique

The governance approach, however, has a number of shortcomings. Although it considerably broadens the analytical horizon as compared to classical integration theory, it has a strong bias towards effective and efficient problem-solving and almost completely ignores questions of political power and rule. It certainly is not alone in this respect. Apart from the neo-Marxist theory of regulation (not to be confused with Majone's approach), some works of a broadly defined post-modern flavor and some individual authors, these questions are almost completely ignored in the contemporary scientific discussion on the EU. Nevertheless, a perspective that starts from the assumption that the EU has developed into a new type of political system different from traditional nation-states should not ignore these issues.

Second, the strong policy orientation has led to a proliferation of case studies. Case studies are a legitimate method of political science and they are of particular importance in the political system of the European Union where we still lack solid microanalyses about how policy-making in the European Union works concretely. There is, however, a strong tendency to replicate the fragmentation of EU policy-making in research. The tendency of policy specialists to dig deeper and deeper into their field of specialization, leaving the rest of the world out of sight, is a phenomenon not confined to EU studies. But it does appear to be even stronger in the EU than in national settings because the mere complexity of the policy processes at stake considerably increases the workload. This is not only a problem for Ph.D. students. Studies covering more than a single policy and including more than two member states are extremely rare. Here we risk increasing information without increasing knowledge.

Third, this tendency is furthered by the fact that the governance perspective offers a *problematique* but does not constitute a coherent theory. It does not even attempt to become one. This is not bad in itself as theory-driven (or worse, meta-theory-driven) debates tend to be sterile and decoupled from empirical reality. A problem-oriented approach such as the governance perspective offers the potential of innovation by recombining elements of different streams of thinking in the social sciences. To do so, it needs a clear focus. Such a single, overarching thematic focus is not visible—governance as such is too broad an issue. The only eligible candidate to my mind, governance in negotiating systems, is still a largely German enterprise with limited international resonance.

Instead, we can observe several streams of discussion that are more or less autonomous. They may be divided along the classical distinction of polity, politics and policy. The policy-oriented literature is flourishing and taking up elements of both international relations and comparative studies of policy-making. A second stream is the literature on political processes, mainly interest group and party politics, and there is a growing literature on legislative politics, particularly from a rational choice perspective. Finally, a polity-oriented perspective looks at constitutional structures and democracy. The challenge for all three discourses is to avoid an exclusive EU orientation and parochialism by adopting a comparative perspective. In the last resort, such a development would integrate the European Union as one object of inquiry among others into standard middle-range theories such as party politics, legislative behavior, democratic accountability, governmental systems and the like—functional instead of territorial organization.

In the end, there would be no theory of European integration just as there is no theory of Swedish politics. However, international relations theory would not be the only broader theory that is able to say something meaningful about the EU. Donald Puchala's famous metaphor, "Of Blind Men, Elephants and International Integration" [Chapter 20] in this perspective is not the statement of a problem but of a desirable state of affairs. The multi-faceted nature of the European Union has no particular relevance to it. A "theory of European integration" is neither feasible nor desirable. What is sometimes subsumed under this label are mostly theories of international relations applied to the European Union. The governance approach offers to integrate the European Union in a number of other theories beyond international relations. This is not a trivial exercise. But it is worth pursuing since the EU is the place where fundamental developments that are transforming the possibilities of effective and responsible governance are probably stronger than elsewhere. In this respect, the EU constitutes a unique laboratory for enhancing our understanding of politics in the twenty-first century. To realize this promise is the great challenge of the governance approach.

31

Europe and Its Empires: From Rome to the European Union

Gary Marks

Federalists and students of comparative politics have compared the EU to other federations, such as the United States and Switzerland (see Chapters 25 and 27). Are there other useful comparisons? Gary Marks (University of North Carolina–Chapel Hill) argues in this piece, first given as a plenary lecture to the European Union Studies Association in 2011, that the EU is an empire (a large composite polity) that can be valuably compared to other composite polities, such as the Roman, Carolingian, Napoleonic, and Nazi empires.

Marks argues that empires exist to reap the significant benefits of jurisdictional scale: when it comes to governance, bigger is better. But their expansion necessarily brings separate communities together under the same authority. Communities can facilitate the expansion of governance within the group perceived as "us," but they can just as easily resist increases in jurisdiction when authority is extended to groups known as "them." Resistance is most pronounced when communities believe they are ruled by "foreigners." This tension between scale and community is magnified in empires. To address the tension, empires have used several strategies, including accommodation (community self-rule in exchange for resources), assimilation (induced identification with the empire), and elimination (community annihilation). The EU pursues a strategy of assimilation, according to Marks, but the euro crisis has exacerbated the tension between the need for scale and the resistance of national communities unwilling to treat all EU citizens as "us." Managing this tension is the challenge of empire—and the European Union.

Introduction

Five large polities have existed in the forests, mountains, valleys and islands that lie north of the Mediterranean and west of what is now Russia (Figure [31.1]). By "large," I mean having a land area no less than one-fifth of the west European landmass of 6 million km^2. By "polity," I mean a government having a reasonable probability of implementing authoritative decisions for the population living in its territory. The five polities are those of Rome, the Franks, Napoleonic France, Nazi Germany and the European Union (EU).

These may be conceived as empires in the Roman sense of exerting *imperium* (power, authority) over a great territory containing diverse communities. Each of them subordinates formerly independent units in a composite polity. Each combines direct and indirect rule. And each uses pre-existing structures and local elites to do so. Empires have a flexible, mosaic quality. They encompass, but do not homogenize, populations with diverse histories, languages and religions, and they adopt a mix of strategies to impose their rule.

Beyond this there is wide variation. Neither the European Union, nor Rome after it extended citizenship to the Italian peninsula in 88 BC and to the empire in 212 AD, are based on the exploitation of one people by another. Unlike most other empires, the EU is not seriously redistributive, but neither were the Franks. True, the European Union is the only one of these polities not based on organized violence. But the extent to which the others used organized violence varies considerably, and might therefore be

Figure 31.1   Europe and Its Empires

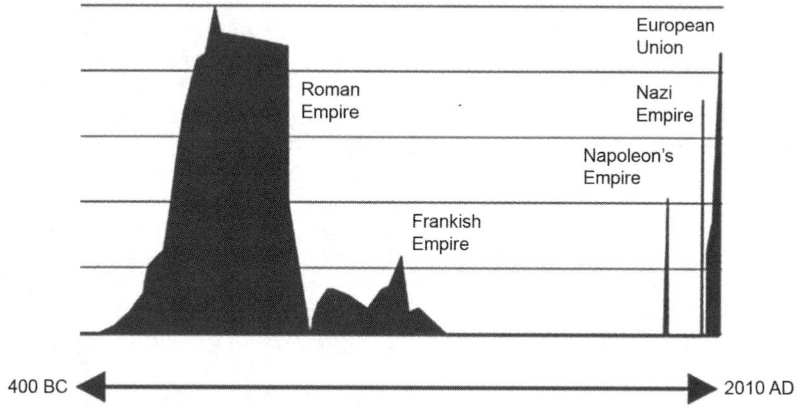

Source: Data from R. Taagepera, "Expansion and Contraction Patterns of Large Polities: Context for Russia," *International Studies Quarterly* 41, no. 3 (1997): 475–504.

Notes: Horizontal lines are increments of 1 million km^2. The figure is approximate because the borders of empires are typically imprecise. At its maximum extent, in 117 AD, around 40 per cent of the territory of the Roman Empire was in Africa and Asia Minor.

considered as something to be explained rather than a definitional trait. Here I wish to examine large composite polities—or empires, if you will— without requiring that they have a redistributive, exploitative and coercive center.

Calling the EU an empire can raise hackles. When José Manuel Barroso, President of the European Commission, observed that "Sometimes I like to compare the EU as a creation to the organisation of empire. [. . .] What we have is the first non-imperial empire. [. . .] I believe it is a great construction and we should be proud of it," the *Sunday Telegraph* declared on its front page that this comment would put the prime minister under pressure to hold a referendum on British membership of the European Union. My purpose here is not to provoke English Eurosceptics, but to understand the tensions that large, composite polities face, no matter how good or evil their purpose. Polities exercising rule over diverse territorial communities are intensely interesting phenomena that allow one to examine the vastly different ways in which humans manage diversity in order to reap the benefits of scale.

The benefits of scale arise from the nature of government. Government exists to provide public goods—that is, goods that are non-rival and non-exclusive. Such goods benefit all, but are not used up by those who consume them. When a public good is consumed, it is not depleted. So your consumption does not reduce my consumption. And this kind of good is no less important, and often more important, than the other kind of good—the one that is used up when it is consumed. Collective security is a public good, as are the institutions that sustain law, economic exchange and knowledge. If my consumption does not diminish your consumption, then the more people who contribute to producing the good, the cheaper it is for each of us. If two groups consume a public good, then the amount produced should reflect the collective benefit—not the benefit for any one group.

Hence, the benefits of jurisdictional scale are profound. By encompassing a greater number of people, larger jurisdictions—whether states, international regimes or empires—expand trade, extend the division of labor, and facilitate economies of scale in production and distribution. The larger a jurisdiction, the greater the benefit of standardization of weights and measures, of a single system of law regarding contracts and of other jurisdiction-wide reforms that reduce the transaction costs of exchange. The same applies to the elimination of tariffs and the suppression of violence. Scale benefits mercantilist as well as liberal regimes because, as the smaller German states found in the first decades of the 19th century, small regimes cannot effectively tax trade.

Scale is fundamental to political power. In wars among great powers, "victory has always gone to the side with the greatest material resources." Analysis of wars since 1816 reveals that countries with greater populations and larger economies usually win. Organization, technology, supply distance, terrain, and much besides, play a role, but scale is usually needed to underpin military power, and military power is usually needed to acquire and protect scale. Scale is a decided advantage when there is rough technological parity, which has been the condition of neighboring tribes and states for most of human history.

Scale provides insurance against disaster. If a polity is large enough it can assist those suffering from flood, earthquake or famine by mobilizing the resources of people living in areas not affected. The same principle applies to exogenous economic shocks. The benefit of scale in disaster relief is well documented.

The European Union exists chiefly to gain the benefits of scale in providing public goods. The Union encompasses countries and their regions in a continental system of economic exchange, individual mobility, dispute resolution, basic research and external representation. Scale enhances efficiency in each of these endeavors because it makes sense to determine the policy for all the people affected by a policy, rather than just one segment, and because the cost of providing a public policy is lower if it is shared across a very large number of people. The economic size of the Union makes it a great power in global economic, financial and environmental governance with "equal bargaining power vis-à-vis the United States."

A second principle of government is that communities—bounded groups of densely interacting humans sharing distinctive norms—facilitate and constrain the provision of public goods. On the one hand, communities diminish free-riding, which is the bane of public good provision, on account of their "shared understandings, [. . .] dense social networks and connective structures." On the other hand, communities constrain the provision of public goods because they resist rule by foreigners. These effects arise because communities are characterized by *parochial altruism.*

Communities are altruistic in that they instill commitment to the welfare of the group that goes beyond rational reciprocity. This idea is as old as the study of politics. Plato and Aristotle agreed that a community in which individuals internalize the common weal is a natural setting for government. Empirical research confirms the link between efficient public good provision and social interconnectedness, community, and norms that raise the cost of defection.

This is perhaps one reason why human beings have an innate propensity to form communities. Charles Darwin makes the telling observation that: "There can be no doubt that a tribe including many members who, from possessing in a high degree the spirit of patriotism, fidelity, obedience, courage, and sympathy, were always ready to give aid to each other and to sacrifice themselves for the common good, would be victorious over other tribes; and this would be natural selection." Altruism—the willingness of an individual to make a sacrifice for his or her community—may be an adaptation to prolonged and existential group competition.

As the term "parochial altruism" suggests, communities are double-edged. The social solidarity that facilitates government within communities, constrains government among them. Communities are parochial in that they divide the social world into "us" and "them," into "insiders" and "outsiders." Distinctive norms and perceptions lead communities not only to prefer particular packages of public goods, but to demand self-rule—that is, the power to provide themselves with the public goods they desire. In the words of the medieval chronicler Thietmar of Merseburg: "Rule by foreigners is the greatest punishment."

Unrestricted power—complete independence—is a chimera to the extent that a community is connected to others. The world has never been divided into non-overlapping, mutually exclusive, communities. Territorial communities exist at different scales, and often their edges are blurred. Patterns of social, economic and political interaction almost never coincide, even in hard states, and most persons consider themselves members of more than one territorial community. So the link between community and identity is open-textured and contested. What then matters for self-rule is the extent to which members of a community have an exclusive attachment, so that they regard an overarching jurisdiction as "rule by foreigners."

The tension between scale and community creates a terrain for strategy. Small polities can try to hide in the skirts of great powers or gain some of the benefits of scale through alliance, by merging into federal regimes or by co-operation in international regimes. Or scale can be created within an overarching polity or empire. The possibilities are many. The premise here is that all can be viewed as solutions to a single problem.

In our research, Hooghe and I have explored these principles of government at the European and sub-national levels. Multi-level governance can be understood as an attempt to reap scale while adapting government to local and regional self-rule. This article engages scale and community where they are most in tension—in empires. Empires are interesting for a political scientist precisely because they confront, in an extreme way, a tension that exists in any polity composed of multiple communities. Just as an astronomer might look for clues to the life of stars by examining supernovae, so empires provide natural experiments in the life of large, diverse polities.

Accommodate, Assimilate, Eliminate?

Scale and community are fundamental to the structure of government. But they clash. Empires have responded to this dilemma by adopting some combination of the following strategies:

- *Accommodate*—that is, allow the community a measure of self-rule in exchange for some share of its financial, physical or human resources.
- *Assimilate*—that is, incorporate the community or its leaders by inducing them to identify with the empire.
- *Eliminate*—that is, destroy the community by dispersing, enslaving or killing its members.

Figure [31.2] models government structure as decision-making under the tension between scale and community. Because communities are rooted in patterns of social, economic and political interaction, they are path dependent. Whereas problems of collective action can emerge rapidly, communities change slowly. The consequence is that government cannot be understood as an efficient response to collective problems. Scale can exert enormous functional pressure, but communities may exhibit intense parochial altruism.

Accommodate

Accommodation is the engine of empire. Why not use the existing political structure of a subject community to exploit its resources? Let the community retain a measure of self-governance, and make its leaders responsible for providing resources to the empire. This relieves the empire of the task of monitoring the community's population, reforming its institutions, collecting its taxes, mobilizing its army and responding to, or suppressing, its discontents.

Indirect rule explains the speed of imperial growth, for an empire can grow by accumulating communities by war or diplomacy, without the costly and time-consuming process of swallowing and digesting the community. Indirect rule explains also the suddenness of imperial collapse. Accommodation leaves the constituent communities and their capacity for strategy intact. Imperial accommodation is continuous implicit negotiation, not a done deal.

Figure 31.2   Scale and Community

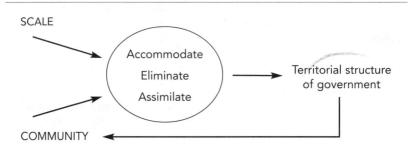

If the leaders of a community perceive the power of empire declining or its rewards fading, they can jump ship.

The European Union has grown by accommodation. The units are the most difficult material for empire yet invented: states. Europe is the crucible in which states melded diverse populations into national communities by inter-state war, religious persecution, national legal systems, and in recent centuries, national systems of communication, education, welfare, industrial relations and economic regulation. It did not always work. Some minority communities were able to resist national integration, but by the middle of the 20th century, western Europe was divided into fewer than 20 states, each of which asserted complete authority within their borders.

The European Union is a response to the following question: how can one realize the benefits of scale while accommodating diverse communities? The answer, in short, is to tax little and redistribute less; legislate by directive as well as uniform regulation; seek consensus and decide by unanimity or supermajority; permit enhanced co-operation by subsets of member states; use soft law and benchmarking; and even then allow member states to include themselves out (for example, by derogation). "[R]ather than applying strictly binding rules of co-ordination in a hierarchical setting or in compulsory negotiation systems, policy-making in the EU aims at a rather flexible combination of co-operation, competition and control." On the one hand, the EU is a regime of mutual adjustment among its member states; on the other, it relies on courts and the rule of law to legitimate and adjudicate its decisions.

Scale in the face of diversity has produced a complex—almost incomprehensible—polity. European legislation must pass through perhaps the most severe obstacle course in the entire history of government. Authority is dispersed *vertically* across three, four or five layers of government depending on the country, and it is dispersed *horizontally* at the European level across two executives, two secretariats, three legislatures and a court.

If an empire must have a center, then the European Union is no empire. In fact, it is distinctly a non-empire, because it makes a fetish of its lack of central direction. There is not one president, but two, sitting in the Commission and the Council. When asked for the telephone number of their leader, Europeans respond with a directory of addresses. The EU is multi-level, multilateral and multi-centered.

If an empire is based on coercion, then the European Union is no empire. The EU "secures its internal domination not through force, but through a *taboo on force*." The EU does not seek to monopolize organized coercion within its territory, but relies on its Member States to enforce their legal obligations. The EU is an empire of the pen, not the sword.

Rome, like the EU, was built by accommodating diversity. The Italian peninsula in the 5th century BC, like Europe in the mid-20th century, was populated by proud, independent polities that were grounded in solidaristic communities. Rome was merely one among numerous Latin and Etruscan city states. City states, then and later, are paragons of parochial altruism—evoking intense solidarity within and prickly independence without.

How did Rome do it? How did it create scale in the presence of city states? Rome practiced accommodation as an art. As it expanded in the Italian peninsula, beginning with the defeat of the Latin League in 498 BC and continuing with the withdrawal of Pyrrhus to Greece in 275 BC, the Roman republic remained a city among other, self-governing, cities. Rome began by annexing the land in its immediate vicinity, but as it expanded, the path to scale was accommodation—not annexation. To extend a term that Schimmelfennig *et al.* apply to the EU, Roman integration was "*differentiated.*" There was no one model, or even two or three, but a set of flexible designs for the *federation*—the treaty that tied an individual city or tribe into the Roman *confederatio*. A number of these survive as inscriptions or are reported second hand. Livy discusses seven arrangements for Latin cities in 338 BC. These involved legally binding arrangements concerning intermarriage, property ownership, voting rights, land redistribution, shipping, whether citizens of a city could join colonies, and the number of troops it had to supply. Each of these elements could vary independently of the others, and they did. The inhabitants of some cities were granted full citizenship, others were *cives sine suffragio*—that is, they paid Roman taxes and served in the army, but could not vote—while others were allies (*socii*) who were exempt from taxes, but who had to provide auxiliary troops to serve under Roman generals.

There was no overarching plan. All roads led to Rome, but there was no attempt to create homogeneity. Rule was indirect and multi-level. "We grant you freedom [. . .] so that you may have in your control the whole organization of your community according to your laws." The Roman bureaucracy was, in any case, tiny. When it peaked in the 5th century AD, there were perhaps 30,000 Roman administrators in the entire empire. City magistrates were chosen under local rules, received no Roman wage, and were responsible for the supply of corn and water, maintaining local order, collecting taxes, recruiting soldiers for the Roman army, and maintaining streets, buildings and markets. In turn, Rome buttressed the magistrate's authority if the plebs revolted.

When the empire expanded to the north and west, a salaried governor was installed in each province to maintain public order and hold judicial sessions. This was direct rule, but of the lightest kind. A governor was expected to respect local legal norms and city liberties, and had to operate within the *lex provinciae*—the treaty incorporating the province in the empire. "Obedience—this was what counted. But outside that, the authorities seem blind to practically all the other things that have led other governments to disqualify, despoil, rob, deport, imprison, torture, burn, impale." Any ambition a governor had to reform a province in the Roman mold was, in any case, constrained by the paltry resources he had at his disposal: a tiny staff, limited military force. At the end of his non-renewable tenure, the locals had a legal right to prosecute the governor for extortion or malfeasance.

Yet accommodation is double-edged, for it leaves the community and its capacity for strategy intact. This almost destroyed the Roman Empire when Hannibal and his army swept down from the Alps into the Po valley in 212 BC. Successive Roman defeats raised the possibility of autonomy for formerly independent towns. And Hannibal was acutely aware that his only hope for success lay in dividing, rather than defeating, his enemy. His aim, according to a contemporary observer, Polybius, "was to restore liberty to the peoples of Italy and give them back possession of the lands and towns confiscated by the Romans. [. . .] By doing so he hoped to draw the Italian populations into his camp by detaching them from the Romans and push into rebellion those who considered that their cities and ports had suffered from Rome's domination." He almost succeeded. After conquering two towns and defeating a Roman army, the Latin town of Clastidium was turned over to him by the commander of the local garrison. More towns followed in 216 BC after Hannibal massacred the principal Roman army at Cannae. These included Capua, the second largest city in Italy after Rome. The Capuans invited Hannibal into their city "not only with obedience, but with zeal, with the full agreement of the common people, and with eagerness to see a general rendered illustrious by so many victories." Capuans demanded, and received, rights denied by Rome. Hannibal consented that "no Carthaginian commander should have any authority over a Campanian citizen, nor any Campanian serve in war or perform any office against his will." This was not lower-class, but elite, revolt, led by town senators, some of whom were connected to great Roman families. Twenty-seven leaders of the revolt committed suicide rather than fall into Roman hands when Capua was recaptured five years later.

In order to support its army and administration, Rome required about 10 per cent of the product of the empire. Imperial income came from a tax on merchants and artisans, revenue from imperial lands and a variety of smaller taxes, but the chief source of revenue was a land tax that amounted to about a quarter of each harvest. A land tax demands accurate assessment of land ownership, and this requires up-to-date public records, including public registration of land sales, and a system for identifying and locating individual peasants. Finally, the tax must be collected from landowners in every town and village.

This system was not reproduced in smaller units when the Roman Empire broke up. "Economic complexity depended on imperial unity." Communities that were previously tied together in imperial networks became autarkic. Cities emptied, trade dwindled, crafts became local, the financial system collapsed, gold coins fell out of circulation, literacy declined, taxation simplified, revenues shrank, towns became fortresses. Local autonomy from barbarian rule was no panacea; the rupture was systemic. The peoples of Europe did, eventually, come to have a higher standard of living than those in the Roman Empire of the 2nd century AD, but this took about a thousand years.

In the Frankish empires, which were the largest Dark Age polities, taxation was limited to tolls, custom dues, a wheel tax, a bridge tax, a port tax, charges on the exercise of justice, penal fines, *seigneurage,* and the obligation to entertain the king and his company. Together these realized a fraction of the Roman land tax. Military campaigns, conducted against Saxons, Avars or Slavs on an annual basis, provided land and booty for imperial stakeholders, and land owned by the church could be confiscated. But the supply of church lands and despoilable neighbors was limited, and Charlemagne and his descendants had to draw on their own landholdings to reward nobles for providing knights. The land remained in the possession of noble families so long as there were heirs.

Community and scale in the post-Roman era. Dark Age empires fragmented in a thousand or more city states, principalities, kingdoms, dukedoms, bishoprics in search of power and resources. The challenge was greatest for independent towns and cities because communal traditions—expressed in city assemblies, popular military mobilization and citizenship—made it difficult for any one of them to swallow its neighbor. "Loyalty to the state was strong; at times it approached the intensity of modern nationalism. But no city-state ever solved the problem of incorporating new territories and new populations into its existing structure, of involving really large numbers of people into its political life."

One path to scale was to combine independent towns into leagues, of which the Hanseatic League was merely one of dozens that were created from the 13th century. These took the form of non-hierarchical coalitions, with the consequence that their durability under external pressure was limited by moral hazard: "[I]n the absence of a single jurisdiction [. . .] each state was liable to free-ride or to default on its obligations."

The constraints on scale beyond the city belt lay in the tangled web of marriage alliance and personal fealty which made the creation of large polities a matter of family circumstance and uncontested succession. In early medieval times, territorial identity appears to have been fluid and emergent. Communal identities were created by common political institutions—above all kingship. As taxes, royal councils, administration and local government were systematized, so one perceives the outlines of more stable and rooted communities. From the 11th century, chroniclers began to describe "permanent, settled inhabitants of a reasonably well-defined territory," forming "a community of custom, law, and descent."

The interaction of community and scale varied across western Europe with decisive consequences for state-building. Repeated conquest of England prevented the emergence of strong regional communities. Danish invasion eliminated the kingdoms of Northumberland, East Anglia and split Mercia; Wessex wiped out the Danish rulers; the Danes won the kingdom back in 1017; then came the Norman Conquest. Local customs and dialects persisted, particularly in the north and west, but regional communities did not resist uniform government. Shire courts, hundred courts and borough courts were generalized throughout the country; aldermen and reeves were royal, not local, agents; the king could call out all able-bodied men in the entire country in time of rebellion or invasion; no tax could be levied without royal permission. When rebellion took place, it was to demand redress against injustice or exorbitant taxation. From the time of the Norman Conquest to the present day, no peripheral elite has aspired to divide England or secede from it.

France, by contrast, was a mosaic state that grew by cobbling together independent provinces through inheritance, marriage, purchase or conquest. These provinces were feudal communities having distinct institutions, laws, languages. Capetian rule beyond the core domain was superficial, because it had to be. Royal suzerainty was sometimes nothing more than recognition of royal rights over justice and public order. In some provinces, the king was able to supply the judges, but the laws were provincial. The king could not raise an army directly, except in the Île-de-France, but had to call on provincial magnates to supply knights.

Communities at the margins of more powerful states were impelled into larger collectivities for mutual security. Britons and Gauls did not have the time to do this under the pressure of Roman conquest, but the Germanic tribes at the northern reaches of the Roman Empire were transformed into larger communities over the course of the 2nd and 3rd centuries AD. The threat of English invasion stimulated cooperation among Picts, Scots, Britons and Angles in the north of Britain, and by the second decade of the 14th century, the lords of Scotland could appeal to the Pope for independence on behalf "of the whole community of the realm." King Robert, they claimed, ruled in a line of kings "unbroken by a single foreigner" and succeeded to the throne "according to our laws and customs which we shall maintain to the death." The Scottish lords go on to declare that "as long as a hundred of us remain alive, never will we on any conditions be subjected to the lordship of the English. It is in truth not for glory, nor riches, nor honours that we are fighting, but for freedom alone, which no honest man gives up but with life itself."

Freedom meant the right of a community to its way of life. If by consequence of dynastic union, independence was not on the cards, then freedom might be contracted. When Edward I arranged for his son to marry the queen of Scots, he signed a treaty with "the whole community" of Scots that their kingdom would remain "separate and apart from the realm of England, and free in itself without any subjection," so that "the rights, laws, liberties, and customs [. . .] shall be fully and inviolably observed for all time." Monarchs sought to create larger kingdoms for their heirs by strategic marriage, but they could not impose uniformity on the communities of the realm. When Henry V of England married the daughter of Charles VI of France, he had to pledge that their heir would guarantee "to each kingdom its rights, liberties or customs, usages and laws, not submitting in any manner one kingdom to the other." The same applied to Philip II of Spain when he married Mary I of England; parliament demanded that Philip would "obey all the laws and English customs, would not admit foreigners as employee in England and would not involve the same one in wars."

Normative diversity in Europe after the break-up of the Roman Empire decisively constrained the scale of government. Figure [31.1] summarizes a coherent path-dependent phenomenon, a prolonged U-curve in which no one polity spanned one-fifth of western Europe for almost a millennium. The nearest thing was Charles the Fifth's Habsburg Empire encompassing Spain, Italy south of Rome, the Low Countries, Bohemia, Transylvania and Austria. The dynasty had immense difficulty in realizing the benefits of scale against the centrifugal demands of its communities to uphold customary rights. Charles, born in Ghent, precipitated a communal revolt in Castile when he imposed Flemish courtiers and married an Iberian princess. His son, Philip II, faced a long and bloody revolt in the Low Countries because he sought to impose Spanish rule on his Flemish subjects. Instead of contributing to Habsburg power, Flanders—the richest part of Europe—drained imperial resources.

The emergence and consolidation of states diminished the benefits and raised the costs of empire. States consolidate and demarcate national communities because they facilitate interaction within their borders and impose costs on that beyond. This produces path dependence of the stickiest kind: an interlocking package of intensified national communication, national laws and institutions, linguistic homogeneity, reinforced by national community. Border disputes and wars were frequent, but until Napoleon and Hitler, no major power annexed another by force. Defeating a power is one thing, absorbing it is another. The main concessions to scale were the creation of states based on communities in Germany and Italy that had previously been divided into multiple states or statelets.

The Napoleonic and Nazi empires appear in Figure [31.1] as spikes in a flat terrain. These spike empires sought scale through conquest, but they were undone by their inability to exploit the resources of the communities they conquered. In a Europe of national states, victories on the battlefield could not produce durable subjugation of national communities.

Eliminate

Eliminationism is the strategy of destroying a subject community by dispersing, enslaving or killing its members. Madness and sadism have played a role, but there are some patterns to eliminationism that explain its incidence. First, it has been used as the ultimate punishment for rebellion in order to strike fear into those who might follow. This is how the Romans considered and practiced it in Corinth and in Judea, Napoleon in Spain, and Hitler in eastern Europe. But its effects are double-edged because elimination provokes not just fear, but the realization that surrender means death. So communities faced with elimination may, if they retain a capacity for strategy, fight to the end.

Second, empires have eliminated defeated communities when their purpose is to exploit the land, not its people. This was precisely Hitler's intention in invading eastern Europe and the Soviet Union. "It is not a matter of acquiring population but of gathering space for agricultural use." However, eliminationism is a fragile basis for empire because it strips the conquered territory of labor, and retains only its raw resources. For the Third Reich the cost was yet greater, for it deprived the Reich of the opportunity to exploit the unfulfilled national aspirations of Ukrainian and Baltic peoples.

The threat of decisive force against rebel communities, up to and including their destruction, is a recurrent theme in the efforts of empires to forestall exit. Empire-building in the age of the national state has been particularly brutal. How much force would have been necessary to quell demands for national autonomy in continental Europe if the Nazi Empire had not been defeated in war? Hitler's interpreter admitted that: "The Nazis kept talking about a 1,000-year Reich, but they couldn't think ahead for five minutes." The Napoleonic and Nazi empires were ephemeral because they were based on a fundamental contradiction: they were nationalist empires in a continent of national communities. Both sought to induce cooperation by framing universal values, but these values were recognized as a fig leaf for aggrandizement. The nationalism that generated the internal solidarity and military power of the Napoleonic and Nazi empires produced hatred and resistance on the part of the peoples they subjugated. This enormously restricted the ability of these empires to mobilize the resources of their conquered communities. Labor productivity in aircraft factories was four times higher in Germany than in occupied France. The gross product of what became Nazi Europe was actually greater than that of the United States before World War II and vastly greater than that of Britain, but it declined considerably under Nazi rule.

Assimilate

Empire builders dream of assimilating subject communities. Not assimilation in the *Star Trek* vision of the Borg—a cybernetic organism that implants components in an individual of another species making it Borg. Assimilation in the more practical sense of directly or indirectly inducing members of a community to adopt a dual identity. Assimilation provides an empire with the capacity to extract more resources as it grows in scale. This is the snowball scenario in which the benefits of scale are unshackled from diversity, so that as the empire grows in size, it gains momentum to grow further.

There are two sides to assimilation: the pull of empire; and the brake of community. The pull of empire is the extent to which an empires is willing, and able, to improve the life chances of those who choose to assimilate. How open is the empire to a person prepared to pay the cost of membership—speaking the right language, wearing the right clothes, adopting an imperial identity, becoming, so to speak, normatively bilingual? And if the empire is open to assimilation, what is in it for a person who chooses to assimilate? What difference does this make to a person's stream of income, or more broadly, his or her life chances? The brake of community is the extent to which a community resists imperial rule as illegitimate. How closed and close-knit is the community? Do the social, economic, religious and linguistic boundaries that demarcate the community coincide? How profound is the normative tension with the empire? What penalties can the community impose on a collaborator?

The Romanization of the culturally and linguistically diverse tribes and cities of the Italian peninsula "in a single civic whole" is one of the most successful instances of assimilation in human history. Roman assimilation had the advantage of pre-modernity: it did not have to contend with the perception of irreducible racial or ethnic difference. And in the era before monotheism, assimilation did not require religious conversion, but simply the extension of an already diverse pantheon of gods. Roman citizenship was based on values, not genes, and could in theory, and eventually in practice, be attained by any person living in the empire.

Conquered cities and peoples were allowed to keep their own languages, cultures, laws and gods, but local rulers had to access the patronage of Roman senators and magistrates to influence land settlement, increase their wealth and sustain their authority within their own communities. As Rome gained military hegemony from the 3rd century BC, local elites learned Latin, adopted Roman manners, copied Greco-Roman architecture and "become integrated, by hook or by crook, into the sphere of Roman political power." However, the process was haphazard, largely unintended, and at one decisive juncture, was fiercely resisted by Rome itself.

The Social War (92–88 BC) was an uprising of Italians demanding the right to Roman citizenship. Depending on the particular treaty by which a tribe or town was tied to Rome, Italians, unlike Romans, were subject to land redistribution and property taxes, and had to pay for the upkeep of their army contingent. Italians were first to be called up to the army in crisis and undertook the most hazardous missions. They could expect harsher punishment for indiscipline. Italian soldiers received an equal share of war booty, but the Senate alone commanded subject cities and distributed their lands. All of this was particularly galling because the cultural distance between Roman citizens and Italians had shrunk to almost nothing. When they went abroad, Italians were perceived as Romans. But in Italy itself, Italians were a class apart and, while they ruled their own towns, they lacked the means to vote on imperial taxation or war. Most Roman senators opposed assimilation because they were unwilling to share the economic boon of empire and were alarmed by the prospect of a greatly enlarged electorate. However, victory for Rome in the Social War paradoxically meant defeat for opponents of assimilation. In order to win allies, Rome felt compelled to offer full citizenship to Italians who joined them. And within a few years, Rome extended citizenship to its erstwhile foes.

This may seem an age away from the question of assimilation in the European Union. There is no mass mobilization, let alone rebellion, demanding European citizenship. But there are some parallels that distinguish both the Roman and the EU experience from the intervening period of state-making. In both Rome and the EU, assimilation is an outcome of processes that are not designed for the purpose. Whereas assimilation was an explicit, often coercively imposed, goal of national states, it is implicit and non-coercive in Europe's bookend empires. In both Rome and the EU, assimilation is "assimilation lite"—that is, assimilation by adopting a dual local-imperial identity, not erasing one identity for another. In both Rome and the EU, the rules regarding assimilation are set out in treaties, with the demand that a community must adopt pre-existing imperial law. In Rome this was the *fundi factio;* in the EU, the *acquis communautaire.* In both Rome and the EU, the chief driver of assimilation is its benefit for members of the elite: Italian rulers and landowners in Roman days, mobile professionals and business owners today.

The Napoleonic Empire sought, with some success, to assimilate northern Italians and the communities of the southern Netherlands. Napoleon saw himself as creating a new Roman Empire, and tried to induce non-aristocratic elites to assimilate by breaking down feudal barriers and offering the possibility of advancement in a meritocratic system of equality before the law. He annexed Piedmont, Tuscany, Umbria, Parma, Rome and the Ligurian Republic; introduced French as the official language and the French franc as currency; provided avenues for new Frenchmen to become rich; compelled elite students to attend French military academies; and arranged marriages between French notables and girls from elite Italian families. However, this policy of *amalgame* was countered by the resentment of local populations against those who collaborated in collecting taxes and forcing conscription. Napoleon's imperial model became unviable when subject populations saw it "as foreign and thus illegitimate."

The consolidation of states in the post-Napoleonic era further limited the possibility of assimilation across national borders. Foreign collaborators of the Third Reich could not aspire to imperial citizenship. Moreover, Hitler's racism ruled out assimilation of non-Germanic communities. Where assimilation was successful, it required pre-existing cultural and linguistic affinities, as in Austria and the Sudetenland prior to their incorporation in the Third Reich.

After World War II, most people in western Europe regarded those living in neighboring states as foreigners. A European polity was created in the absence of Europeans. Even today, if one wishes to predict how a person views the EU, the most pertinent line of inquiry concerns how that person perceives his or her national community and its relation to other communities. Most Europeans have a strong attachment to their national community and a weaker attachment to Europe. What appears to be decisive is how these attachments fit together. Does an individual conceive of national identity as one among a set of attachments or as an exclusive attachment? Is membership of the national community conceived as civic, and hence acquired by residing in a country, speaking its language and respecting its laws, or as an inherently ethnic characteristic?

Those individuals who interact with others on a regular basis are most likely to conceive a European community alongside their national community. Individuals who travel within Europe, who speak a second European language, who spend a year studying in Europe, who live in a European country that is not their country of origin, are more likely to take on a European identity alongside their national identity. Around 10 per cent of Europeans (around 50 million people) say that they feel European only or European first and national second. If interaction across national borders continues to increase one would expect this proportion to grow. But the vast majority remains rooted in national conceptions of identity, and this has brought community into tension with further shifts of authority to Europe.

In the years when European decisions were made by elites, these questions did not count for much. But today things are different. A permissive consensus in which conceptions of community were inert has become a constraining dissensus in which nationalism is mobilized by populist political parties and Eurosceptic groups in referendums and national elections.

Collapse of Empire

There are more theories of imperial collapse than there are empires. No less than 210 reasons have been given for the fall of the Roman Empire. No theory can tell us precisely when and why empires collapse unless it can account for the exogenous shocks—succession crises, rise of new powers, changes in military technology, alliance politics, resource depletion, financial crises and so forth—that have historically brought this about. A theory of empire that predicts the fall of empire is a theory of almost everything.

A useful theory makes claims about what is likely to be causally important in explaining a phenomenon while pointing out things that otherwise might have been taken for granted or missed altogether. Scale and community, as theorized here, are basic principles of government, but they provide a setting for strategic choice rather than deterministic prediction. Both are in flux as patterns of human interaction change, and government itself shapes those patterns.

The Roman Empire transformed its own communities and those of its neighbors in ways that intensified the tension between imperial scale and local community. The problems that confronted Rome in the 4th century AD did not arise from imperial overreach—territorial expansion had been off the cards since Hadrian's reign (117 AD)—but from internal division and external threat. Each army group located in a border region—Britannia, the Danube, the Rhine—came to see itself as a community of fate with popular leaders and common interests. "A century of stable frontiers, fixed garrisons and local recruitment [. . .] had forged strong bonds between soldiers and the districts where they served. Many men were defending families, homes and farms nearby." Succession crises took on the character of regional wars among legions mobilizing different parts of the empire. Rome did not determine the outcome; it was the prize.

There was worse. The barbarian peoples of the north were scaling up. Tacitus, writing in the 1st century AD, identified more than 50 Germanic tribes which were just as likely to fight each other as fight Romans. Barbarian alliances could inflict the occasional defeat on Roman legions (as in the Teutoburg Forest in 9 AD), but these alliances "had no capacity to formulate and put into practice sustained and unifying political agendas." Ominously, by the 4th century the number of tribes described in written records and identified in archaeological sites decreased to a handful. Partly as a result of contact with Rome, barbarian farming intensified, population density rose, iron production increased and, most importantly, the sheer scale of tribal organization grew. The northern tribes had become a serious threat.

All of this might not have led to collapse but for a totally unanticipated development: the displacement of Goth tribes into the Roman Empire to escape the Huns. The first to come were the Tervingi in 376 who begged to be allowed to cross the Danube and settle in Thrace. To gain time to assemble his forces, Emperor Valens agreed. Two years later, the Tervingi and Goth allies defeated the main Roman army at Hadrianople, killing the Emperor and 35 tribunes. The peace of 382 established the mechanism by which Rome would break into pieces: a Gothic state within the empire, an independent community with its own leaders, its own laws and its own army.

The Frankish empire of the Carolingians was torn to pieces by a series of succession wars and by Vikings, Saracens and Magyars, who began by plundering and ended up carving out territories for settlement. However, by the time that the empire was eaten piecemeal by marauders, security was already organized on a local basis. If there is a systematic element to the collapse of the Frankish Empire, it lies in the independence of the local bosses who supplied its fighting power. The Frankish Empire relied on booty to reward supporters, but the supply dried up by the end of Charlemagne's reign, and there was no alternative but to provide gifts of non-renewable assets—above all, land from the royal fisc.

"Candy is dandy, but liquor is quicker." Napoleon's spike empire was launched in his Italian campaign of 1800, reached its maximal extent in 1812, and lasted for just three more years. Hitler's empire compressed even this rapid history: beginning in the autumn of 1939, peaking in 1943, and by the summer of 1945 in ruins. Neither empire effectively exploited its scale, but the proximate cause of collapse was military defeat. Yet even if these empires had not generated overwhelming counter-alliances, it is difficult to believe that they could have long endured.

The EU has no mortal enemy, and unlike former empires, it does not face a fiery end. Yet it is facing an economic shock that exacerbates the tension between scale and community. Monetary union reveals that the benefits of scale may involve redistribution across communities, and that while there is a willingness within each national community to help those in need, this does not extend beyond national borders. Parochial altruism constrains scale. Monetary union reduces economic transaction costs, but makes it impossible for a country experiencing recession to devalue its currency. Yet there is no routinized fiscal mechanism in the EU to subsidize a country that is suffering recession. The fundamental problem of the sovereign debt crisis is not economic, but political. The combined debt of Greece, Portugal and Ireland is currently ⇔680 billion – just 7 per cent of eurozone output. A European bond would assure markets that the debt would be repaid, and therefore lower interest costs, but the major European governments are unwilling. They oppose creating a public good that is vulnerable to defection. Governments of the weaker economies might not resist the temptation to draw on the European weal rather than engage in politically costly reform. A European fiscal government could limit this moral hazard, but it is considered politically infeasible because it would diminish national self-rule.

The EU was established on the ruins of Nazi Europe. The European states system and its vaunted balance of power had proved an unimaginable disaster. Not one of the six founding states had avoided occupation by a foreign power. Institutions that were considered utopian before the war now seemed worth trying. The logic of reform was to gain the benefits of scale among densely interacting peoples: could states create a European-wide territory of prosperity and peace? As one problem was addressed, as one externality was internalized, so others came to the fore. European integration has been rolling integration. It has been driven by its underlying purpose—not by a conception of the final outcome.

The assumption was that community would follow. Trust among Europeans has grown, and individuals who interact across borders and who have the most to gain from doing so have assimilated a European identity alongside their national identity. However, powerful populist currents run in precisely the opposite direction, framing national identity in opposition to European integration, and appealing to those who perceive little benefit in Europe or who fear loss of national self-rule. Solidarity that would enable the Union to redistribute in order to sustain scale is conspicuously lacking.

The hard edges of European states have been softened in a system of multi-level governance, but the current crisis reveals how difficult it is to bring normatively diverse communities under a single jurisdictional roof. How can a large polity endure if it combines states with populations having parochial identities? Will it break apart, or be eroded by resurgent nationalism? For the bulk of Europe's history, empire has been associated with coercive subjugation of unwilling peoples, but the experience of the EU suggests that government reflects not only circumstances, but human ingenuity in adapting to them. The art of scale under community is an evolving one. Nationalism is being mobilized, but it would be foolish to presume that benefits of scale will be any less compelling in the future than they are at this moment.

32

What Is
European Integration Really About?
A Political Guide for Economists

Enrico Spolaore

Political scientists are not the only scholars examining the tension between scale and community (see Chapter 31). Contemporary economists, using a different vocabulary, have also explored the costs and benefits of establishing a "federation across heterogeneous populations, sharing diverse social and economic structures, languages, cultures, and identities."

Economist Enrico Spolaore (Tufts University) explores the costs and benefits of European integration. He argues that integration occurs when the benefits of scale are greater than the costs associated with integrating heterogeneous populations. Integration stalls, however, when heterogeneity costs rise or remain too high. Functionalism (the "chain-reaction method") historically overcame the cost of heterogeneity by starting with economic integration in limited sectors and solving new problems with deeper integration that diverse populations accepted out of ignorance or apathy. European elites from Jean Monnet to Helmut Kohl intentionally left unaddressed certain economic problems (such as the absence of a fiscal union to backstop monetary union) that could only be solved by creeping political union. But the strategy of political integration by stealth, according to Spolaore, is flawed because it rests on the questionable assumption that the benefits of gradual integration will continue to outweigh the costs of heterogeneity. In his view, heterogeneity costs must come down through the convergence of values and policies, or integration will peter out.

The euro crisis, argues Spolaore, has uncovered the weaknesses in the functionalist method of integration. Resistance to solving the crisis through political integration has risen, making the cost of fiscal union entirely too great. He suggests elites should "focus on a narrower set of minimum

Reprinted with permission from *Journal of Economic Perspectives* 27, no. 3 (2013): 125–144. Notes omitted.

requirements" to "ensure the stability of monetary union in Europe" without pressing the case for becoming a "sovereign federation."

As an economic and financial crisis unfolds across the European Union, critics argue that European institutional integration has gone too far, blame misguided political motivations, and assert that the monetary union has failed. On the other side, supporters of European integration attribute the euro crisis to institutional incompleteness—what Bergsten called a "half-built house." They argue that the solution to Europe's woes should be sought in additional integration: a banking union, a fiscal union, or perhaps even a full political union, and the formation of a federation. In sum, the political design of European institutions is at the center of the current debate about the euro.

In fact, Tommaso Padoa-Schioppa, the economist and central banker who played a key role in the birth of the euro, wrote: "[T]he euro was the result of a long-term development that started in the aftermath of World War II. After experiencing political oppression and war in the first half of the twentieth century, Europe undertook to build a new order for peace, freedom, and prosperity. Despite its predominantly economic content, the European Union is an eminently political construct. Even readers primarily interested in economics would hardly understand the euro if they ignored its political dimension." This political guide for economists takes a step back and looks at the creation of the euro within the bigger picture of European integration. How and why were European institutions established? What is European integration really about?

The history of European integration is complicated, with a big cast of actors including governments, technocrats, interest groups, and voters, who in turn pursue a range of economic and political goals. This complexity is reflected in a variety of interpretations by political scientists and political economists. This article discusses facts and theories about European integration from a political economy perspective, building on ideas and results from the economic literature on the formation of states and political unions. Specifically, we look at the motivations, assumptions, and limitations of the European strategy of partially integrating policy functions in a few areas with the expectation that more integration will follow in other areas in a sort of chain reaction towards an "ever-closer union." The euro with its current problems is a child of that strategy and its limits.

A European Federation?

The idea of a new sovereign federation across Europe goes back a long time, but it received a big push from the first half of the twentieth century.

At the end of World War II, the promoters of European integration looked back at the previous decades and saw a continent fragmented in independent and unconstrained nation states which had pursued costly beggar-thy-neighbor policies during the Great Depression and engaged in two major wars. The goal of European integration was to create a system where nation states would no longer follow such unilateral and destructive policies.

In 1943, a group led by Altiero Spinelli founded the European Federalist Movement. In 1946, Winston Churchill argued for the creation of "the United States of Europe" (which in his view did not include Britain). By definition, a federation would have eliminated national borders and international conflict (but not civil conflict) among Europeans. However, no European federation was created immediately after World War II.

Instead, the founding document of European integration is the Schuman Declaration of May 9, 1950, named after France's foreign minister Robert Schuman and inspired by Jean Monnet, a businessman and civil servant who played a crucial role in starting European institutions in the following years. The declaration proposed that "Franco-German production of coal and steel as a whole be placed under a common High Authority, within the framework of an organization open to the participation of the other countries of Europe." The plan was motivated by security as a way "to make it plain that any war between France and Germany becomes not merely unthinkable, but materially impossible." The pooling of coal and steel production was ambitiously defined as "a first step in the federation of Europe."

The Schuman Declaration led in 1951 to the European Coal and Steel Community (ECSC) among six countries: France, West Germany, Italy, the Netherlands, Belgium, and Luxembourg. The ECSC was then used as the institutional template for two proposed communities: the European Defense Community and the European Political Community, which included the formation of a common army, a common budget, and common institutions with significant legislative and executive powers. It would have basically amounted to a European federation. A treaty was signed among the six countries in 1952 but failed to obtain ratification in the French parliament and never took effect. In 1955 several politicians, including Jean Monnet, created an "Action Committee for the United States of Europe." But, again, no United States of Europe actually formed.

The fundamental reasons behind these failures to form a federation have bedeviled the supporters of a United States of Europe, then and since. Two issues are key to understanding the beginning of the integration process, its setbacks, and the following path of European integration. One issue is a general problem in political economy: the trade-off between costs and benefits when heterogeneous groups are politically integrated under a common authority. The other issue involves the particular role of Germany, the country that played a central role in World Wars I and II.

The Political Economy of Heterogeneous Populations

The formation of a European federation across heterogeneous populations, sharing diverse social and economic structures, languages, cultures, and identities, would come with several benefits, but also with high costs. The trade-off between these costs and benefits is central to the political feasibility and stability of institutional integration among these populations.

Potential benefits from full political unification include economies of scale in the provision of federal public goods, such as defense and security, and the ability to internalize positive and negative externalities over a large area. A European federation with its own budget and redistribution policies could also provide insurance against asymmetric shocks that only affect some of its regions, whether natural like an earthquake or man-made like the bursting of a housing bubble. These benefits from fiscal federalism are often stressed when comparing Europe to the United States and are now at the forefront of the debate about the European sovereign debt crisis.

However, political unification comes with significant costs when various groups speak different languages, share different cultural norms and identities, and have different preferences for public policies and institutions that cannot be decentralized at the sub-federal level. Among those institutions is the ultimate "public good": the federal government itself, with all its constitutional and legal traits, policies, official language(s), and so on, about which German or Dutch people may have very different views from those prevalent in France or Italy.

A growing literature has explored the links between measures of heterogeneity and political outcomes such as the provision of public goods, the extent of redistribution, the quality of government, and the likelihood of civil and international conflict. . . . The bottom line of this literature is that measures of ethnic, linguistic, and cultural diversity have significant effects on policy outcomes, redistribution, and the provision of public goods. A European federation would be quite heterogeneous by most of these measures and likely to face significant political costs when choosing common public goods and policies at the federal level.

The example of defense and security—which played a fundamental role in Europe's early attempts to integrate—can illustrate these issues. These public goods have high economies of scale, but also high heterogeneity costs stemming from diverse preferences across populations. Military power has historically been a central tool to ensure a government's monopoly of legitimate use of coercion over a territory. Integration of defense and security under one authority usually goes hand in hand with the centralization of this monopoly of coercion—that is, with the formation of a sovereign state or federation. However, different populations with different histories, cultures, and identities are likely to disagree over the type of government in charge of such a federation. Moreover, coercion can then be used to collect taxes, finance a larger set of other public goods, and redistribute resources across different groups. This redistribution is more likely to be resisted when groups are different not only economically but also along ethnic and linguistic lines. For instance, western Germans may be more willing (or less unwilling) to redistribute resources to eastern Germans than to Greeks or Italians. Consequently, centralized provision of defense and security across large and diverse populations usually takes place when dictatorial rulers are able to ignore the heterogeneity costs of the populations they conquer, and/or when there are overwhelming benefits of scale from defense that offset high heterogeneity costs. The two most successful federal republics, Switzerland and the United States, emerged in response to external security threats, and the unification of Germany in the nineteenth century resulted from conquest by Prussia.

Military and political union is not the only way to deal with security threats. Heterogeneous sovereign states can benefit from economies of scale in defense by forming military alliances while still maintaining their political and fiscal independence. But military alliances, where each state can autonomously decide its own level of military spending and pay for it, can lead to undersupply of defense from the perspective of the whole alliance because of free riding. Western Europeans failed to form a federation even when faced with an existential threat from the Soviet Union and relied instead on an international alliance (NATO) where issues of undersupply and free riding were in part addressed by the dominant role of the United States.

If heterogeneity can explain failures to integrate in the past, does it need to be an obstacle to future political integration? Over time, couldn't a federal Europe change political and social interactions and affect cultures and identities among Europeans, leading to a shared identity within a "European nation"? After all, nineteenth-century France famously turned "peasants into Frenchmen" through public policies and modernization.

This question is part of the broader debate on the persistent political and economic effects of historical and cultural traits, and the extent to which culture itself can be changed by policies and institutions. In the long run, people can learn new languages, modify their cultural traits and identities, and transmit different traits to their children in response to changing incentives, including public policies. However, it is at best a gamble to hope that political integration of modern democratic nations will lead to cultural integration. Historically, nation building and attempts to "homogenize" populations were implemented by rulers of undemocratic societies who had an interest in reducing heterogeneity costs in order to maximize their own rents or pursue their own preferences. Realistic supporters of European integration understand that convergence of political preferences through reduction of linguistic and cultural barriers, if it is going to occur at all, will be a slow and gradual process, which should take place naturally and consensually.

For Europeans, heterogeneity has been a source of benefits as well as of costs. When people have different preferences and traits, societies can benefit economically and culturally through specialization, learning, and exchange of goods and services, as well as ideas and innovations. Benefits from heterogeneity, however, are mostly about interactions over rival goods, not public goods, which are nonrival. Similar preferences over the same rival goods can lead closely related groups to conflict and war, while different preferences over rival goods can facilitate peaceful exchanges and a better allocation of resources. In contrast, diverse preferences over public goods, like a federation's government, laws, and public policies, will be much harder to reconcile because one kind must apply to everyone within the federation, whether everyone likes it or not. As a result, heterogeneity of preferences is mostly beneficial when people interact about rival goods, but costly when sharing nonrival goods. This is an important reason why, as we will see, the European project has been much more successful when fostering economic exchanges and a common market, while it has stalled when attempting to pool "federal" public goods, such as defense and security.

The Role of Germany

In hindsight, as we look back at the 1952 treaty that would have established a European Defense Community and a European Political Community, what's perhaps more surprising is not that France rejected it, but that other states ratified the treaty. A reason is that the other two largest states at that time, West Germany and Italy, had just emerged from a severe military defeat and faced significant constraints to their own defense and foreign policy. West Germany was the more extreme case: a divided country, technically under military occupation until 1955. In those circumstances, the costs of constraints on German sovereignty by pooling defense and security were low and could be traded against other political and economic benefits. As Germany's status as a sovereign state "normalized" over time, its incentives to join a security-based federal union decreased.

The agreement for a European Coal and Steel Community is often interpreted from a similar perspective. According to Milward, France proposed the coal and steel community to constrain German control of its own industry in response to US plans in 1949 to allow a Germany relatively free of Allied supervision. Germany agreed to the Schuman plan because, by sharing management of its coal and steel, it could obtain important concessions, such as "the removal of ceilings on permissible levels of industrial production." According to Berger and Ritschl, French access to German coal was "the most important element of the Monnet Plan for France's reconstruction."

These examples illustrate a continuing issue in the history and politics of European integration: the extent to which European supranational institutions can be interpreted as tools to constrain German power in the interest of its neighbors, especially France. This theme has come to the forefront again with the creation of the euro. A popular view is that giving up its currency was the price that Germany had to pay to overcome France's opposition to German reunification, a deal summarized by the witticism quoted by Garton Ash: "[T]he whole of Deutschland for Kohl, half the deutsche mark for Mitterrand." Literally taken, as a quid pro quo, this interpretation is not held by most scholars. It is questionable that a French threat to veto the reunification of Germany could be credible. Moreover, key decisions about the single currency had already been taken before the fall of the Berlin Wall in 1989, and German politicians and interest groups (like exporters) had other strong reasons to favor a monetary union.

However, it is not fully coincidental that the implementation of the euro took place during and right after German reunification and the opening of political and economic relations between Western and Eastern Europe. Germany's chancellor at that time, Helmut Kohl, viewed the euro as a big step in the broader process of European integration, which he considered essential to reassure Germany's neighbors about his enlarged country's commitments to peace, security, and economic cooperation. And even though the process leading to economic and monetary union had started before the fall of the Berlin Wall, a detailed analysis of the interactions among key participants in the negotiations show that German reunification led to a reassessment of the relative payoffs from economic and monetary union, and was used "to reshape . . . negotiations."

The increase in Germany's potential power might also have affected the borders of the future euro area, making it much larger than predicted by efficiency criteria, such as the theory of optimal currency areas. For example, Eichengreen mentions the view that France and others pushed for the inclusion of many countries at the "periphery," like Southern Mediterranean countries, to "balance" Germany's larger size and influence within the monetary union.

Whether these Realpolitik interpretations are fully persuasive, the French government saw a close link between German reunification and European integration. According to an adviser to the French President, "Mitterrand did not want [German] reunification without advances toward greater European integration, and the currency was the only topic that was open to debate."

How had a monetary issue become "the next step" in the process of European integration? What was (and is) such a process about? To answer these questions we need to go back to what happened after the rejection of the defense and political communities in the mid-1950s.

From Common Market to Economic and Monetary Union: Jean Monnet's Chain Reaction?

From the successful creation of the European Coal and Steel Community and the rejection of the European Defense Community, Jean Monnet and the other supporters of European integration learned a lesson in political realism. Partial integration in narrowly defined areas, such as coal and steel, was feasible, while more ambitious integration in broader areas such as defense and policy coordination would meet too much political opposition. Their next step was the creation in 1957 of a community similar to ECSC for civilian atomic energy (EURATOM) and, more importantly, a European Economic Community (EEC) to set up a customs union: the "common market." The institutions of the three communities were later merged and became known as the European Community. The treaties of Maastricht (1992) and Lisbon (2009) reorganized and replaced the European Community with the European Union.

The Treaty of Rome of 1957 establishing the European common market no longer referred to steps "toward a federation" but included the vaguer objective of laying the "foundations of an ever-closer union among the peoples of Europe." The signatories' main stated goal was "to ensure the economic and social progress of their countries by common action to eliminate the barriers which divide Europe," while claiming that this would strengthen peace and security. To foster those goals, European states created two sets of institutions: supranational institutions such as the European Commission, Parliament, and Court of Justice, and intergovernmental institutions, such as the Council of Ministers and, later, the European Council, formed by the heads of state or government of the member states.

Over time, policy functions have been delegated to European institutions in an increasing range of areas. Nonetheless, national governments have kept control over fundamental decisions and must decide unanimously on all changes to the international treaties that set Europe's informal "constitution." An attempt to establish a formal "Constitution for Europe" failed when it was rejected by French and Dutch voters in 2005.

The history of European integration reflects this tension between the role of supranational institutions and the power of national governments. The conflict is also mirrored by the two most influential political theories about European integration: functionalism and intergovernmentalism. This terminology can be confusing for the uninitiated. In a nutshell, the theories are distinguished by how they answer the question: who is in charge of European integration?

Intergovernmentalists believe that national governments are in charge, and that supranational institutions are tools of the national states, which use them to pursue their own goals. Moravcsik, an influential proponent of this theory, believes that national governments have built European institutions to pursue the economic interests of their domestic constituencies. In this spirit, Moravcsik views the euro as an economic gamble, mostly reflecting the interests of powerful national producers. This interpretation fits within a broader literature emphasizing the link from domestic economic interests to national attitudes and policies towards European integration. The political economy approach to regional integration based on domestic economic interests is familiar to the economics profession, and therefore I will not say more here. I will focus instead on the alternative theory of functionalism, which is much less known among economists, even though it has played a significant role in the ideology and practice of European integration and the creation of the euro.

Functionalists believe that European integration is not primarily driven by national governments and their voters, but mostly pushed by elites and interest groups that transcend national boundaries. They stress the role of supranational entrepreneurs and civil servants like Jean Monnet in the 1950s and Jacques Delors in the 1980s and 1990s. The theory is called "functionalism" because it is about the dynamic effects of transferring specific "functions" to supranational institutions: for example, regulation of coal and steel production to the European Coal and Steel Community or monetary policy to the European Central Bank. Although this integration starts in economic areas, integration in one area may well lead to further integration in many other areas, not only economic but also political. Thus, while intergovernmentalists believe that European integration is rooted in the pursuit of national economic interests, functionalists believe that it is about economic integration as a path towards political integration.

The theory of functionalism was directly inspired by Jean Monnet's strategy to delegate specific functions to supranational institutions in relatively narrow areas, mostly technical and economic, with the expectation that it would lead to more institutional integration in other areas over time. Functionalists believe that moving only some policy functions to the supranational level while leaving other functions at the national level creates pressure for more integration through positive and negative mechanisms. A positive mechanism would work through learning: as politicians and interest groups observe the benefits of integrating a few functions, they will want more. This idea is implicit in the Schuman Declaration, which stated that "Europe will not be made all at once, or according to a single plan. It will be built through concrete achievements." Another mechanism is assumed to work by changing people's preferences: as groups cooperate on specific functions, barriers to communication and interaction will decline, which will bring an "endogenous" convergence of values and norms and a demand for more integration. This rather optimistic outlook was inspired by Deutsch's influential research on communication theory and political integration.

A darker mechanism through which partial integration could lead to more integration is, paradoxically, by generating problems and crises.

Because integration is only partial, important complementary functions are missing at each step. For the functionalists, such incompleteness is not a bug but a feature, because it creates pressure for further integration. Monnet's method was explained by his collaborator George Ball:

> There was a well-conceived method in this apparent madness. All of us working with Jean Monnet well understood how irrational it was to carve a limited economic sector out of the jurisdiction of national governments and subject that sector to the sovereign control of supranational institutions. Yet, with his usual perspicacity, Monnet recognized that the very irrationality of this scheme might provide the pressure to achieve exactly what he wanted— the triggering of a chain reaction. The awkwardness and complexity resulting from the singling out of coal and steel would drive member governments to accept the idea of pooling other production as well.

A challenge for this story is to explain why national politicians don't anticipate Monnet's chain reaction. The implicit assumptions here are that integration is irreversible and that national politicians or voters would prefer limited integration to either more integration or no integration. But then, if politicians see that limited integration will lead to more integration, they should either agree to the outcome of more integration right away or they should object to starting the process at all. What factors could allow elites and supranational technocrats to move ahead with initiatives leading to outcomes that national politicians or voters would not have approved in advance? A first possible explanation proposed by functionalists is that national politicians have short horizons: they approve the first step but do not care about the next steps. A second explanation is asymmetric information. The initial steps of functional integration are taken in narrow and technical areas, such as coal and steel in the 1950s or, later, antitrust regulations and monetary issues. In those matters, national politicians and voters are much less informed than technocrats, political elites, and supranational entrepreneurs. Hence, it is difficult for them to monitor these agents and anticipate the consequences of their actions. A third, even less-flattering reason why the mechanism may work is that European supranational institutions and bureaucracies have been set up (on purpose?) with little democratic accountability—the so-called "democratic deficit"—reducing the opportunities of national voters to monitor the technocrats, who can therefore move ahead with integration in areas that would not have been approved in advance by the voters.

Functionalism was the dominant theory of European integration in the 1950s and 1960s, then came to seem less plausible following a series of political setbacks to integration. A major setback was the "Empty Chair Crisis," when French President Charles de Gaulle boycotted European institutions because he objected to their plans for more supranational integration.

The crisis was resolved in a truly "intergovernmentalist" way with the Luxembourg compromise of 1966, in which de facto veto power was given to every member state on issues of "very important national interest." However, the functionalist view returned to fashion with the revival of European integration in the 1980s and 1990s when Jacques Delors was head of the European Commission. Functionalism continues to be very influential not only academically but also among European policymakers and supranational civil servants (perhaps not surprisingly, given that they play the main role according to the theory).

In 1992, the members of the European Community signed a Treaty on European Union at Maastricht, which reorganized European institutions and designed an Economic and Monetary Union (EMU) establishing the institutional foundations for the euro. Jacques Delors and his Committee for the Study of Economic and Monetary Union, also known as the "Delors Committee," played a crucial role, as documented in a detailed analysis of the negotiations leading to the economic and monetary union. The design and rationale for the European economic and monetary union, as laid out in official documents and studies, was deeply influenced by the functionalist view of European integration.

An important functionalist argument was based on the "inconsistent quartet": the mutual incompatibility of free trade, mobility of capital, fixed exchange rates, and independence of national monetary policies. Assuming that fixed exchange rates were essential for Europe's single market, then moving from commercial integration to liberalization of capital movements had to lead to the loss of national monetary autonomy. In fact, Padoa-Schioppa, one of the architects of the economic and monetary union and key member of the Delors Committee, explained the path to the euro in terms that explicitly echoed the chain-reaction metaphor: "[T]he road toward the single currency looks like a chain reaction in which each step resolved a preexisting contradiction and generated a new one that in turn required a further step forward. The steps were the start of the EMS [European Monetary System] (1979), the re-launching of the single market (1985), the decision to accelerate the liberalization of capital movements (1986), the launching of the project of monetary union (1988), the agreement of Maastricht (1992), and the final adoption of the euro (1998)." Also, in the functionalist tradition, each step in this chain reaction was viewed as irreversible. A joke attributed to Padoa-Schioppa refers to how EMU, the economic and monetary union, was like the Australian bird with the same name, in that neither could walk backward.

Not only was the path to the euro explained in functionalist terms from a technical perspective, but it was also viewed, in Schuman and Monnet's tradition, as "a further step—and as a prerequisite for yet other steps—in the political unification of Europe." Wim Duisenberg, the first President of the European Central Bank, said: "EMU is, and was always meant to be a stepping stone on the way to a united Europe." German Chancellor Helmut Kohl famously said in 1991: "It is absurd to expect in the long run that you can maintain economic and monetary union without political union."

From the perspective of Monnet's method, such an "absurd" economic and monetary union without political union should create pressures for still more integration. The euro area lacked many institutions historically associated with a successful monetary union: for example, a central bank that could really act as market maker and lender of last resort, a banking union, and a fiscal union. But this incompleteness could be rationalized as a natural and unavoidable feature of partial integration in the functionalist tradition. Even though present political constraints prevented the immediate implementation of a more comprehensive design, the launching of an "incomplete" monetary union would set the steps for further integration in due course, as predicted by functionalist theories. For example, people would learn with time about the large benefits from economic and monetary union and ask for more integration in other areas. Also, supporters of the euro embraced two arguments mirroring the long-standing functionalist view that preferences and behavior endogenously converge following integration. First, regions will become economically more homogeneous after they share a common currency. Secondly, the economic and monetary union was supposed to provide discipline to governments, including those that used to pursue erratic policies. As a result, all member states would eventually converge to common values and policies emphasizing macroeconomic stability. Supranational institutions could provide the necessary sanctions if national governments deviated from agreed rules of stability. No-bailout rules would also be enforced. If, in spite of these positive effects and precautions, future crises were to occur, they could be resolved with more institutional integration.

Assuming that such logic could really work—and events of the last few years certainly sound a skeptical note—where would Jean Monnet's chain reaction lead in the long run? Monnet himself was ambiguous about his long-term vision of European integration. He oscillated between two visions. One was the original federalist dream of the United States of Europe, in which the current Europe was an "incomplete federation" to be completed. The other vision was of a "post-modern" world where traditional sovereign states, including classic federations like the United States of America, would play a marginal role compared to supranational institutions and norms, which would represent a novel way to organize interdependence among individuals and groups—a vision of Europe as a "post-federation." This same ambiguity is present in the conflicting views about the euro among its supporters: is it a currency without a state yet, or is it a currency without a state ever?

The Limits to Monnet's Chain Reaction

Since the Schuman Declaration of 1950 which launched the Monnet strategy of partial integration, European institutions have grown from a coal and steel community of six countries to a European Union of 28 countries (as of summer 2013), building along the way a customs union, a single market, an economic and monetary union, and much more. This list of achievements has brought several benefits, to which we will return. Nonetheless, the "functionalist" view, deeply embodied in the ideology and practice of the European Union, that each step is part of a chain reaction leading to ever closer integration has serious limitations.

As a starting point, the functionalist emphasis on the rising power and autonomy of supranational institutions compared to national governments must be taken with a grain of salt. National governments do agree to delegate responsibilities to supranational institutions as commitment devices to achieve collective goals which are in each government's long-term interest. To be credible, those institutions must have some autonomous power and independence; the rules for the autonomy of the European Central Bank come to mind. In addition, as in all complex organizations, supranational agents cannot be perfectly monitored by their principals (in this case, national governments and voters), and some principal–agent slack always exists. However, none of this means that Europe's supranational institutions can go very far against the ultimate interests of national governments. While supranational institutions and procedures are important in the day-by-day working of Europe, they "could not work for a week in the absence of the will to cooperate of the member states, especially the largest ones— Germany and France above all."

A well-known illustration of how centralized discipline does not work when ultimate power is in the hands of sovereign governments is the spectacular failure of the Stability and Growth Pact, which came into force in the late 1990s and included mechanisms to ensure that member states would hold their annual budget deficits below 3 percent of GDP and their accumulated government debt below 60 percent of GDP. The Stability and Growth Pact was never credible, and became moot after 2003, when France and Germany used their political power to prevent sanctions against their own violation of the pact's fiscal rules. In general, the success of supranational agents' ability to take autonomous decisions can only be sustained in matters where the extent of disagreement among national governments over policy outcomes is relatively low, like the enforcement of trade liberalization agreements. But success in those areas does not imply that supranational institutions and rules could also trump national institutions and rules in other areas with much higher heterogeneity of preferences and interests, like fiscal policies.

The role of the European Court of Justice is instructive. In a series of landmark cases, the Court enunciated the doctrine that European Community norms have direct effect in member states and trump domestic law and that individuals can directly invoke European law before national and European courts. For example, the 1963 case of Van Gend en Loos v Nederlandse Administratie der Belastingen was decided in favor of a Dutch importer of German chemical products that had objected to a tariff charged by the Dutch authorities in violation of article 12 of the Treaty of Rome, which forbids member states from raising customs duties between themselves or introducing new ones. The aggressive interpretation of its role by the European Court of Justice in this and other cases went beyond the legal framework that had been formally agreed with the Treaty of Rome, and, according to some scholars, brought Europe close to a federal system from a legal perspective, expanding supranational powers beyond the control of national governments. However, these new legal doctrines were established to enforce norms consistent with national governments' own collective objectives, such as trade liberalization. The acceptance of these decisions by national governments and courts did not imply that any European norms would be as easily accepted in the future. In more recent years, the German Constitutional Court has elaborated the legal theory of conditional acceptance of European Union norms, according to which Germany only accepts the supremacy of EU law insofar as it is consistent with fundamental German rights. In a famous decision on the constitutionality of the Maastricht Treaty, the German Court ruled that there is a legal limit to the powers of EU norms, defined by their effects on national democratic sovereignty. In a landmark ruling on the Lisbon Treaty, the German Court explicitly stated that the national states are "the masters of the treaties" and "therefore must see to it that there are no uncontrolled, independent centralization dynamics" within the European Union, a clear and explicit brake on functionalist dynamics.

In general, the central problem with the chain-reaction method is the unwarranted expectation that gradual integration, which has been successful in areas with low costs of heterogeneity, can continue unabated when moving to areas with much higher heterogeneity costs. The source of this problem is the lack of a realistic assessment. Successful integration is more likely to take off in areas such as commercial integration, where heterogeneity costs are relatively low, and partly offset by the benefits from diversity. As integration proceeds to other areas, after low-hanging fruits are picked, heterogeneity costs continue to increase along a convex curve. At some point, those high costs become politically prohibitive, and the pressure from spillovers, inefficiencies, and crises will no longer lead to further integration, but just to losses—and possibly even the collapse of the whole system. The chain-reaction approach does not anticipate that heterogeneity costs and constraints will eventually become binding and stop the process for good. Followers of this approach are therefore prone to setting up incomplete and inefficient arrangements, relying on the overoptimistic expectation that such inefficiencies can always be addressed at a later stage through additional integration.

For these reasons, there is no guarantee that regional integration in economic areas, such as a common market, should lead to political unification down the road. The example of the German customs union (Zollverein) in the nineteenth century, often mentioned in this respect, is misleading, because the main force behind commercial integration was political integration pushed by Prussia's military power. In fact, international cooperation and political unification can be viewed as substitute ways to lower barriers to trade. If two regions can already agree to reduce their trade barriers with each other while remaining independent, they are going to obtain smaller additional gains from trade if they also form a political union with a unified domestic market. This is a direct negative effect of economic integration on the incentives to form a political union. In practice, this negative effect is likely to be larger than possible indirect effects of economic integration in lowering the costs of political integration through communication and coordination, which were stressed by Monnet and his followers.

The historical record up to now indeed suggests that international economic integration is more likely to go hand in hand with political disintegration.

The euro is a child of the functionalist method. The method of partial integration provided the institutional framework and rationale for monetary integration. Without Monnet's idea of delegating specific policy functions and prerogatives to supranational institutions, the euro would not have come into existence. Of course this does not mean that the euro was created exclusively for "functionalist" reasons and goals, nor that the decisionmakers were only supranational civil servants and elites. There would be no euro without the actions of powerful national politicians pursuing their own geopolitical and domestic objectives or without the backing of powerful economic interests (like German exporters). However, statesmen with political goals and producers with economic interests exist elsewhere but do not end up with a "currency without a state." Such a currency was only possible—politically, technically, and intellectually—in the exceptional institutional framework provided by European integration.

By creating the euro, the chain reaction crossed the border between "pure" economic integration, which can be achieved through international cooperation in the form of liberalization of trade and capital flows, and the form of monetary integration that historically had only been obtained by a sovereign state using its power of coercion to establish one currency within its borders.

The exceptional nature of the euro does not mean that Europe's monetary union is unsustainable in the long run or only sustainable if Europe becomes a sovereign federation. The parameters of the questions have been well stated by Mario Draghi, the head of the European Central Bank, who said that "those who claim only a full federation can be sustainable set the bar too high." Instead, Draghi focuses on the "minimum requirements to complete economic and monetary union." In such framework, the future of the euro depends on a key political variable: the heterogeneity costs associated with the minimum set of functions that must be pooled or delegated for a currency union to work.

If the costs associated with heterogeneity were small, the euro area crisis of the last few years could perhaps be addressed with deep fiscal and political integration. This outcome seems out of reach at present given the historical experience of European integration. In principle, monetary union could lead to a fiscal and political union, even if heterogeneity remains high, if the costs from leaving the euro are even higher and fiscal and political integration are perceived by national governments and voters as the only solution. That outcome could be seen as a vindication of the darker version of Monnet's chain reaction: heterogeneous Europeans would have been "trapped" in a fiscal and political union because they took an irreversible decision to enter a monetary union without anticipating the spillover to further integration. However, political union on such grounds would hardly be a solid start for a European federation; it would be very unlikely that such political union could trigger the positive cultural changes that would be the only sustainable foundation for a cohesive federation in the long run.

A more promising way to ensure the stability of monetary union in Europe is to focus on a narrower set of minimum requirements, as suggested by Draghi. High priority is likely to be given to banking and financial integration. Those gains could in part be secured with tools and institutions similar to those already profitably employed in areas where the European Union has been most successful, like commercial integration, antitrust regulation, and the formation of a single market. At the same time, though, the close links between banks and sovereign states in Europe can create dangerous spillovers, crises, and clashes between supranational authorities and national governments.

Back Where We Started:
The Benefits from European Integration

European integration in the aftermath of World War II was encouraged to counteract the threats of war and protectionism. We saw the timid beginnings with coal and steel, the defeat of the ambitious plan to pool defense, the establishment of a common market, and the building of ever more complex and ambitious supranational institutions—eventually including monetary union. We discussed the serious problems with the expectation that this would necessarily be a chain reaction towards ever closer political integration. Now, it is time to offer a few final comments on the sources of strengths of the European integration project.

While the chain-reaction method can be carried too far, key aspects of Monnet's strategy have in fact contributed to the concrete successes of the European project when the tools of integration have been applied to the appropriate areas: those with lower heterogeneity costs and higher economies of scale. These aspects include: partial integration with a focus on economic areas; deep "institutionalization," with the delegation of substantial prerogatives to supranational institutions going well beyond the institutional framework of more traditional international organizations; and integration of several functions, creating useful "linkages."

Trade integration is a good example of the effectiveness of partial integration in economic areas. Trade is an area where costs of heterogeneity are offset by benefits from heterogeneity and large economies of scale. The removal of trade barriers was in the general interest of Europeans even though specific sectors and groups within each country benefited from protectionist policies. European supranational institutions provided a way to coordinate trade liberalization and to lock in the commitment not to raise barriers unilaterally when faced with domestic political pressure. In this respect, European integration was one of the earliest and most successful examples of regional arrangements set up to solve coordination problems and to provide credible commitments. Partial institutional integration in different areas also allowed "linkages" between issues and provision of credible side-payments to potential losers from commercial integration. For instance, the notoriously wasteful Common Agricultural Policy has been often explained as a political compromise between France and Germany: German manufacturers gained access to the French market, and German taxpayers helped subsidize French farmers.

Trade integration within Europe has also benefited peace and security. The view that international trade can reduce the risk of war goes back to Montesquieu and Kant and has spurred a large empirical literature. Multilateral openness (or "globalization") does not reduce the risk of war between pairs of countries. However, bilateral trade, by increasing the opportunity cost of conflicts between two partners, reduces the probability of conflict between that pair of countries, even when controlling for historical, linguistic, and cultural similarities between populations. In fact, Martin, Mayer, and Thoenig find that country pairs with a high frequency of old wars are more likely to sign regional trade agreements, and this can be explained as a consequence of the complementarity between economic and political gains from trade. They also show that multilateral trade openness reduces the opportunity cost of bilateral conflict, thereby increasing the risk of war between pairs of countries which can trade with third partners. Therefore, globalization also increases the political incentive to sign regional agreements for security reasons.

This interaction between economic and political factors can explain important aspects of European integration. For instance, it can shed light on why Konrad Adenauer, the Chancellor of West Germany from 1949 to 1963, pushed for a geographically narrower but institutionally deeper customs union with France, Germany's old enemy, therefore reducing the risk of war between the two countries. Adenauer overruled his economic minister Ludwig Erhard, who was primarily interested in economic benefits and would have preferred a broader free-trade area, which France would have been unlikely to join given its own commercial and political interests.

An open question is whether European integration has played a central or only a marginal role in securing peace in Europe. Skeptics of the "pacifying" effect of European institutions stress the crucial involvement of the United States and NATO in Europe during the Cold War and afterwards, and the failure of Europeans to deal with the breakup of Yugoslavia on their own. Moreover, peace has also held between Japan, the other loser of World War II, and its neighbors, and trade has prospered among them in the absence of Asian institutions analogous to the European Union. However, the Cold War ended in Europe with the fall of the Berlin Wall, Germany is now unified, and European institutions have played a very significant role in the process of democratization and integration of Eastern and Central Europe. In contrast, the relation between a still formally communist China and Taiwan remains tense and unresolved, and Korea is still divided and even at risk of a nuclear war, which could spread to Japan and other neighboring countries. On balance, whether because of European integration or other factors, in recent decades Europe has fared quite well in terms of peace and democracy relative to other areas of the world.

In general, pooling and delegating functions and policies to supranational institutions to take advantage of economies of scale and scope while maintaining other prerogatives at the national (or subnational) level has brought substantial benefits to Europeans when appropriately implemented in areas with relatively low heterogeneity costs. Those benefits have been obtained while keeping ultimate sovereign control and the monopoly of the legitimate use of coercion at the national state level. A centralized European authority could provide a broader range of public goods with large economies of scale and scope while using coercion to prevent free riding. But that would come with much higher heterogeneity costs. Europeans probably have been wise in not yet traveling all the way to a sovereign federation given their existing differences in preferences and cultures. If those preferences change, Europe may benefit from a reorganization in a federal direction, but of course that should be decided only through broad and democratically expressed consensus.

At the moment, Europeans are sticking to the current system of cooperation among sovereign states within a supranational organization. Within those boundaries, and in spite of the serious limitations that we discussed, European institutions have provided useful commitments to overcome some (but not all) problems from free riding and beggar-thy-neighbor policies. European cooperation has at least turned out better than the alternative system of destructive unilateral national policies plaguing European history until 1945. In this respect, Moravcsik, a leading "intergovernmentalist" scholar of European integration, is hopefully not far from the truth when he writes: "Whatever the outcome of the crisis, the EU will remain without rival the most ambitious and successful example of voluntary international cooperation in world history."

Index

About the Book

The fourth edition of this popular reader, thoroughly updated, introduces students to both the concept of a united Europe and to integration theory.

The expanded first two sections of the book now present the visions of the primary shapers of the union and its fundamental documents, as well as early currents in integration theory. The completely revised third and fourth sections explore recent theoretical developments in theory and practice as the EU wrestles with economic crises, political unrest, cultural conflict, and international competition.

Brent F. Nelsen is professor of political science at Furman University. His writings focus on European integration, religion and politics in Europe, and European public opinion. **Alexander Stubb** is Finland's minister for European affairs and foreign trade. He previously served as minister of foreign affairs (2008–2011) and as a member of the European Parliament (2004–2008). He is author of several books on European integration.